Family Life Education

Integrating Theory and Practice

National Council on Family Relations, Minneapolis, MN

The National Council on Family Relations (NCFR) was established in 1938 as a multi-disciplinary professional association to provide a forum for family researchers, educators, and practitioners to share in the development and dissemination of knowledge about families and family relationships, to establish professional standards, and to promote family well-being. NCFR publishes three journals, *Journal of Marriage and Family*, *Family Relations,* and *Journal of Family Theory & Review,* and sponsors the Certified Family Life Educator (CFLE) program.

ISBN# 0-916174-69-7

ncfr
catalyzing research,
theory and practice

NATIONAL COUNCIL ON FAMILY RELATIONS
3989 Central Avenue NE., #550
Minneapolis MN 55421
Toll-free: (888) 781-9331
Fax: (763) 781-9348
www.ncfr.org
info@ncfr.org

Table of Contents

Family Life Education Teaching and Practice Resources

About The Editors

Dr. David Bredehoft is chair and Professor of the Social and Behavioral Sciences Department at Concordia University, St. Paul, Minnesota. Prior to CSP he was employed as a marriage and family therapist and family life educator at Lutheran Social Service in Wichita, Kansas. He earned the Ph.D. in Family Social Science from the University of Minnesota in 1983. Dr. Bredehoft became a Licensed Psychologist in the State of Minnesota in 1988 and a Certified Family Life Educator in 1998. Along with the responsibilities of his teaching, Dr. Bredehoft has been active in both the fields of family and psychology publishing over 100 articles in journals, magazines, and newspapers. He is editor of the second edition of ***Life Span Family Life Education Framework*** poster published by the National Council on Family Relations. Currently he is conducting a series of research studies on the overindulgence of children. The results of these studies can be found at www.overidnulgence.info. He is also a coauthor of a book on overindulgence titled ***How much is enough? Everything you need to know to steer clear of overindulgence and raise likeable, responsible, and respectful children*** (Marlowe & Company, 2004). Dr. Bredehoft served as president of the Minnesota Council on Family Relations in 1992-1993 and was named Certified Family Life Educator of the year by NCFR in 2003.

Dr. Michael Walcheski is Associate Dean and Professor of Psychology and Family Studies in the College of Education at Concordia University, St. Paul, Minnesota. Prior to CSP he was employed as a family life educator and director of Christian education at Zion Lutheran Church in Kalamazoo, Michigan. He earned the Ph.D. in Counselor Education and Supervision from Western Michigan in 1998. Dr. Walcheski is a Clinical Member of the American Association of Marriage and Family Therapists; a Certified Family Life Educator through the National Council on Family Relations; a licensed marriage and family therapist and an approved supervisor in the state of Minnesota. Along with the responsibilities of teaching, Dr. Walcheski has been active in both the fields of family therapy and family life education presenting papers at national and regional conferences. He is active in the practice of marriage and family therapy and family life education. Dr. Walcheski directs the first NCFR approved distance education program in family life education. He is co-author of ***Stepping Into Wholes: An Introduction to Complex Systems***, *and was named Certified Family Life Educator of the year by NCFR in 2008.*

Dedications

David J. Bredehoft

I dedicate this book to my first family life education teachers, my parents, John and Elsie Bredehoft; and to Dr. Richard Hey who inspired me to learn about family life education; to Jean Illsley Clarke who showed me how to do it; and to my wife Adena who has demonstrated infinite patience.

Michael Walcheski

I dedicate this book to Mrs. Emily LaBudde and Mr. Leslie Erickson who has demonstrated the time tested lessons of family life education; to Dr. Karen Blaisure who taught me about the complexity of families; and to my wife, Elizabeth Walcheski who inspires me to see how important family life education is for families in the here and now.

Family Life Education: Integrating Theory and Practice

INTRODUCTION

MICHAEL J. WALCHESKI AND
DAVID J. BREDEHOFT

Over the past 40 years, family professionals (Arcus, Schvaneveldt, & Moss, 1993) have attempted to find a common definition that clarifies the work of family life education (FLE). The object of definition and debate, family life education continues to evolve as that work intended for the well being of families and those individuals comprising the family. Modern definitions have emerged regularly since 1962 (Powell & Cassidy, 2007). Broad encompassing definitions of family life education were criticized for being too vague, while narrow more specific definitions have been criticized for being too restrictive and limiting (Thomas & Arcus, 1992; Arcus, Schvaneveldt, & Moss, 1993; Powell & Cassidy, 2007).

In their review of the literature, Arcus, Schvaneveldt and Moss (1993) examined the practical and programmatic features of family life education in the context of what is and what should be family life education. They arrived at these principles:

- Family Life Education is relevant to individuals and families throughout the life span.
- Family Life Education should be based on the needs of individuals and families.
- Family Life Education is a multidisciplinary area of study and multiprofessional in its practice.
- Family Life Education programs are offered in many different settings.
- Family Life Education takes an educational rather than a therapeutic approach.
- Family Life Education should present and respect differing family values.
- Qualified educators are crucial to the successful realization of the goals of Family Life Education (p. 15-20).

Currently, the National Council on Family Relations (NCFR) "considers family life education work experience to be paid employment that involves **prevention and education** for individuals and families relevant to the ten FLE content areas" (NCFR, n.d., ¶ 2).

The evolution of family life education and its practice is reflected in the similarities and changes in the first (NCFR, 1993) and second editions (Bredehoft & Cassidy, 1995) of the Family Life Education Curriculum Guidelines. The first edition, part of the application materials for Certified Family Life Educators, included a framework of seven interdependent topics specifying the major content areas: Human Development and Sexuality; Interpersonal Relationships; Family Interaction; Family Resource Management; Education about Parenthood; Ethics; and Family and Society. Within each topic, categories and key concepts were identified to further clarify each content area. Key concepts were intended as emphases within the subject matter across three general age levels: children, adolescents, and adults. A working knowledge of the entire framework was intended to encourage family life educators to: "plan programs to fit the developmental levels of their learners, to reflect community norms; as well as to demonstrate sound family life education programming" (NCFR, 1993, p.1). In addition to the content areas of the framework, the College and University Curriculum Guidelines (NCFR, 1984) were included to provide direction for college and university curriculum planning and as a guide for certification of family life educators. The College and University Curriculum Guidelines were intended to provide "knowledge about the research and theory" (NCFR, 1993, p.1) in each of the ten content areas. The first addition also included curriculum guidelines for human growth and sexuality and interpersonal relations as well as annotated family life education references and resources.

The second edition of the Family Life Education Curriculum Guidelines followed in the footsteps of the first edition with the purpose "to assist family life educators" (Bredehoft & Cassidy, 1995). The second edition reflected a formalizing direction in family life education materials. It highlighted an article reprinted from *Family Relations*, which expanded the definitions and major concepts of the *Framework for Life Span Family Life Education* and a formal statement of belief concerning families and family policy approved by the NCFR Board. Further, the second edition included articles outlining contemporary parent education programs, identifying bias and exclusivity in family life education curriculum, and developing ethical guidelines for family educators. As in the first, the second edition included related articles, books, media resources, and curriculum materials for family life education.

Family Life Education: Integrating Theory and Practice (2nd ed.) is written to address many of the issues involved in the training of family life educators and the needs of the practicing family life educator. This book outlines an approach that integrates family theory with the practice of family life education. Following in the footsteps of the first edition, the purpose of *Family Life Education: Integrating Theory and Practice* (2nd ed.) is twofold. First, it provides a text for the preparation of family life educators. Second, it provides a resource for the practice of family life education. We have been intentional about using the phrase family life education as the professional identifier throughout the document. However, it is not intentional to be dismissive of other family professionals. We are confident this book will be a benefit for all family professionals.

Historically, NCFR has played a significant role in shaping and defining family life education and the professionalization of family life educators. NCFR has been diligent in advocating the content of family life education, clarifying family life education substance areas for certification, and contributing to the professionalization of family life educators through research. Twenty-five years have passed since NCFR's Board of Directors approved the Certification of Family Life Educators, the University Curriculum Guidelines, Standards and Criteria for certifying Family Life Educators, and content areas for family life education. In 1997 (Bredehoft) NCFR revised and expanded the *Framework for Life Span Family Life Education* and in 2000, NCFR established plans to revise and expand the *Family Life Education Curriculum Guidelines* (2nd ed.). Most recently in preparation of the CFLE exam, based on the CFLE job analysis survey the exam committee clarified several of the content area titles (e.g., changed "Families in Society" to "Families and Individuals in Societal Contexts").

Family Life Education: Theory and Practice (2nd ed.) is a resource integrating theory and practice with an emphasis toward the practitioner. Our focus on the needs of the practitioner parallels a similar direction stated in the revised mission statement for the journal *Family Relations.* The editors state in their instruction to authors:

> Our shared view of applied family research and the key sentence in the mission statement, "Articles should be conceived and written with the needs of practioners in mind," is that all manuscripts must include the identification and thorough discussion of a series of implications for professionals who work with families. No manuscripts will be published that lack explicit implications (Pasley, 2001, p. 1).

Three overarching concepts formed the development of this book: recognizing the integration of theory and practice as a necessary dynamic for effective family life education; identifying the intended audiences as the pre-professional family life educator and the practicing family life educator; and reflecting the prescriptive work of family life education across the life span.

A primary purpose for editing the *Family Life Educaton Curriculum Guidelines* (2nd ed.) (Bredehoft & Cassidy, 1995) was to update and expand its content and utility. For example, we have included the current edition of the *Framework for Life Span Family Life Education* (Bredehoft, 1997, 2001). By relying on current research and practice, revising the *Family Life Education Curriculum Guidelines* (2nd ed.) makes a contribution to the professionalization of family life education by extending the development of technical skills to "focusing on the assumptions and beliefs that underlie decision-making at all stages of family life education, program development and delivery" (Arcus & Thomas, 1993, p.28). The process of identifying current thinking, approaches, tools, and materials for the preparation of family life educators was intended to be a collaboration of family scholars and professionals involved in the practice of family life education and/or the preparation and training of family life educators.

As editors, we have organized *Family Life Education: Integrating Theory and Practice* (2nd ed.) in three sections. Section one is a collection of chapters representing current themes in family life education. These chapters are a starting point for discussing essential concepts central to the teaching and practice of family life education beginning with David Bredehoft's chapter: The Framework for Life Span Family Life Education Revised and Revisited. In the second chapter of section one, Dawn Cassidy reviews the current state of the profession including the CFLE exam. In addition, this chapter discusses current perceptions within the field and poses future challenges for family life education. In the third chapter Jean Illsley Clarke, a family life educator with thirty years' experience looks in the rearview mirror and shares with us things she has learned about being a family life educator and provides directions to pursue in the future. Deborah Gentry offers models of how to teach financial literacy in chapter four. Hawkins, Carroll, Doherty, & Willoughby present a comprehensive framework for marriage education in chapter five. What are the challenges for marriage education is the question and focus of the sixth chapter in which Jeffry Larson updates a previous article addressing innovations in marriage education. Following these chapters we have assembled a collection of articles that address issues surrounding the balancing of work and family. This group of articles was authored by the following family work life experts: Shelly MacDermid, Phyllis Moen, and Michael Lane Morris. The final chapters in this section, written by Jody Johnston Pawel and Nancy Gonzalez address the practical concepts and techniques for marketing Family Life Education programs as well as promoting yourself as a family life educator.

Section two contains the ten Family Life Content Areas reflecting the integration of the Framework for Family Life Education and the Curriculum Guidelines for the practice of family life education. Authors were asked to follow the same template; the uniqueness each author brought to the task produced distinctive results. As editors, we attempted to provide a sense of continuity without disturbing the distinct contribution of each author. Many of the content areas overlap and integrate with each other and are not mutually exclusive categories. As was stated in the first edition of the Curriculum Guidelines, the framework consists of interdependent topics. In this section, each content area includes:

- The specific Curriculum Guideline's definition and objectives.
- The specific life span framework's concepts and area goals.
- An introduction of the curriculum guideline topic and the life span framework concepts.
- A discussion, integrating the curriculum guidelines (e.g., Internal Dynamics of Families) and the concepts from the life span framework (children, adolescents, adulthood, and later adulthood) for the practice of family life education. Authors were asked to provide application examples that highlight the integration of the two.
- Key resources, theoretical and practical, that inform and support the work of the family life educator. These resources include: books, research articles, websites, films and media sources, and curriculum materials.
- Suggested tips for new professionals.
- Future issues and challenges for family life educators.
- Future program needs to equip family life educators.
- References.

Section three includes resource articles for teaching and practice. These articles are intended as support for the first two sections. Family Life Educators and the Development of Cultural Competency; In the Best Interests of Children and Their Families: Merging Program Development and Program Evaluation; Ethical Thinking and Practice for Family and Parent Educators; The Development and Teaching of Ethical Principles and Guidelines for Family Scientists; Boundaries Between Parent and Family Education and Family Therapy comprise the third section.

This book continues the rich history of writing about work with families. For family life educators, it is necessary to question and discuss changing definitions; to review old and offer new approaches to program and delivery; to evaluate work and effectiveness with individuals and families across the life span; and to assess the relevancy of training programs. Margaret Arcus (personal communication, November 23, 2002) referred to these as "enduring questions," certain to keep family life education sharp and vibrant. We think so too.

As a profession, family life educators are consistently faced with pioneers who leave, the arrival of new explorers, and the ever-changing territory of work with families. It is imperative that we remain vigilant to these enduring questions.

References

Arcus, M. E., Schvaneveldt, J. D., & Moss, J. J. (Eds.). (1993). *Handbook of family life education: The practice of family life education* Vol. 1. Newbury Park, CA: Sage Publications, Inc.

Arcus, M. E., & Thomas, J. (1993). The nature and practice of family life education. In M. E. Arcus, J. D. Schvaneveldt & J. J. Moss (Eds.), *Handbook of family life education: Foundations of family life education* (Vol. 2. pp. 1-32). Newbury Park, CA: Sage Publications, Inc.

Bredehoft, D. J. (Ed.). (1997). *The framework for life span family life education* (2nd ed.) [Poster]. Minneapolis: National Council on Family Relations.

Bredehoft, D., & Cassidy, D. (Eds.) (1995). *Family life education curriculum guidelines* (2nd ed.). Minneapolis: National Council on Family Relations.

Hawkins, A. J., Carroll, J. S., Doherty, W. J., & Willoughby, B. (2004). A comprehensive framework for marriage education. *Family Relations*, *53*, 547-558.

National Council on Family Relations. (1993). *Family life education curriculum guidelines* (1st ed.). Minneapolis: Author.

National Council on Family Relations. CFLE Certification (n.d.). *Family life education work experience*. Retrieved January 8, 2008, from http://www.ncfr.org/index.asp

Pasley, K. (2001). Editorial. *Family Relations*, *50*, 1-2.

Powell, L. H., & Cassidy, D. (2007). *Family life education: An introduction* (2nd ed.). Long Grove, IL: Waveland Press Inc.

Thomas, J., & Arcus, M. (1992). Family life education: An analysis of the concept. *Family Relations, 41*, 3-8.

About the Authors

Michael J. Walcheski, Ph.D., CFLE is Professor of Psychology and Family Studies and Chair, Department of Graduate Studies in the College of Education at Concordia University, St. Paul, MN. He is co-editor of *Family Life Education: Integrating Theory and Practice*. E-mail: Walcheski@csp.edu.

David J. Bredehoft, Ph.D., CFLE is Professor of Psychology and Family Studies and Chair, Department of Social and Behavioral Sciences at Concordia University, St. Paul, MN. He is the editor of *The Framework for Life Span Family Life Education* (2nd ed.), coeditor of *Family Life Education: Integrating Theory and Practice*, and coauthor of *How much is enough? Everything you need to know to steer clear of overindulgence and raise likeable, responsible, and respectful children*. E-mail: bredehoft@csp.edu.

Current Themes in Family Life Education

Section I

The Framework for Life Span Family Life Education

Revisited and Revised

David J. Bredehoft

The family life education movement began around the turn of the 20th century as a means of strengthening family living. This movement was created to respond to a variety of social conditions that were placing stress on individuals and families (Arcus, 1992; Darling, 1987). The origins of the movement began in home economics, but quickly spread beyond the boundaries of home economics as widespread academic interest in the family increased. Today, the family life education movement encompasses a broad range of disciplines such as health science, sociology, psychology, counseling, biology, anthropology, medicine, law, religion, social work, history, economics, mass communication and others (Darling, 1987; Somerville, 1971). The content and focus of family life education curricula today are also very diverse. Examples of family life education include but are not limited to pre-marriage education, marriage enrichment, parent education, sexuality education, financial management, time management, anger management, stress reduction, communication, and conflict resolution workshops. As this movement grew, so did the need for a conceptual framework that would embrace and integrate its diverse knowledge and conceptual base. From this need then the *Framework for Life Span Family Life Education* was conceived, not as curriculum but as a guide for program development, delivery, and assessment.

The *Framework for Life Span Family Life Education* was first published in 1987 by the National Council on Family Relations (NCFR) and has been used extensively by theorists and practitioners alike to develop and evaluate family life education programs (Arcus, 1995; Thomas & Arcus, 1992). The framework has also been a useful tool for counselors who as part of their role provide family life education to the community or refer clients to family life education courses for their psychoeducational value. In addition, the framework also provides a conceptual foundation to those representing professionals in a variety of fields such as health care, ministry, counseling, and community education who are committed to prevention. The first edition of the framework (NCFR, 1987) emanated from work by the Committee on Standards and Criteria for Certification of Family Life Educators (NCFR, 1984). The framework's goal according to Arcus (1987) was to clarify and specify the content of family life education while further expanding the definition of family life education. Early on in its development, scholars (Arcus, 1987, 1995; Thomas & Arcus, 1992) recognized that the first edition of the framework would not be its last. Thus, as scientific knowledge, theory, and experience concerning family life amplified, so too would the need to revisit and revise the *Framework for Life Span Family Life Education*. To set a foundation for the revisions made in the second edition of the framework, a definition of family life education is presented followed by a brief history of the first edition.

Definition of Family Life Education

Today, family life education is defined by NCFR (2000) as "preventative and educational activities including program development, implementation, evaluation, teaching, training, and research related to individual and family well-being." However, from its early inception in the 1960's, the definition of family life education has undergone revision and refinement, with little agreement (Bredehoft & Cassidy, 1995; Powell & Cassidy, 2001), and not without problems (for a more in-depth discussion on the definition of family life education and associated problems see Arcus, Schvaneveldt & Moss, 1993a, 1993b). The nature of family life education, and its subsequent definition (Arcus et al., 1993b), has evolved from a vague position of meaning different things to different family life educators who deliver family life education almost exclusively in a school setting (Avery, 1962, Avery & Lee, 1964; Lee, 1963), to teaching activities that are "devoted to enabling adults to increase the effectiveness of their skills in daily living, that is, in relating to others, in coping with life events, and in realizing personal potential" (Tennant, 1989, p. 127). Even though there is not an agreement on one definition of family life education most family life educators subscribe to a set of operational principles (Arcus et al., 1993b) and use them to guide the delivery of their work in a wide range of settings (e.g., schools, churches, community and counseling settings), on a broad number of topics, to a diverse number of populations. Arcus et al., (1993b) identified and described seven such principles: (a) family life education is relevant to individuals and families throughout the life span, (b) family life education should be based on the needs of individuals and families, (c) family life education is a multidisciplinary area of study and multiprofessional in its practice, (d) family life education programs are offered in many different settings, (e) family life education takes an educational rather than a therapeutic approach, (f) family life education should present and respect differing family values, (g) qualified educators are crucial to the successful realization of the goals of family life education. These principles form the basis for both the first (NCFR, 1987) and second (Bredehoft, 1997) editions of the *Framework for Life Span Family Life Education.*

A Brief History of the First Edition

The basic structure for the first edition of the Framework (1987) was based on the philosophy, principles, and purposes from the field, and the collective wisdom of experienced family life education scholars and practitioners (for an in-depth discussion of the history and development of the first edition of the Framework see Arcus et al., (1993b). The substance for this edition came from the work of many scholars and practitioners cited in a series of works including Kerckhoff (1964), the National Commission on Family Life Education (1968), the National Council on Family Relations (1970), Somerville (1971), and Davidson (1989).

The first edition responded to Fisher and Kerckhoff's (1981) call to further clarify and define family life education while articulating its basic context, assumptions, and propositions. Fisher and Kerckhoff postulated that family life education would advance if scholars pursued four modi operandi: (a) the organization of current knowledge in the field; (b) the construction of methods of program development, delivery, and assessment; (c) the improvement of training of family life educators; and (d) the facilitation of the development and testing of theoretical models in family life education. The first edition of the framework addressed two of these strategies by facilitating the organization of current knowledge in the field and by assisting with the construction of methods of program development, delivery, and assessment (Arcus, 1987).

Finally, it is important to note that the following three guiding principles (Arcus, 1987) were used during the construction and development of the first framework; (a) a broad conception of family life education would be reflected in the framework, (b) the framework should include all dimensions of learning: knowledge, attitudes, and skills, and (c) the framework would represent family members of all ages and their need to learn about family life. These principles were highly influential in the revision process of the framework.

The Need for Revision

The impetus to revise the framework emanated from a number of sources. First, routine feedback and assessment from Certified Family Life Educators (CFLE's)[2] working in the field of family life education indicated it was time to revise the framework (D. Cassidy, NCFR Certification Director, personal communication, September 28, 1996). Second, a review of the literature indicated that scholars working in the family life education field had identified cultural shifts and demographic changes that the first edition had not adequately anticipated. This feedback did not say the whole framework was flawed, rather, that the following four changes needed to be made: (a) the framework should be expanded to include the "later adulthood" age-group, (b) the conceptual areas should more closely parallel in scope and sequence the nine categories identified in the College and University Curriculum Guidelines (NCFR, 1984), (c) the framework should include a system/ecosystem perspective, and, (d) the framework should provide a more diverse lens from which to view content and concepts (Thomas, 1995; Walker, 1998).

Revision Process

The revision process began with the assumption that conceptually the second edition of the framework (Bredehoft, 1997) would retain as much of the original Framework (NCFR, 1987) as possible. This assumption was based on feedback from CFLEs suggesting the framework needed fine-tuning and adjustment; not radical revision. The process involved four steps: (a) focus groups were used to identify concepts for the "later adulthood" age group; (b) the editor identified a conceptual method to include both a systemic and a multicultural lens to the model; (c) a working committee of family life education experts reviewed, revised, and refined the work of the focus groups and the editor; (d) the editor synthesized the input from the working committee and then circulated it for final review.

The first review goal was to identify key concepts for the expanded age group in the Framework titled "later adulthood." Participants were invited to attend one of three focus groups to generate concepts and themes pertaining to this new age group. Participants comprised a mixture of university academics and field practitioners working in family gerontology identified from a mailing list from the Minnesota Gerontological Society. So that all participants would be familiar with the first edition of the framework and a body of family life education literature for later adulthood, each participant was sent a packet of information for review prior to meeting with the focus group. The packet included the *Life Span: Family Life Education* poster (NCFR, 1987), *A Framework for Life Span Family Life Education* (Arcus, 1987), and *Family Life Education for the Later Years* (Brubaker & Roberto, 1993).

Each focus group session lasted between two and three hours. Participants sat around a table that had a poster-sized model of the first edition framework and its concepts. A blank fourth row was added to the bottom of the poster for the later adulthood age group. A facilitator encouraged the group to generate concepts and themes relevant to later adulthood. The discussion focused on and paralleled the framework's conceptual areas (families in society, internal dynamics of families, human growth and development, human sexuality, interpersonal relationships, family resource management, parent education and guidance, family law and public policy, and ethics). A separate individual recorded the concepts as they were generated by the group. Data from the three focus groups were then collated.

The next step of the review process involved a working committee of family life education experts at the 1996 NCFR Annual Meeting. The committee's task was to review, revise, and refine the focus group's data. Utilizing the committee's input and suggestions, the editor wrote a draft of the second edition of the framework. This draft was sent to the committee and to all NCFR section chairs for review and response. Responses were noted and a final draft was completed for publication.

Changes to the Second Edition

Professional family life educators recognized from the outset that modifications to the framework would be necessary, "...[that] additional concepts might be added to the framework and, over time, modifications will need to be made as new knowledge develops" (Arcus, 1987, p. 8). As a result of new information, a number of significant changes appear in the second edition of the Life Span Family Life Education Framework (Bredehoft, 1997).

First, following an Eriksonian conceptualization of adulthood (1950), the age group of "later adulthood" was added to the framework expanding the life span age categories from three to four. In addition, the four categories were changed from descriptors of individuals (i.e., children, adolescents, adults) to that of the life stage (childhood, adolescence, adulthood, later adulthood). The addition of the fourth life stage was in response to assertions made by numerous scholars including Brubaker and Roberto (1993), Arcus (1992), and Schvaneveldt & Young (1992) that "older people and their families will benefit from the efforts of family life educators. As knowledge about retirement, widowhood, intergenerational relations, and caregiving grows, family life education programs can be better tailored to the later years" (Brubaker & Roberto, 1993, p. 220). Furthermore, Arcus cited important demographic changes resulting from increasing individual life spans that family life educators have to consider. The fastest growing U.S. cohorts are those 70 years of age and older. And, as a result, Schvaneveldt & Young (1992) cautioned ..."in addition to putting strain on the family, the large numbers of the population moving into the ranks of the elderly have also had a societal effect" (p.385).

Second, compared to seven conceptual areas in the first edition of the framework, the 1997 edition has nine conceptual areas. The first edition of the framework (Arcus, 1987) was prepared for the National Council on Family Relations (NCFR, 1984) and included the following seven conceptual areas: (a) human development and sexuality, (b) interpersonal relationships, (c) family interaction, (d) family resource management, (e) education about parenthood, (f) ethics, and (g) family and society. The processes of communicating, decision-making and problem-solving were not listed as separate concepts, but rather incorporated into each conceptual area. The second edition (Bredehoft, 1997) identifies key concepts in nine areas. These nine areas more closely parallel, in both sequence and number, the key concepts from the College and University Curriculum Guidelines developed by the NCFR Committee on Standards and Criteria for Certification of Family Life Educators (NCFR, 1984). The nine areas in sequence are as follows: (a) families in society, (b) internal dynamics of families, (c) human growth and development, (d) human sexuality, (e) interpersonal relationships, (f) family resource management, (g) parent education and guidance, (h) family law and public policy, and (i) ethics. The second edition handles communication, decision-making and problem solving in the same manner as the first in that it is subsumed and incorporated into all major conceptual areas.

Third, the first edition of the framework was strong on individual development but lacked a systemic viewpoint. It stressed individual life span development, "children" "adolescents" and "adults," but omitted an important conceptualization for family scholars: Individuals function within a family system and a family system operates within a greater ecosystem (Bubolz, Eicher & Sontag, 1979; Darling, 1987; Paolucci, Hall & Axinn, 1977). According to systems theory, family members have reciprocal relationships with one another, meaning change occurring for one individual family member impacts other family members and the family as a whole (Kerr, 1981; Kerr & Bowen, 1988; Satir, 1988). The family system is also part of a larger ecosystem (Bubolz, et al., 1979; Darling, 1987; Paolucci, et al., 1977). "This approach [an ecosystem approach] can provide a framework in which multidisciplinary study can be accomplished and in which various theories and approaches can also be combined" (Darling, 1987, p.819). In response, the second edition integrates both a systemic, and an ecosystemic perspective into the framework. This is accomplished graphically by symbolically wrapping the entire framework with the phrase "reciprocal interactions between family and ecosystem – within the context of the family system."

Fourth, a diversity lens has been added to the framework through which to view the process of family life education in response to the growing number of diverse voices struggling to be heard (Allen & Baber, 1992; Berry, 1992; Bubolz & McKenry, 1993; MacDermid, Jurich, Myers-Walls & Pelo, 1992; Mirfin-Veitch, Brey, & Watson, 1997). This is accomplished graphically by symbolically weaving the phrase "multicultural - gender fair - special needs aware" horizontally throughout the framework. In today's changing world, family life professionals are expected to demonstrate a range of knowledge and skills needed to understand, affirm and provide educational services to people bringing experiences and worldviews from increasingly diverse communities and backgrounds (Dilworth-Anderson, Burton & Turner, 1993; Hildreth & Sugawara, 1993; Smith & Ingoldsby, 1992; Thompson, 1995). In addition to cultural diversity, family life educators can strengthen family life by adopting both a feminist and a special needs perspective. Both perspectives value diversity, equality, and the full participation in mainstream of society for everyone (Allen & Baber, 1992; Berry, 1992). These disparate perspectives have and will continue to shape the way we view, plan and deliver family life education.

Fifth, all category concepts have been reviewed, updated, and reordered. As in the first edition, the three processes of communicating, decision-making and problem-solving were not listed as separate concepts; rather, they were incorporated into the conceptual areas and are expected to be an integral part of all family life education programs.

Uses of the Framework

Program Development and Assessment

Like the first edition before it, the second edition of the framework may be used in numerous ways and it is helpful to those who engage in family life education on a full-time basis (e.g., a parent educator) as well as those who do it on a part-time basis (e.g., a counselor offering a marriage enrichment workshop). The framework can be an important tool in program development and assessment by aiding program developers in determining appropriate curriculum content for age-specific programs. For example, a parent educator charged with developing and teaching a curriculum for parents of adolescents may use the following concepts found in the framework to guide and focus their work: parent-adolescent communication, meeting children's needs at different stages of development, responding to individual differences in adolescents, rewards and demands of parenthood, understanding marital and parenting roles, teaching skills to adolescents (self sufficiency, safety, decision-making, family conflict and conflict resolution, varied parenting situations) single parenting, step-parenting, adoption, and caretaking of disabled children. Concepts found in the framework are equally effective in identifying and guiding the curriculum choices of a practicing counselor who offers a marriage enrichment seminar in a local community setting (e.g., communicating effectively, evaluating choices and alternatives in relationships, responsible sexual behavior – choices, consequences, shared decision-making).

The framework also provides assistance in assessing both breadth and depth in family life education curricula. When systematically used, it can be used to identify missing pieces in a curriculum, or segments that may need to be strengthened. For example, a social service agency may use the framework to analyze its educational workshop offerings. And, after identifying a missing piece, it may decide to offer educational opportunities to its clients who are children, adolescents, adults and older adults in any one of the following conceptual areas: (a) families and society, (b) internal dynamics of families, (c) human growth and development, (d) human sexuality, (e) interpersonal relationships, (f) family resource management, (g) parent education and guidance, (h) family law and public policy, or (i) ethics.

A Resource for Training and Promotion of Family Life Education

For those involved in family life education, the framework is a wonderful resource for training. It can be used in the preparation of family life educators entering the field, or as a tool to guide and assess continuing education.

It also is a valuable resource to explain, promote and justify family life education to other professionals interested in families, but who are not professional family life educators (e.g. doctors, lawyers, social workers, politicians, school boards and county commissioners, etc.). The framework is capable of helping these professionals understand the needs of families at each developmental stage, as well as their complexity. Thus, a variety of settings may benefit from using the framework with their unique clientele (child-care centers, youth groups, religious settings, health-care and assisted care centers for individuals in later adulthood, etc.). Further, business and industry could benefit from using the framework as a measure for assessing how family friendly the work place and it's policies are.

Family Life Education as Prevention

Counselors and mental health professionals have had a long-standing interest in the area of prevention (Felner, Jason, Moritsugu, & Farber, 1983). Special issues of the Journal of Counseling and Development (Myers, Emmerling, & Leafgren, 1992) have focused exclusively on prevention. And, family life education is a major prevention tool. So it would make sense that counselors would then endorse the use family life education.

Gibson & Mitchell (1995) discuss a widely accepted prevention model that has been borrowed from public health. It identifies three levels of prevention: primary, secondary and tertiary. Primary prevention efforts target groups who are not currently affected for the purpose of helping them to function in healthy ways. Secondary prevention utilizes early identification and intervention with individuals who are exhibiting initial signs of the problem, and tertiary prevention relies on rehabilitation of the individual with the goal of reducing residual effects of the disorder (Felner et al., 1983). Counselors can only enhance their primary and secondary prevention efforts by referring clients to family life education venues like pre-marriage, marriage enrichment, parenting, time management, anger management, stress reduction, communication and conflict resolution workshops.

Conclusion

The second edition of the framework builds on the work of many distinguished individuals and continues a long, rich history in family life education. It expands on definitions of family life education by specifying major content for broad life span family life education programs including later adulthood. It reflects current conceptual development and empirical knowledge in each conceptual area, and gives attention to relevant knowledge, attitudes, and skills. It incorporates both a systemic and an ecosystemic viewpoint along with a cultural-diverse, feminist-, special-needs-aware lens from which to view all conceptual areas.

The framework is a guide for program development, delivery, and assessment. It is assumed that practitioners will select the most appropriate organization of concepts and types of methodologies in order to meet the needs of their specific audiences. The framework should be used as a guide to provide practical assistance to family life practitioners, theorists and counselors as we face the challenges of the 21st century.

Note: The Life Span Family Life Education Framework is available in poster format as well as a PowerPoint slide presentation through the National Council on Family Relations (www.ncfr.org).

References

Allen, K. R., & Baber, K. M. (1992). Starting a revolution in family life education: A feminist vision. *Family Relations, 41*, 378-384.

Alvy, K. T. (1988). Parenting programs for black parents. In L. A. Bond & B. M. Wagner (Eds.), *Families in transition* (pp. 135-169). Newburry Park, CA: Sage.

Arcus, M. E. (1987). A framework for life span family life education. *Family Relations, 36*, 5-10.

Arcus, M. E. (1992). Family life education: Toward the 21st century. *Family Relations, 41*, 390-393.

Arcus, M. E., Schvaneveldt, J. D., & Moss, J. J. (1993a). The nature of family life education. In M. E. Arcus, J. D. Schvaneveldt, & J. J. Moss (Eds.), *Handbook of family life education: Vol. 1. Foundations of family life education* (pp. 14-20). Newbury Park, CA: Sage.

Arcus, M. E., Schvaneveldt, J. D., & Moss, J. J. (Eds.). (1993b). *Handbook of family life education: Vol. 2. The practice of family life education*. Newbury Park, CA: Sage Publications, Inc.

Arcus, M. E. (1995). Advances in family life education: Past, present, and future. *Family Relations, 44*, 336-344.

Avery, C. E. (1962). Inside family life education. *The Family Life Coordinator, 11*(2), 27-39.

Avery, C. E., & Lee, M. R. (1964). Family life education: Its philosophy and purpose. *The Family Life Coordinator, 13*(2), 27-37.

Barozzi, R. L., & Engel, J. W. (1985). A survey of attitudes about family life education. *Social Casework, 66*, 106-110.

Berry, J. O. (1992). Preparing college students to work with children and families with special needs. *Family Relations, 41*, 44-48.

Bredehoft, D. J., & Cassidy, D. C. (Eds.). (1995). *Family life education curriculum guidelines* (2nd ed.). Minneapolis, MN: National Council on Family Relations.

Bredehoft, D. J. (Ed.). (1997a). *Life span family life education* (2nd ed.) [Poster]. Minneapolis, MN: National Council on Family Relations.

Brubaker, T. H., & Roberto, K. A. (1993). Family life education for the later years. *Family Relations, 42*, 212-221.

Bubolz, M. M., Eicher, J. B., & Sontag, M. S. (1979). The human ecosystem: A model. *Journal of Home Economics, 71*, 28-30.

Bubolz, M. M., & McKenry, P. C. (1993). Gender issues in family life education: A feminist perspective. In M. E. Arcus, J. D. Schvaneveldt, & J. J. Moss (Eds.), *Handbook of family life education: Vol. 1. Foundations of family life education* (pp. 131-157). Newbury Park, CA: Sage Publications, Inc.

Czaplewski, M. J., & Jorgensen, S. R. (1993). The professionalization of family life education. In M. E. Arcus, J. D. Schvaneveldt, & J. J. Moss (Eds.), *Handbook of family life education: Vol. 1. Foundations of family life education* (pp. 51-73). Newbury Park, CA: Sage Publications, Inc.

Cromwell, B. E., & Thomas, V. L. (1976). Developing resources for family potential: A family action model. *The Family Coordinator, 25*, 13-20.

Darling, C. A. (1987). Family life education. In M. B. Sussman & S. K. Steinmetz (Eds.), *Handbook of marriage and the family* (pp.815-833). New York: Plenum.

Davidson, J. K., Sr. (1989). The certification of family life educators: A quest for professionalism. *Family Science Review, 2*, 125-136.

Dilworth-Anderson, P., Burton, L. M., & Turner, W. L. (1993). The importance of values in the study of culturally diverse families. *Family Relations, 42*, 238-242.

Erikson, E. (1950). *Childhood and society*. New York, Norton.

Famighetti, R. (Ed.). (1997). *The world almanac and book of facts: 1998*. Mahwah, NJ: K-III Reference Corporation.

Family life education programs: Principles, plans, procedures, A framework for family life education. (1968). *The Family Coordinator, 17*, 211-215.

Felner, R. D., Jason, L. A., Moritsugu, J. N. & Farber, S. S. (Eds.). (1983). *Preventive psychology: Theory, research, and practice*. New York: Pergamon.

Gibson, R. L., & Mitchell, M. H. (1995). *Introduction to counseling and guidance* (4th ed.). Englewood Cliffs, NJ: Prentice-Hall, Inc.

Herold, E. S., Kopf, K. E., & deCarlo, M. (1974). Family life education: Student perspectives. *Canadian Journal of Public Health, 65*, 365-368.

Hildreth, G. J., & Sugawara, A. I. (1993). Ethnicity and diversity in family life education. In M. E. Arcus, J. D. Schvaneveldt, & J. J. Moss (Eds.), *Handbook of family life education: Vol. 1. Foundations of family life education* (pp. 162-186). Newbury Park, CA: Sage.

Hughes, R., Jr. (1994). A framework for developing family life education programs. *Family Relations, 43*, 74-80.

Hughes, R., Jr., & Perry-Jenkins, M. P. (1996). Social class issues in family life education. *Family Relations, 45*, 175-182.

Kerckhoff, R. K. (1964). Family life education in America. In H. T. Christensen (Ed.), *Handbook of marriage and the family*. Chicago: Rand McNally and Company.

Kerr, M. E. (1981). Family systems theory and therapy. In A. S. Gurman & D. P. Kniskern (Eds.), *Handbook of family therapy* (pp. 226-264). New York: Brunner/Mazel.

Kerr, M. E., & Bowen, M. (1988). *Family evaluation*. New York: W. W. Norton & Company.

Lee, M. R. (1963). How do experts define "family life education?" *The Family Life Coordinator, 12*(3-4), 105-106.

MacDermid, S. M., Jurich, J., Myers-Walls, J. A., & Pelo, A. (1992). Feminist teaching: Effective education. *Family Relations, 41*, 31-38.

Manchester, J. (1993). *Baby boomers in retirement: An early perspective*. Washington, D.C.: Congress of the United States, Congressional Budget Office.

Mirfin-Veitch, B., Brey, A., & Watson, M. (1997). "We're just that sort of family" intergenerational relationships in families including children with disabilities. *Family Relations, 46*, 305-311.

Morgaine, C. A. (1992). Alternative paradigms for helping families change themselves. *Family Relations, 41*, 12-17.

National Council on Family Relations. (1970). Position paper on family life education. *The Family Coordinator, 19*, 186.

National Council on Family Relations. (1984). *Standards and criteria for the certification of family life educators, college/ university curriculum guidelines, and content guidelines for family life education: A framework for planning programs over the life span*. Minneapolis: Author.

National Council on Family Relations. (1987). *Life span: Family life education* [Poster]. Minneapolis: Author.

National Council on Family Relations. (1998). *Standards and criteria for the certified family life educator program*. Minneapolis: Author.

National Council on Family Relations. (2000). *NCFR homepage*. [Online]. Available: http://www.ncfr.org.

Paolucci, B., Hall, O. A., & Axinn, N. (1977). *Family decision making: An ecosystem approach*. New York: John Wiley & Sons, Inc.

Satir, V. (1988). *The new peoplemaking*. Mountain View, CA: Science and Behavior Books, Inc.

Simon Market Research Bureau. (1992). *The new American family: Significant and diversified life styles*. New York: Author.

Schvaneveldt, J. D., & Young, M. H. (1992). Strengthening families: New horizons in family life education. *Family Relations, 41*, 385-389.

Smith, S., & Ingoldsby, B. (1992). Multicultural family studies: Educating students for diversity. *Family Relations, 41*, 25-30.

Somerville, R. M. (1967). The relationship between family life education and sex education. *Journal of Marriage and the family, 29*, 374-389.

Somerville, R. M. (1971). Family life and sex education in the turbulent sixties. *Journal of Marriage and the Family, 33*, 11-35.

Stern, E. E. (1969). Family life education: Some rationales and contents. *The Family Coordinator, 18*, 39-43.

Tennant, J. (1989). Family life education: Identity, objectives, and future directions. *McGill Journal of Education, 24*, 127-142.

Thomas, J. (1995). Toward inclusive curriculum: Identifying bias and exclusivity in family life education curriculum material. In D. J. Bredehoft & D. C. Cassidy (Eds.), *Family life education curriculum guidelines* (2nd ed.) (p. 15). Minneapolis, MN: National Council on Family Relations.

Thomas, J., & Arcus, M. (1992). Family life education: An analysis of the concept. *Family Relations, 41*, 3-8.

Thompson, L. (1995). Teaching about ethnic minority families using a pedagogy of care. *Family Relations, 44*, 129-135.

Walker, A., J., Martin, S. S. K., & Thompson, L. (1988). Feminist programs for families. *Family Relations, 37*, 17-22.

About the Author

David J. Bredehoft, Ph.D., CFLE is Professor of Psychology and Family Studies and Chair, Department of Social and Behavioral Sciences at Concordia University, St. Paul, MN. He is the editor of *The Framework for Life Span Family Life Education* (2nd ed.), coeditor of *Family Life Education: Integrating Theory and Practice*, and coauthor of *How much is enough? Everything you need to know to steer clear of overindulgence and raise likeable, responsible, and respectful children.* E-mail: bredehoft@csp.edu.

This article was originally published in *The Family Journal*, 9(2), 134-139, and is reprinted with permission.

Challenges in Family Life Education: Defining and Promoting the Profession

Dawn Cassidy

Family life education is a growing and developing field. When this chapter was first written in 2003, the profession of family life education was likened to a pre-teen, or at best, an adolescent. Five years have passed, and family life education has matured into young adulthood. There have been some important advancements resulting in increased recognition and value. While the profession of family life education is far from realizing its full potential, it is well on its way!

There have been numerous advances in the field in the last half-century including advances in the scholarship on family life education, advances in practice, and advances in the preparation of family life educators (Arcus, 1995). Through the efforts of the pioneers of family life education and those currently working in the field, this profession strives to become as recognized, understood, and accepted as marriage and family therapy, counseling, social work and teaching.

The focus of family life education is on the development of individual potential and the prevention of problems through education (National Commission on Family Life Education, 1968). Family life educators provide skills and knowledge to enrich individual and family life. The scope of family life education includes knowledge about how families work; the interrelationship of the family and society; human growth and development throughout the life span; both physiological and psychological aspects of human sexuality; interpersonal relationships, the impact of money, time management, goal-setting and decision-making skills on daily life; the importance and value of education for parenting; the effects of policy and legislation on families; ethical considerations in professional conduct; and a solid understanding and knowledge of how to teach and develop curriculum for what are often sensitive and personal issues (NCFR, 2008).

Family life education applies a preventive approach to promote family well-being. Historically, service delivery to families has operated primarily from an "intervention" mode – addressing the needs of families once problems begin. Waiting for pathology to set-in is more expensive to society – and more detrimental to individual families. Family life education attempts to provide individuals and families with the skills and knowledge they need to live successfully within their individual families, which in turn contributes to societal well-being. As CFLE Deborah Cashen of Parenting Partnerships says "Families do better when they know better."

Family life education is carried out in a variety of settings including health care, community education, public education, faith communities, social services, the military, and increasingly, business. But rarely is it referred to as family life education and rarely are the providers called "family life educators." Perhaps the biggest struggle faced by family life educators is the lack of awareness and understanding of who they are, what it is they do, and what they have to offer.

What needs to happen in order for family life education to be widely understood and valued? What will it take to make parent education commonplace, for all engaged couples to take marriage education courses, and for marriage and relationship enrichment weekends to be the norm? Imagine the personal and societal problems avoided if all high school graduates completed a course in communication skills and conflict resolution or if more people had the skills and knowledge needed to efficiently manage their time and their finances? This chapter will consider progress made to date, as well as future efforts needed in order for family life education to reach its true potential as a profession.

Current Status

There are numerous published accountings of the history of family life (Arcus, 1993: Powell & Cassidy, 2007). The focus of this chapter will be on the current status and future expectations for family life education as a profession including issues relevant to professional development and academic program development.

The National Council on Family Relations (NCFR) has played an important role in the advancement of family life education. NCFR is a non-profit, nonpartisan, professional membership organization that provides a forum for family researchers, educators and practitioners to share in the development and dissemination of knowledge about families and family relationships. NCFR has established professional standards and works to promote family well-being. NCFR has been in existence since 1938, publishes the *Journal of Marriage and Family, Family Relations: Interdisciplinary Journal of Applied Family Studies* and, beginning in 2009, the *Journal of Family Theory & Review*. NCFR holds an annual conference for family professionals from around the world and sponsors the Certified Family Life Educator (CFLE) credential. The National Council on Family Relations has been actively involved in promoting the field of family life education since the 1960's.

Definitions

Family Life Education

NCFR defines family life education as follows:

> *Family life education has as its primary purpose to help individuals and families learn about human growth, development, and behavior in the family setting and throughout the life cycle. Learning experiences are aimed at developing the potential of individuals in their present and future roles as family members. The core concept is relationships, through which personality develops, about which individuals make decisions to which they are committed, and in which they develop self esteem.* (National Commission on Family Life Education, 1968, p. 211).

While the NCFR definition is often cited, it is by no means definitive. For example, back in 1964 Kerckhoff identified the lack of consensus on the definition of family life education and the division of labor within the field as one factor that might inhibit advancement of the field (Arcus, 1993). Numerous definitions have followed (see Arcus, 1993, p. 5–6) but there is still no single widely-accepted definition for family life education.

Definition of a profession

First, let us consider the question; is family life education a profession? How do we know? East (1980) defined eight criteria that should be in place in order for a field or occupation to be considered a profession. They include:

1. the activity becomes a full-time paid occupation;
2. training schools and curricula are established;
3. those who are trained establish a professional association;
4. a name, standards of admission, a core body of knowledge, and competencies for practice are developed;
5. internal conflict within the group and external conflict from other professions with similar concerns lead to a unique role definition;
6. the public served expresses some acceptance of the expertise of those practicing the occupation;
7. certification and licensure are the legal signs that a group is sanctioned for a particular service to society and that it is self-regulated; and
8. a code of ethics is developed to eliminate unethical practice and to protect the public.

The scope of this chapter does not allow a thorough discussion of each of these criteria. However, Table 1 provides an overview of East's criteria and family life education's current status within each of these criteria. While not all criteria have been met, it is clear that considerable progress has been made.

Table 1. Family Life Education: Defining the Profession

East's Criteria (East, 1980)	Progress Made	Room to Grow	Criterion 1= no progress 5 = Criterion has been fully met
1. The activity becomes a full-time occupation	Though rarely called family life education, many professionals practice family life education on a full-time basis under such descriptions as parent education, sex education, marriage enrichment, etc.	Family life education is often only part of a family life educator's job responsibilities or employment specifically in family life education may only be available on a part-time basis.	4
2. Training schools and curricula are established.	Family-related degrees have been offered since 1960s. NCFR began recognizing academic programs that meet the criteria needed for the CFLE designation, beginning in 1996. To-date there are 101 NCFR approved programs.	Few degrees are called *family life education* but rather Child and Family Studies, Human Development and Family Studies, Human Services, Family Studies, etc.	4
3. Those who are trained establish a professional association.	Numerous family-related associations have been in existence since the early 1900s. NCFR established itself as the premier family life education association in 1985 with the establishment of the CFLE program.	There are numerous other family-related associations and organizations which can cause a fragmented identity.	4
4. A name, standards of admission, a core body of knowledge, and competencies for practice are developed.	NCFR developed the *University and College Curriculum Guidelines* and *Standards and Criteria for the Certification of Family Life Educators* in 1984. In 2007 NCFR conducted a practice analysis and created the CFLE Exam. The results of the CFLE Practice Analysis Survey confirmed the validity of the ten family life content areas as representing the knowledge base needed for family life education.		5
5. Internal conflict within the group and external conflict from other professions with similar concerns leads to a unique role definition.	Numerous organizations and credentials exist with some overlapping content. Development of *University and College Curriculum Guidelines* and the *Standards and Criteria for the Certification of Family Life Educators* defined the family life education content areas.	Employers and the public are still unclear on what family life education is and how family life educators differ from social workers, therapists, counselors, etc.	3
6. The public served expresses some acceptance of the expertise of those practicing the occupation.	The increased popularity of parent education and marriage education programs throughout the country reflects the public's increased acceptance of education related to family issues.	Participation in family life education programs including parenting education, sex education, marriage and relationship education, financial literacy programs, etc. is still not the norm.	4
7. Certification and licensure are the legal signs that a group is sanctioned for a particular service to society and that it is self-regulated	The CFLE designation was developed to regulate qualifications of family life education providers. CFLEs must meet continuing education requirements in order to maintain their designation. The CFLE credential is becoming recognized as a valid credential for those working in parenting coordination.		5
8. A code of ethics is developed to eliminate unethical practice and to protect the public.	The Family Science Section of NCFR established *Ethical Principles and Guidelines* in 1995. In 1997 the Minnesota Council on Family Relations finalized their work on *Ethical Thinking and Practice for Parent and Family Educators,* which was adopted by NCFR for use with the CFLE program in 1997. In 2008 NCFR began the process of developing a formal code of ethics for the CFLE credential.		5

Standards and Criteria for Family Life Education

Establishment of Curriculum Guidelines

Perhaps the largest obstacle to getting family life education recognized as a profession comes from the multidisciplinary nature of the field. Initially, and still in many cases today, those carrying out the practice of family life education have come to their vocation through a variety of disciplines (Arcus, 1995). Until fairly recently, few people were trained specifically in family life education. Rather, professionals practicing family life education held degrees in child or human development, family relations, education, psychology, social work, sociology, etc. They responded to a need for preventative education and attempted to strengthen their knowledge in family life education through in-service trainings, workshops, conferences, etc. (Czaplewski & Jorgenson, 1993).

This variety of disciplines led to recognition of the need for standards of practice: a comprehensive and cohesive body of knowledge deemed necessary for effective practice. In 1984, the National Council on Family Relations developed *University and College Curriculum Guidelines* (NCFR, 1984), which are used as a guideline for coursework by academic programs and in the development and implementation of family life education curriculum (Bredehoft, 1997, 2001). In 1998 faculty at Weber State University modified the NCFR University and College Curriculum Guidelines, identifying knowledge, skills and abilities needed for practice. NCFR incorporated the Competencies for Family Life Educators into a publication called "Tools for Ethical Thinking and Practice for Family Life Educators." (NCFR, 1999).

Establishment of Certification for Family Life Educators

In 1984 NCFR also introduced Standards and Criteria for certification of family life educators. Rather than focusing on curriculum content, the Standards and Criteria represented the knowledge base needed for effective practice as well as guidance and directions for completing the CFLE certification application process. The development of a certification credential for family life educators helped to define the practice of family life education and the skills needed. The first Certified Family Life Educators (CFLE) were approved in 1985. There are currently approximately 1,425 active Certified Family Life Educators practicing throughout the world.

There are two levels of CFLE certification, Provisional and Full. **Provisional Certification** is available to CFLE applicants who have demonstrated content knowledge in each of the ten family life content areas, but who have not yet earned sufficient work experience hours in family life education to qualify for Full status. **Full Certification** is available to CFLE applicants who have demonstrated *both* content knowledge and sufficient work experience in providing family life education. The number of hours of work experience needed varies depending upon the relevancy and level of the degree.

The criteria needed for the CFLE designation parallel the University and College Curriculum Guidelines (NCFR, 1984/2007) and include ten family life content areas. These areas include:

1. Families and Individuals in Societal Contexts (previously titled: Families in Society)
2. Internal Dynamics of Families
3. Human Growth and Development Across the Life Span
4. Human Sexuality
5. Interpersonal Relationships
6. Family Resource Management
7. Parent Education and Guidance
8. Family Law and Public Policy
9. Professional Ethics and Practice (previously titled: Ethics)
10. Family Life Education Methodology

The broad range of these content areas reflects the multidisciplinary nature of family life education. Without conscious effort it is difficult for someone not trained specifically in family life education to be knowledgeable in these ten family life content areas.

There are a number of other family-related credentials available. Professionals can be certified in Family and Consumer Sciences (CFCS) or Human Development and Family Studies (HDFS) through the American Association of Family and Consumer Sciences. Those working specifically with families with children facing health issues might pursue certification as a Child Life Specialist through the Child Life Council. Certifications also exist for employee assistance personnel through the Employee Assistance Professionals Association (EAPA), for counselors through the National Board for Certified Counselors, for sex educators through the American Association of Sex Educators, Counselors and Therapists, for marriage and family therapists through the American Association of Marriage and Family Therapy; and for social workers through the National Association of Social Workers. These professions all encompass various aspects of family life education.

Until 2007, the CFLE credential was awarded through a portfolio review process which required the applicant to document their background in each of the ten family life content areas through academic preparation, professional development, and work experience.

In 2007, the National Council on Family Relations replaced the CFLE portfolio process with a standardized exam. The decision to move to an exam reflected another level of advancement for the profession of family life education. An examination process is often the most effective and cost-efficient method for awarding professional credentials. The development and administration of the exam provides a valid, reliable, objective and legally defensible process for evaluating adherence to the criteria needed for the CFLE credential which will increase the likelihood of having the CFLE designation recognized by official and government agencies.

In looking back on East's criteria for defining a profession cited earlier in this chapter, (see Table 1) establishment of the Certified Family Life Educator designation could be considered one of the first steps in the professionalization of the field as it helped to identify a core body of knowledge and standards for practice (criteria # 4) and solidified the National Council on Family Relation's role as a key professional association for those in the field (criteria # 3).

Increased Opportunities for Family Degrees

Pursuing formal training in family has become easier over the past decade because of the increase in the number of family-related degree programs. Touliatos and Lindholm (1991) identified 104 colleges and universities in the U.S. and Canada that included specific graduate-level coursework in the family. Though not a comprehensive list of all programs, it did include the majority. In 2002, *Graduate and Undergraduate Study in Marriage and Family: A Guide to Bachelors', Masters', and Doctoral Programs in the United States and Canada* (Hans, 2005) included 235 family programs (121 undergraduate, 190 masters level, and 71 doctoral programs). While these programs are not all focused specifically on family life education, they do represent a more cohesive and focused approach to the preparation of family professionals. A great number of these programs focus their coursework specifically on concepts and issues deemed core to family life education. They have been approved by the National Council on Family Relations for including coursework needed for the Certified Family Life Educator designation through the NCFR Academic Program Review.

NCFR introduced the Academic Program Review in 1996 in order to recognize university and college degree programs that offer a combination of coursework that covers the ten family life content areas needed for certification through NCFR. As of February, 2008, the National Council on Family Relations has approved 83 schools, representing 101 undergraduate and graduate programs. This increase in NCFR-approved programs has resulted in an increase in the number of CFLE applicants with specific training in family. Graduates of these approved programs are able to apply for Provisional Certification through an abbreviated application process. Since the first school was approved in 1996, approximately 900 applicants have received Provisional Certification through the Abbreviated Application process. Provisional certification provides recognition to designees with a solid academic foundation in family in order to increase their job opportunities, which in turn, provides them with the family life education work experience needed to upgrade from Provisional to Full Certification. An increased number of professionals who formally identify themselves as family life educators through certification will help to increase the visibility of the profession.

Family Life Education Practice Analysis Survey

In 2007 the National Council on Family Relations set about the task of developing a standardized examination to replace the portfolio application process as the means for awarding the Certified Family Life Educator designation. As a first step, NCFR contracted with Schroeder Measurement Technologies (SMT) to conduct a Practice Analysis Study. The goal of this study was to develop an instrument that appropriately assessed the skills and knowledge required for competent entry-level family life education practice. The survey results, which we'll review below, provided a helpful insight into the experience, practice settings and demographics of those currently practicing family life education. In addition, it confirmed the validity of the family life content and sub-content areas.

The study intended to describe the practice of family life education and determine if there was a core set of competencies required for entry-level practice. While NCFR had identified the content areas determined to be necessary for practice when they developed the CFLE Standards and Criteria back in 1984, this determination had been based on a more theoretical approach. NCFR did not conduct any kind of practice survey when first developing the CFLE program. According to professional standards, a Practice Analysis should address those competencies that are needed by the professionals to practice safely and effectively in order to protect the public. At the same time, the Practice Analysis should address the importance and frequency with which elements are used or performed (SMT, 2007).

The *Competencies for Family Life Educators*, developed by faculty at Weber State University, served as the foundation for the CFLE Practice Analysis. A committee of Subject Matter Experts (SME) assisted in the research, organization, and review of the competencies resulting in a comprehensive list of skills and knowledge elements required for competent practice. A rating scale was adopted to provide a means for measuring how often a skill was performed and how important the skill was for practice.

The Subject Matter Experts converted the comprehensive listing into a survey instrument in order to analyze the skill and knowledge elements required for competent entry-level CFLE practice. Included in the survey was a demographic questionnaire designed to gather confidential data describing the survey respondents. This survey was sent to current CFLEs as well as family life educators who were not certified.

The survey received a total of 522 responses from CFLEs in 47 states, as well as responses from Canada, Switzerland, Jamaica, Japan, and Turkey. The email-based survey achieved a response rate of 47.2% of the CFLE population.

NCFR requested the development of a mirror survey so they could request participation from non-certified practitioners who were practicing in the field of family life education. The sampling plan targeted non-certified practitioner participation through community websites and Listservs. The final analysis included 369 practitioners in the field of family life education who were not NCFR- Certified. Respondent demographic information and element ratings from the mirror survey were used by NCFR to compare to the finding from the certified sample.

Level of Certification

Of the 522 current CFLEs, 79% held Full Certification (demonstrated knowledge and experience) with 21% indicating Provisional Certification (demonstrated knowledge but not meeting the minimum work experience requirements needed for Full certification).

Years of Experience

Respondents were asked "How many years have you been a family life educator?" Of the 522 respondents, four did not answer. About 22% had two years of experience or less, about 17% had between three and five years' experience, about 33% indicated six to ten years and approximately 28% indicated over ten years' experience as a family life educator. The mean was 9.16 and the median was seven years.

Organizational Structure

Respondents were asked about the structure of their organization. Of the 522 respondents, twelve did not answer this question. From the three options listed, approximately 53% reported non-profit organizations while 30% indicated Government and 17% indicated for-profit organizational structures.

Primary Funding Source

Respondents were asked to identify their organization's primary funding source. Of the 522 respondents, ten did not answer this question. The largest group of respondents (about 32%) reported State funds and about 12% reported Federal funds as their primary source, while about 21% indicated fee-for-services and about 16% indicated "other" sources, most indicating a combination of sources.

Primary Focus

Respondents were asked to identify their organization's primary focus. Of the 522 survey respondents, 12 did not answer this question. About 65% reported Education and about 14% reported Intervention as their primary focus while about 11% indicated Prevention and about 10% indicated "Other."

Primary Practice Setting

Respondents were asked to describe their primary practice setting. Of the 522 survey respondents, four did not answer this question. Approximately 34% or respondents indicated Education (post-secondary) as their primary practice setting and about 11% indicated Education (e.g. birth through secondary) settings. Practitioners in Community-based Services made up about 20% of the sample. Other settings included Faith-based organizations (8.5%), Government/Military, (5.4%), Health Care and Family Wellness (4.25%), Private Practice (9.65%) and Other (6.56%).

Primary Area of Practice

Respondents were asked to identify their primary area of practice from 43 options provided in a pull-down menu. Of the 522 survey respondents, four did not answer this question. About 19% indicated College/University Education as their primary area of practice, about 12% Parenting Education, while about 9% indicated Counseling and Therapy as their primary area of practice.

Education Level

Respondents were asked to describe their highest level of education. Of the 522 survey respondents, six did not answer this question. About 37% indicated a Doctorate degree and about 42% indicated a Master's degree, while just 21% indicated a Bachelor's degree.

Degree

As a follow-up to the education level question, respondents were asked to identify the field in which their highest degree is in. Of the 522 respondents, a majority (57.47%) indicated their highest degree was in Human Development and Family Studies. About 16% indicated Marriage and Family Therapy/Social Work as the field of their highest degree while about 14% indicated Education.

Age

Respondents were asked to identify their age. Of the 522 survey respondents, two did not answer this question. About 11% reported their age was under 30; about 15% reported their age was 30 to 39; about 20% 40 to 49; and about 40% were 50 to 59 years old. About 2.5 % indicated they were over 70 years old. The mean age was 48.08 years and the median was 51.

Gender

Of the 522 survey respondents, four did not answer the question regarding gender. About 82% of the respondents were female and 18% were male.

Ethnic Background

Respondents were asked to identify their ethnic background. Of the 522 respondents, twelve did not answer this question. The majority, (87.25%) of respondents were Caucasian, while about 7% were African American, and about 2% reported Hispanic ethnicity.

Client Age

Respondents were asked to describe the age range of the clients to whom they provided care. Respondents were asked to select all that applied. Of the 522 respondents, about 66% indicated providing care to Young Adults and 58% indicated providing care to Adults, 33% to Infants/Children, and 15% to Newborns. About 8% of the sample indicated care for the Elderly over the age of 85.

Survey Findings and Decision Criteria

The demographic data gathered from the survey was helpful in providing a picture of those practicing family life education, but the main objective of the practice analysis survey was to identify elements of practice including frequency of performance and importance.

Survey respondents were asked to review a comprehensive list of 77 tasks that may be performed by a family life educator using the following scale: **Not Performed, Of No Importance, Of Little Importance, Moderately Important, Very Important** and **Extremely Important**. A sampling of the 77 tasks included: "Assess the impact of demographics (e.g. class, race, ethnicity, generation, gender) on contemporary society," "Evaluate family dynamics in response to crises," "Identify developmental stages, transitions, tasks and challenges throughout the life span," "Recognize the biological aspects of human sexuality," "Recognize the developmental stages of relationships," "Apply goal-setting strategies and evaluate their outcomes" "Promote various parenting models, principles and strategies," "Identify current laws, public policies, and initiatives that affects families," "Identify and apply appropriate strategies to deal with conflicting values," and "Employ techniques to promote application of information in the learner's environment."

Summary of the Practice Analysis

The 2007 entry-level CFLE Practice Analysis collected data on the frequency and importance of CFLE element performance. A SME Committee reviewed statistical analysis of the 77 elements and established statistical criteria for frequency and importance rating. Of the 77 elements, four did not meet the criteria for inclusion set by the SME Committee and were removed from the content outline. Two of the four were rewritten and included by SME Committee decision. Two other elements were rewritten and one element was included based on respondent suggestions.

The SME Committee developed several criterions for determining if an element would be included or eliminated. Most notable were the following:

Decision Criteria - Percent Not Performing

The SME Committee's first decision criterion was based on the percentage of respondents who indicated that they did not use or perform an element. To qualify for inclusion, the element had to have at least 94% of the respondent population indicating that the element was performed. No elements were eliminated based on this decision criterion.

Decision Criterion - Mean Importance Rating

The second decision established that the mean importance rating must be at least 3.65 (0.65 Higher than Moderate Importance on the rating scale) to be included on the final content outline. Three elements were eliminated based on this decision criterion:

- Analyze how individuals and families manage resources using various theoretical perspectives
- Promote consumer rights, responsibilities, and choices of action/advocacy
- Recognize the biological and psychosocial aspects of sexual dysfunction

These elements were determined to be outside the scope of family life education practice and were not included in the final CFLE Exam Content Outline (p. 261).

The elements included in the final content for the NCFR CFLE met the statistical criteria of importance and frequency of performance established by the SME Committee of Subject Matter Experts.

Use of the results of the Practice Analysis survey as the base for the Certified Family Life Educator Exam ensured that the exam accurately represents the knowledge, skills and abilities needed for effective practice. The results of the survey completed by non-certified family life educators proved to be very consistent with the results of the survey completed by CFLEs, further reinforcing the validity and reliability of the content elements.

Current Challenges

Lack of Identity as a Discipline

As demonstrated, substantial progress has been made in establishing consensus on the content of family life education and the standards needed for effective practice. However, there is less agreement on what an academic degree meeting these standards is called. Very few degree programs are specifically titled "family life education." Rather, family-related degree programs carry a myriad of titles including family science; family studies; individual and family studies; family and consumer sciences; family and child development; human ecology; family, youth and community sciences; family and child sciences; child, adolescent, and family studies; family relations, and more. The overall field of family studies has struggled with the issue of identity for many years with no clear consensus. For example, the *Graduate and Undergraduate Study in Marriage and Family: A Guide to Bachelor's, Master's, and Doctoral Programs in the United States and Canada* (Hans, 2002), includes within the 235 programs listed, over 100 different titles for their departments and/or degrees awarded. The establishment of a core body of knowledge and the advancement of the profession through standards of practice will help with the promotion of family life education as a profession within itself but as a field of study within the broader family field, family life education would benefit from a clearer identity.

Diversity of Settings in Which Family Life Education Takes Place

There are probably numerous instances of family life education occurring in your community on any given day. There are family life educators working in health care settings - doing workshops and classes at hospitals, in community education, faith communities, junior and senior high schools, colleges and universities, social service agencies, corporate settings, government agencies, corrections, retirement communities, and in the military (see Appendix A for examples of employment settings for those trained in the family field).

The multidisciplinary nature of family life education and the variety of settings in which it takes place can be seen as both a plus and a minus. The positive side is that there are numerous opportunities for those with the broad training normally included in a family degree. The negative side is that this variety of settings can make it difficult to target efforts when job seeking. Do you apply with hospitals or through community education programs? Which job titles do you look for in the classifieds or when searching the Internet? The Department of Labor's 2008-09 Occupational Outlook Handbook www.bls.gov/oco does not include family life education as an occupation (Bureau of Labor Statistics, 2008-2009). In fact, the only occupations listed with family in the title include Family and General Practitioners, Family Services Social Workers, and Family Therapists. The occupation of Family Services Social Worker only includes information on social work with no reference to any other family-related positions. As those involved in family life education know, the social work field has done an excellent job of branding itself and incorporating social work training (and in many cases social work licensure) into many state and federal jobs dealing with families. While this works well for jobs focusing on intervention and case management, it excludes a great many well-qualified family professionals who possess the skills and knowledge needed to help families through a preventative approach. A new licensure requirement for non-social work family professionals is not likely. Generally, most legislators are not interested in creating new licensure requirements in any fields that do not involve significant health or welfare risks to the public.

An NCFR marketing consultant once recounted a story about the Certified Public Accountant (CPA) designation, which is possibly the most widely recognized certification in the United States. A representative of the American Association of Certified Public Accountants was asked, "What did it take to get the CPA designation so widely recognized?" His response: about 100 years.

Strategies for Growth

Ideally it will not take 100 years for family life education to become a widely-recognized profession. There are a number of strategies that can be implemented to increase the visibility and value of educational and preventative efforts focused on the family, including the promotion and support of standards of practice, education of employers and the general public, incorporation of family life education into intervention settings, inclusion of family life educators as recognized service providers in legislation dealing with families, increased funding for programs focused on prevention and with that increased attention to the importance of evaluation, and the development of a niche or specialty area for CFLEs.

Promote and support standards of practice

While the Certified Family Life Educator program does not entirely represent the field of family life education, it does provide the most focused effort at increasing the awareness and value of family life education as a profession. Since licensure for family life educators may not be feasible, at least in the near future, other efforts will be needed. Family professionals can support the field of family life education by recognizing the need for established standards of practice. This might involve pursuing certification themselves and/or recognizing and rewarding those who carry the CFLE designation. Increasing the number of people who identify themselves as family life educators, and actively promoting this identification through the use of CFLE initials after their name, in their promotional materials, on their resumes and vitae as well as in their job titles, will help to increase awareness of family life education as a profession. Likewise, increasing the number of qualified Certified Family

Life Educators is an important strategy to increasing the recognition and value of family life education as a profession. The CFLE initials after a designee's name brings attention to family life education as a practice with identified standards and requirements. Likewise, credentials like Certified Family and Consumer Scientist (CFCS) and Human Development Family Studies (CFCS-HDFS) help to bring awareness to professions that bring a preventive and educational approach to family issues.

Educate employers and the public

Family life educators will find that they need to do a fair amount of educating about family life education and its value. They may need to be creative in finding employment settings and be willing and able to market themselves to potential employers. Often employers will not really understand what a family degree or certification represents. They need to be educated on the fact that these credentials represent a solid understanding of families, a life span perspective, and the skills and knowledge needed to develop and present educational workshops. Most family life educators trained specifically in family will work from a systems perspective, i.e., individual system, couple system, family system, and social service, business and government systems. Graduates of family degree programs need to see themselves working as a family life educator at *any* system level in *any* organization (C. Campbell, personal communication, May, 9, 2002). They need to be encouraged to see themselves very broadly in terms of training and skills and to encourage employers to do the same. Employers that experience the benefit of hiring an employee with such skills and knowledge will be more likely to hire similar candidates in the future.

Incorporate family life education into intervention settings

Family life educators working in settings that focus primarily on intervention or counseling might be able to identify opportunities for offering family life education within that same setting. For example, an agency that works primarily with families struggling with financial issues might want to offer money-management workshops to the community. Those offering home visits to parents identified as at-risk might also sponsor "family fun nights" that provide opportunities for all families to gather together to share information and friendship. There is usually no shortage of families needing the assistance of a social worker or counselor, so there is little risk that inclusion of preventative measures by the same agency will result in a shortage of clients.

Inclusion of family life educators as providers in legislation

The growing field of marriage education may provide opportunities to get family life educators legally recognized as well. A number of states have passed or are considering legislation that mandates or provides incentives for people completing marriage education or parent education classes. Typically this legislation includes a listing of recommended providers of these services. Unfortunately, legislators tend to favor bills that include a limited list of qualified providers. These providers are usually people who possess credentials such as licensure that are already sanctioned and recognized by state or federal bodies. It simplifies the passage of the bill but unfortunately may not provide the best measure of who is qualified to provide these services.

Important progress has been made within the field of parenting coordination. Parent Coordinators work within the court systems with divorcing parents. They focus their efforts on minimizing the effects of divorce on children by working with the parents. In addition to educating parents about the effects of divorce, they work with them to establish procedures and policies to increase the likelihood that ongoing relationships will be positive. Until recently mandated parent education programs, required in some states for divorcing couples with children, often identify licensed social workers, therapists, and clergy as the only approved providers. While many of these providers may very well be qualified to provide educational classes dealing with parenting, being licensed as a social worker, therapist, or clergy does not guarantee any specific knowledge in parenting or the ability to develop and implement educational workshops. Someone trained specifically in family life education is at least as qualified, and most likely more qualified, to provide parenting education workshops than a social worker, therapist or pastor who are identified as providers simply by virtue of their licensure in that particular state. Through the efforts of family life educators in the state of Texas, Certified Family Life Educators are now specifically included in legislation identifying qualified providers for parenting coordination. This is an important advancement for family life education because it recognizes professionals who use a preventive and educational approach.

Those interested in promoting family life education can monitor relevant legislation and take the opportunity to educate those who initiate the bills to include family life educators among the list of approved or recommended providers. Inclusion of family life educators as approved providers in legislation will open the door for similar provisions throughout the country.

Increased funding for programs focused on prevention – Evaluation

Prevention can be difficult to prove. Granting agencies usually require thorough documentation of program outcomes to support funding efforts. "The potential benefits of family life education must be more clearly linked to predefined program goals (e.g., the reduction of teenage sexual activity or pregnancy, more effective parenting behavior, or stronger, more fulfilling interpersonal relationships) in a way that shows such education to be good for society by fostering the development of individuals and families (Czaplewski & Jorgensen, 1993). If a clear and direct linkage through family life education could be made to a reduction in at least the financial costs (let alone the emotional costs) associated with divorce, substance abuse, teen pregnancy, child abuse, violence, bankruptcy, and many other individual and societal problems, funding of preventative and educational programs would no longer be an issue (for an excellent discussion on program evaluation see Treichel, 2009 in this publication).

Carve a niche

As noted, family life education takes place in a myriad of settings. Its multidisciplinary nature means that family life educators might find themselves competing for jobs with, or working along side, those trained in social work, psychology, child development, sexuality, or therapy. One approach to increasing the visibility of family life education is to establish or identify a setting where family life educators are uniquely qualified to provide services. Health care providers are increasingly offering workshops on parenting and stress management. Community education catalogs list numerous classes related to family life. Youth programs and church and faith communities are some of the most common settings for family life education.

The area of work/life holds tremendous potential for family life educators. Corporations and businesses are beginning to understand the interconnectedness of work and family life. They recognize that the personal life of an employee can have a detrimental effect on their work life, especially if that personal life is riddled with substance abuse, domestic violence or serious financial difficulties. However, less-serious or problematic issues related to normative family stresses, such as couple relationships, parenting, elder care and more can affect work life as well. Investment in brown bag lunch workshops on "communicating with your adolescent" or "time management" can pay back in increased productivity or decreased employee absence. Family life educators are uniquely qualified to provide these types of workshops.

Conclusion

Few can argue with the merits of providing individuals and families with the knowledge and skills needed to lead satisfying and productive lives. But general acceptance of, or the lack of argument against such efforts, is not enough to ensure the advancement of the field of family life education. The challenge before advocates of family life education lies in converting this rather soft support of preventative efforts into acceptance and promotion of something that can be seen, felt and truly understood. We need people to readily recognize what is meant by parent education, marriage enrichment, and life skills and to actively participate in such activities on a regular basis. We need professionals in related fields to acknowledge and value the knowledge and skills possessed by those who identify themselves as family life educators and to recognize the place that family life education can hold in a variety of settings and situations. Family life education is not in competition with other fields such as social work, therapy, counseling, or ministry. Rather it should be seen as a complement and part of a collaborative collection of resources and services available to help families function as effectively as possible.

Like all worthy goals, the elevation of family life education to a recognized and valued profession cannot be accomplished quickly or through the efforts of just a few individuals. It requires a grass-roots effort of multiple players: individuals, agencies, organizations, businesses, schools and government. Perhaps someday, in place of the response "What do you mean – take a class on parenting — everyone knows how to parent," we instead hear "Which parent education class will you be taking?" If each player can do his or her part, family life education may someday be a household word and an activity in which we all willingly take part.

References

Arcus, M. E., Schvaneveldt, J D., & Moss, J. J. (Eds.). (1993). *Handbook of family life education* (Vol. 1). Newbury Park, CA: Sage.

Arcus, M. E. (1995). Advances in family life education: Past, present and future. *Family Relations*, *44*, 336-344.

Bredehoft, D. J. (Ed.). (1997). *The framework for life span family life education* (2nd ed.) [Poster]. Minneapolis, MN: National Council on Family Relations.

Bredehoft, D. J. (2001). The framework for life span family life education revised and revisited. *The Family Journal*, *9*(2), 134-139.

Bureau of Labor Statistics. (2008-2009). *Occupational outlook handbook*. Retrieved January 26, 2008 from http://www.bls.gov/oco

Czaplewski, M. J., & Jorgensen, S. R. (1993). The professionalization of family life education. In M. E. Arcus, J. D. Schvaneveldt & J. J. Moss (Eds.), Handbook of family life education: Vol. 1, (pp. 51-75). Newbury Park, CA: Sage.

East, M. (1980). *Home economics: Past, present and future*. Boston: Allyn & Bacon.

Eiklenborg, L. L., Bayley, B., Cassidy, D., Davis, J. C., Hamon, R., Florence-Houk, A., et al. (2004). *Family science: Professional development and career opportunities*. Minneapolis: National Council on Family Relations.

Hans, J. D., (2005). *Graduate and undergraduate study in marriage and family: A guide to bachelor's, master's and doctoral programs in the United States and Canada*. Columbia, MO: Family Scholar Publications.

National Commission on Family Life Education. (1968). Family life education programs: Principles, plans, procedures: A framework for family life educators. *The Family Coordinator*, *17*, 211-214.

National Council on Family Relations. (1984). *Standards and criteria for the certification of family life educators, college/university curriculum guidelines, and an overview of content in family life education: A framework for planning life span programs*. Minneapolis, MN: Author.

National Council on Family Relations. (1999). *Tools for ethical thinking and practice in family life education*. Minneapolis, MN: Author.

National Council on Family Relations. (2008). *Certified family life educator program* [Brochure]. Minneapolis, MN: Author.

Powell, L. H., & Cassidy, D. (2007). *Family life education: Working with families across the life span*. Long Grove, IL: Waveland Press.

Schroeder Measurement Technologies. (2007). *National council on family relations certified family life educator (CFLE) practice analysis report*. Dunedin, FL.

Touliatos, J., & Lindholm, B.W. (1991). Graduate study in marriage and the family. *Family Science Review*, *4*, 165-176.

Treichel, C. (2009). In the best interests of children and their families: Merging program development and program evaluation. In D. J. Bredehoft & M. J. Walcheski (Eds.), *Family life education: Integrating theory and practice* (2nd ed.) (pp. 221-231). Minneapolis, MN: National Council on Family Relations.

Related Websites

American Association of Family and Consumer Sciences: www.aafcs.org

American Association of Marriage and Family Therapy: www.aamft.org

American Association of Sex Educators, Counselors and Therapists: www.aasect.org

Child Life Council: www.childlife.org

Coalition for Marriage, Family and Couples Education (CMFCE) www.smartmarriages.com

Employee Assistance Professionals Association: www.eap-association.com

National Association of Social Workers: www.naswdc.org

National Board for Certified Counselors: www.nbcc.org

National Council on Family Relations www.ncfr.org

About the Author

Dawn Cassidy, M.Ed., CFLE, is the Director of Education for the National Council on Family Relations where she administers the Certified Family Life Educator (CFLE) program and the Family Life Education Department. She is co-author, with Dr. Lane Powell, CFLE, of *Family Life Education. Working with Families Across the Life Span* (2nd ed.). E-mail: Dawncassidy@ncfr.org.

Appendix A

Family Life Education Career Opportunities – Employment Settings[1]

4-H Development
Adoption and Foster Care
Adult Education Centers
Child Protective Services
Civic Groups
Colleges and Universities
Community Action Programs
Community Education/Extension
Community Health Centers
Consumer Credit and Protection
Correctional Facilities
Criminal Justice
Crises Centers
Crisis or Hotline Services
Day Care Centers
Disability Services
Divorce Mediation
Domestic Violence Prevention
Drug/Alcohol Rehab Centers
Early Childhood Family Education
Economic Opportunity
Employee Assistance Programs
Extension
Faith Communities
Family Life
Family & Individual Therapy
Fathering Programs
Funeral and Mortuary Services
Girl Scouts/Boy/Scouts/Campfire Girls
Halfway Houses
Health Care
Health Promotion Organizations
Hospices
Hospitals
International Agencies
Latch Key Programs
Mental Institutions
Military Family Support
Neighborhood Youth Corporations
Nursing Homes
Parenting Centers
Peace Corp.
Planned Parenthood
Pre-School/Day Care
Project Head Start
Recreation Programs
Religious Organizations
Research
School Dormitories
Schools - Public & Private
Schools for Deaf/Blind
Senior Citizen Programs
Social Security
Social Welfare Offices
Sororities/Fraternities
Student Services
Vocational Guidance
Women's Centers
YMCA/YWCA
Youth Organizations

[1]For an extended discussion on careers and family life education see Eiklenborg, Bayley, Cassidy, Davis, Hamon, Florence-Houk, et al. (2004). *Family Science: Professional Development and Career Opportunities.* Minneapolis: National Council on Family Relations

The Rearview Mirror: "Things I Wish I Had Known 30-Years-Ago"

Jean Illsley Clarke

"As an experienced parent educator, will you write about what you know now that you wish you had known when you were just beginning?" Umm…. What an interesting challenge. What do I wish I had known thirty years ago? And what do I wish I could know now?

"Yes, I'll write." Which to think about first—content or process? Try as I would, I couldn't stay focused on content or process. Changes and challenges resulting from either new content or new process were constantly pushed aside by thoughts about the changes in me. Okay, so start with the educator. Since it is generally accepted that humans learn best in a relationship, and since some have asserted that those in family life education classes learn more from their relationship with the teacher than from the subject matter that is taught, let's start with the personal. Content and process; the what and the how of parent education, will come later.

Who Is This Educator?

I knew, in 1948 when I was a student in Juliet Myron's intriguing adult education class at the University of Minnesota, that I wanted to become an adult educator. In 1950, I started teaching adult sewing classes in the evenings. I must have done an adequate job; my classes always filled. But I had an important lesson to learn from my day job as a high school teacher before I could begin to understand why the women in my classes did not seem interested in some of the fine tailoring skills I assumed everyone would be delighted to learn. I wasn't thinking about parent education then. I was busy trying to understand those women who came to make garments that their families needed.

Part of my day job was to visit the home of each of my high school students, the affluent in their fine brick homes above Lexington Avenue and the poor who lived on the river flats.

I knew, intellectually, that children grow in differing environments, but the day I couldn't find a house number until I discovered the front door lying flat on the ground, partly obscured by unmowed grass, was the day that I "got it" emotionally. On some deep level, I had assumed that everyone grew up like I did. The little girl who lived in the house without a front door hadn't given me a clue - at least not one that I could read. I knew right then that I had a lot to learn about other people and about myself. I'm still busy doing that.

Uniqueness Means There Is Only One

I wish I had understood more about other people. But, even more, much more, I wish I had understood about myself.

I wish I hadn't assumed that other people think like I do. I can be sequential or random (Tobias, 1994) depending on the situation, but not everyone can. When I was young I thought as fast as the wind and waited impatiently for other people to catch up. Age and two accidents involving minimal brain damage have changed that! Now, in my classes, I enjoy the people who think right past me and I make time and space for the ones who think more slowly (and frequently come up with better answers than the racers).

I wish I had understood how unique I am. Then I could have recognized sooner that *everyone* is unique. Now I know that every person, including me, has a story, and every story, if you really get to know it, is fascinating. Every person is on a journey, and the story of every journey is unique. We educators may have something to offer, something to enhance the stories, but people have the right to grow through their own stories. We may offer information or help, we may invite or nudge, but each person's story is her own story. Even if we might have to intervene on specific behaviors that involve hurting self, other, or property, we still need to hold individuals and their journeys in deep respect.

I wish I had understood how many things shape the stories. The *individual's* specific self, his sex, health, appearance, temperament, birth order, and all of the quotients: the EQ, emotional quotient; SQ, spiritual quotient; IQ, intelligence quotient (recent readings suggest that only 48% of IQ is genetic; Devlin, Daniels, & Roeder, 1997); TQ, temperament quotient; DQ, developmental quotient; XQ, experiential quotient, etc.

I wish I had understood how much the *family's* situation, values, interpretation of sex roles, combinations of parenting practices, comfortable or uncomfortable place in the extended family, expressions of ethnicity, religious or spiritual practices, responses to or uses of violence, or frequency of overindulgence shapes the individual's story.

I didn't appreciate the significance of the roles of the individual and the family and in the *community* – from the person's immediate peer group to the community at large. What are the communities' expected mores, its tolerance or intolerance of deviant patterns, the rigidity of its economic, class, race, or ethnic structures? What brings the beggar to the streets? Generational poverty? Situational poverty? Depression? An injury? Chronic illness? Lack of skills? Hopelessness? An addiction? Loss of a job? An economic downturn in the community? (Payne, 2005). Sometimes the adult has contributed to his unfortunate position, but for a child, homelessness is just bad luck! I didn't know to think about all these possibilities. And I certainly didn't understand the ubiquitous role of culture.

Unconscious Culture Codes

I wish I had learned earlier how very American I am, how I see and interpret and respond to everything through my American lens. Then I could have had deeper respect for how much everyone's culture is crucial to her sense of identity or his map for survival.

> One can look at a culture as a survival kit passed down from one generation to the next. . . . The Culture Code is the unconscious meaning we apply to any given thing—a car, a type of food, a relationship, even a country—via the culture in which we are raised. . . . All of the different codes for all of the different imprints, when put together, create a reference system that people living in these cultures use without being aware of it. These reference systems guide different cultures in very different ways (Rapaille, 2006, pp. 5, 11).

Rapaille (2006) has invented a method for discovering codes for some of the deep associations people of a specific culture make with specific topics. For example, he says that the French code for food is ENJOYMENT. The preparation, presentation, and eating of the food is attended to in a way that will produce pleasure. At the end of the meal, the French say, "That was delicious." Americans, on the other hand, view food as ENERGY. At the end of a meal we commonly say, "I'm full." We eat to get us through our activities. "Oh, no," thought I. "I like food that is flavorful." Then I realized that I was carrying my breakfast toast in my left hand while I pulled up the shades with my right. I was in a hurry – I had many things to do and skipping breakfast is not an option. I get tired if I skip breakfast. Okay Rapaille, I do use food for ENERGY, at least part of the time. Not that I agree with all of his codes. I wish, when this Frenchman-became-American observed the various cultural groups, he had been joined by say, a Mexican person, an English person and a Japanese person. (I wish I had always known how to be as skeptical of all research, including my own, as I am now).

However, I do believe that a survival kit of culture codes exists so deeply within us that we barely know they are there. And, since the drive to survive is in the brainstem, we can heed our codes without automatically running them past the cortex. We can act on them, without realizing that people from other cultures are probably acting on different codes.

Immigrants

Except for Native Americans, we are all immigrants here. Even though my ancestors came to America many generations ago, when I visit England and Scotland I feel comfortable in ways I can't replicate in other foreign countries. I think I have some of those old codes deep in my being. The idea of culture codes helps me have greater respect for every new immigrant. In 2008 the estimate is that twelve percent of people living in America were born in another country. How do we help them adjust to their new culture when, even if they come willingly, the brainstem messages come with them from their culture of rearing?

How do they relate to the new culture? Is this a *foreigner* who looks different and thinks differently? A *hidden immigrant* who looks "American" but thinks differently? An *adopted immigrant* who looks different but thinks like mainstream Americans? A *mirror immigrant* who looks and thinks like the main culture? Even if we parent educators don't practice color-based prejudice, our immigrants of color do have to deal with it. How do we help them as well as the immigrants who "pass" but have to deal with misunderstandings springing from cultural differences?

First Generation Children

If 12% of the current population was born in a foreign country, how many first generation children do we have? My husband and my son-in-law (or as the old Scottish tradition has it, my "good-son") are both first generation. If I had known what I have finally been able to identify (Boss, 1999) about the first generation experience when I was first married, I would have understood my husband better, and I would have been more aware of and sensitive to the needs of the first generation people I work with. I'm exploring that now. So far my interviewees include:

- A person who views being first generation as an opportunity and an exciting challenge
- A person who finds the mix of cultures confusing
- A person who, even as an adult, never feels sure what "normal" is
- The one whose parents told stories of the old country and who feels comfortably connected with both the old and the new
- The ones whose parents were lost or who never told their stories and who long to have the holes in their identities filled in

I think we need to learn more about our first generation children and adults. I need to learn more about first generation children whose parents come from two different cultures.

Third Culture Kids

In addition, if I had understood culture codes, I could have made more sense of the special challenges and abilities of *Third Culture Kids* (Pollock & Van Reken, 2001), those children whose parents move them to another country so they grow up in a culture other than their home culture—missionary children, military children, diplomats' children, foreign business people's children. Their parents, firmly grounded in their home culture, may be oblivious to the mixed cultural messages their children are experiencing. Pollock and Van Reken (2001) tell us that these children have more in common with other third culture kids than they have with people from either their home or their host culture, even if one is an American who lived in Saudi Arabia and her friend is from England but grew up in India. I meet many third culture kids who are now adults and when I ask them if this is true they say, "Oh, yes," and go on to list other qualities that sound right out of the book: restlessness, difficulty settling down, high degree of adaptability , lack of true cultural balance, expanded work view, confused loyalties (Pollock & Van Reken, 2001). These people seem to have wonderfully creative approaches to problem solving. I believe they have an important role to play in our culture.

Christian Lenses

I wish I had realized how Christian I am. I had studied about other religions, but only when I traveled in Muslim and Buddhist countries, and in places steeped in Confucianism, did I start to realize how deeply held my Christian attitudes are. I'm not talking about, "Do you believe in Jesus Christ?" I'm talking about realizing day after day that I was seeing the world in which these people live differently than they were seeing it. They seemed unimpressed by things that shocked me. They were calm where I was anxious. They were excited or joyful about I knew not what. I was seeing through a Christian lens. Like glasses-Christian lens over one eye, American lens over the other. I can't separate the two. I know too that others see me through their cultural and religious lenses. I know that some of my foreign friends find Americans (no doubt that includes me) arrogant and vulgar. Now, rather than thinking, "What did I just do?" I ask myself, what lens are they looking through that makes sense to them? I remind myself that they don't have our whole picture, but that their lens is true for them, at least until they learn differently.

Of course, I wish I had been more aware of the diversity in my classes, particularly the types I couldn't see. I like to look at a group of ten; pretend they represent all of the people in America, and guess which one might be which. Which one holds far left or far right political or religious views? Which three have dyslexia? Which three have adopted, been adopted, or relinquished a child? Which one is an immigrant? It may not be the person of color (for an extended discussion see Clarke & Bredehoft, 2009, pp. 199-206).

I wish I had realized that every person is individually unique and culturally-scripted. I like that. I celebrate having learned that.

Some of the New Content I Wish I Had Known

The Brain

I can't keep up with the burgeoning brain research. Every week I learn new things that I wish we all could have known long ago. For example, we think logically with the cortex and store feelings in the amygdala, but the drive to survive is in the brainstem, and, when push comes to shove, the brainstem rules. When the brainstem says, "Survive!" we act, even if later we wish we had stopped to consider options. Think of this in relation to post traumatic stress flashbacks such as when a recently returned Iraq veteran sees a red traffic light and hits the gas instead of the brakes. Scary! However, most of the time that good old brainstem just keeps us alive.

Then there are the new findings about the cortex, the seat of impulse control and logical thought. We are told that it is not fully formed until the mid-twenties. The conventional wisdom was that teenagers were mature enough to separate so we should back off and let them make their own decisions. According to Small (personal communication, 2004) and his research team at the University of Wisconsin, we now know that adolescents need monitoring. They also need strong connections with parents (Miller, 1997), and the research about the reorganization of the adolescent brain makes the teen's mercurial moods more understandable (Walsh, 2004). No parents, you didn't do something terrible to cause this unpredictable behavior. It is reassuring to read David Walsh's (2004) book *Why Do They Act That Way?*

It used to be assumed that IQ was set at birth. Now we learn that only 17% of the brain is connected at birth (Walsh, 2004). Included in that basic set is the need to be in *connection* and a need to be *competent*. This is powerful information for parent educators. I currently work with the findings from the Overindulgence Research Studies (Bredehoft, 2006; Bredehoft & Armao, in press; Bredehoft & Leach, 2006; Bredehoft, Mennicke, Potter, & Clarke, 1998; Clarke, Dawson, & Bredehoft, 2004; Walcheski, Bredehoft, & Leach, 2007). The new information about the brain gives added urgency to my teaching about the impact of overindulging children. Consider the need for connection and think about children who were overindulged with things that cost money. As adults they told us, "They gave me things, but what I wanted was them."

Also, consider that over-nurture, doing things for children that they should be doing for themselves, can result in *learned helplessness* (Clarke, Dawson, & Bredehoft, 2004). Not the directly taught learned helplessness created in the laboratory, but an induced learned helplessness from not allowing children to learn the tasks crucial to their stage of development. Since a need to be competent is part of every child's birthright, creating learned helplessness causes them to go against their very nature. The same thing happens from soft structure, fuzzy boundaries, no rules or no regular enforcement of rules, no chores, no standards. The outcome is *learned irresponsibility* (Clarke, Dawson, & Bredehoft, 2004). That also overrides a need to be competent. It requires a child to go against her brain's basic program.

Think about the 83% of the brain that is not connected at birth but is hooked up after birth by the combination of genetics and responses to the environment. Huge amounts of basic learning are done early (Walsh, 2004), but the brain continues to generate new cells, and our capacity to learn continues into old age (Cohen, 2005). Think how just those few examples of brain research can influence how we help parents understand children and themselves.

Sex and Sexism

We have known for a long time that girls exhibit earlier language facility than boys do. The family story is that my older sister talked before she walked. I know that my younger brother didn't bother to speak early. Perhaps, with two older sisters, he didn't need to. Boys do, on average, learn to read later than girls. The question was, is the difference in boys' and girls' brains, or is it seated in cultural practices?

Now Burman, Booth, and Bitan (2008) tell us that there are unambiguous findings that when boys and girls are learning language tasks, different areas of the brains are doing the work. The functional magnetic resonance images revealed that the girls showed greater activation in the language areas of their brains, and the boys used visual areas when they were reading and auditory areas when they were listening. The girls used abstract thinking areas while the boys seem to be creating meanings just from seeing or hearing the word (Burman, Booth, & Bitan, 2008). Does this mean we should try schooling boys and girls separately in the early grades? What do I say to the parent in my class who is fretting because son Billy isn't reading as early as his sisters did? I try to keep some helpful reading at my fingertips. Currently I'm finding Helen Neville's (2007) *Is This A Phase?* to be a book that is easy for parents to use. Neville combines temperament and child development.

If Burman, Booth and Bitan (2008) are correct in linking brain function differences in learning to read with the observation that women often provide more context and abstract representations than men, then we have some clues about helping parents communicate with their sons and daughters. If the daughter isn't understanding her dad's directions, he may need to be less terse and give more peripheral information. If the son isn't following his mother's directions, she may be speaking in a way that is over-detailed for him. She could try giving specific directions in fewer words.

Male and female brains *are* different, so each gender has essential gifts to offer. Sexism, however, is a separate issue. Separate! It is about power and not about brain structures or differing abilities. I become more and more aware of how insidious and damaging sexism is. Same for all the "isms." Racism, ageism, etc. All are about power and hierarchy and a false sense of self-esteem (Clarke, 1978), not about brain superiority of one group over the other.

Family Systems

When I started doing parent education, my understanding of family systems was purely academic. It took me a long time to understand that the child who had been fed, bathed, read to, and tucked in and still called for a glass of water, may not have been thirsty for water but for something else—love, recognition, structure, clarity? "Of course the children don't know we are getting a divorce." Ha! Also, it took me an even longer time to understand how dramatically the family system is impacted by systems that surround it. For example, the ways in which current media and marketing practices pull and tug and shape family systems (Dungan, 2003; Lamb & Brown, 2006; Linn, 2004; Schor, 2004; Thomas, 2007; Walsh, 2004).

In classes it seems that the child's behavior is always the presenting problem, but children really are cogs in their family system and are doing their best to function with their limited skills and limited understanding. If drugs or depression or grief hang heavily over the family, simple suggestions about behavior management either won't help much or the "child's" problem just moves over to pop out somewhere else. From the Overindulgence Research Studies (Bredehoft, 2006; Walcheski, Bredehoft, & Leach, 2007) we have learned how goodhearted parental wishes for their children to be happy have led some parents to give-in to their children, to neglect to provide firm structure. Now when I hear someone say, "That child is running the family!" I quickly rephrase in my head or say aloud, "That is a child whose parents are having him run the family (Clarke, Dawson, & Bredehoft, 2004)." How many parents do I have in my Group of Ten who came because of their child's demanding behavior when the child is doing the best she can in the face of lack of parental structure?

I wish I had understood more about the depth of differences between generations. In this time of tremendous cultural flux (Land & Jarman, 1992), when I watch my granddaughters do things I don't understand, it calms me to recognize that I really *don't* understand and that they and I can learn to live with that. I am frequently stopped by their casual approach to computers, electronic games, the Internet, the websites of MySpace and YouTube, chat rooms, explicitly sexual behavior, violence, the ubiquity of drugs, digital cameras, cell phones, text messages, teen buzz (the cell phone ring that the teacher can't hear), all those things that didn't exist when I was their ages. So I send emails to remind them that it is time to build a gingerbread house, and they call to announce how many friends they are bringing. They love the rituals.

I love creativity, change, and spontaneity! All fine, but I wish when our children were young I had had a deeper appreciation of the role of rituals in strengthening family systems, and in keeping individuals and families grounded and emotionally healthy. Now when my granddaughters say, "Grandma, we always...," I listen and I pay attention. I wish I had done more all through the years to encourage families to develop and maintain meaningful family rituals. I hope that children who are not regular participants in a faith community are getting enough rituals in other ways. I wish I had been more aware of the importance of keeping some regular rituals in my parent education classes, such as always mentioning ground rules to remind people the setting is a safe place (Clarke, 1984), and relating ground rules to the subject matter of the day to provide a transition from the world outside to the class or workshop, and always using developmental affirmations to feed the spirits of the adults and to remind them of the reinforcements children need.

About content

I Wish I Had Known More About

I would have been a more helpful parent educator if I had had an earlier and greater understanding of:

- Personality types (Myers & Myers, 1995)
- Temperament types (Neville, 2007)
- Emotional and social intelligence (Goleman, 2006)
- Relationships (Gottman, 2002)
- Overindulgence (Clarke, Dawson, & Bredehoft, 2004)
- Unconditional love – that it means being willing to be the parent, it means holding children in high regard, providing opportunities for them to grow and it means being able to tolerate their discomfort. Neither love nor building self-esteem means keeping children entertained or turning having fun into a childhood job by constantly asking, "Did you have fun today?" Or, "How did school go?" School didn't go anywhere, but the question implies that the quality of the child's day was up to someone else. "What did you learn, and how did you help someone today?" are the questions of high regard.
- Sensitive topics – how I respond to them, what makes them sensitive, and what my own areas of vulnerability are (Clarke, 2005).
- The ability to know what I know and what I don't know and the sureness to say, "I don't know about that. Would you like us (the whole class) to give you some ideas about where to go for help?"
- The reality that I can only invite.
- The reality that parent educators can't fix people. If I offered my best and it didn't help, I can mourn for them and wish I had known more. I can learn more without throwing a heavy guilt trip on myself.
- That the family is one unit, but it is a different experience for every person in it (Saunders & Saunders, 2005). I know my experience of my family (how tough and how wonderful it is) and I know my experience of my marriage (how tough

and how wonderful it is), but I can't, cannot really know how anyone else's family, relationship, or parenting are. I can only be a helpful onlooker and cheerleader. As the old toast goes: *Not above you, or below you, but beside you.*

- The idea that things all fit together somehow. It's my job to figure out how.

I'm Glad I Knew

What I'm glad I knew about and continue to learn about:

- Human development
- Human behavior
- Nature and nurture, or as I choose to call it now, Nurature (Nobel Conference, 2002)
- Sorrow and suffering
- The process of grieving
- Color, joy, hope, and laughter (heard any new jokes?)
- Transactional Analysis, my main psychological theory base which views individuals as having intrapsychic systems and being in relationship systems

Process, the Challenge

Keeping up with the research, the fast moving cultural changes, the world, is a challenge. But adjusting my processes, my methods of making the content available, is a far greater challenge for me. Before I became a parent educator, I had a firm base in adult education methods from Juliet Myron, from further study, and from my father who was a superb teacher and facilitator of adult groups in his role as a master farmer. In my youth, I spent scores of evenings watching him, learning from him. Many of the methods presented in *Who, Me Lead a Group?* (Clarke, 1984) started with him. He had no formal education in group leadership, and I had no formal education in parent education, but I take him with me, in my head, every time I lead.

I didn't come to parenting early in my life, and I came to parent education even later. Parenting our children was a challenge. I was always playing catch-up with them. At that time there were a few books and a few classes, but they didn't seem to fit for us. On my 50th birthday I was attending a workshop on Transactional Analysis (TA) (Berne, 1961; James & Jongeward, 1971). The concepts sounded so helpful! But they were all in the language of the therapist – mostly how to help people who got it wrong during childhood. I wanted to hear it as a parent, to get more of it right while my children were young. That day I decided to translate Transactional Analysis into parenting language, to write the book that would help me and that might help others. That book was *Self-Esteem: A Family Affair* (Clarke, 1978). One book. That was all I envisioned. But the other books came tumbling after. (Well, they didn't really tumble. Each took a lot of effort, but looking back on it, it seems as if they tumbled.) The most recent are *How Much Is Enough?* (Clarke, Dawson, & Bredehoft, 2004) and the *How Much Is Enough? Leader's Guide* (Clarke, 2008) with the Developmental Parenting Highway. Oh, that Highway! Finally I got it! I found a way to get child development, temperament, health, the current family situation, affirmations, and parenting skills all on one page. One page! Look at the whole child! It is so exciting to create new processes! I have continued to study TA, all the way through to international level certification. Although the theories and language of Transactional Analysis have been widely absorbed into the American scene, TA has been largely dismissed as a serious theoretical study here. In many parts of the world, however, it is alive and growing, so I continue to learn with my colleagues from many countries and diverse cultures.

Some of the new methods I find helpful are presented in the chapter family life education methodology in this book (Clarke & Bredehoft, 2009). Most of these process pieces I have learned or honed since I became a parent educator. The many degrees, certificates, courses, and workshops that are available now were nonexistent then. When I started I did know how to give lectures, do demonstrations, teach procedures, design curricula and handouts, and create simulations. But as I learned more about myself and more about other people, I had to invent new ways of teaching, and to adapt my methods to include what other people were discovering. Probably no single body of information has improved my teaching as much as Dunbar's (1996) collection of the research on group sizes (see discussion in Clarke & Bredehoft, 2009). When I stay mindful of it, side conversations disappear, and the group usually stays on task.

One thing has not changed—preparation. Each lesson, each class, each workshop deserves preparation. Thought and preparation! Winging it is for the birds, and leading by the seat of the pants is for motorcycle rides. Preparation, done with an open mind, opens the way for intuition, flexibility, creativity, assuredness and responsiveness.

Once a Parent, Always a Parent

Now I am at the age of parenting children who are adults. Yes, once a parent, always a parent. I am learning from my own life and from friends that parenting changes but it never stops.

Sometimes my new awarenesses come not from statistics, but from personal encounters or people's stories. For example, among my friends are four who have lost adolescent or young adult children. I ask, especially at anniversary times, "How are you doing?" Then I listen. I hurt for them. Sometimes I celebrate with them. Recently, I was in a distant city drinking tea with a longtime friend whom I see infrequently. I asked, "How are you doing with Kate? (I do have permission to tell this story.) My friend stared at her teacup and smiled. She looked up and her eyes grew serious. "I think of her every day. I want to tell her about something, or discuss something with her." Then she smiled again, "I've been wanting a teapot. Hadn't got around to buying one. A couple of weeks ago I noticed that Kate's blue and yellow teapot was sitting in the middle of the shelf where I keep mementos of her. I thought, 'I can use Katy's teapot!' So, I do. Every morning I have a cup of tea with Kate. Sometimes I feel sad for five minutes, but it makes my day better. Kate's tea nourishes me. I love it. It's been five years you know."

I asked, "If someone had suggested you use Kate's teapot right after she died, what would you have done?" She bristled, "Smashed it! Broken it! It would have been on the floor in pieces!"

Drew knew I was flying home that night, but I asked softly, "May I join you and Kate tomorrow for your morning cup of tea?" A quick smile crinkled my friend's face, "Kate would like that."

Then I told my friend about how amused and amazed and proud I am of my granddaughter who recently quit her high level job as a graphic artist to become a firefighter. Gressa is the same age Kate would be if she were alive. Drew was able to marvel and celebrate with me. And I marvel and celebrate Drew's ability to grieve and grow.

Sometimes we learn from a story in the newspaper. I know lots about the early years of life, but not so much about death. Think about Fred's parents. Fred is in first grade. He will not go to second grade. Fred has terminal brain cancer. Fred has a thing about hair, and when he learned that the treatments he is receiving will cause his hair to fall out, he was distraught. His best buddy announced that he would have his head shaved so he and Fred could be bald together. His school picked up on the idea and declared a Saturday to be Fred's Day. Fred's dad was first in line to get his head shaved. The gym was buzzing. Those who didn't get shaved got a hair cut or had their hair dyed some weird color. Amazing. The community supporting a family—as we should. But, how long will we remember? Five years from now will Fred's family have the equivalent of a blue and yellow teapot?

Two years from now, if I'm leading a workshop where we are talking about eight-year-olds and a certain mom gets misty-eyed or a certain dad folds his arms across his chest and stares hard at his shoes, what will I do? When I started teaching I might have asked the mom what was wrong or urged the dad to participate. Now, I think, if I am alert and healthy, that I can distinguish the difference between boredom and going-inside. I try to watch for signs that signal if they want to speak, to be available as they leave the room, to hold them in respect. Always behind that are the questions: What is our contract? This is not a therapy group so how can I be available without prying? What does the educator offer? How is my role as a teacher different from my role as a friend? What are my skills? How do I hold people in respect? Why wasn't I aware earlier that parents lose children but never stop being parents? What about our military losses now—the child, the spouse, the parent who lost eyesight, or cognitive ability, or limbs, or focus, or life?

I add to that Group of Ten regularly. I find a statistic I should have known – 12% of the people currently in the United States were born in another country. Oh, yes, that makes sense. We parent educators have been working on that. But, one of every 150 children being born now is some place on the autism continuum? Are you sure? Yes, say the researchers at the University of Minnesota (Reiff, personal communication, 2007). What does this mean for me? I listen to a parent's story and realize that I know zip about the four-year-old boy who is talking to his dad, looking at him and seems to be connecting with him, and suddenly turns away, walks to the wall, and talks directly at the wall for twenty minutes. I don't know how to help with that boy. But I do know about his six-year-old sister who is trying to learn to read, knowing that recess is approaching, and there will be bullying on the playground. Do her needs get minimized as her parents cope and grieve and struggle and try to keep some balance in a home where the visitor autism has become a permanent resident? Would it help them also focus on the six-year-old if, for each child, they had one of my Developmental Parenting Highways (Clarke, 2008) taped on the cupboard door? So, I make my offers, and when I am teaching, I remember to replace, "Four-year-olds do . . . ." with "Many four-year-olds do. . . ."

How many people in my Group of Ten are grieving something?

The Future

What I Am Afraid Of

- Entitlement! Children and adults who feel entitled to any privilege they didn't earn
- Okay! Adults mushing a direction to a child by adding *okay*? "Time to get in the car, okay?"
- The viciousness of sexism and racism
- Greed
- Childhood overindulgence! The message to the child is, "You are not competent." It can leave big holes in the adult's skill set and cause great dissatisfaction. Adults surveyed in the overindulgence studies (Bredehoft, 2006;

Bredehoft, Mennicke, Potter, & Clarke, 1998) who had been overindulged as children resented it. They said it was done for the needs of the parents, not for theirs, the child's welfare.

What I Am Not Afraid Of

- I am not afraid of Orange Alert. I fly anyway.
- I am not afraid of the rapid growth of technology. I have enough faith in the human brain and in human goodness to believe we will harness it to work for our health and welfare.
- Most importantly, I am not afraid of "the disintegration of the family." Our world is flattening, like it or not, and this means we are in a time of great cultural flux (Land & Jarman, 1992). This much flux feels chaotic and to some, frightening. However, each time a culture goes through a great time of change, the family has looked as if it is disintegrating, but it comes through changed and better adapted to keeping people alive in the next age. I believe we are in the middle of that change. This is a difficult time to be a parent, but I believe we will muddle, dance, complain, and create a way through. We parent educators are doing our best to help that happen.

Hope for the Future

I hope high quality parent education becomes the norm. I hope all parents expect it to be available and useful at all stages of family life. Parenting is our most important job. It is nurturing our planet's most crucial resource. Surely that enterprise deserves our most thoughtful and widespread educational effort.

"So after a searching look in our rearview mirrors, let's focus on what's ahead! Let's take what we know and continue to grow!"

References

Berne, E. (1961). *Transactional analysis: A systematic individual and social psychiatry.* New York: Grove Press.

Boss, P. (1999). *Ambiguous loss: Learning to live with unresolved grief.* Cambridge, MA: Harvard University Press.

Bredehoft, D. J., Mennicke, S., Potter, A. M., & Clarke, J. I. (1998). Perceptions attributed by adults to parental overindulgence during childhood. *Journal of Family and Consumer Sciences Education, 16*(2), 3-17.

Bredehoft, D. J., & Leach, M. K. (2006). *Influence of childhood overindulgence on young adult dispositions – Executive summary: Study 2.* Retrieved from http://www.overindulgence.info/AboutOurResearch.htm

Bredehoft, D. J. (2006). *Becoming a parent after growing up overindulged: Executive summary - Study 3.* Retrieved from http://www.overindulgence.info/AboutOurResearch.htm

Bredehoft, D. J., & Armao, C. K. (2008). What teachers can do when overindulged children come to school. *Lutheran Education. 142*(1), 25-35.

Burman, D. D., Booth, J. R., & Bitan, T. (March, 2008). Sex differences in neural processing of language among children. *Neuropsychologia.* Available online at http://dx.doi.org/10.1016/j.neuropsychologia.2007.12.021.

Clarke, J. I. (2008). *How much is enough? leader's guide.* Seattle, WA: Parenting Press, Inc.

Clarke, J. I. (2005, January). Dealing with sensitive subjects. In *Family information services professional resource materials* (pp. 1-4). Minneapolis, MN: Family Information Services.

Clarke, J. I. (1984). *Who, me lead a group?* Seattle, WA: Parenting Press, Inc.

Clarke, J. I. (1978). *Self-Esteem: A family affair.* Center City, MN: Hazelden.

Clarke, J. I., & Bredehoft, D. J. (2009). Family life education methodology. In D. J. Bredehoft & M. J. Walcheski (Eds.), *Family life education: Integrating theory and practice* (2nd ed.) (pp. 199-206). Minneapolis, MN: National Council on Family Relations.

Clarke, J. I., Dawson, C., & Bredehoft, D. J. (2004). *How much is enough? Everything you need to know to steer clear of overindulgence and raise likable, responsible, respectful children.* New York: Marlow and Company.

Cohen, G. (2005). *The mature mind: The positive power of the aging brain.* New York: Basic Books.

Devlin, B., Daniels, M., & Roeder, K. (1997). The heritability of IQ. *Nature, 388*, 468-471.

Dunbar, R. (1996). *Grooming, gossip and the evolution of language.* London: Faber and Faber.

Dungan, N. (2003). *Prodigal sons & material girls: How not to be your child's ATM.* Hoboken, NJ: John Wiley & Sons, Inc.

Goleman, D. (2006). *Social intelligence: The new science of human relationships.* New York: Bantam Books.

Gottman, J. (2002). *The relationship cure: A 5 step guide to strengthening your marriage, family, and friendships.* New York: Three Rivers Press.

James, M., & Jongeward, D. (1971). *Born to win: Transactional Analysis with Gestalt experiments*. Reading, MA: Addison-Wesley Publishing Company.

Lamb, S., & Brown, L. M. (2006). *Packaging girlhood: Rescuing our daughters from marketers' schemes.* New York: St. Martin's Griffin.

Land, G., & Jarman, B. (1992). *Breakpoint and beyond: Mastering the future today.* New York: HarperBusiness.

Linn, S. (2004). *Consuming kids: The hostile takeover of childhood.* New York: The New Press.

Miller. J. B. (1997). *The healing connection: How women form relationships in therapy and in life.* Boston, MA: Beacon Press.

Myers, I. B., & Myers, P. B. (1995). *Gifts differing: Understanding personality type.* Palo Alto, CA: Davies-Black Publishing.

Neville, H. (2007). *Is this a phase? Child development & parent strategies, birth to 6 years.* Seattle, WA: Parenting Press, Inc.

Nobel Conference. (2002). *The nature of nurture*. Gustavus Adolphus College.

Payne, R. K. (2005). *A framework for understanding poverty* (4th ed.). Highlands, TX: Aha! Process.

Pollock, D. C., & Van Reken, R. E. (2001). *Third culture kids: The experience of growing up among worlds.* Yarmouth, ME: Intercultural Press, Inc.

Rapaille, C. (2006). *The culture code: An ingenious way to understand why people around the world live and buy as they do.* New York: Broadway Books.

Saunders, K. , & Saunders, B. (2005). *The grace of ordinary days: An invitation to celebrate life's journey.* Maple Plain, MN: Center for Living Art, Inc.

Schor, J. B. (2004). *Born to buy: The commercialized child and the new consumer culture.* New York: Scribner.

Thomas, S. G. (2007). *Buy, buy, baby: How consumer culture manipulates parents and harms young minds.* New York: Houghton Mifflin Company.

Tobias, C. (1994). *The way they learn.* Colorado Springs, CO: Focus on the Family Publishers.

Walcheski, M. J., Bredehoft, D. J., & Leach, M. K. (2007). *Overindulgence, parenting styles, and parent sense of competence: Executive summary: Study 4.* Retrieved from http://www.overindulgence.info/AboutOurResearch.htm

Walsh, D. (2004). *Why do they act that way? A survival guide to the adolescent brain for you and your teen.* New York: Free Press.

About the Author

Jean Illsley Clarke, Ph.D., CFLE is a parent educator, teacher trainer, the author of *Self-Esteem: A Family Affair*, and co-author of *Growing Up Again: Parenting Ourselves, Parenting Our Children, How Much is Enough? Everything You Need to Know to Steer Clear of Overindulgence and Raise Likeable, Responsible, and Respectful Children* and the *How Much is Enough? Leader Guide*. E-mail: Jiconsults@aol.com.

Teaching for Financial Literacy

DEBORAH B. GENTRY

The National Council on Family Relations' (NCFR) *Framework for Life Span Family Life Education* (Bredehoft, 1997) specifies family resource management throughout the life span as one of the fundamental knowledge areas of Family Life Educator; this expertise is also required knowledge for NCFR's Certified Family Life Educator credential. While individuals and families manage, on a continuum of poor to exceptionally well, human, economic, and environmental resources, it is the management of economic or financial resources that is the focus of this chapter. Too many youth, adolescents, young adults and older adults are financially illiterate and, as a result of such a condition, potentially rendering themselves and their families financially insecure. Family life educators have an important role to play in working to remedy this situation.

Defining Financial Literacy and Security

Vitt, Reichbach, Kent, and Siegenthaler (2005) define financial literacy as the "ability to read, analyze, manage, and communicate about the personal financial conditions that affect material well-being. It includes the ability to discern financial choices, discuss money and financial issues without (or despite) discomfort, plan for the future, and respond competently to life events that affect everyday financial decisions, including events in the general economy" (p.7). *Financial security* is the ability to meet future needs while keeping pace with day-to-day financial obligations (eXtension, 2008). As the term *security* in general usage is synonymous with "safety," the ultimate goal of financial literacy is to have one's financial well-being protected against danger and loss. However, the relationship between financial literacy and financial security is not a guaranteed one. Certain beliefs, behaviors and choices can keep financially literate persons from achieving financial security for themselves and their families.

Poor Financial Literacy: Nature and Scope of the Problem

Problems associated with poor financial literacy fall into two categories: problems of omission or problems of commission. Problems of omission occur when people are not doing what they should be doing (Nichols, 2000). In the circumstance of managing financial resources, not engaging in savings or banking, neglecting to ensure that assets are protected, or failing to seek credible financial information and advice would be examples of acts of omission that lead to negative outcomes. Problems of commission occur when people are doing something that they should not be doing (Nichols, 2000). In the situation of managing financial resources: over-consumption, impulse buying, excessive use of credit, and taking on risky loans would be examples of acts of commission that often have negative outcomes for individuals and their families. When analyzing problems of omission and commission in a teaching-learning context, it is reasonable to suggest that lack of knowledge, lack of skills, and/or counterproductive attitudes are at the core of such problems and carry a high price tag.

The "Price Tag" for Poor Financial Literacy

Saving Little or Nothing

The personal savings rate in the U.S. has been falling for 20 years, and since 2005 the rate has been near or below zero (Bureau of Economic Analysis, 2008). This suggests that Americans have been spending all of their earnings after paying taxes…and more. Taylor, Fund, and Clark (2007) believe the situation among the young and poor is most worrisome. Forty-two % of 18 to 49 year-olds and forty-five % of households reporting annual incomes below $30,000 say they tend to spend more than they can afford. Debt is increasing among Americans of all adult age groups. Consumer debt in America is projected to be in the trillions. In 2005, for the first time ever recorded, household debt levels surpassed those for household income.

It is one thing not to set aside savings for luxury items and other "wants," but quite another matter not to set aside funds for emergencies. Emergency funds consist of liquid assets that can easily and quickly be converted to cash when major unexpected expenses and crises arise (e.g., layoff or loss of job, injury, illness, property damage as a result of disaster or accident). According to the Consumer Federation of America (2007) 40 % of adults specifically set aside monies to cover emergencies, though such funds seldom reach the commonly recommended amount sufficient to cover three months of living expenses.

Highlighting concerns about adequate savings for retirement, the Employee Benefit Research Institute (2007) found 72 % of respondents reported being very confident or somewhat confident of having enough money for a comfortable retirement. Yet almost half of workers saving for retirement report total savings and investments (excluding the primary residence and defined benefit plans) of less than $25,000. Based on these data, financial experts believe many people are underestimating their financial needs during retirement.

From 1992 to 2004, the percentage of households headed by persons age 55 and older with overall debt grew faster than the rate of the overall population. In households headed by persons 65 and older, the average amount of credit card debt more than doubled during this time period (Demos, 2008). Much of such debt can be attributed to rising health care, housing, and energy costs. Excessive debt is forcing some seniors to delay retirement as well as nudging others who already exited to reenter the workforce. More and more older persons are filing for bankruptcy. Though many resist turning to their middle-age children for assistance, those that do often find their offspring struggling with their own debt, especially if they are also assisting with underestimated and sky-rocketing college expenses for their own children.

Being Unbanked

Estimates of the number of "unbanked" Americans range from 22 to 45 million. Barr (2004) reports that nearly 10 million households lack checking and/or savings accounts, this includes 22 % of low income families earning less than $25,000 per year. Instead, unbanked persons conduct their financial transactions with check-cashing stores, payday lenders, title lenders, rent-to-own stores, and tax preparers. Among low-to-moderate income households, the unbanked tend to be minority, immigrant, and/or less educated, particularly with regard to financial matters (Bucks, Kennickell, & Moore, 2006). Further, they are more likely to be unemployed, rent their homes, and have young children. Many unbanked persons reason that it is too costly to use mainstream banking services, especially if they do not write many checks, cannot maintain expected minimum balances, have had a previous account closed due overdrafts or other problems, and/or cannot easily access such institutions. However, without a bank account, it is more difficult and costly to establish credit or qualify for a loan. Moreover, alternative financial service providers also charge fees, often considerably higher than conventional institutions. For those inclined to save, traditional banks and credit unions offer far more safety than a shoebox or cookie jar.

Failing to Protect Assets

DeNavas-Walt, Proctor, and Smith (2007) report the number of Americans without health insurance has increased. Forty-six and a half million people were uninsured, of which 11.7% were children under the age of 18, and 1.5% were adults over the age of 65. Conditions of poverty certainly contribute to individuals' and families' decisions to forego insuring assets, both property and health. Decline in employer-sponsored coverage was a reason reported by many leading to their new uninsured status. Though it is difficult to ascertain, it seems reasonable to suggest that some element of financial illiteracy contributed to the decision to forego health insurance made by the 17.7 million persons with annual incomes of $50,000 or more (DeNavas-Walt, Proctor, and Smith, 2007). Having examined several problems of omission, the following problems of commission are worthy of attention: over-consumption, impulse buying, overuse of credit, and taking on risky loans.

Consuming Too Much

"Affluenza" is a term recently coined by de Graff, Wann, and Naylor (2002) and Hamilton & Denniss (2005) to describe "a painful, contagious, socially transmitted condition of overload, debt, anxiety, and waste resulting from the dogged pursuit of more" (p.2). People are buying goods and services beyond that which they truly need. Purchasing is often done impulsively or spontaneously. Consumer Federation of America (2007) acknowledged respondents were not saving adequately, 37 % cited impulse buying as a reason, 29 % mentioned spending to "feel good," and 20 % attributed spending rather than saving to "social pressure from friends or family." Persons of all income levels admitted to such tendencies with nearly equal frequency.

For some, shopping can become a compulsion or addiction. Impulse buyers find reasons to justify their spending, try to forget about the cash they just dropped, or hide the purchase from others (Yi & Baumgartner, 2004). Compulsive shoppers have little control over their spending habits and will "binge buy." The rush that impulsive and compulsive shoppers get from buying an item is followed by feelings of regret, guilt, shame, and anxiety. Their only relief from this is to make yet another purchase. It is estimated that from 1.8 to 16 % of U.S. adults are compulsive shoppers. Koran, Faber, Aboujaoude, Large, and Serpe (2006) report nearly 6% of their survey respondents experienced such tendencies. Enticing advertisements, easy access to credit, and the conveniences of shopping by phone or computer enhance temptations.

Using Credit Too Liberally

One of the U.S.' three major credit reporting bureaus, Experian, cites a National Score Index study based on a nationwide sampling of 3 million consumer credit files. Data collected in late 2006 indicated approximately 51% of the U.S. population have two cards in their wallet, while about 14 % have 10 or more cards (Greer, 2007). Having credit cards, in and of itself, is not a problematic. However, there are significant negative consequences that arise when balances are not paid off promptly: interest charges accumulate and credit ratings decline. Credit cards are increasingly being used for a greater variety of purchases than ever before. Instead of being limited to purchases such as furniture, appliances, clothing and jewelry, credit cards are more readily being used for groceries, gasoline, fast food, other everyday necessities and even college tuition.

A credible source of information about state of U.S. family finances is the Federal Reserve Board. Its triennially conducted Survey of Consumer Finances (SCF) has provided comparative data on the balance sheet, pension, income, and other demographic characteristics of U.S. families since 1983. Data collected from the 2007 survey are under analysis. When 2007 and 2004 data are eventually compared, the volatility of the U.S. and other global economies since 2004 may well be shown to have had serious impact. In 2004, 46.2 % of families surveyed reported credit card debt of some amount, up from 44.4 % in 2001. Of the households that did owe money on credit cards at the time of the 2004 survey, the median balance was $2,200, up from $2,000 three years earlier. For a worrisome 8.3 % of surveyed households, the balance on their credit cards totaled $9,000 or more (Bucks, Kennickell, & Moore, 2006). Though the results from the 2007 survey will not be available until 2009, other data sources (e.g., CardTrak, CardData, CardWatch, and so on) shared troubling figures about the number of delinquencies and defaults in credit card payments in early 2008. As a result, especially in light of the recent subprime mortgage crisis that has developed, card issuers are toughening their lending policies and raising their interest rates. For many credit card holders, reading and understanding complex credit card disclosure statements presents major challenges and, regrettably, are not adequately undertaken.

Being Tempted by Predatory Lenders

Predatory lending involves abusive lending practices, including excessive or hidden fees, refinancing at no benefit to the borrower, offering a loan knowing the borrower lacks the means to repay it, and high-pressure sales tactics. It is difficult to arrive at an accurate figure for the number of persons or households victimized by predatory lending and other scams each year, as many victims do not report their situation. There are indications that predatory loan practices have become increasingly prevalent. While home buying is a common context for unfair, deceptive lending practices, car loans and payday loans are frequent contexts as well. In such situations, when the borrower is unable to make loan payments in full or on time, foreclosure or repossession is often the outcome.

RealtyTrac Inc. (2008) documents a total of 2,203,295 foreclosure filings (e.g., default notices, auction sale notices and bank repossessions) related to 1,285,873 properties nationwide during the year, up 75 % from 2006. The report also shows that more than 1 % of all U.S. households were in some stage of foreclosure during the year, up from 0.58 % in 2006. Families living in poor and minority neighborhoods have been particularly vulnerable and the consequences reach beyond those that lose their homes. Efforts to revitalize neighborhoods and promote home ownership are weakened when numerous home foreclosures and repossessions occur as an outcome of risky loan practices.

Though the number of personal bankruptcy filings each quarter and year has fluctuated, the overall picture has been one of steady increase since the mid-1980s. According to figures maintained by the U.S. Courts, improvement that had taken place after implementation of the Bankruptcy Abuse Prevention and Consumer Protection Act of 2005 is now fading. In the 12-month period ending September 30, 2007, the number of non-business filings was 775,344. This figure represents a 28 % decrease from the year prior. However, filings during the quarter July through September were up 28% compared to the same quarter in 2006 (see http://www.uscourts.gov/bnkrpctystats/bankruptcystats.htm). Bankruptcy poses lasting repercussions for individuals and families. It typically takes considerable time to recover.

A number of manifestations of poor financial fitness have been described above. The extent to which individuals and families do not engage in saving or banking, fail to adequately insure assets, spend beyond their financial means, and allow themselves to become vulnerable to financial exploitation is important to note, but the overall problem is far more complex. Few problems exist in isolation. Were this discussion not confined to a chapter, correlating problems associated with poverty, physical and mental ill-health, various loss-related crises (e.g., divorce, death, job), and inadequate cultural experience could be addressed.

Who Cares? What Can Be Done?

Who cares about financial literacy and security as a policy issue? And, what do these interested parties have to say about the best ways to optimize both for individuals and families? Lots of people in public, private, and non-profit settings care about this issue. Among them are family professionals who believe financial literacy and security are family policy issues, or certainly deserving of a family perspective or lens when analyzed. Educators are interested in these issues, particularly family life educators, but also math, finance, business, and consumer educators as well. Financial advisors and planners, counselors specializing in personal and family finance problems, as well as attorneys and judges observe the costs of financial illiteracy each day. Banking, real estate, and community development professionals are involved in analyzing this issue and have ideas about possible solutions. Employers want their employees to be financially fit. Many local, state, and federal policymakers, agency staff, and organizational leaders make financial literacy and security a focus of their work-related endeavors.

To develop a deliberation guide pertaining to financial literacy and security (Gentry, 2007), I solicited the insight and vision of persons employed with the Federal Reserve Board, Federal Deposit Insurance Corporation, Visa USA, Wachovia Corporation, the National Endowment for Financial Education, Jump$tart Coalition for Personal Financial Literacy, three universities, and the National Council on Family Relations. Public deliberation guides produced by the Kettering Foundation and promoted by the National Issues Forums Institute served as a model for this guide, *Financial Fitness...It's Priceless*. After tapping the analytical abilities of my consultants, I identified four strategic approaches that could be undertaken in an effort to improve the financial literacy and security of U.S. citizens: 1) promote prevention through education, 2) provide counseling and advice, 3) expand and improve regulations, 4) support asset building and other innovative measures. Each approach has its champions and critics. Each approach presents various tradeoffs.

When problems of omission and commission related to financial resource management are rooted in poor attitudes and negative behaviors that are well-engrained, they are likely to be more difficult to counteract. Professional counseling and peer support groups (e.g., Debtors Anonymous) can help individuals and family members to bring about attitudinal and behavior modification with some degree of staying power. People can be protected, in a sense, from their own neglectful and imprudent behaviors by governmental regulations, securing paid financial advisors to undertake financial transactions on their behalf, and being automatically enrolled into employer benefits programs unless they formally opt-out (e.g., automatic savings programs). In order to prevent problems from developing in the first place, or having to remedy them before they have become too severe, family life educators are more apt to promote strategies that transmit relevant, useful information and facilitate the development and refinement of skills related to financial resource management.

Financial Education: Defining the Term and Establishing the Need

In *Goodbye to Complacency,* Vitt, Reichbach, Kent, and Siegenthaler (2005) share that consumers and program directors they interviewed consistently indicated a dislike for the term "literacy" when used in conjunction with financial education. As a result, throughout the report, they made the choice to interchangeably use "financial education" or "personal finance education." The definition they arrived at for *financial education* is instruction that "equips individuals and families with the ability to negotiate the money management issues necessary for them to make self-enhancing life choices" (Vitt, Reichbach, Kent, & Siegenthaler, 2005, p. 9). Former Chairman of the Board of Governors of the Federal Reserve, Alan Greenspan, once said that financial education is a learning process "that should begin at an early age and continue throughout life. This cumulative process builds the skills necessary for making critical financial decisions that affect one's ability to attain the assets, such as education, property, and savings, that improve economic well-being" (Financial Literacy and Education Commission, 2006, p. 83).

In 2003 FleetBoston Financial, a Massachusetts-based bank, undertook the Smarter Decisions with Fleet National Survey, to which more than 1,000 respondents replied. Though 73 % of the participants said parents should be the ones primarily responsible for teaching children about basic finance, only 26 % of those with children aged five and older at home indicated they were very well prepared to do so. Additionally, only 27 % of all respondents perceived themselves as very well informed about managing household finances. When asked if they were to take a quiz on how the stock market or mutual funds work, nearly 70 % projected they would receive a grade of "C" or worse. An equal number expressed a desire to learn more about smarter financial decision-making.

Two well-known non-profits, the Jump$tart Coalition for Personal Financial Literacy and the American Association of Retired Persons (AARP), have assessed the financial knowledge and skills of differing age groups. Jump$tart, located in Washington, DC, seeks to assess and improve the personal financial literacy of students in kindergarten through college. Among its efforts is a biennial survey of high school seniors from across the nation that features questions aimed at assessing respondents' knowledge of and behavioral practices related to money management. The results of surveys conducted in 1997, 2000, 2002, 2004, and most recently, 2006 have been analyzed and compared. While average scores have fluctuated over the course of the ten years, they have never been higher than 57.3 % nor lower than 50.2%. Similar findings surface from the Teens & Money Survey conducted by Charles Schwab & Co. (2006) and the Boys & Girls Clubs of America. Teens overestimate their preparedness to deal with personal finance issues once they graduate from high school when compared to what they really know and, in practice, do about such matters.

Also headquartered in Washington, DC, AARP is an organization dedicated to making life better for people aged 50 and over. In 2003, the organization conducted the Consumer Experiences Survey featuring questions related to credit behavior, fraud, and financial planning. While results indicated most of the 1,500 respondents were managing their debts and credit responsibly, as well as attempting to protect themselves from fraud and identity theft, a significant number lacked knowledge of basic financial and investment terms and practices. Most admitted to not having enough money set aside for aside for future retirement needs or long-term care expenses (AARP, 2003).

Vitt et al. (2005) note financial education was not commonly addressed in U.S. literature prior to the close of the 1990s. Though they do not use the term "tipping point" as it has been coined by Gladwell (2002), they do sense a surge of strategic policy education and advocacy efforts between 2000 and 2005 has brought about "big differences" in awareness of problems associated with poor financial literacy and actions to remedy them, particularly education as a means of prevention. As evidence, they point to numerous pieces of state and federal legislation; concerted efforts to train more financial educators and to train them well; proliferation of educational programs and materials, as well as a clearinghouse to track their existence and availability; numerous research studies; and active networking and coalition building among a diverse group of interested parties.

There are numerous entities (e.g., government agencies, businesses, corporations, schools, not-for-profit organizations, and more) taking up this call to action and are often doing so in collaboration or partnership with one another. Alhough there are too many to identify adequately within the space confines of this chapter, a reasonably comprehensive list of such entities can be found in *Goodbye to Complacency* (Vitt et al., 2005). One federal government agency working to facilitate communication and networking among the key players in this nationwide effort is the Financial Literacy and Education Commission (FLEC). It was established by the Financial Literacy and Education Improvement Act of 2003, is chaired by the U.S. Secretary of the Treasury, and comprised of heads of 20 relevant entities such as the Board of Governors of the Federal Reserve System; the Federal Deposit Insurance Corporation; the Federal Trade Commission; and the Departments of Education, Agriculture, Defense, Health and Human Services, Housing and Urban Development, Labor and Veterans Affairs.

Since its creation, the FLEC has convened quarterly meetings and hosted summits to discuss best practices; developed a national strategy for financial literacy entitled *Taking Ownership of the Future* (FLEC, 2006); established a website to serve as a clearinghouse and coordinated point of entry to information about financial literacy and education programs, grants, and other resources; established an informational hotline available to the members of the public seeking personal finance information; and helped to establish and convene the first meeting of the National Financial Education Network of State and Local Governments in 2007. To further enhance these efforts, in early 2008, President Bush announced the establishment of the President's Advisory Council on Financial Literacy, which brings together members of the business, faith and non-profit communities to make recommendations regarding the best means to improve financial education in the United States. The Council is charged with advising the President and Secretary of the Treasury on ways to improve public understanding of mortgages, credit cards, retirement planning and other financial tools. It will also recommend ways to better measure the progress of U.S. financial literacy. It should be heartening to family life educators to know that Tahira Hira, Professor of personal finance and consumer economics at Iowa State University, is among the inaugural members of the Council. She has a long history of teaching and conducting research in the areas of family financial management, consumer credit, gambling, and consumer bankruptcy in the United States, Japan, United Kingdom, Canada, and New Zealand.

Financial Education: Where, What, Who, How and How Well

Powell and Cassidy (2007) list a variety of settings or contexts wherein family life education, in the broad sense, takes place. Financial education occurs in every arena they identify: Health care settings, community outreach settings, social service agencies, churches, schools (primary, secondary, and post-secondary), workplace settings (e.g., corporate, business, government, and military), correctional settings, and residential settings (e.g., private homes, retirement and other group living communities). Financial education is delivered to learners, either individually or in groups, via classroom, workshop, seminar, online, and self-study instruction. There are educational offerings for children, adolescents, younger adults and older adults. In *Goodbye to Complacency,* Vitt et al. (2005) provide a matrix of financial education initiatives that demonstrate such multiplicity of setting, format, and audience. While it appears variety, as an element of instructional best practice, has been considered as recent financial education efforts have been undertaken, there are surely instances of unmet need. Persons committed to improving the financial literacy and security of individuals and families living in their communities would be wise to conduct a needs assessment to determine the degree to which financial education is optimally and widely delivered to diverse audiences, with suitable frequency, in locations that are easily and safely accessed, and at little or no cost.

In her book entitled *Implementing a Financial Education Program in Your Community: A Step-by-Step Resource Guide for Making Connection Sites,* Murrell (2005) also advocates a needs assessment be undertaken as an important first step toward putting a financial education program into place. Identifying and clarifying program goals, objectives, and content is a second step that follows quickly on the heels of the first. Having been, at one time, senior director for outreach and education with the Fannie Mae Foundation, Murrell knows the benefits of developing partnerships and, as a result, has much good advice regarding ways to bring such partnering about. Effective partnering can also facilitate the development of creative and innovative strategies to market a newly planned financial education program. One step that must not be neglected is evaluation, both formative and summative. Murrell is not alone in noting that too few financial education programs in existence today have undertaken the design and implementation of high quality evaluation studies (Lyons, 2005 and Lyons, Palmer, Jayaratne & Scherpf, 2006). The Jump$tart Coalition for Personal Financial Literacy has recently solicited information about curricula and programs for which formal evaluation studies have been conducted and results readied. The organization intends to eventually disseminate the findings associated with these studies from its website (see http://www.jumpstart.org/).

The National Council on Family Relations (NCFR) provides guidance to family life educators by establishing professional standards for knowledge of ten content areas. As to the content area of family resource management, NCFR suggests the primary objective is to help learners arrive at an understanding of the decisions individuals and families make about developing and allocating resources including time, money, material assets, energy, friends, neighbors, and space, to meet their goals.

This entails, for example, teaching the concepts of goal-setting and decision-making processes; acquisition and allocation of resources; social-environmental influences; life cycle and family structure influences; and consumer issues and decisions (Bredehoft & Cassidy, 1995). The organization's framework for life span family life education provides more detailed direction about topics appropriate for learners based on the life span stage they are currently experiencing (Bredehoft, 1997) (See sidebars Family Resource Management, p. 165-166).

For family life educators needing guidance that more narrowly focuses on just financial resource management, the Jump$tart Coalition for Personal Financial Literacy has developed national K-12th grade curricular standards and accompanying competencies for learners at the benchmark milestones of 4th, 8th, and 12th grades. There are 29 standards that fall within six conceptual categories: financial responsibility and decision-making (6 standards), income and careers (3 standards), planning and money management (7 standards), credit and debt (4 standards), risk management and insurance (3 standards), and saving and investing (6 standards). Revised in 2007, the latest edition of the standards and competencies can be found on the organization's website: http://www.jumpstart.org/. Jump$tart is also considering the formulation of post-secondary standards and competencies. It should be noted, too, that the National Business Education Association, National Council on Economic Education, National Council of Teachers of Mathematics, and the American Association of Family and Consumer Sciences have also developed curricular standards related to financial education.

Variety or diversity was spoken of earlier as an element of instructional best practice to be attended to when designing and delivering financial education. There are other best practices that financial educators should abide by as well. Jump$tart (2003) has identified nearly 30 best practices that address such elements of curriculum and instruction as objectivity, ethical standards, cultural sensitivity, accuracy, timeliness, relevance, accessibility, understandability, interactivity, and usefulness. The FLEC has identified eight components of a successful financial education program (FLEC, 2006) as shown in Table 1.

Table 1. Eight Components of a Successful Financial Education Program

Content	1. Focuses on basic savings, credit management, home ownership and/or retirement planning.
	2. Is tailored to its target audience, taking into account its language, culture, age and experience.
Delivery	3. Is offered through a local distribution channel that makes effective use of community resources and contacts.
	4. Follows up with participants to reinforce the message and ensure that participants are able to apply the skills taught.
Impact	5. Establishes specific program goals and uses performance measures to track progress toward meeting those goals.
	6. Demonstrates a positive impact on participants' attitudes, knowledge or behavior through testing, surveys or other objective evaluation.
Sustainability	7. Can be easily replicated on a local, regional or national basis so as to have broad impact and sustainability.
	8. Is built to last as evidenced by factors such as continuing financial support, legislative backing or integration into an established course of instruction.

Murrell (2005) estimates more that 400 financial education curricula and/or programs are available for instructional use. Approximately 75 % of them have come to fruition since the late 1990s or early 2000s (Vitt, Anderson, Kent, Lyter, Siegenthaler, & Ward, 2003). It would appear the tipping point has been met. However, many educators, including family life educators, positioned to implement financial education curricula and programs are not adequately trained to do so. Some indicate they are not comfortable or confident about their abilities to teach related content and skills to a variety of audiences. Some question their own level of financial literacy and doubt they can cover most or all content areas with proper authority (FLEC, 2006).

The FLEC has identified, as priorities, the need to provide better training for teachers or financial educator roles as well as the importance of supporting them once they are involved in such roles. To that end, state level offshoots of the Jump$tart Coalition for Personal Financial Literacy have facilitated partnerships between state agencies, financial institutions, businesses, and academics from institutions of higher education for purposes of providing K-12 teachers with training, curricula, instructional materials, and other resources. For example, a series of week-long summer financial teacher education classes have taken place in Wisconsin. In West Virginia, such partnerships brought about free personal finance courses for elementary and secondary teachers that offered the possibility of college or professional development credits (FLEC, 2006).

While financial counselors and advisors across the nation are expected to be properly credentialed in order to practice, concerted efforts to establish, implement, require, and monitor a process for certifying personal finance educators have not been widespread or particularly visible. Certainly, persons designated as Certified Family Life Educators (CFLE) have demonstrated their knowledge of family resource management concepts among a host of concepts related to individual and family well-being. The Association for Financial Counseling and Planning Education provides an opportunity for financial educators to acquire certification. The Association of Family and Consumer Sciences also offers a certification that, in part, verifies proficiency with regard to family resource management content and skills. Finally, through its Center for Financial Certifications, the Institute for Financial Literacy offers a Certified Educator in Personal Finance designation (CEPF) that abides by the standards and best practices associated with both K-12 and adult financial literacy education.

It appears, however, that more can and should be done to ensure competency among tomorrow's financial educators. When the New America Foundation convened a roundtable meeting of financial education experts in early 2007, one of ten "policy ideas" put forward by participating practitioners, researchers, and financial institution representatives focused on credentialing as a means of improving financial education and helping consumers make wise financial decisions. More specifically, a report resulting from this roundtable discussion suggested the following occur:

> Establish a process to provide credentials and ongoing training and certification to financial education counselors and educators. The credentialing process would promote quality standards and be implemented in a manner that acknowledges the time and cost constraints of nonprofit financial educators. The process should identify standard core financial management topics necessary for all consumers, as well as additional financial management topics that can be tailored to the needs of different target audiences and different environments. Financial education programs that employ credentialed counselors and educators would be officially certified and otherwise recognized, for example, as automatically eligible for government funds (New American Foundation, 2007, p. 3-4).

Another policy idea voiced by this same roundtable group convened by the New America Foundation was to mandate financial education in schools. They advocated federal funds be provided to enable states to ensure that comprehensive, integrative financial education be taught to every child in grades K-12 by well-trained, capable teachers such that personal finance questions could be included in standardized tests revealing progress in learning (New America Foundation, 2007). The Jump$tart Coalition for Personal Financial Literacy tracks legislative efforts regarding state requirements for financial education. Currently, the organization's website reports that three states (Missouri, Tennessee, and Utah) require at least a one-semester course devoted to personal finance, while 14 states (Georgia, Idaho, Illinois, Kansas, Louisiana, New York, North Carolina, Ohio, Oklahoma, South Carolina, South Dakota, Texas, Virginia, and West Virginia) require personal finance instruction to be incorporated into other subject matter. The website also provides a brief synopsis of the legislation approved in each of these states. Though such legislation may fall short in some ways, these efforts are commendable in the eyes of many.

Two more policy ideas articulated by this group, as well as other policy advocates and educators (Gentry, 2007), also deserve attention here. First, relevant financial instruction should be provided, possibly even required, as a step in the process of securing loans such as home mortgages and college financial aid. Other teachable moments that are ripe for financial education occur when consumers are setting up bank accounts or making arrangements for retirement savings. Second, financial education, including but not limited to retirement planning, should be provided in the workplace. New America Foundation (2007) roundtable participants suggested that every publicly-traded corporation in the U.S. be required to include in its annual report a description of the strategies and activities it undertakes to enhance the financial literacy and security of its workforce. Likewise, parallel requirements should be established for all government entities, including the military. Even employers of small workforces should be encouraged, possibly by offering incentives such as tax credits, to facilitate financial education for their employees. Instruction need not necessarily be given on-site, but offered elsewhere by other providers.

What Remains to Be Done

The need for financial education is apparent and the case for it well made (Fox, Bartholomae, & Lee, 2005). To meet this need, an ample number of financial education programs, curricula, and resource materials have been developed and marketed. Efforts to ensure adequate numbers of competent educators to deliver such programs and utilize instructional materials have been and continue to be underway. However, while these forces have been on the rise, local, state, and national economic conditions have declined and budgets have been cut (Lyons, 2005). As committed to sponsoring financial education programs as many potential funders are, their resources are limited. As a result, they want help in identifying programs that have been shown to work well with the audiences they hope to reach. They are not solely content with information about numbers of sessions taught, participants served, or print materials distributed. Rather, they want documentation of knowledge gain and retention, as well as evidence of improvement in attitude and behaviors leading to better financial decision-making (Lyons, 2005). To a degree, these expectations held by funders are being met. In their review of a handful or two of programs, Fox, Bartholomae, and Lee (2005) conclude there are some that have demonstrated noteworthy effectiveness. More often than not, however, "a significant number of financial education providers still do not have in place the evaluation capacity and resources to conduct more effective and rigorous evaluations, especially smaller, non-profit organizations" (Lyons, 2005, p. 56). Developing and maintaining this capacity is a task for immediate and future undertaking.

For those willing to engage in such capacity building, there are barriers and challenges to be addressed. Lyons (2005) enumerates five common ones. First, there is difficulty in reaching consensus among researchers and practitioners regarding how program success is to be defined. Second, considerable care must be taken to appropriately match projected program outcomes and their indicators with the targeted population and their particular financial situations. Third, for a variety of reasons, some participants may be unwilling and unmotivated when it comes to completing program evaluation paperwork. Fourth, more rigorous evaluation designs are time, labor, and expertise intensive to set up and carry out. Finally, such demands are costly, unless innovative strategies such as partnering and pooling resources are employed.

There are ways to address and counteract such barriers and challenges (Fox, Bartholomae, & Lee, 2005; Lyons, 2005; Lyons & Neelakantan, 2008). A crucial first step would be to establish a standardized, consistent, yet flexible approach to program evaluation at the national level. To accompany this national evaluation strategy, a set of "tools" could be devised and promoted. According to Lyons, such tools would include a website offering, all in one place, exemplary survey instruments, best practices, informational webinars, and other evaluation related resources and materials. Face-to-face trainings, seminars, forums, and discussions could be conducted on a regular basis to focus on emerging issues related to financial education and program evaluation. A journal or periodical devoted to financial education program evaluation could be developed. Finally, a referral list of national experts/researchers in program evaluation could be created and utilized. Simultaneous to endeavors to establish a national evaluation strategy and toolkit, another important action would be to seek consensus regarding the theory(ies) and framework(s) that are most suitable to guide program design, development, delivery, and evaluation activities.

Though applications of life cycle theory to these enterprises have proven useful, applications of the Transtheoretical Model of Change (TTM) have yielded insightful results for various financial education practitioners and scholars. Integrating major psychological theories into a theory of behavioral change, TTM posits such change occurs in these five stages: precontemplation, contemplation, preparation, action, and maintenance. Though this model originally provided guidance to efforts to help individuals gain control over harmful health-related behaviors such as smoking, alcohol and drug abuse, and over eating, it has recently been helpful in examining changes in financial management behaviors (Lyons, 2005; Lyons & Neelakantan, 2008). The work of Schockey and Seiling (2004) and Xiao, Newman, Prochaska, Leon, Bassett, & Johnson (2004) provide illustration of how TTM can be applied in this context.

Jacobs' (1988) framework for program evaluation has been well received by many scholars and practitioners. For example, Hughes (1994) has demonstrated its usefulness to family life education program development and evaluation. Fox, Bartholomae, and Lee (2005) have applied the framework to personal and family financial education specifically. Just as TTM features five stages, so does Jacobs' framework, though she uses the term "tiers" instead of stages: preimplementation; accountability; program clarification; progress toward objectives; and program impact (Jacobs, 1988). *Preimplementation* involves conducting needs assessments. *Accountability* consists of documenting facts and figures related to the means of instruction provided, types of materials and services shared, nature and number of participants served, and costs incurred to deliver a given educational program. The *program clarification* tier necessitates revisiting the mission, goals, objectives, and strategies initially devised for a particular program to determine if they remain worthy of continued pursuit. During the *progress-toward-objectives* stage, program evaluators collect evidence of participant learning. This stage provides the foundation for activities associated with the last one. *Program impact* involves deeper, more rigorous inquiry regarding both short-term and long-term impacts of a program. While intake information received from participants at the time of registration, exit surveys, focus group commentary, and pretest-posttest approaches may be sufficient means of data collection for lower tiers, the final tier of this evaluation enterprise benefits from formal experimental, or quasi-experimental methods that are, perhaps, carried out by external researchers. This five-tier framework for program evaluation is appreciated for its comprehensiveness, as it is both formative and summative in nature. Another strength is its expectation, as the process moves from tier to tier, that data collection and analysis efforts become increasingly impartial, independent, and rigorous (Jacobs, 1988; Fox, Bartholomae, and Lee, 2005). In doing so, results of evaluative inquiry are more powerful and, potentially, more persuasive.

Roles Family Professionals Can Play

Family professionals, be they educators, scholars, or policy specialists, have multiple and intertwining roles to play in furthering financial literacy and security for individuals and their families. Family life educators are well-positioned, particularly if they have acquired certification status, to design and deliver financial education curricula and programs. For those who lack adequate exposure to one or more important content areas, there are courses, workshops, and other forms of training that they can avail themselves of in an effort to enhance their competency as an educator. Family scholars can envision new theories and frameworks, or refine existing ones, that can lend insight to the problems of financial illiteracy and mismanagement, as well as give guidance to program development and evaluation processes. Evaluation experts in the family realm can serve as consultants and external reviewers when called upon by financial education providers and funders. Lastly, family policy specialists can organize deliberative forums and impact seminars to educate both members of the public as well as policymakers about problems associated with poor financial literacy and security. They can facilitate the objective analysis of these problems and help to generate workable solutions. The momentum that currently exists on the financial education front should not be allowed to ebb away. A state of complacency must not be allowed to return. More work remains to be done and family life professionals can be among those to carry the movement forward.

References

American Association of Retired Persons. (2003, October 21). *Americans ages 45+ score a "C" grade on consumer issues.* Retrieved from http://www.aarp.org/research/press-center/presscurrentnews/a2003-10-31-news-consumerissues.html

Barr, M. S. (2004, September). *Banking the poor: Policies to bring low-income Americans into the financial mainstream.* Washington, D.C.: The Brookings Institution. Retrieved from http://www3.brookings.edu/metro/pubs/20041001_Banking.pdf

Bredehoft, D. (Ed.). (1997). *The framework for life span family life education* (2nd ed.). [Poster]. Minneapolis, MN: National Council on Family Relations.

Bredehoft, D., & Cassidy, D. (Eds.). (1995). *Family life education curriculum guidelines* (pp. 12-14). Minneapolis, MN: National Council on Family Relations.

Bucks, B. K., Kennickell, A. B., & Moore, K. B. (2006). Recent changes in U.S. family finances: Evidence from the 2001 and 2004 Survey of Consumer Finances [Electronic version]. *Federal Reserve Bulletin, 92*, A1-A38.

Bureau of Economic Analysis. (2008). *National economic accounts.* Retrieved from http://www.bea.gov/national/index.htm#personal

Charles Schwab & Co. (2006, April 19). *Schwab survey reveals new insights into money behavior and concerns of teens.* Retrieved from http://www.businesswire.com/portal/site/schwab/index.jsp?epi-content=GENERIC&beanStrID=schwabNdm&viewID=news_view&ndmConfigId=1002458&newsId=20070919006225&newsLang=en&vnsId=4608

Consumer Federation of America. (2007, February 26). *National survey reveals emergency savings needs and effective saver strategies.* Retrieved from http://www.consumerfed.org/pdfs/America_Saves_Week_Press_Release_2.26.07.pdf

Consumer Federation of America. (2007, December 10). *More than half of Americans say they are not saving adequately.* Retrieved from http://www.consumerfed.org/pdfs/CFA_Wachovia_Savings_Press_Release_12_10_07.pdf

de Graff, J., Wann, D., & Naylor, T. (2002). Affluenza: The all-consuming epidemic. San Francisco, CA: Berrett-Koehler Publishers, Inc.

DeNavas-Walt, C., Proctor, B. D., & Smith, J. (2007). *Income, poverty, and health insurance coverage in the United States: 2006.* U.S. Census Bureau, Current Population Reports, P60-233. Washington, D.C.: U.S. Government Printing Office.

Demos. (2008). *Faces of debt: Students, people of color, and older Americans.* Retrieved from http://www.demos.org/page43.cfm#older

Employee Benefit Research Institute. (2007). *Saving for retirement in America.* Retrieved from http://www.ebri.org/pdf/surveys/rcs/2007/RCS07_FS_4_Sav.pdf

eXtension. (n.d.). *Personal finance.* Retrieved February 28, 2008 from http://www.extension.org/personal+finance

Financial Literacy and Education Commission. (2006). *Taking ownership of the future: The national strategy for financial literacy.* Washington, D.C.: U.S. Department of the Treasury.

Fox, J., Bartholomae, S., & Lee, J. (2005). Building the case for financial education. *The Journal of Consumer Affairs, 39*(1), 195-214.

Gentry, D. (2007). *Financial fitness...It's priceless: A guide to conducting deliberative forums.* American Association of Family & Consumer Sciences. Alexandria, V.A. Retrieved from http://www.aafcs.org/policy/financialfitnessguide.html

Gladwell, M. (2002). *The tipping point: How little things can make a big difference.* New York: Little, Brown and Company.

Greer, H. (2007, February 15). *Experian's National Score Index shows 14 % of U.S. population has more than 10 credit cards.* Retrieved from http://www.nationalscoreindex.com/ScoreNews_Archive_13.aspx

Hamilton, C, & Denniss, R. (2005). *Affluenza: When too much is never enough.* Crows Nest, Australia: Allen & Unwin.

Hughes, R. (1994). A framework for developing family life education programs. *Family Relations: Interdisciplinary Journal of Applied Family Studies, 43*(1), 74-80.

Jacobs, F. H. (1988). The five-tiered approach to program evaluation: Context and implementation. In H. B. Weiss and F. H. Jacobs (Eds.), *Evaluating Family Programs* (pp. 37-68). New York: Aldine DeGruyter.

Jump$tart. (2003). *National best practices guidelines for personal finance education materials.* Retrieved February 28, 2008 from http://www.jumpstart.org/bp.cfm

Koran, L. M., Faber, R. J., Aboujaoude, E., Large, M. D., & Serpe, R. T. (2006). Estimated prevalence of compulsive buying behavior in the United States. *American Journal of Psychiatry, 163*(10), 1806-12.

Lyons, A. C. (2005). Financial education and program evaluation: Challenges and potential for financial professionals. *Journal of Personal Finance, 4*(4), 56-68.

Lyons, A. C., Palmer, L., Jayaratne, K. S. U., & Scherpf, E. (2006). Are we making the grade? A national overview of financial education and program evaluation. *Journal of Consumer Affairs, 40*(2), 208-235.

Lyons, A. C. & Neelakantan, U. (2008). Potential and pitfalls of applying theory to the practice of financial education. *Journal of Consumer Affairs, 42*(1), 106-112.

Murrell, K. L. (2005). *Implementing a financial education program in your community: A step-by-step resource guide for making connection sites.* Baltimore, MD: Annie E. Casey Foundation.

New America Foundation. (2007). *Public policy ideas to improve financial education and help consumers make wise financial decisions.* Retrieved from http://www.newamerica.net/files/Public%20Policy%20Ideas%20to%20Improve%20Financial%20Education.pdf

Nichols, F. (2000). *Changing someone else's behavior: Factors to consider.* Retrieved February 28, 2008 from http://home.att.net/~nickols/changing.htm

Powell, L. H., & Cassidy, D. (2007). *Family life education: Working with families across the life span* (2nd ed.). Long Grove, IL: Waveland Press, Inc.

RealtyTrac Inc. (2008, January 29). *U.S. foreclosure activity increases 75 % in 2007.* Retrieved from http://www.realtytrac.com/ContentManagement/pressrelease.aspx?ChannelID=9&ItemID=3988&accnt=64847

Schockey, S. S., & Seiling, S. B. (2004). Moving into action: Application of the transtheoretical model of behavior change to financial education. *Financial Counseling and Planning, 15*(1), 41-52.

Taylor, P., Funk, C., & Clark, A. (2007, January 24). *We try hard. We fall short. Americans assess their saving habits.* Retrieved from http://pewresearch.org/assets/social/pdf/Saving.pdf

Vitt, L. A., Anderson, C., Kent, J., Lyter, D. M., Siegenthaler, J. K., & Ward, J. (2003). *Personal finance and the rush to competence: Financial literacy education in the U.S.* Middleburg, VA: Institute for Socio-Financial Studies.

Vitt, L. A., Reichbach, G. M., Kent, J. L., & Siegenthaler, J. K. (2005). *Goodbye to complacency: Financial literacy education in the U.S. 2000-2005.* Washington, D.C.: American Association of Retired Persons.

Xiao, J. J., Newman, B. M., Prochaska, J. M., Leon, B., Bassett, R. L., & Johnson, J. L. (2004). Applying the transtheoretical model of change to consumer debt behavior. *Financial Counseling and Planning, 15*(2), 89-100.

Yi, S., & Baumgartner, H. (2004), Coping with negative emotions in purchase-related situations. *Journal of Consumer Psychology, 14*(3), 303-317.

About the Author

Deborah B. Gentry, Ed.D., CFLE, CFCS is Director of the Instructional Development Center at Heartland Community College, Normal, Illinois. An experienced educator and scholar of teaching and learning, she has presented and published on the scholarship of teaching and learning, family life education, and family conflict. She has served in various leadership roles within the National Council on Family Relations, Family Science Association, the Groves Conference on Marriage and Family, and the American Association of Family and Consumer Sciences. E-mail: Deborah.Gentry@heartland.edu.

A Comprehensive Framework for Marriage Education*

ALAN J. HAWKINS, JASON S. CARROLL,
WILLIAM J. DOHERTY, AND BRIAN WILLOUGHBY

In a progressive society such as the United States, we usually take problems, such as high divorce and non-marital childbearing rates, as a cause for action rather than a reason for resignation. Thus, it should surprise no one that the beginnings of a marriage movement have emerged in the United States over the last decade (Gallagher, 2000). A prominent part of this emerging movement has been a wide array of educational initiatives; however, to date there has been no formal effort to develop an integrative conceptual framework of marriage education. Some efforts to articulate the overarching paradigm of the marriage movement have occurred (Gallagher; Doherty, & Carroll, 2002), but there has been less emphasis on the development of theoretical models or heuristics to organize marriage education.

In this article, we attempt to provide marriage educators with a set of concepts to help them better understand their craft and discover unseen possibilities. Too often, educators have only a narrow view of the breadth of what marriage education actually might encompass. We offer a map or framework, depicted in Figure 1, to help marriage educators think more thoroughly, systematically, broadly, and creatively about opportunities to strengthen marriage. We draw attention to the elements of content, intensity, method, timing, setting, target, and delivery in marriage education. We note that we have much to learn about marriage education for lower income couples who potentially have the most to benefit from educational initiatives. We emphasize the value of developing marriage education with greater specificity in content, timing, and target, and we call for intervention that embeds marriage education in diverse institutional settings with access to couples across the socioeconomic spectrum. We end by addressing the need to take marriage education beyond a valuable helping profession —and even an expanding educational service integrated into the human services—to a vibrant social movement.

First, we highlight a few caveats. The focus of our framework is educational intervention. Although we value other forms of intervention that seek to strengthen marriage, such as therapy and policy, our focus here is on education. Our framework stresses possibilities for marriage education more than description, because the field remains open to creative effort. We use

*This article was prepared while the first author was a visiting scholar with the Office of Planning, Research, and Evaluation, Administration for Children and Families, U.S. Department of Health and Human Services. The views expressed are those of the authors and not necessarily those of the Administration for Children and Families.

Figure 1.
A Comprehensive Framework for Marriage Education

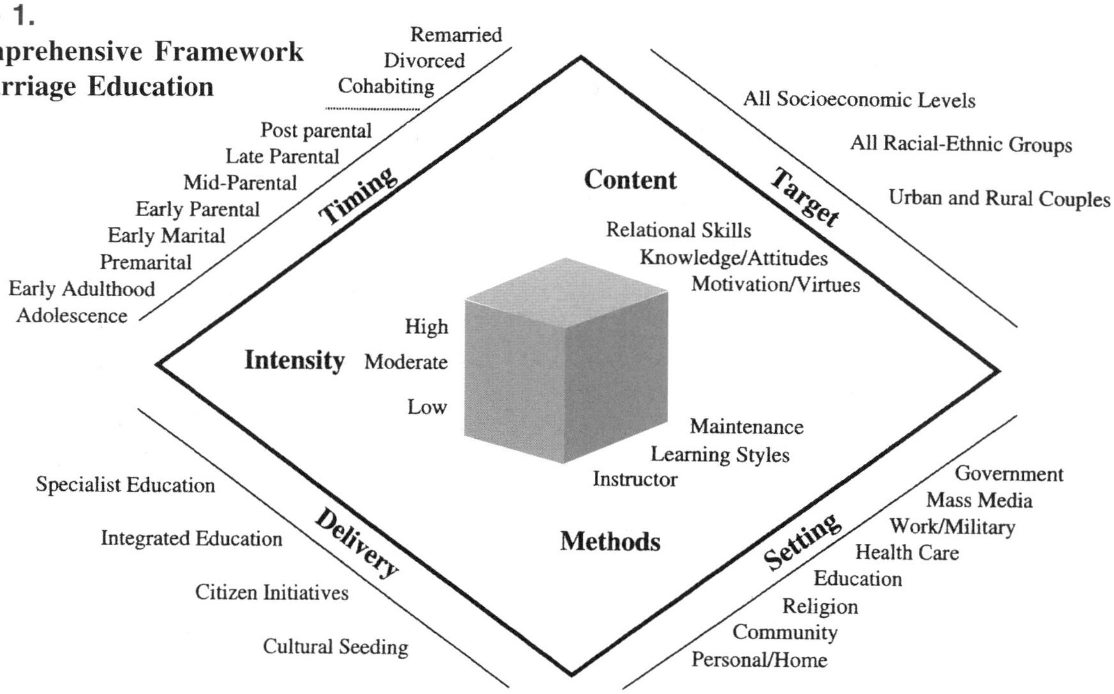

the term marriage education here rather than relationship education to capture both the relational and institutional dimensions of marriage with a life course perspective to facilitate covering issues of importance to youth and unmarried adults. We acknowledge our positive bias toward marriage education. We also acknowledge the need for more data to confirm the general efficacy of marriage education, especially for low-income and minority couples. While we wait for those data to accumulate, however, we believe that enough is known to continue the work that has begun. Finally, we clarify that our use of the word marriage is short-hand for healthy marriage—a generous, respectful, equal partnership free of abuse.

Dimensions of Marriage Education

Dimension I: Content—What is Taught?

The content of most marriage education is based in some way on the excellent research over the past 20 years that has illuminated couples' interactional processes as central in the breakdown of marital relationships. However, less attention has gone to basic knowledge about the institutional features and benefits of marriage, or to the virtues that sustain healthy marriages. We discuss three subdimensions of content: relational skills; awareness/knowledge/attitudes; and motivations/ virtues. Importantly, whatever the content, we acknowledge the importance of empirically derived curricula rather than personal, idiosyncratic content.

Relational skills

Relationship skills have been the primary emphasis of most marriage education efforts. A generation of good research points to the importance of interactional processes, communication patterns, and problem-solving behaviors that sustain or weaken marriages (Gottman & Notarius, 2000). The importance of relationship skills has increased concomitant with our cultural expectations for marriage. We expect marriage to bring us lifelong joy, companionship, growth, and sexual fulfillment. This might be an unrealistic standard, but most couples hold it and, thus, need better skills to achieve their vision of marital success.

Evaluation research provides hope that vital relationship skills can be learned (Halford, Moore, Wilson, Farrugia, & Dyer, 2004; Stanley et al., 2001). Still, Browning (2003) argued that a skills education perspective tends to see marriage in a therapeutic worldview that is less attentive to the institutional features of marriage and the virtues that undergird healthy marriages, which also are important content domains. Some skills-based programs are sensitive to this concern and have upgraded curricula accordingly (e.g., PREP, PREPARE/ENRICH).

Awareness, knowledge, and attitudes

We believe that relational skills will develop and work best in the context of a good understanding about healthy marriage and attitudes that foster it. Even when they focus primarily on relational skills, most programs still teach participants some basic knowledge and attitudes about marriage. For instance, most programs make couples aware of common problems to avoid. Awareness of basic problems helps to motivate couples to work harder on their relationships (Halford et al., 2004). In addition, virtually all programs discuss or imply that sustaining healthy marriages requires effort. In essence, most marriage education invokes a principle of marital entropy: Marriages naturally decay unless we put energy into them. Understanding that marriage requires regular effort might be gaining importance in a society with increasing acceptance of the notion that a perfect soulmate is available with which to form an effortless marriage (Whitehead & Popenoe, 2001).

There are other areas of knowledge that appear to be less integrated into current marriage education despite the real possibility that mental and ethical elements of the marital infrastructure that support healthy marriages (e.g., realistic expectations, a willingness to make significant personal sacrifices) need shoring up (Fowers, 2000). One domain of knowledge that is usually taken for granted is a discussion of the basic institutional and societal features of marriage (Nock, 2002). For instance, what societal purposes does a strong, stable marriage serve? What public responsibilities are inherent in this private relationship? With the roots of marriage education in clinical psychology (DeMaria, 2003) rather than sociology or anthropology, it is not surprising that marriage educators have given less attention to basic knowledge about the public dimension of marriage. However, in some communities, healthy marriages are a minimal feature of the social environment. Some low-income couples have virtually no models of healthy marriage (Edin & Kefalas, in press). Understanding how one's marriage makes an important contribution to one's community and society might provide greater motivation to maintain a healthy relationship.

Motivation/Virtues

In addition to needed skills and basic knowledge, the motivations and virtues brought to marriage are important content domains for marriage education. Doherty (2000) argued that we are in danger of deeding marriage over to the consumer culture that governs many other aspects of our affluent lives. Further, he asserted that a consumer marriage is weak because individuals are in it for present personal benefits. If a consumer ethic is a dominant motive in marriage, even good skills and knowledge might be insufficient to keep spouses together.

Commitment is one important motivation that usually is addressed in marriage education. A growing body of research finds that commitment is crucial to healthy, stable marriages (Amato & Rogers, 1999; Stanley, Whitton, & Markman, 2004). Fowers (2000) argued that character and the motivations that individuals bring to relationships are fundamental to understanding healthy marriage. He put virtues, such as generosity, justice, and loyalty, at the center of marriage, implying that marriage educators teach relational skills and knowledge in a moral domain, not just an instrumental one. We believe that these and other virtues deserve more attention from educators.

Dimension II: Intensity—What is the Dosage?

Proper dosage is an important part of any intervention; too little means ineffective treatment, but too much can be costly or even dangerous. Like public health practitioners, marriage educators also need to think carefully about the resources needed for an intervention to achieve its goals with as wide a group as possible. For instance, some hypothesize that marriage intervention for disadvantaged low-income couples needs to be more intensive than traditional approaches to be effective (Dion et al., 2003). On the other hand, practical concerns suggest the need for some marriage education to be less intense. Lower dosage offerings might attract couples less inclined to seek out marriage education, especially preventive education targeting less distressed couples who might not sense an immediate need. Dishion (2003) showed how shorter interventions for parents of adolescents can attract more participants and still be effective.

If more intense programs are beneficial to recipients, they still might have limited impact because they reach relatively few. A common response to this problem is to teach educators more effective marketing; however, better marketing does not override the need to question whether treatment dosages fall within the resource budgets of potential participants. In short, we are calling for a creative and flexible approach to marriage education that varies the dosage along a continuum of intensity. Moreover, we argue that intervention researchers should regularly include dosage as a design feature in their studies.

Low Level

Public health educators strive to increase population health with low-level educational interventions such as media campaigns (e.g., Hornik, 2002). We believe that marriage educators also should explore the potential of lower dosage interventions. There are some noteworthy efforts beginning to emerge. For instance, First Things First (http://www.firstthings.org) of Chattanooga, Tennessee, has used creative low-level media messages to teach basic principles of healthy marriages and encourage greater involvement in marriage education services as part of their communitywide marriage initiative. They also have produced a pamphlet, *What You Need to Know About Living Together*, for wide distribution to youth, that addresses popular misconceptions about cohabitation. The potential of these kinds of efforts for strengthening marriage is largely uninvestigated, but we believe that the documented successes with public health campaigns (Hornik) could be replicated in marriage education.

Moderate Level

Providing specific cutoffs that distinguish low-level from moderate-level interventions might be impossible; intensity is more fluid than solid and resists categorization. However, we provide some possible examples of moderate-dosage efforts and some elements that tend to produce higher dosages. For example, a half-day marriage-enhancement seminar does not demand the time of a multisession workshop, but it accommodates more content than low-level efforts. In addition, flexible self-guided interventions might fit well here. Larson's (2003) *The Great Marriage Tune-Up Book* shows promise as a self-guided intervention. A pilot study of the flexible self-guided Couple CARE program in Australia (Halford et al., 2004) provides evidence that these kinds of interventions can strengthen couple relationships. Web-based programs that capitalize on flexibility and self-guided participation also might fit in a category of modest-level education. (For example, see a Web-based marriage preparation course, "Saying 'I Do': Consider the Possibilities" at (http://www.utahmarriage.org.) Educational offerings in the middle of the intensity continuum might make interventions more attractive to work or healthcare organizations whose primary missions lie elsewhere.

Moderate-dosage intervention also should be identified by some assessment of the psychological costs required of participants. Our experience has been that programs that ask participants to explore psychologically sensitive areas scare away some potential participants. Thus, moderate-intensity programs should avoid psychologically intense activity.

Finally, moderate-level intervention might restrict the scope of the curriculum. When marriage education programs try to be comprehensive in their coverage of crucial content, they require more time and energy of the participants. We believe that there also is a need for marriage education that focuses on just one or two topics. For instance, money management and debt are serious problems that influence marital quality and stability (Johnson et al., 2002). In addition, interventions aimed at couples with special circumstances, such as couples caring for a special-needs child or elderly parents, are needed. Moderate-intensity formats focused on specific problems would fill an important niche in a comprehensive set of marriage education offerings. They might be better attended, because they are more likely to address a concrete challenge experienced by many couples.

High Level

High-dosage educational offerings also will be crucial to a comprehensive marriage education strategy. More intense marriage education allows for in-depth exploration of a fuller range of topics. It also might allow for individuals and couples to explore personal issues at deeper levels with trained facilitators, and it might allow educators to build supportive structures into their curriculum, such as mentor couples (McManus, 1993). Although individuals will differ on an exact delineation of high-dosage intervention, we hinted at relevant factors in the previous section. They include time commitment, psychological security, and the amount of professional training required of program leaders. One example is the Becoming Parents program (Jordan, Stanley, & Markman, 1999), which is a marriage and parenting curriculum adapted from the Premarital Relationship and Enhancement Program (or PREP) model (see http://www.PREPinc.com) and targeted specifically to couples transitioning to parenthood. Seminars require 27 classroom hours. Moreover, this intervention requires specialized training for instructors who must complete an extensive for-fee 3-day training workshop. These kinds of interventions can be effective for couples with the personal desires and resources to invest in them. It might be that lower dosage education that reaches more individuals also could serve to increase interest in more intensive learning experiences.

Dimension III: Methods—How is it Learned?

Regardless of the content of marriage education offerings, decisions need to be made about how the content is presented and learned. Our experience teaches us that teaching processes might be as crucial to educational outcomes as the content itself. Although our list of topics is not exhaustive, we discuss three important method issues: instructor, learning styles, and maintenance. (Note that most of our comments assume a higher dosage educational format.)

Instructor

We believe that the more instructors are familiar with the particular issues that participants face, the more credibility they will have. They also will be able to adapt and present curricular content to fit the lived experiences of participants most effectively. For instance, lower income African American couples face daunting challenges to forming and sustaining marriages (Fein, Burstein, Fein, & Lindberg, 2003). An instructor who relates to these complex barriers might be as important to the success of the program as the content offered. Hispanics reflect many different cultural traditions related to marriage, and unless marriage educators understand these differences and can tailor instruction and program materials in relevant ways, they will struggle to help important groups. Gender also can be an important issue. Our experience suggests that some men are more responsive to the content of a program if delivered by a male-female team of co-instructors instead of just a woman instructor. Similarly, couples who share a particular faith might be served best by an educator who can communicate content within the culture and language of their religious beliefs and practices. In short, messages are enhanced or inhibited by messengers. Importantly, all instructors must receive training to assure competence.

Learning styles

Curricula differ in how much emphasis they place on cognitive versus experiential learning. Most marriage education programs that we know of include a variety of methods tailored to diverse learning styles, such as didactic presentation of information, showing examples (e.g., in a video), interactive discussion, and role-playing. The choice of methods requires careful and empirically informed tailoring. Well-educated individuals and couples are accustomed to more cognitive and didactic approaches typical of higher education. However, this approach might be less effective for individuals without extensive formal education, who might prefer more active, experiential learning methods. Similarly, our experience is that individuals in some non-Western cultures are uncomfortable with public disclosure of personal lives and emotions, a method that marriage educators commonly rely on to normalize issues. Some work suggests that lower income U.S. couples are less comfortable in formal settings with self-disclosure of intimate and emotional aspects of their lives (Dion et al., 2003). No firm rules exist for making these decisions, but one guiding principle is that such decisions should be made by those who are well connected to and experienced with typical participants, reprising the earlier point about the need for culturally sensitive instructors.

Maintenance

Although there is encouraging initial evidence that marriage education helps couples build and sustain healthy relationships (Carroll & Doherty, 2003; Halford et al., 2004), research is less clear about how long intervention effects are maintained. Given the steady stream of new stresses that couples face and the short duration of interventions, diminishing effects are not surprising. For some time, marriage educators have speculated about the benefits of follow-up "booster" sessions to reinforce learned ideas and behaviors (Silliman, Stanley, Coffin, Markman, & Jordan, 2001). However, few programs integrate booster sessions into their curricular process. Cowan and Cowan (2000) effectively included postnatal booster sessions in their intervention that strengthened marriages during the transition to parenthood. And Jordan (Jordan et al., 1999) also includes booster sessions in her Becoming Parents program, which is now being evaluated. Because attendance at follow-up sessions might be spotty, other ways to deliver booster curriculum deserve consideration. Newsletters sent periodically to program graduates might reinforce program effects and encourage ongoing maintenance activities. Marriage educators could employ e-mail and the Internet efficiently and creatively to follow up with participants and reinforce learning. Building virtual communities of graduates who can support each other over time also might be effective. Doherty and Carroll (2002) took the concept of booster sessions in a different direction. They urged consideration of another model in which couples who first receive education then give back to their communities by reaching out to help other couples in some fashion, such as mentoring other couples, becoming educators themselves, and advocating in their communities for healthy marriages.

Marriage educators need to give more attention to methods that can help participants maintain program benefits. In addition, as a profession, marriage education can extend this work temporally to think about multiple interventions across the life cycle because regular marital inoculations may be needed to cope successfully with normal changes over time.

Dimension IV: Timing—When Does it Occur?

Marriage educators frequently teach general principles and skills for building and sustaining healthy marriages that appear to transcend temporal and circumstantial boundaries; however, marriages are not static. General principles exist, but there are good reasons for marriage educators to temporally tailor their work. An important reason for temporal specificity is that it makes curricula more concrete. For example, learning general problem-solving skills is important, but young engaged couples who are blinded by new love might be least aware of their differences. For them, it might be as important to attend to such issues as assessing risk and protective factors in the relationship and understanding the basic duties that marriage imposes. Similarly, couples beginning a second marriage with responsibilities to children from a previous union bring challenges to their union that childless couples do not face. The more tailored educational offerings are to the temporal and life circumstances of their participants, the more likely they are to meet perceived needs. By extension, they also might attract more participants.

Life Course Changes

We believe that marriage education has focused primarily on young engaged or newly married couples. Reaching adolescence and young adults who are forming attitudes about marriage, as well as couples whose children have been launched, will reveal rich educational possibilities.

Adolescence. We see adolescence as a fertile time to begin to reach out to youth with relationship and marriage eduation. Some high school curricula, such as the PREP-based *Connections*, integrate relationship and marriage education into the classroom. Healthy relationship skills are a staple of these programs, but it might be equally important that they address other issues, such as common marriage and divorce myths and guidelines for effective marriage preparation. Many adolescents have experienced parental divorce and an absent father personally, and some struggle to point to any healthy long-term marriages in their families and neighborhoods. Further, they are large consumers of television and other media (Roberts, 2000) that give confusing and false messages about intimate relationships (Harris & Scott, 2002). Under these circumstances, many adolescents lack a solid understanding of what marriage means, how society benefits from it, and how healthy, stable marriages are sustained. Accordingly, Pearson (2000) has argued that marriage educators should attend to adolescents' basic understanding of marriage and not ignore difficult issues that weigh on adolescents. Pearson also argued that adolescents are bored by the typical sex education curriculum that focuses on body parts and diseases; instead, they need and want to understand a fuller and richer meaning of sexuality. Marriage education for adolescents carries the potential of wiser choices leading to stronger marriages.

Early adulthood. There is now a 12–15-year period between the onset of sexual capacity and the time that most young adults choose to marry. This lengthened period of the life course coincides with great sexual freedom. It is not surprising that marriage scholars are studying this changing life course period (Glenn & Marquardt, 2001; Whitehead & Popenoe, 2000). However, marriage educators could give greater attention to this period, because young adulthood is not a period of cognitive and behavioral latency regarding marriage; they are forming attitudes about marriages and engaged in behaviors that might impact their future marriages. Marriage educators could address in more concrete ways topics introduced to adolescents, such as dating patterns, sexual involvement, and cohabitation. An important need is to help young adults understand how to make good marriage partner choices and avoid partners who carry a significant risk of being abusive. Van Epp's How to Avoid Marrying a Jerk program tries to do this (see http://www.nojerks.com). Colleges and universities would be a prime setting to fill this educational gap.

Another educational possibility during young adulthood is helping some to develop clearer cognitive models of healthy marriages and greater confidence that they can succeed. Research indicates that young adults are less confident than previous generations about their chances for marital success (Glenn, 1996), in part because of childhood experience with divorce and fatherlessness. For some, especially lower income African Americans, marriage is missing from their childhood experience and is nearly absent from their communities (Fein et al., 2003). These young adults still hold aspirations for marriage (Bendheim-Thoman Center for Child Wellbeing, 2002), but they might need help to understand more clearly what the institution of marriage is and what it could hold for them personally. Clearly, there is a need for more marriage education opportunities in this period of the life course.

Premarital and early marital. Couples in these periods of the life course are obvious candidates for sound, preventative intervention. Unfortunately, too many engaged couples are blinded by romance, so they fail to see potential pitfalls; they focus on the wedding rather than the marriage. To help, religious organizations have been leading the way in turning wedding planning into marriage preparation. The best preparation programs combine religious instruction on the sacred nature of marriage with secular wisdom on building and sustaining healthy marriages. They also include couples taking a relationship inventory to help them identify strengths and challenges in their relationship, and encourage efforts to address potential problems. (See Larson, Newell, Topham, & Nichols, 2002, for a critical review of the major inventories.) Some couples are discouraged from marrying because they come to see dangerous flaws in their relationships (Center for Marriage and Family, 1995; Stanley, 2001). In addition to premarital education, some faith communities assign newlyweds a mentor couple trained to be a personalized support system (McManus, 1993). However, premarital educators in religious or other settings need to adjust or augment their efforts for many couples who come to marriage with more complications, such as childhood abuse or stepchildren.

Enrichment education in the early years of marriage could prevent little troubles from growing into long-standing problems that eventually threaten the marriage. For many couples, issues that seem insignificant before marriage, such as the division of domestic labor or in-law relations, can become major sources of conflict after wedding vows are exchanged. For some couples, even more complex problems must be addressed early on, such as dividing time between biological children from a previous union and time with stepchildren or biological children in a current union. Further, the early years might be an ideal time to encourage couples to work on foundational relationship skills, such as effective problem solving and compassionate listening. Religious organizations could capitalize on their successes with premarital education by extending their programs to include booster sessions during the first year of marriage.

Early parental years. Marriage educators are beginning to give more attention to the marital challenges associated with becoming parents (Shapiro & Gottman, in press). The challenge that this transition presents to couple relationships is one of the most well-established findings in the family sciences (Cowan & Cowan, 2000; Shapiro, Gottman, & Carrére, 2000; Twenge, Campbell, & Foster, 2003). A recent meta-analysis (Twenge et al.) suggested that recent cohorts of transitioning parents appear to experience more of a decline in their marital satisfaction compared with their parents' generation, perhaps because cultural changes make parenting feel more restrictive of personal freedom and cause more gender conflict than in the past. Even when it does not create a crisis, the transition to parenthood stresses the marital relationship for most couples, potentially setting in motion future marital breakdown, especially for couples whose relationships were already stressed (Cowan & Cowan).

Because couples are already stretched with the demands of caring for a new infant, topical, moderate-dosage educational offerings that address issues such as the division of domestic labor and added financial stress might be necessary. A natural setting for reaching couples before the birth of their child is the healthcare system (Hawkins, Gilliland, Christiaens, & Carroll, 2002). Many transitioning couples in low-income communities who are not married live together with hopes for marriage (Bendheim-Thoman Center for Child Wellbeing, 2002). We discuss these couples later.

Midparental years. It would be easy for marriage educators to view the middle parenting years as uneventful, with minimal need for intervention. However, there are good reasons to reject this perspective. Doherty (2001) asserted that this period is becoming known for its time-starved quality, when more children and more commitments mean less couple time. He argued that the daily investments of couple time that lubricate marital functioning dry up with chauffeuring overscheduled children, increasing work demands, and so forth. Lower income families who struggle constantly to meet the economic needs of their families might be even more likely than middle-income families to be affected by this time crunch. Accordingly, marriage education that addresses ways to prioritize marital time would be valuable for couples in the midparental years. Ironically, these couples might have little time to accommodate the luxury of marriage education, so educators need to be creative in how they overcome this barrier. Embedding lower dosage topical curricula in other settings where active parents are involved is worth considering. For instance, parents might already be involved in religious groups to encourage their children's religious education. This setting might offer a temporal cloister for marriage education. Marketing lunchtime seminars in a workplace setting also might attract time-impoverished parents.

Late- and postparental years. Launching children can be disorienting for couples, especially if parenthood has become the primary bond between spouses, and the marital bolts have become rusty through neglect. There is evidence that marital quality declines somewhat with the duration of the marriage (Glenn, 1998; VanLaningham, Johnson, & Amato, 2001). Yet, diminishing parenting demands hold possibilities for reprioritizing and reinvigorating long-term marriages. Marriage curricula that revisit the fundamentals of marital communication and problem solving is an intriguing possibility for curriculum in this time (Arp, Arp, Stanley, Markman, & Blumberg, 2000). Over time, couple interaction patterns become entrenched but still produce chronic conflict. Marriage educators could help couples unlearn less functional, ingrained interaction patterns and replace them with healthier ones. Further, retirement might be as disorienting to familiar marital patterns as children leaving the home (Kulik, 2001). In addition, health issues increase in importance for later-life couples (Goldin & Mohr, 2000) and challenge relationship skills. Clearly, marriage curricula on these and other topics could be helpful. Programs like MATE (Olson & Adams, 1996), specially modified from the PREPARE/ENRICH program to help couples in the later years, have an educational niche. Because of their knowledge, gerontology educators would be good recruits to develop and deliver marriage education.

Life Course Changes

Contemporary unions often follow more diverse temporal and developmental paths than in the past. Cohabitation, divorce, and remarriage introduce greater complexities that marriage educators must accommodate in their efforts to help all couples.

Cohabitation. More than 5 million couples are currently cohabiting (U.S. Census Bureau, 2001). About half of cohabiting couples are likely assessing their relationship with a view to marriage (Bumpass, Sweet, & Cherlin, 1991), and nearly two thirds of high school seniors believe that living together before marriage improves the odds of marital success (Popenoe & Whitehead, 2002). However, research shows that cohabitation before marriage, unless one eventually marries his or her first partner, puts individuals at more, not less, risk for divorce (Teachman, 2003). In fact, Dush, Cohan, and Amato (2003) concluded that the experience of cohabitation is responsible for the greater risk of divorce, more so than selection effects of higher risk individuals into cohabitation. Apparently, cohabitation by itself is unlikely to prepare people effectively for a lasting marriage. For this reason, marriage educators serving cohabiting adults need to emphasize reality versus myth and provide empirically based principles for good marriage preparation.

Recent research from the Fragile Families Study (Bendheim-Thoman Center for Research on Child Wellbeing, 2002) documents that most urban single mothers are intimately involved with their baby's father at the time of the birth. About half are cohabiting; 30% of fathers are frequently visiting and romantically linked to the mother; and almost 75% believe that there is a good chance that they will eventually marry. Unfortunately, only about 15% ever do so (Bendheim-Thoman Center for Research on Child Wellbeing, 2003a), but only about one third of them have serious problems that make them poor prospects for marriage (Bendheim-Thoman Center for Child Wellbeing, 2003b). Some policymakers find these statistics encouraging and are anxious to experiment with ways to help low-income unmarried parents form and sustain healthy marriages (see Horn, 2003). Clearly, there are large barriers to marriage with this population, and marriage education alone cannot overcome them all. However, a large, long-term federal research project is under way to explore the kinds of educational efforts that can be successful with these couples (see Ooms & Wilson, 2004). Marriage education programs will require helping many of them figure out how to manage obligations to other children from previous relationships. In addition, recent research suggests that there is a higher level of distrust, in particular about sexual fidelity, among lower income families, especially among African Americans (Cazenave & Smith, 1990; Edin, England, & Linenberg, 2003). Further, a disproportionate number of these poor unmarried mothers have experienced childhood abuse (Cherlin, Burton, Hurt, & Purvin, 2003). As such, existing curricula will need to be modified substantially or new curricula developed, to help these individuals and couples. Marriage educators will need to think more ecologically than is their norm, supplementing their educational offerings with links to support services for these couples, such as job training or substance abuse treatment (Bendheim-Thoman Center for Child Wellbeing, 2003b).

Divorce. In our experience, marriage educators see their roles primarily as preventing divorce. However, there might be untapped educational opportunities for them among individuals who have recently experienced a divorce. Some research suggests that one third of divorced individuals say they had some regrets about their decision to divorce, and many marriages do go from bad to good (Waite et al., 2002). Individuals who have recently divorced might value the assistance of educators to help them maintain a functional coparenting relationship with a former spouse and understand what went wrong in their marriage and how to avoid such problems in the future. In addition, we encourage educators to try harder to reach couples thinking about divorce by enlisting the cooperation of legal practitioners who are as wearied by the sadness of their day-to-day work as they are profited by it.

Remarriage. Remarriage might be the triumph of hope over experience (Visher & Visher, 1979), but hope is hardly in short supply. Because nearly half of marriages today are remarriages for one or both spouses (U.S. Census Bureau, 1999), there is a growing need for tailored marriage education to serve this large population. The complexities of remarriage call for enhanced communication and problem-solving skills (Pasley, Dollahite, & Ihinger-Tallman, 1993), we believe, which are a staple of numerous marriage education programs. Programs will be more attractive if they integrate these skills with topical content that addresses the added challenges of remarriage, such as dealing with former spouses, obligations to children from a previous marriage, stepparenting, and blending finances.

Dimension V: Setting—Where Does it Take Place?

For at least three reasons, it behooves marriage educators to think more concretely about the location of their activities. First, there are settings that lend themselves well to particular educational topics (e.g., workplace seminars on balancing work and marriage, religious sermons on sexual fidelity). Second, it is easy to overlook fruitful venues for marriage education, such as the military or healthcare settings. Finally, the more settings in which effective marriage education occurs, the more individuals will be reached. Marriage education needs intervention that weaves itself naturally into the systems and sectors of professional work and human services, where opportunities exist to strengthen marriages—a point made in the context of an overall strategy to help divorcing families (Haine, Sandler, Wolchik, Tien, & Dawson-McClure, 2003).

Personal/Home

An important purpose of our framework is to shed light on educational opportunities that marriage educators easily overlook. This is the case with personal and home-based interventions to strengthen marriage. Weiner-Davis (2002) encouraged informal personal interventions when she speaks about "guerilla divorce busting" strategies (i.e., brief, informal interchanges with friends or associates thinking out loud about divorce to suggest that there are effective ways to solve marital problems other than divorce). Similarly, Weiner-Davis encouraged marriage educators to reinforce the value of marriage in their ordinary daily interactions with people. The informal, spontaneous nature of these efforts makes it difficult to see them as formal education. Yet, we believe that marriage education should be avocational and vocational. Marriage educators could help teach others how to do these personal microinterventions, including knowing when they are inappropriate because of a dangerous relationship. Creative research is needed to determine how effective microinterventions can be.

Similarly, marriage educators could help parents to be more intentional about teaching healthy marriage to their children. Pearson (2000) expressly called for parents to be primary educators to their adolescents about love, sexuality, commitment, and marriage, but intriguing educational possibilities also emerge in midlife mentoring of adult children. Glenn (2002) noted that young adults receive little monitoring and input from parents about courtship and marital choices, and parents have much to offer their children as they prepare for marriage. Marriage educators could develop curricula to help parents be a supportive—as opposed to intrusive—resource to help their children build their own healthy marriages.

Neighborhood/Community

The more accessible and familiar a setting is, the more likely it is to attract people to marriage education, perhaps especially lower income couples who might struggle with convenient transportation. There are possibilities in organizing educational efforts on a smaller, geographically more intimate basis within neighborhoods. Topics can be tailored to specific personal interests, and it might be easier to recruit when people and settings are familiar. In addition, we sense that when neighbors participate together in a program, they are more likely to interact with each other in the future and reinforce lessons learned.

We believe that a community saturation model of marriage education has emerged recently that holds promise (see http://www.lewin.com/Spotlights/Features/Spotlight_Feature_CHMI.htm). In this model, marriage activists recruit sectors of a community and its leaders to support marriage education efforts, and then flood a community with messages and opportunities to build and sustain healthy marriages. One of the premier examples of this is First Things First (see http://www.firstthings.org). Through work with local media, businesses, religious and civic institutions, and other organizations, activists produce a sustained communitywide effort to support healthy marriages. An intriguing feature of these initiatives is that they seek a cultural-level change and individual exposure to marriage education. They seek to shift the culture from one that sees marriage as only a private concern to one that sees marriage as an important part of a healthy civic infrastructure. The federal government has begun a major study of the effectiveness of these community initiatives (Dion, 2004).

Religion

Religious institutions are an important civic component of any community. The religious setting undoubtedly is where most premarital education occurs, but more religious leaders could adopt this valuable role. The efforts of individual faith communities sometimes have grown into larger community networks of support. For example, Marriage Savers (http://www.marriagesavers.org) has trained hundreds of communities to organize local congregations to band together to require premarital education and provide mentoring for newlyweds. An initial study of these community marriage policies suggests that they might reduce divorce rates (Birch, Weed, & Olsen, 2004). In addition, the Catholic-based ministry, Retrouvaille, supports an intensive educational effort to repair marriages on the verge of divorce and claims a high short-term success rate (Rubin, 1998).

Religious settings hold particular strengths as venues for marriage education (Stanley, Markman, St. Peters, & Leber, 1995). First, recruitment of more participants is easier because such settings are already associated with the faith community. In addition, some research provides optimism that lay marriage educators in religious settings can be as effective as professionally trained secular ones (Stanley et al., 2001). Second, when participants end their formal participation in a marriage program, they are more likely to maintain ongoing involvement with congregants who also were involved and can serve as a support system, and we believe that this can help to maintain program effects. Third, religious settings invite the ethical and moral domains into the curricula, providing powerful supports for learning. For many who associate with a religious community and imbue marriage with spiritual meaning, a religious setting is an ideal place for marriage education.

Education

Secondary and higher education are obvious natural settings for marriage education curricula. Scholars recently examined what is being taught in high schools and colleges in the United States (Glenn, 1997; Larson & Hickman, 2004; Mack, 2000; Pearson, 2000). These reports critiqued the adequacy of textbooks commonly used and provided constructive suggestions, so improved materials might be forthcoming. Florida, Oklahoma, and a few other states are building relationship and marriage education capacity into high school curricula (Ooms, Bouchet, & Parke, 2004). Family life educators in the national Cooperative Extension Service embedded in land-grant universities are giving increasing attention to marriage education. They are experienced in reaching underserved individuals in remote rural locations who are easily left out of services.

We believe that institutions of higher education could offer much to marriage education, if they were more dedicated to teaching future human service professionals in various disciplines about the importance of healthy marriages to adults, children, and their communities, and informing them about research-based interventions to strengthen marriages. As college students move into their various professions, they would be better prepared to support marriage education initiatives.

Educational settings present an important benefit to marriage education. Marriage curricula embedded in high schools and colleges can reach a large proportion of adolescents and young adults across the socioeconomic spectrum (see Nielsen, Pinsof, Rampage, Solomon, & Goldstein, 2004). Educated youth possess an appetite for reliable information to help them prepare for their life goal of a healthy marriage. The more marriage educators can reach these eager students with solid information before they begin forming intimate relationships, the more they will encourage attitudes and behavior patterns that lead to healthy marriages.

Health Care

The healthcare system is extensively involved in public education. Because healthy marriages are linked to a host of physical and emotional health advantages, and divorce is linked to notable health problems for adults and children (Keilcolt-Glaser & Newton, 2001; Waite & Gallagher, 2000), the healthcare system is a natural venue for addressing concerns about strengthening marriage, especially when curriculum content is linked to health issues. For example, substance abuse puts relationships at serious risk; yet, successful recovery is enhanced by a positive social support system (Richardson, 2001), and marriage can be one source of such support. In addition, we argue that public health campaigns should be harnessed to strengthen marriage (Hawkins, Barnes, & Gilmore, 2004). A potential strength of the healthcare setting for marriage education is that it is well suited to reach out to the racial, ethnic, and economically diverse populations that it regularly serves.

Work and Military

The workplace also is a profitable setting for marriage education. However, to date the potential of a marriage education and workplace merger is largely unexploited. The rationale for educational services in the workplace to strengthen marriages is straightforward. Employee productivity is reduced directly by domestic problems and indirectly by health problems and other issues connected to marital breakdown (Forthoffer, Markman, Cox, Stanley, & Kessler, 1996). Hence, marriage education could yield a productivity return on investment. From a broader perspective, corporations demonstrate their social responsibility by acknowledging that work has significant impact on marriage and family, and then seeking to help individuals manage this challenge. The educational infrastructure to support workplace-based marriage education already exists, at least in larger corporations with well-developed employee assistance programs (EAPs). Many EAPs support counseling for employees struggling with serious problems, which could include marriage problems. Preventative educational services focused on strengthening marriages are emerging, but more are needed.

The workplace setting offers some potential advantages for marriage education. To the extent that work organizations make education available at work during the workday, this facilitates recruitment, which often is a major barrier to preventive intervention. Similarly, marriage education in the workplace, such as lunchtime seminars, might diminish barriers to involvement, including arranging child care, enrollment fees (if underwritten or subsidized), and the understandable desire to spend precious nonwork time with family. More convenience and reduced costs will help attract lower wage employees—another challenge for marriage educators. In addition, the workplace might be a natural setting to address contemporary topics, such as balancing work and personal lives, managing family finances, and training managers to be more accommodating of employees' family situations.

Of course, there are educational liabilities to the workplace setting. One pragmatic challenge is the difficulty of including both spouses, because few couples work for the same employer. Because marriage education usually assumes delivery to a couple, educators will need to accommodate this difference or find ways to involve nonemployee spouses when they are not actually present. As such, programs might need to emphasize unilateral change that strengthens marriages rather than mutually learned skills, such as self-regulation processes (see Halford, Wilson, Lizzio, & Moore, in press).

The military consumes a significant proportion of the U.S. workforce, so it is a substantial setting for marriage education. In fact, we sense that marriage education in the military is considerably advanced compared with the private workforce. The rationale for marriage education in the armed forces is similar to that of the corporate world: Military service places stresses on marriages, and marital problems impinge on force readiness (McCarroll et al., 2000; Stanley et al., 2004). As with other settings, the military has both advantages and challenges. One advantage is that an educational infrastructure exists in family support services attached to military bases. Many professionals in these settings are beginning to offer marriage education to military personnel (Stanley et al.). In addition, these programs typically are available at no cost to military personnel, lowering a barrier to program participation. One challenge is that the unique circumstances of military service might diminish the applicability of off-the-shelf marriage education programs. These circumstances include long deployments with spousal separations, and combat stress that heightens the risk of divorce (Wilson, Ruger, & Waddoups, 2002). Marriage educators must address both generic marriage skills and knowledge and specific help with how to cope with these challenges.

Mass Media

Mass media in our society educates and entertains. As a media-saturated society, this has a substantial power to shape beliefs and behaviors. Marriage education in the media ranges from billboard messages and 30-second public awareness campaigns to information-filled Web sites and television documentaries. Some marriage educators build Web-based marriage resource centers for their communities, an inexpensive way to begin a community initiative (see http://www.OCmarriage.org). Still others broaden their educational influence by building helpful, ongoing relationships with reporters and producers, like Diane Sollee, director of the Coalition for Marriage, Family and Couples Education in Washington, DC (http://www.smartmarriages.com).

One of the advantages of mass media for marriage education is its potential to reach large numbers of individuals at relatively low costs. This suggests the exciting potential of media-based marriage education to facilitate cultural-level change that can support forming and sustaining healthy marriages. There is ample evidence of how media help shape attitudes and behavior (Hornik, 2002). However, there are limits to this educational setting. Initial production costs can be a daunting barrier for marriage educators, and media consumers demand that programming be new and current, so ongoing attention to the message is required. We believe that marriage educators will be most effective when building positive working and consulting relationships with reporters and producers who have the specialized knowledge and connections required for success in the mass communications industry. In addition, marriage educators need to partner with public relations professionals who understand how to attract and enlist mass media.

Government and Public Services

Marriage is both a public institution and a private relationship. A strong institution of marriage supports important governmental purposes (Browning, 2003). Thus, it is not surprising when government gets involved in marriage education efforts. (Strictly speaking, government is more involved as a catalyst for marriage education in other settings than a setting in itself.) For example, under current Temporary Assistance to Needy Families (TANF) policy, Arizona helps pay for premarital education programs for lower income couples. Oklahoma has made a major commitment to building a statewide network of marriage educators formally trained in the PREP (Markman, Renick, Floyd, Stanley, & Clements, 1993) to make this intervention available to as many individuals and couples as possible, with clear attention to lower income individuals (see http://www.okmarriage.com/OklahomaMarriageInitiative.asp). Other states (e.g., Arizona, Utah) are providing helpful free information booklets to marrying couples. A few state legislatures have reduced the cost of a marriage license if couples invest in premarital education (Ooms, et al., 2004). Government policy also is encouraging social service agencies, including child and family support entities serving at-risk populations, to explore the potential of marriage education (Ooms, Bouchet, & Parke).

One invaluable consequence of such government support is that marriage educators are encouraged to serve more economically disadvantaged individuals and couples. In turn, marriage educators need to adapt their curricula to be more sensitive to challenges that work against a healthy marriage in the social contexts of disadvantaged individuals. An important way that government encourages marriage education is through direct funding, and programs that serve the poor need such funding. In addition, governments are paying for studies to evaluate these interventions. Marriage educators working under the auspices of government support undoubtedly will experience frustrations from the ubiquitous bureaucratic entanglements and requirements, which can be discouraging. However, stamina to work within these constraints will open up possibilities for reaching lower income populations who otherwise would be difficult to help.

Dimension VI: Target—Who Receives It?

There is a need for marriage education to meet the needs of all racial, ethnic, and socioeconomic groups (Wiley & Ebata, 2004). Empirical work over the next decade will tell us whether interventions developed primarily for White, middle-class couples are as effective for low-income groups and other racial and ethnic groups (see Ooms & Wilson, 2004; Seefeldt & Smock, 2004). Having labored for half a century to gain respect among social scientists, marriage education finally might gain it by demonstrating the efficacy of marriage education in service to lower income and minority populations, whom marriage educators have been slow to reach (Ooms, 2002). Marriage educators need to direct primary attention to those who can benefit the most from their efforts, and assistance from basic researchers studying marriages in diverse populations will benefit their efforts (see Fein et al., 2003).

Throughout this article, we have suggested ways that marriage education needs to be modified to serve more disadvantaged groups. One additional point is that marriage educators need to understand that racial and ethnic minorities probably have as much within-group diversity as between-group diversity. As such, the work of diversifying curricula is likely to be more fine-grained than many marriage educators anticipate.

Last, an overlooked population is rural Americans whose lives are substantially different from those in urban settings and who have less access to services. Ironically, discovering over time what an array of curricula tailored for diverse populations share in common might yield greater appreciation for principles of healthy marriages that approach universal understanding.

Dimension VII: Delivery—How is it Disseminated to the Public?

Marriage educators have much to consider in relation to the content, intensity, methods, timing, setting, and target of marriage education. Delivery is a final, crucial dimension. This dimension addresses the broader issue of how marriage education will be disseminated to the public to impact the institution of marriage. We identify four general approaches to delivering marriage education, each essential to strengthening marriages. In discussing these four approaches, our purpose is to acknowledge that more than formal educational programs are needed, even ones that reach out to larger and more diverse groups of people. Also needed are initiatives led by citizens and community activists concern with meeting a pressing local need. Moreover, educational efforts directed broadly at seeding the culture with influential messages about healthy marriage will be essential.

Specialist Marriage Education

We see a need for formal marriage education led by trained and often certified specialists. Specialized marriage educators are helping professionals with a depth of knowledge and skill that can provide a valuable opportunity to couples. Specialized marriage education offers interested individuals and couples programmatic instruction with significant content breadth and intensity. Like most family life educators, specialized marriage educators work at the retail level of the marriage education movement. Yet, the inevitable limitation of this approach, we believe, is that it will struggle to reach large numbers of people; it will be more like a specialty boutique than a large retailer like Wal-Mart. Even with creative marketing, the number of people who will seek out these specialized services and invest the time, money, and energy they require will be limited. Thus, we need additional approaches to delivering marriage education that can reach further.

Integrated Marriage Education

This approach recognizes that marriage education needs to be integrated into a more comprehensive set of human services provided to individuals in multiple settings and multiple times of the life course. Generally, the more an educational initiative attaches itself to an established setting that already serves individuals and couples, the greater its potential outreach. When other institutions take on the goal of strengthening marriages as a valued part of their mission, marriage education becomes a component of a larger system with resources and momentum rather than an entrepreneurial enterprise continually striving to find new customers. For instance, professionals working with individuals and couples in religious, healthcare, employment, and community settings can provide valuable marriage education services as a natural supplement to their primary work. These professionals already know and understand their clients and can adapt marriage education to meet their particular circumstances. Generally, integrated marriage education will be less intense than specialized marriage education because it is only a component of an overall service. However, because it is more available to people in the course of their everyday lives through professionals and institutions with which they are already familiar, we believe that this approach to marriage education holds promise.

Specialized marriage educators will still play a role in this integrated approach. Specialists can take the lead in helping various professionals recognize the value and potential of marriage education as a part of their services. They also can provide training to professionals in various settings to help them deliver marriage education. Further, specialist marriage educators also could consult with professionals to adopt and adapt educational offerings to meet their unique situations, and assist other professionals to integrate marriage education into their repertoires of services.

Citizen Marriage Initiatives

A third approach to delivering marriage education to the public recognizes that not all effective educational experiences are managed by professionals. Rather, grassroots citizen-led initiatives responding to a shared local problem can be an effective way of reaching neighbors and community members with valuable educational experiences (Doherty & Carroll, 2002). Moreover, citizen marriage initiatives can go beyond providing educational opportunities to consumers by inviting those consumers to enlist in the cause and become producers or supporters of marriage education (Doherty & Carroll). An interesting distinction with this approach is that marriage education is about more than strengthening an isolated marriage; it also has the purpose of uniting communities and making them better environments to nurture all marriages (see Doherty & Anderson, 2004). In other words, citizen marriage initiatives attempt to create microcultural change. We believe that the strength of citizen-led initiatives is that they are closely linked to local problems shared by neighbors and community members. Hence, the educational offerings are more likely to meet a real-time immediate need and attract enthusiastic learners. Then these learners often go on to become a part of the initiative, thus increasing its reach.

Again, specialist marriage educators have a role to play in the citizen marriage approach. One role is to help community members articulate a shared problem. Then, the specialist can provide whatever support citizen leaders require, including cheerleading. They also can provide citizen leaders a summary of marriage research to help them grasp the bigger picture of their local efforts. In this approach, specialist marriage educators are resources and consultants rather than experts and leaders; they are on tap rather than on top, supporting grassroots efforts rather than supervising them.

Marriage Culture Seeding

A final approach to delivering marriage education is the least active at this time, but we believe that it remains crucial. Marriage education has its origins in the therapeutic helping professions. Thus, marriage educators generally think of themselves as helping professionals, with clients who seek out their services. The integrated marriage education approach invites specialist marriage educators to draft other professionals to assist in this helping profession. The citizen marriage initiative approach stretches specialist marriage educators to move beyond the helping professional role to assist in generating microcultural change as supporters of grassroots initiatives. The fourth approach—cultural seeding to strengthen the institution of marriage—refers to both formal and informal attempts to spur macrocultural change. For example, formal attempts at cultural change could include media-based public awareness campaigns. Formal attempts often generate informal intervention that gets people talking and acting in ways that build a momentum of positive cultural change. The marriage educator who helps generate a stronger macroculture of marriage ultimately helps all individuals in the mainstream to achieve their personal goals for a stable, healthy marriage.

The cultural seeding approach uses a different set of tools than is common in traditional marriage education. Tools from public health and mass communications are central to this approach, because they allow education, condensed and reduced to summaries and sound-bites, to reach large numbers of people. For instance, a broad public awareness campaign that discredits myths that contribute to marital dissolution could shift the common perception away from marriage being primarily about romance and impervious to rational processes. Similarly, if journalists over a sustained period drew attention to the value of better preparation for marriage (rather than mere preparation for an elaborate wedding), they could help create a norm of more intentional preparation for marriage. Public policy also can be a cultural seeding tool. For example, legislation encouraging involvement in premarital education in exchange for a reduced marriage license fee sends a public message about the seriousness of this decision. The strength of delivering marriage education in a cultural seeding approach lies in its potential for slowly moving the cultural ground under people's feet in directions that ultimately strengthen all marriages.

We believe that the specialist marriage educator has an essential role in this approach. The specialist can be a catalyst who brings attention to important issues by attracting the notice of the media and cultivating relationships with local and national media professionals to get out important ideas. Similarly, specialists can be catalysts and consultants to public communication campaigns to strengthen marriage.

Despite the growth of marriage education over the last decade as a helping vocation, and even with signs that it is integrating itself into various institutions that provide human services to broader segments of the population, this is not enough to make a substantial impact on the institution of marriage if it is not accompanied by cultural change. We believe that a social movement that infuses marriage education into the normative infrastructures of everyday lives is needed, and that a cultural seeding approach to marriage education is needed to fuel this movement.

Toward an Integrated Strategy for Marriage Education

At this early stage of the marriage education movement, we would be presumptuous to propose a population-level treatment plan for marriage education, although there are hints of what such a model could resemble. One possible template comes from the emerging public health issue of obesity. Scientists and public health officials recently realized that an epidemic with deleterious consequences for generations is here (U.S. Department of Health and Human Services, 2001). The best treatment is prevention. The importance of this issue is such that government is unwilling to simply watch the efforts of health practitioners. In fact, the federal government will spend more than $100 million over the next few years for programs and research to prevent and control obesity (National Center for Chronic Disease Prevention and Health Promotion, 2003). States also will invest funds. The U.S. Surgeon general has issued a comprehensive strategic plan that calls for private and public partners to address obesity. This plan involves large public communication campaigns, along with moderate- and high-level educational initiatives with multiple messages delivered in numerous settings and sectors of society. These campaigns, tailored to different age, socioeconomic, and racial groups, would be accompanied by substantial public and private resources to promote and evaluate these efforts (see U.S. Department of Health and Human Services). We strongly believe that the effort to promote healthy marriages deserves no less of a comprehensive plan.

The goal of marriage education is to give individuals and couples the knowledge and skills needed to build and sustain a healthy marriage. Our initial framework does not have all of the details right, nor does it fully specify all of the broad strokes to guide the marriage education movement. However, we hope that it can serve as a catalyst to assist marriage educators to think more systematically and creatively about their work. We likely have missed some important details in our comprehensive framework for marriage education, and we look forward to improving it over time. In the meantime, we hope that this framework will spur marriage educators to explore and experiment with a broader range of educational possibilities to reach larger numbers of individuals and couples.

References

Amato, P. R., & Rogers, S. J. (1999). Do attitudes toward divorce affect marital quality? *Journal of Family Issues, 20*, 69–86.

Arp, D. H., Arp, C. S., Stanley, S. M., Markman, H. J., & Blumberg, S. L. (2000). *Empty nesting: Reinventing your marriage when the kids leave home*. San Francisco: Jossey-Bass.

Bendheim-Thoman Center for Child Wellbeing. (2002, July). Is marriage a viable option for fragile families? *Fragile Families Research Brief, No. 9*. Princeton, NJ: Princeton University.

Bendheim-Thoman Center for Child Wellbeing. (2003a, January). Union formation and dissolution and in fragile families. *Fragile Families Research Brief, No. 14*. Princeton, NJ: Princeton University.

Bendheim-Thoman Center for Child Wellbeing. (2003b, May). Barriers to marriage among fragile families? *Fragile Families Research Brief, No. 16*. Princeton, NJ: Princeton University.

Birch, P. J., Weed, S. E., & Olsen, J. (2004). Assessing the impact of community marriage policies on county divorce rates. *Family Relations, 53*, 495–503.

Browning, D. S. (2003). *Marriage and modernization*. Grand Rapids, MI: Eerdmans.

Bumpass, L. L., Sweet, J. A., & Cherlin, A. (1991). The role of cohabitation in declining rates of marriage. *Journal of Marriage and the Family, 53*, 913–927.

Carroll, J. S., & Doherty, W. J. (2003). Evaluating the effectiveness of premarital prevention programs: A meta-analytic review of outcome research. *Family Relations, 52*, 105–118.

Cazenave, N. A., & Smith, R. (1990). Gender differences in the perception of Black male-female relationships and stereotypes. In H. E. Cheatham & J. B. Stuart (Eds.), *Black families: Interdisciplinary perspectives* (pp. 149–170). New Brunswick, NJ: Transaction.

Center for Marriage and Family. (1995). *Marriage preparation in the Catholic Church: Getting it right*. Omaha, NE: Creighton University.

Cherlin, A., Burton, L., Hurt, T., & Purvin, D. (2003, September). *Domestic abuse and patterns of marriage and cohabitation: Evidence from a multi-method study*. Paper presented at the National Poverty Center Conference, Washington, DC.

Cowan, C. P., & Cowan, P. A. (2000). *When partners become parents: The big life change for couples*. Mahwah, NJ: Earlbaum.

DeMaria, R. (2003) Psychoeducation and enrichment: Clinical considerations for couple and family therapy. In T. L. Sexton, G. R. Weeks, & M. Robbins (Eds.), *Handbook of family therapy* (pp. 411– 430). New York: Brunner-Routledge.

Dion, M. R. (2004, March). *Federal policy efforts to improve outcomes among disadvantaged families by supporting marriage and family stability*. Paper presented at the Families and Poverty Research Conference, Provo, UT.

Dion, M. R., Devaney, B., McConnell, S., Ford, M., Hill, H., & Winston, P. (2003). *Helping unwed parents build strong and healthy marriages: A conceptual framework for intervention, final report*. Washington, DC: U.S. Department of Health and Human Services, Administration for Children and Families.

Dishion, T. J. (2003). *Intervening in adolescent problem behavior*. New York: Guilford.

Doherty, W. H. (2000, August). Consumer marriage. *Marriage and Families*, 16–22.

Doherty, W. H. (2001). *Take back your marriage: Sticking together in a world that pulls us apart*. New York: Guilford.

Doherty, W. H., & Anderson, J. R. (2004). Community marriage initiatives. *Family Relations*, *53*, 425–432.

Doherty, W. H., & Carroll, J. S. (2002). The Families and Democracy Project. *Family Process 41*, 579–589.

Dush, C. M., Cohan, C. L., & Amato, P. R. (2003). The relationship between cohabitation and marital quality and stability: Change across cohorts? *Journal of Marriage and Family*, *65*, 539–549.

Edin, K., England, P., & Linnenberg, K. (2003, September). *Love and distrust among unmarried parents*. Paper presented at the National Poverty Center Conference, Washington, DC.

Edin, K., & Kefalas, M. (in press). *Promises I can keep: Why poor women put motherhood before marriage*. Berkeley: University of California.

Fein, D. J., Burstein, N. R., Fein, G. G., & Lindberg, L. D. (2003, March). *The determinants of marriage and cohabitation among disadvantaged Americans: Research findings and needs*. Bethesda, MD: Abt Associates.

Forthoffer, M. S., Markman, H. J., Cox, M., Stanley, S. M., & Kessler, R. C. (1996). Associations between marital distress and work loss in a national sample. *Journal of Marriage and the Family*, *58*, 597–605.

Fowers, B. L. (2000). *Beyond the myth of marital happiness*. San Francisco: Jossey-Bass.

Gallagher, M. (2000). *The marriage movement: A statement of principles*. New York: Institute for American Values.

Glenn, N. (1996). Values, attitudes, and the state of American marriage. In D. Popenoe, J. B. Elshtain, & D. Blankenhorn (Eds.), *Promises to keep: Decline and renewal of marriage in America* (pp. 15–33). Lanham, MD: Rowman & Littlefield.

Glenn, N. (1997). A critique of twenty family and marriage and family textbooks. *Family Relations*, *46*, 197–208.

Glenn, N. (1998). The course of marital success or failure in five American 10-year marriage cohorts. *Journal of Marriage and the Family*, *60*, 569–576.

Glenn, N. (2002). A plea for greater concern about the quality of marital matching. In A. J. Hawkins, L. D. Wardle, & D. O. Coolidge (Eds)., *Revitalizing the institution of marriage for the 21st century: An agenda for strengthening marriage* (pp. 45–58). Westport, CT: Praeger.

Glenn, N., & Marquardt, E. (2001). *Hooking up, hanging out, and hoping for Mr. Right*. New York: Institute for American Values.

Goldin, E., & Mohr, R. (2000). Issues and techniques for counseling long-term later-life couples. *The Family Journal: Counseling and Therapy for Couples and Families*, *8*, 229–235.

Gottman, J. M., & Notarius, C. I. (2000). Decade in review: Observing marital interaction. *Journal of Marriage and the Family*, *62*, 927– 947.

Haine, R. A., Sandler, I. N., Wolchik, S. A., Tien, J., & Dawson-McClure, S. R. (2003). Changing the legacy of divorce: Evidence from prevention programs and future directions. *Family Relations*, *52*, 397–405.

Halford, W. K., Moore, E., Wilson, K., Farrugia, C., & Dyer, C. (2004). Benefits of flexible delivery relationship education: An evaluation of the Couple CARE Program. *Family Relations*, *53*, 469–476.

Halford, W. K., Wilson, K. L., Lizzio, A., & Moore, E. M., (in press). Does working at your relationship work? Relationship self-regulation and relationship outcomes. In J. Feeney & P. Noeller (Eds.), *Marriage*. Cambridge, UK: Cambridge University.

Harris, R. J., & Scott, C. L. (2002). Effects of sex in the media. In J. Bryant & D. Zillmann (Eds.), *Media effects: Advances in theory and research* (pp. 307–331). Mahwah, NJ: Erlbaum.

Hawkins, A. J., Barnes, M. D., & Gilmore, D. (2004). Media campaigns to strengthen marriages: What can we learn from public communication campaign evaluation research? [Working Paper]. Office and Research, Planning, and Evaluation, Administration for Children and Families, Washington, DC.

Hawkins, A. J., Gilliland, T., Christiaens, G., & Carroll, J. S. (2002). Integrating marriage education into perinatal education. *Journal of Perinatal Education*, *11*(4), 1–10.

Horn, W. (2003). Closing the marriage gap. *Crisis: Politics, Culture and the Church*, *21*(6), 32–37.

Hornik, R. C. (2002). *Public health communications: Evidence for behavior change*. Mahwah, NJ: Erlbaum.

Johnson, C. A., Stanley, S. M., Glenn, N. D., Amato, P. R., Nock, S. L., Markman, H. J., & Dion, M. R. (2002). *Marriage in Oklahoma: 2001 baseline statewide survey on marriage and divorce*. Oklahoma City: Oklahoma Department of Human Services.

Jordan, P. L., Stanley, S. M., & Markman, H. J. (1999). *Becoming parents*. San Francisco: Jossey-Bass.

Kielcolt-Glaser, J. K., & Newton, T. L. (2001). Marriage and health: His and hers. *Psychological Bulletin*, *127*, 472–503.

Kulik, L. (2001). The impact of men's and women's retirement on marital relations: A comprehensive analysis. *Journal of Women and Aging, 13*(2), 21–37.

Larson, J. H. (2003). *The great marriage tune-up book.* San Francisco: Jossey-Bass.

Larson, J. H., & Hickman, R. (2004). Are college marriage textbooks teaching students the premarital predictors of marital quality? *Family Relations, 53*, 385–392.

Larson, J. H., Newell, K., Topham, G., & Nichols, S. (2002). A review of three comprehensive premarital assessment questionnaires. *Journal of Marital and Family Therapy, 28*, 233–239.

Mack, D. (2000). *Hungry hearts: Evaluating the new high school curricula on marriage and relationships.* New York: Institute for American Values.

Markman, H. J., Renick, M. J., Floyd, F., Stanley, S., & Clements, M. (1993). Preventing marital distress through communication and conflict management training: A four and five year follow-up. *Journal of Consulting and Clinical Psychology, 62*, 70–77.

McCarroll, J. E., Ursano, R. J., Liu, X., Thayer, L. E., Newby, J. H., Norwood, A. E., & Fullerton, C. S. (2000). Deployment and the probability of spousal aggression by U.S. Army soldiers. *Military Medicine, 165*, 41–44.

McManus, M. (1993). *Marriage savers.* Grand Rapids, MI.

National Center for Chronic Disease Prevention and Health Promotion. (2003). *Physical activity and good nutrition: Essential elements to prevent chronic diseases and obesity 2003.* Atlanta, GA: Centers for Disease Control and Prevention.

Nielsen, A., Pinsof, W., Rampage, C., Solomon, A. H., & Goldstein, S. (2004). Marriage 101: An integrated academic and experiential undergraduate marriage education course. *Family Relations, 53*, 485–494.

Nock, S. L. (2002). The social costs of the de-institutionalization of marriage. In A. J. Hawkins, L. D. Wardle, & D. O. Coolidge (Eds.), *Revitalizing the institution of marriage for the 21st century* (pp. 1–14). Westport, CT: Praeger.

Olson, D. H., & Adams, E. (1996). *Mature Age Transition Evaluation (MATE) couple inventory.* Minneapolis, MN: Life Innovations.

Ooms, T. (2002). Strengthening couples and marriage in low-income communities. In A. J. Hawkins, L. D. Wardle, & D. O. Coolidge (Eds.), *Revitalizing the institution of marriage for the 21st century* (pp. 79–99). Westport, CT: Praeger.

Ooms, T., Bouchet, S., & Parke, M. (2004). *Beyond marriage licenses: Efforts in states to strengthen marriage and two-parent families, a state-by-state comparison.* Washington, DC: Center for Law and Social Policy.

Ooms, T., & Wilson, P. (2004). The challenges of offering relationship and marriage education to low-income populations. *Family Relations, 53*, 440–447.

Pasley, K., Dollahite, D. C., & Ihinger-Tallman, M. (1993). Bridging the gap: Clinical applications of research findings on the spouse and stepparent roles in remarriage. *Family Relations, 42*, 315–322.

Pearson, M. (2000). *Can kids get smart about marriage? A veteran teacher reviews some leading marriage and relationship education programs.* Piscataway, NJ: The National Marriage Project.

Popenoe, D., & Whitehead, B. D. (2002). *Should we live together? What young adults need to know about cohabitation before marriage* (2nd ed). New Brunswick, NJ: The National Marriage Project.

Richardson, L. (2001). Social network characteristics and substance abuse treatment outcome. Doctoral dissertation, New School for Social Research, New School University.

Roberts, D. F. (2000). Media and youth: Access, exposure, and privatization. *Journal of Adolescent Health, 27*, 8–14.

Rubin, B. (1998). Ties that bind: Program to keep marriages together. *Good Housekeeping, 226*(4), 108–111.

Seefeldt, K. S., & Smock, P. J. (2004). *Marriage on the public agenda: What do policy makers need to know from research?* Ann Arbor, MI: National Poverty Center, University of Michigan.

Shapiro, A. F., & Gottman, J. M. (in press). "Bringing baby home": Effects on marriage of a psycho-educational intervention with couples undergoing the transition to parenthood, evaluation at 1-year post-intervention. *Journal of Family Communication.*

Shapiro, A. F., Gottman, J. M., & Carrére, S. (2000). The baby and the marriage: Identifying factors that buffer against decline in marital satisfaction after the first baby arrives. *Journal of Family Psychology, 14*, 59–70.

Silliman, B., Stanley, S. M., Coffin, W., Markman, H. J., & Jordan, P. L. (2001). Preventative interventions for couples. In H. Liddle, D. Santisteban, R. Levant, & J. Bray (Eds.), *Family psychology: Science-based interventions* (pp. 123–146). Washington, DC: American Psychological Association.

Stanley, S. M. (2001). Making a case for premarital education. *Family Relations, 50*, 272–280.

Stanley, S. M., Markman, H. J., Prado, L. M., Olmos Gallo, P. A., Tonelli, L., St. Peters, M., Leber, B. D., Bobulinski, M., Cordova, A., & Whitton, S. (2001). Community based premarital prevention: Clergy and lay leaders on the front lines. *Family Relations*, *50*, 67–76.

Stanley, S. M., Markman, H. J., Saiz, C. C., Schumm, W. R., Bloomstrom, G., & Bailey, A. E. (2004). *Building strong and ready families evaluation report*. Washington, DC: SAIC.

Stanley, S. M., Markman, H. J., St. Peters, M., & Leber, B. D. (1995). Strengthening marriages and preventing divorce: New directions n prevention research. *Family Relations*, *44*, 392–401.

Stanley, S. M., Whitton, S. W., & Markman, H. J. (2004). Maybe I do: Interpersonal commitment levels and premarital or non-marital cohabitation. *Journal of Family Issues*, *25*, 496–519.

Teachman, J. (2003). Premarital sex, premarital cohabitation, and the risk of subsequent marital dissolution among women. *Journal of Marriage and Family*, *65*, 444–455.

Twenge, J. M., Campbell, W. K., & Foster, C. A. (2003). Parenthood and marital satisfaction: A meta-analytic review. *Journal of Marriage and Family*, *65*, 561–573.

U.S. Census Bureau. (1999). *Statistical abstract of the United States: 1999* (119th ed.). Table No. 156. Washington, DC.

U.S. Census Bureau. (2001). *Census 2000 profile* (Publication No. CB01-CN.67). Washington, DC: Public Information Office.

U.S. Department of Health and Human Services. (2001). *The Surgeon General's call to action to prevent and decrease overweight and obesity*. Rockville, MD: U.S. Department of Health and Human Services, Public Health Service, Office of Surgeon General.

VanLaningham, J., Johnson, D. R., & Amato, P. (2001). Marital happiness, marital duration, and the U-shaped curve: Evidence from a five-wave panel study. *Social Forces*, *79*, 1313–1341.

Visher, E. B., & Visher, J. S. (1979). *A guide to working with stepparents and stepchildren*. New York: Brunner/Mazel.

Waite, L. J., Browning, D., Doherty, W. J., Gallagher, M., Luo, Y., & Stanley, S. M. (2002). *Does divorce make people happy? Findings from a study of unhappy marriages*. New York: Institute for American Values.

Waite, L. J., & Gallagher, M. (2000). *The case for marriage*. New York: Doubleday.

Weiner-Davis, M. (2002, July). *Guerilla divorce busting*. Keynote address presented at the Smart Marriages Conference, Crystal City, VA.

Whitehead, B. D., & Popenoe, D. (2000). Sex without strings, relationships without rings: Today's young singles talk about mating and dating. *The state of our unions 2001* (pp. 6–20). Piscataway, NJ: National Marriage Project.

Whitehead, B. D., & Popenoe, D. (2001). Who wants to marry a soul mate? *The state of our unions 2001* (pp. 6–16). Piscataway, NJ: The National Marriage Project.

Wiley, A. L., & Ebata, A. (2004). Reaching American families: Making diversity real in family life education. *Family Relations*, *53*, 273–281.

Wilson, S., Ruger, W., & Waddoups, S. (2002). Warfare and welfare: Military service, combat, and marital dissolution. *Armed Forces and Society*, *29*, 85–107.

About the Authors

Alan J. Hawkins, Ph.D., CFLE, is Professor in the School of Family Life at Brigham Young University. E-Mail: hawkinsa@byu.edu.

Jason S. Carroll, Ph.D., is an Associate Professor in the School of Family Life at Brigham Young University. E-Mail: jcarroll@byu.edu.

William J. Doherty, Ph.D., CFLE, is Professor in the Department of Family Social Science and Director of the Citizen Professional Center at the University of Minnesota. E-Mail: bdoherty@umn.edu.

Brian J. Willoughby, M.A., is a doctoral candidate in the Department of Family Social Science at the University of Minnesota. E-Mail: bwilloug@umn.edu.

This article was originally published in *Family Relations*, 2004, *53*(5) 547–558 and is reprinted with permission.

Innovations in Marriage Education: Current Status and Challenges for the Future

JEFFRY H. LARSON

Professional and public interest in marriage is high today. Marriage education is said to have its own movement (Brotherson & Duncan, 2004) whose purpose is to strengthen marriage as a fundamental institution in our country. This movement is evident in the hundreds of community marriage initiatives that are developing in a variety of states (Doherty & Anderson, 2004; Birch, Weed, & Olson, 2004) with the intention of strengthening marriage and lowering the divorce rate. Other evidence of a movement is the national conference called Smart Marriages, held yearly since 1995 with increasing attendance each year from religious and lay leaders, educators, government officials, researchers, program developers, and the general public. In fact, the term, marriage education, is now used regularly by members of the Coalition for Marriage, Family and Couples Education (CMFCE, sponsor of the Smart Marriages conference) and others (Doherty & Anderson, 2004). Recently, government and private funding for marriage education programs and evaluation studies has increased (Brotherson & Duncan, 2004) and the need for such support is more highly recognized. This recognition has included professional organizations, for example, in 2003, when the National Council on Family Relations held its annual conference in Vancouver, BC, Canada, with the theme of The Future of Marriage. Cumulatively, these events inspired a special issue of the journal *Family Relations: Interdisciplinary Journal of Applied Family Studies (Family Relations)* in 2004. Because much has happened in the field of marriage education in the last 10 years, the purpose of this paper is to bring some order, awareness, and suggestions for the future development of marriage education to this rapidly developing field.

What Is Marriage Education?

For our purpose here, marriage education is defined broadly as including both skills-based group programs for the prevention and remediation of marital distress and marital support groups normally labeled as marriage enrichment (Larson, 2007). Obviously, these two approaches overlap. Marriage enrichment groups often incorporate skills-based activities that are found in marriage education (DeMaria, 2003). Marriage education though usually skills-based, often includes group activities and support common to marriage enrichment groups. Finally, because research usually has made no distinction between education and enrichment, these terms will be used synonymously in this paper. Whether called education or enrichment, it can be metaphorically conceptualized as, "working upstream" (D. Sollee, personal communication, June 15, 2003). This refers to working with couples before problems become too serious and entrenched and focuses on an educational and preventive rather than a remedial approach to helping couples.

Why Marriage Education Is Important

Mental health professionals are faced with an enormous challenge in reaching the many couples who need marital therapy. Unfortunately, most couples with marriage problems never seek therapy. Between 80% and 90% of divorcing couples report they have not consulted with a therapist for their marital problems (Halford, Markman, Kline, & Stanley, 2003). In addition, there are several other limitations of couple's therapy. In general, only about two-thirds of couples report improvements in their marital satisfaction as a result of therapy (Johnson, 2002), and a substantial number of couples who successfully complete marital therapy do not attain the levels of satisfaction reported by nondistressed couples (Van Widenfelt, Markman, Guerney, Behrens, & Hosman, 1997). Finally, relapse after treatment is quite common (Jacobson, Schmaling, & Holtzworth-Munroe, 1987). These limitations of marital therapy suggest that additional approaches to helping couples avoid or overcome marital distress must be used to augment therapists' work.

Further, there are several good reasons to promote marriage education before couples become distressed. First, it is probably easier for couples with no distress or mild distress to enhance their marriage than it is for couples who have severe relationship problems to alter entrenched, negative patterns and feelings (Van Widenfelt et al., 1997). Second, most couples experiencing problems do not seek professional help because they fear that treatment may do more harm than good, that it will not work, or doing so will violate their privacy. Add to these issues fears of being stigmatized as being dysfunctional and the high cost of treatment, it is no wonder that few couples seek professional help for marital distress. In fact, most couples with marital problems are more likely to see a member of the clergy for help than a therapist (Glenn et al., 2002).

Compared to marital therapy, marriage education is less likely to provoke these fears, is less stigmatizing, less risky, less intrusive in a couple's private life and less expensive. In addition, some forms of marriage education may be successfully acquired from lay leaders or clergy members (e.g., Stanley et al., 2001). Finally, education may help reduce barriers to receiving more intense professional help later.

Current Status of Marriage Education Research

Marriage education is becoming increasingly available in most Western countries but most programs offered have not been rigorously evaluated within randomized controlled trials (Halford, 2004). Many providers develop their own programs, often in response to perceived local needs, and most of these programs are not documented in a way that permits evaluation.

Existing evidence-based marriage education is usually of two forms. The first is the use of structured inventory-based assessments with one or more hours of feedback sessions used to provide couples with information about their level of risk for future relationship problems (Larson, Newell, Topham, & Nichols, 2002). This approach is based on the assumption that such feedback can guide couples to take appropriate remedial action. The most widely used inventories provide scores on dimensions like shared realistic relationship expectations, effective communication and conflict resolution skills, emotional health, and effective personal stress management (Larson & Halford, in press). Scores on these questionnaires predict couples' future relationship satisfaction and stability (Larson et al., 2002), showing they do assess relevant aspects of couple relationships.

There have been three recent studies evaluating the effects of assessment and feedback on couple relationships. The first was a quasi-experimental study by Knutson and Olson (2003) who found that assessment and feedback using the PREPARE inventory program significantly improved premarital couples' relationship satisfaction. Two randomized controlled trials evaluated assessment with feedback with the internet-based, self-interpretive RELATE inventory. Both studies showed increases in relationship satisfaction and commitment in couples in early stage committed relationships (Busby, Ivey, Harris, & Ates, 2007; Larson, Vatter, Galbraith, Holman, & Stahmann, 2007). The Busby et al. (2007) study was the only one to evaluate maintenance of effects, and they found relationship satisfaction and commitment were sustained at a high level for at least six months after completing RELATE. Each of the samples of couples in these three studies were well-educated and in early stage committed relationships (long-term dating or engaged), and the generalizability to less educated or longer-lasting established relationships is untested. Whether the effects of assessment and feedback persist for years also is unknown. It is known that some couples lack key relationship skills such as effective communication and conflict management (Halford et al., 2003). Assessment and feedback might be insufficient to allow such couples to sustain high relationship satisfaction, and thus they might benefit from relationship skills training.

The second evidence-based approach to marriage education seeks to teach couples crucial relationship skills, typically in a face-to-face course of 12 to 15 contact hours with the use of procedures like modeling, rehearsal, and feedback on skills. It is well established that skill-focused relationship education can teach couples key relationship skills such as positive communication and conflict management, and these skills are maintained for at least a year or two after training (Halford et al., 2003).

Moreover, couples that initially have somewhat low relationship satisfaction show immediate increases in relationship satisfaction (Giblin, Sprenkle, & Sheehan, 1985).

There are benefits from skill-based marriage education in helping couples sustain long-term relationship satisfaction, but these benefits seem to be primarily for couples not at high risk for future relationship difficulties. Several quasi-experimental studies have shown long-term (3 to 4 year) universal benefit for couples from skill-based education (e.g., Bodenmann, Pihet, Shantinath, Cina & Widmer, 2006; Markman, Renick, Floyd, Stanley & Clements, 1993). However, as Halford et al (2003) noted these effects might be due to couples self-selecting into receiving marriage education. Only randomized controlled trials with adequate follow-up can clearly establish an effect of marriage education on maintaining relationship satisfaction and stability. (See Larson and Halford (in press) for information on trials with at least 6 month follow-up evaluations).

Challenges for the Future

My evaluation of the state of marriage education is that, like stated in the novel (p.1), *A Tale of Two Cities*, by Charles Dickens (1859), "It is the best of times, and it is the worst of times." I believe it may be the best of times because:

- Public and private funding for marriage education programming and evaluation has increased over the last 15 years (Brotherson & Duncan, 2004; Doherty & Anderson, 2004).
- Risk and resiliency factors related to marital quality and stability are now well-known and programs are being tested to address these factors (Halford, 2004).
- The unique needs and preferences of at-risk couples (e.g., low income and minorities) are starting to be assessed, and programming for them is in the development and evaluation stage now. Old myths about who wants marriage education and who values from it are being challenged (Ooms & Wilson, 2004).
- A new standard has been suggested for providing evidence of program effectiveness—"empirically-supported programs" (Jakubowski, et al., 2004).
- A heterogeneous group of professionals and lay leaders are discussing, debating, planning, organizing, designing, offering, and evaluating marriage education programs. Many diverse voices are being heard (Doherty & Anderson, 2004).
- Programs are available for individuals and couples from junior high school to late marriage (Halford, 2004).
- Comprehensive, flexible, stepped, customized, and empirically-derived and supported are important adjectives for use with marriage education programs (Larson, 2007).

However, it also may be the worse of times because:

- Although there is a plethora of marriage education programs, there is a dearth of peer-reviewed, published research on the short-term and long-term effectiveness of these programs. Generally, only a few programs with a strong skills-based focus have been evaluated in controlled research trials (Halford, Markman, Kline, & Stanley, 2003). Randomized controlled trials are still rare in this field. For most programs, only customer satisfaction and anecdotal evidence is provided to show program effectiveness. Further, studies using pre and post evaluations typically collect only program participant data rather than collecting data from a control or nonparticipant group.
- We still know little about the specific components of a marriage education program that produce the most change in relationship dynamics, satisfaction, and stability.
- We have yet to adequately test and publish research on programs that work best with at-risk couples. We also lack comparisons of marriage education formats with diverse racial, ethnic, and economic groups. In fact, only recently have we recognized that marriage education content and format may require customization for couples done in a stepped manner (see Larson & Halford (in press) for details).
- There is evidence that marriage education programs, especially premarital programs, may not be reaching couples most at risk for marital distress (Halford, O'Donnell, Lizzio, & Wilson, 2004; Sullivan & Bradbury, 1997). A focus on understanding these at-risk individuals and couples and their perceptions of premarital and marital education and counseling has only just begun.

Future Directions

In addition to the insightful and important recommendations for marriage education in the future described by Halford (2004), I offer several suggestions. First, an increased focus on empirically-informed foundations and empirical evaluations of marriage education programs using randomized controlled trials is needed. With increased public and private funding available, this seems more possible. Sources of information on funding opportunities can be found in the Brotherson and Duncan (2004) article. Until most programs are subjected to greater scrutiny, their effectiveness remains uncertain.

Second, less use of "shotgun approaches" in marriage education is warranted. This approach assumes all couples need the same intervention. This is highly unlikely (Halford, 2004; Larson & Halford, in press). Whereas some couples may need communication skills training, others do not; instead they may need to be trained in stress management techniques or how to deal with conflict with in-laws, emotional problems, etc. More customized programming suggests a renewed emphasis on pre-program assessment. The advantage of assessment-based marriage education is that couples can avoid the typical "one size fits all" kind of marriage education by first becoming aware of their unique strengths and weaknesses. Their marriage education can be customized for maximum effectiveness (Larson & Halford, in press).

Since not all couples need all components of a program, participating in a fixed curriculum program means many couples may waste valuable time and money. Couples report that it is unhelpful to work through materials that are not directly applicable to their unique relationship needs (Larson & Halford, in press). Learning concepts and skills irrelevant to their unique needs may de-motivate the learner to participate in other curriculum components more relevant to their needs. For example, individuals who have excellent communication skills but poor financial management skills may show low engagement with, or even drop out of programs practicing communication skills.

A challenge in offering customized marriage education is that many current providers of relationship education do not have the professional skills to carry out relationship assessments that might guide customizing (Doherty & Anderson, 2004). One possible solution to this problem is for marriage educators to use easily accessed, web-based assessments like RELATE (see Larson et al., 2002) that are relatively easy for couples to do in a short time. They are private, inexpensive, self-interpretive, and also provide clear interpretative guidelines to educators and couples.

Third, increased use of comprehensive ecosystemic models to assess couple needs and provide educational interventions (e.g., Bradbury, 1995; Karney & Bradbury, 1995; Larson & Holman, 1994) is needed. The ecological or ecosystemic perspective provides the educator with an overarching theoretical scheme for organizing the predictors of marital outcomes and developing interventions. This theory helps us to understand a couple as a developing unit that can and does respond to influences from within and outside the system. Their relationship develops at a number of levels, including the individual, couple, and contextual levels. Their relationship at all levels is dynamic rather than static, changing and evolving in a nonlinear fashion. To fully understand marital process and predict probable outcomes demands an understanding of as many of the levels of environments or ecosystems with which the couple comes into contact. The couple system reflects both individuals and a relationship, and these parts and the whole are interdependent. Too often, marriage educators have ignored "the self in the system" (Gurman & Fraenkel, 2002), p. 247. Marriage educators must consider individual factors such as emotional health and the ability to cope with stress (Gurman & Fraenkel, 2002), couple interaction factors such as communication skills and conflict resolution styles (Gottman & Notarius, 2002), the context or environment in which the couple is embedded (e.g., level of stress in the environment, and the level of conflict with extended family members, etc. (Bodenmann & Shantinath, 2004).

Fourth, increased use of comprehensive program development and evaluation criteria as suggested by the American Psychological Association (APA) Task Force on Promotion, Prevention, and Intervention Alternatives (Price, Cowen, Lorion, & Ramos-McKay, 1989) and Berger and DeMaria (1999) is essential. These criteria include demonstrating empirical evidence for both the short-term and long-term effects of the program and evidence of the program's cost effectiveness. In addition, for well-established and empirically supported programs (e.g., the Prevention and Relationship Enhancement Program, Couple Communication, and Relationship Enhancement, (see Berger & Hannah, 1999 for descriptions), future research should focus on components of the program that produce the most change in relationships. Marriage educators have made little progress in answering Arcus' (1995) call to answer the question: . . . "which programs work best for which people and under what conditions. . ?" (pg. 342-342).

Fifth, more flexible and innovative programs are needed like those recently tested by Bodenmann and Shantinath (2004), Halford et al (2004), and Nielsen et al. (2004). Silliman and Schumm (2004) suggest an even bolder idea: Training and supporting parents, mentors, and peer educators in teaching marriage education concepts to adolescents. Such an approach has been successfully used in related areas like sex education and drug education.

This is an exciting time to be involved in marriage education as a program designer, practitioner, or researcher. I hope this paper provides a new baseline for what we know and do not know about the field of marriage education and a launching pad for future program development and evaluation.

References

Arcus, M. E. (1995). Advances in family life education: Past, present and future *Family Relations*, *44*, 336-344.

Berger, R., & DeMaria, R. (1999). Epilogue: The future of preventive interventions with couples. In R. Berger & M. T. Hannah (Eds.), *Preventive approaches in couples therapy* (pp. 391-428). Philadelphia: Brunner/Mazel.

Berger, R., & Hannah, M. T. (1999). *Preventive approaches in couples therapy*. Philadelphia: Brunner/Mazel.

Birch, P. J., Weed, S. E., & Olsen, J. (2004). Assessing the impact of community marriage policies on county divorce rates. *Family Relations*, *53*, 495-503.

Bodenmann, G., Pihet, S., Shantinath, S. D., Cina, A., & Widmer, K. (2006). Improving dyadic coping in couples with a stress-oriented approach: A 2-year longitudinal study. Behavior *Modification*, *30*, 571-597.

Bodenmann, G., & Shantinath, S. D., (2004). The Couples Coping Enhancement Training (CCET): A new approach to prevention of marital distress based upon stress and coping. *Family Relations*, *53*, 477-484.

Bradbury, T. N. (1995). Assessing the four fundamental domains of marriage. *Family Relations*, *44*, 459-468.

Brotherson, S. E., & Duncan, W. C. (2004). Rebinding the ties that bind: Government efforts to preserve and promote marriage. *Family Relations*, *53*, 459-468.

Bulbolz, M. M., & Sontag, M. S. (1993). Human ecology theory. In P. G. Boss, W. J. Doherty, R. LaRossa, W. R. Shumm, & S. K. Steinmetz (Eds.), *Sourcebook of family theories and methods* (pp. 419-448). New York: Plenum.

Busby, D. M., Holman, T. B., & Taniguchi, N. (2001). RELATE: Relationship evaluation of the individual, family, cultural and couple contexts. *Family Relations*, *50*, 308-317.

Busby, D. M., Ivey, D. C., Harris, S. M., & Ates, C. (2007). Self-directed, therapist-directed, and assessment-based interventions for premarital couples. *Family Relations*, *56*, 279-290.

DeMaria, R. (2003). Psychoeducation and enrichment: Clinical considerations for couple and family therapy. In T. L. Sexton, G. R. Weeks, & M. S. Robbins (Eds.), *Handbook of family therapy* (pp. 411-431). New York: Brunner-Routledge.

Doherty, W. J., & Anderson, J. R. (2004). Community marriage initiatives. *Family Relations*, *53*, 425-432.

Giblin, P., Sprenkle, D. H., & Sheehan, R. (1985). Enrichment outcome research: A meta-analysis of premarital, marital, and family interventions. *Journal of Marital and Family Therapy*, *11*, 257-271.

Glenn, N. D., Nock, S., Waite, L, Doherty, W, Gottman, J., & Markey, B. (2002). Why marriage matters: Twenty-one conclusions from the social sciences. *American Experiment Quarterly*, *5*, 34-44.

Gottman, J. M., & Notarius, C. I. (2002). Marital research in the 20th century and a research agenda for the 21st century. *Family Process*, *41*, 159-198.

Gurman, A. S., & Fraenkel, P. (2002). The history of couple therapy: A millennial review. *Family Process*, *41*, 199-260.

Halford, W. K. (2004). The future of couple relationship education: Suggestions on how it can make a difference. *Family Relations*, *53*, 559-571.

Halford, W. K., Markman, H. J., Kline, G. H., & Stanley, S. M. (2003). Best practice in couple relationship education. *Journal of Marital and Family Therapy*, *29*, 385-406.

Halford, W. K., O'Donnell, C., Lizzio, A., & Wilson, K. (2004). Do couples at high-risk of relationship problems attend premarriage education? *Journal of Family Psychology*, *20*, 160-163.

Jacobson, N. S., Schmaling, K. B., & Holtzworth-Munroe, A. (1987). Component analysis of behavioral marital therapy: Two year follow-up and prediction of relapse. *Journal of Marital and Family Therapy*, *13*, 187-195.

Jakubowski, S. F., Milne, E. P., Brunner, H., & Miller, R. B. (2004). A review of empirically supported marital enrichment programs. *Family Relations*, *53*, 528-536.

Johnson, S. M. (2002). Marital problems. In D. H. Sprenkle (Ed.), *Effectiveness research in marriage and family therapy* (pp.163-190). Alexandria, VA: American Association for Marriage and Family Therapy.

Karney, B. R., & Bradbury, T. N. (1995). The longitudinal course of marital quality and Stability: A review of theory, method, and research. *Psychological Bulletin*, *118*, 3-34

Knutson, L., & Olson, D. H. (2003). Effectiveness of PREPARE program with premarital couples in community settings. *Marriage and Family*, *6*, 529-546.

Larson, J. H. (2007). Couple enrichment approaches. *Journal of Couple and Relationship Therapy*, *6*, 197-206.

Larson, J. H., & Halford, W. K. (in press). One size does not fit all: Customizing couple relationship education for unique couple needs. *Handbook of clinical issues in couple therapy (2nd ed.).*

Larson, J. H., & Holman, T. B. (1994). Premarital predictors of marital quality and stability: An applied literature review. *Family Relations, 43*, 1-10.

Larson, J. H., Newell, K., Topham, G., & Nichols, S. (2002). A review of three comprehensive premarital assessment questionnaires. *Journal of Marital and Family Therapy, 28*, 233-239.

Larson, J. H., Vatter, R. S., Galbraith, R. C., Holman, T. B., & Stahmann, R. F. (2007). The Reationship Evaluation (RELATE) with therapist-assisted interpretation: Short-term effects on premarital relationships. *Journal of Marital and Family Therapy, 33,* 364-374.

Markman, H. J., Renick, M. J., Floyd, F. J., Stanley, S. M., & Clements, M. (1993). Preventing marital distress through communication and conflict management training: A 4- and 5-year follow-up. *Journal of Consulting and Clinical Psychology, 61,* 70-77.

Nielsen, A, Pinsof, W., Rampage, C., Solomon, A. H., & Goldstein, S. (2004). Marriage 101: An integrated academic and experiential undergraduate marriage education course. *Family Relations, 53,* 485-494.

Ooms, T., & Wilson, P. (2004). The challenges of offering relationship and marriage education to low-income populations. *Family Relations, 53,* 440-447.

Price, R. H., Cowen, E. L., Lorion, R. P., & Ramos-McKay, J. 1989). The search for effective programs: What we learned along the way. *American Journal of Orthopsychiatry, 59*, 49-58.

Silliman, B., & Schumm, W. R. (2004). Adolescents' perceptions of marriage and premarital couples education. *Family Relations, 53,* 513-520.

Stanley, S. M., Markman, H. J., Prado, L. M., Olmos-Gallo, P. A., Tonelli, L., St. Peters, M., Leber, B. D., Bobulinski, M., Cordova, A., & Whitton, S. W. (2001). Community-based premarital preparation: Clergy and lay leaders on the front lines. *Family Relations, 50*, 67-76.

Sullivan, K. T., & Bradbury, T. N. (1997). Are premarital prevention programs reaching couples at risk for marital dysfunction? *Journal of Consulting and Clinical Psychology, 65*, 24-30.

Van Widenfelt, B., Markman, H. J., Guerney, B., Behrens, B. C., & Hosman, C. (1997). Prevention of relationship problems. In W. K. Halford & H. J. Markman (Eds.), *Clinical handbook of marriage and couples interventions* (pp. 651-675). New York: John Wiley & Sons.

About the Authors

Jeffry H. Larson, Ph.D., LMFT, CFLE, is a Professor of Marriage and Family Therapy at Brigham Young University. He is the editor of *the Journal of Couple and Relationship Therapy. Innovations in Clinical and Educational Interventions*, and author of *Should We Stay Together? A Scientifically Proven Method for Evaluating Your Relationship and Improving its Chances for Long Term Success* (San Francisco: Jossey-Bass, 2000). Email: jeffry_larson@byu.edu.

This article is based on an article originally published in the journal *Family Relations: Interdisciplinary Journal of Applied Family Studies*, 2004, *53*, 421-424, and is reprinted with permission.

Work-Family Research: Learning from the "Best of the Best"

SHELLEY MACDERMID

Over the past few decades there has been an explosion of research on the relationships between work and non-work life. The Rosabeth Moss Kanter Award for Excellence in Work-Family Research was created to raise awareness of high quality work-family research among the scholar, consultant, and practitioner communities.

The award is administered by the Center for Families at Purdue University and the Center for Work and Family at Boston College and currently sponsored by the Alliance for Work-Life Progress, the professional organization of corporate work-life practitioners. The purpose of the award is to foster debate about what the standards of quality for work-family research should be and ultimately to raise those standards. Here is an overview of what we have learned in the past few years from the "best of the best."

Overload is more problematic than *overwork*

Role overload is defined as having too much to do in the amount of time available. Although there is considerable public debate about long work hours, several studies suggest that role overload and the resulting stress are just as important. For example, a study of police officers and their wives found that while exhaustion actually seemed to improve the emotional climate of the relationship, job stress produced signs of marital distress.

According to another study, although husbands who spent more than 60 hours a week in work-related activities spent less time in shared activities with their wives, couples did not evaluate their relationships less positively *unless* the husband also reported high role overload. Then, wives reported feeling less loving, and there was more marital conflict.

In relationships with adolescent children, fathers who worked long hours but reported low overload were seen just as positively as fathers who worked less. But fathers who worked long hours and felt overloaded were seen as less accepting. These fathers were as seen as less effective in perspective-taking, that is, the ability to entertain the psychological point of view of another person.

These studies suggest that work overload and stress may corrode family relationships, and that researchers and practitioners would be wise not to overlook them.

Work situations differ more than men and women do

During the past 40 years mothers of young children have joined the labor force in rapidly increasing numbers. But recent Kanter studies suggest that it would be a mistake to conclude that men and women will respond differently to work-family demands. A 2003 study found that men and women who faced similar demands tended to respond in similar ways. Fathers and mothers were both more likely to refuse promotions than nonparents. Men and women in predominantly male occupations were more likely than those in predominantly female occupations to miss a family gathering.

In the winning article from the most recent competition, researchers studied the gender gap in eldercare, trying to understand why women consistently provide more care than men. Proposed explanations have included both "nature"—women are biologically predisposed to provide care—and "nurture"—women are trained and socialized to provide care. But researchers found that gender gap disappeared for men and women who worked in similar jobs. In other words, the gender gap in eldercare occurs largely because women and men differ in their employment conditions. Women tend to earn lower wages, are more likely to work part-time, and are less likely to be self-employed than men.

Motherhood can be costly

Considerable research has focused on a persistent gender gap in wages that disadvantages women. Two recent Kanter studies have focused explicitly on mothers to examine the costs of motherhood in wages and wage growth.

The first study found that unless mothers were college-educated, they faced wage penalties of 3 to 6 percent for several years following their return to the labor force. The wage penalties were sometimes smaller if mothers stayed out of the labor force longer.

The second study followed mothers for 10 years following the birth of their children to see what happened to their wage increases, taking into account any special work arrangements mothers used. Mothers who used policies that reduced their presence in the office—for example, telecommuting or working part-time—faced substantial penalties in wage growth. Penalties were most severe for mothers in managerial or professional jobs, who sacrificed 27 percent of their wage growth for telecommuting and 22 percent for working part-time at any time during the study period. Telecommuting or working part-time for the entire study period reduced wage growth by 58 percent or 50 percent respectively.

Wives' employment does not lead to marital breakdown

According to a 2002 study, wives working 20 hours a week had a 13 percent greater risk of divorce than wives who did not work outside the home. Wives who worked full-time had a 27 percent greater risk of divorce than wives who did not work outside the home. These differences were significant, but did not take marital happiness into account.

A 2003 study found that when marital happiness was taken into account, wives' employment status had no effect on marital disruption when both partners were happy. If either partner was dissatisfied with the marriage, the wife's employment significantly increased the risk of marital disruption. Thus, women's employment was a factor in divorce only when one or both members of a couple were dissatisfied with the marriage. An earlier Kanter nominee showed that marital dissatisfaction tended to precede rather than follow increases in wives' involvement in employment.

And finally, a 2004 study found that increases in marital satisfaction contributed to increases in job satisfaction. Similarly, increases in marital discord decreased job satisfaction over time. Unexpectedly, the influence of marital quality on job satisfaction was similar for married men and women.

For both women and men, the work-family relationship extended beyond daily interactions to affect long-term satisfaction. More satisfying marriages seemed to produce greater job satisfaction, suggesting that employers may realize benefits by reducing work conditions—such as work overload—that interfere with marital quality.

Supportive policies, programs or practices do not have to be bad for business

A creative study using longitudinal data revealed a positive relationship between work-family initiative announcements and subsequent shareholder returns. Between 1981 and 1996, the average three-day return was 0.48 percent. This compared to average decreases in share price of 0.38 percent associated with layoff announcements and 0.33 percent associated with discrimination lawsuits.

Returns were higher in high-tech firms and in industries with large proportions of women. There was no evidence that shareholder returns due to work-family announcements were significantly greater (or less) during times of low unemployment. Firms named the "best company for working mothers" reaped an increase in share price of 0.69 percent.

In 1998, children spent more time with their parents than in 1965

A 2001 study found the time mothers spent in child care activities declined between 1965 and 1975. But this was followed by a steady increase in the succeeding years. The time spent by fathers in child care activities increased in the late 1990s, rising from 41 percent to 53 percent of total child care activities in the household.

In addition, children of employed mothers in 1998 spent more time with their mothers than the average child spent in 1965, even though most mothers then were not employed. Much of the time parents have freed up for children appears to have come out of their own leisure time.

References

Anderson, D. J., Binder, M., & Krause, K. (2003). The motherhood wage penalty revisited: Experience, heterogeneity, work effort, and work-schedule flexibility. *Industrial and Labor Relations Review, 56*(2), 273-294.

Crouter, A. C., Bumpus, M. F., Head, M. R., & McHale, S. M. (2001). Implications of overwork and overload for the quality of men's family relationships. *Journal of Marriage and Family, 63,* 404-416.

Glass, J. (2004). Blessing or curse? Work-family policies and mother's wage growth over time. *Work and Occupations, 31*(3), 367-394.

Mennino, S. F., & Brayfield, A. (2002). Job-family trade-offs: The multidimensional effects of gender. *Work and Occupations, 29*(2), 226-256.

Roberts, N. A., & Levenson, R. W. (2001). The remains of the workday: Impact of job stress and exhaustion on marital interaction in police couples. *Journal of Marriage and Family, 63,* 1052-1067.

Sarkisian, N., & Gerstel, N. (2004). Explaining the gender gap in help to parents: The importance of employment. *Journal of Marriage and Family, 66,* 431-451.

About the Author

Shelley M. MacDermid, Ph.D., CFLE is Professor of Family Studies, Director of the Center for Families, and Co-Director of the Military Family Research Institute at Purdue University, West Lafayette, IN. She served as editor of the Families in Society sections of two previous teaching resources published by the National Council on Family Relations. E-mail: shelley@purdue.edu.

This article was originally published in the *NCFR Report*, 2006, *51*(2), and is reprinted with permission.

Between the Career Mystique and Reality: Minding the Gap

PHYLLIS MOEN

Over 40 years ago, in *The Feminine Mystique,* Betty Friedan (Friedan, 1965) pointed out the cultural contradictions of assigning full-time homemaking to half the adult population. The story line of the feminine mystique went something like this: Marriage and motherhood (for white, middle-class women, at least) were to be totally fulfilling, a life peopled by children and other mothers, isolated in the new residential suburbs sprouting up in post-war America. But Friedan paid scant attention to its mirror image: the *career mystique* (Moen & Roehling, 2005) the cultural contradictions of jobs that require employees to invest all their time, energy, and commitment to moving up seniority or job ladders.

In the almost half century since Friedan labeled "the problem with no name," the feminine mystique has become a cultural relic, or else a short-term project for mothers while their children are young. By contrast, the career mystique remains an integral aspect of the American way of life, today embraced by women as well as men, as the path to success, even for those who know they can never attain it.

While myths are important—providing a vision of what is possible— the career mystique as a **false myth**, standing in the way of creating new, alternative workplace and career flexibilities. It is "false" for five reasons. First, climbing the ladder of occupational success was never possible for all workers, even in the 1950s. Hard work paid off only for a select group of mostly white, mostly middle-class men.

Second, the feminine mystique provided the platform undergirding the career mystique. It is no accident that those most successful in climbing career ladders in business and in government have been men with either homemaking wives or else wives who put their own careers on the back burner.

Third, the old "contract" trading continuous, hard work for wage increases and seniority is long gone. Americans must now compete for jobs on a global playing field.

Fourth, neither men nor women want to live with the old gender divide. Women have not simply traded one mystique for another – moving from strictures about the "good" mother or the "good" wife to those embodied in the "good" worker. Rather, many American women are trying to have it all – to be the good wife, the good mother, *and* the good employee. Growing numbers of American men are trying to be all as well—egalitarian husbands and caring fathers *as well as* productive and competitive on the job. They too find it almost impossible to do so.

Fifth, very few men or women *can* live by the old rules. One job per family—the old breadwinner/homemaker model—is often a ticket to economic privation, since wages have not kept pace with inflation or living costs, the minimum wage is a poverty wage, and "middle-class" today means something very different in today's consumption economy.

Nevertheless, the career mystique remains institutionalized in policies and practices rewarding continuous full-time dedication to paid work, bracketed by education and retirement at both ends of the life course. This myth is interwoven into the very fabric of the American way of life, making it hard to envision any alternatives. Thus, Americans perceive it as "normal" that people in the primary labor market (historically white-collar and unionized blue-collar men) following lock-step occupational paths have typically reaped benefits: health-care insurance, pensions, vacations, sick leave, as well as seniority, promotions, and job security. By contrast, those in the secondary labor market—mostly women and minorities, as well as the poorly educated, unskilled, and immigrants — working part time or in temp or casual jobs, receive none of these things. But increasingly all of us are in the "secondary" workforce... even those in what were formally "good" jobs now live in a climate of uncertainty and ambiguity. Most American families confront job or income insecurity and stress as they contend with the moving platform of change characterizing life thus far in the 21st century.

Why do Americans cling to this patently false mystification of careers as the path to the good life? In part, it epitomizes the American Dream. The career mystique embraces an endurance ethic and a work ethic, both crucial to American values of individualism and free enterprise. Sacrifice by working hard, the myth goes, and you'll reap wealth, security, status, health insurance, pensions, respect, love, admiration, happiness. Like the sitcom reruns of the 1950s, the mystique remains. But the mid-20th century bargain of trading a lifetime of paid work for a lifetime of income security is probably gone forever. Still, children, young people, adults, retirees—along with CEOs, managers, union leaders, and government policy makers—"buy into" the career mystique.

Most men and women typically go along to get along, adopting "*work*-friendly" strategies. They try to "fit into" taken-for-granted blueprints of jobs, careers, and success that are now ill fitting at best. Some draw on new information technologies to manage the multiple strands of their lives. Picture a leading TV commercial; a mother at the beach with her two children frolicking in the waves while she is on a cell-phone conference call. Such technological advances permitting people to work anywhere, anytime may be family-friendly, but they are also *work*-friendly, encouraging employees to work everywhere, all the time. Other key family-friendly business innovations, such as child care and flextime, are also *work*-friendly, making it possible for employees to devote more time to their jobs.

Even the watchword "balance" itself is *work*-friendly. Single-parents aren't expected to "balance," but to work full-time, full year to support their families. And rarely do both spouses in a marriage "balance" their work and family goals and obligations. Rather, one spouse (usually the wife) typically scales back ("balances") in order that the other spouse (the husband) can put in long hours, travel, be on call, and try to climb or at least hang onto an increasingly shaky career ladder. The metaphor of "balance" is a cultural convention reinforcing the notion that conflicts and strains are private troubles, not public issues.

The (false) career mystique remains part of the human experience of Americans at all ages and stages, interwoven into customs, policies and practices as both a gender divide and an age divide. What is key is that both the breadwinner/homemaker *gender divide* (of paid work and unpaid family care work) and the life course as a three-part sequential *age divide*: (education, employment, and retirement) are social inventions, products of 20th century forces (industrialization, urbanization, suburbanization, and bureaucratization). These are, in fact, imaginary divides—between home and workplace, between men and women, between paid work and unpaid care or community work, between students, employees and retirees.

Social inventions, like technological inventions, can become obsolete. The career mystique stands in the way of imagining and implementing more sustainable ways of organizing paid work, family care work, and community engagement, as well as better safety nets for families. Can our nation bridge the gaps – between paid work and unpaid family and community work, between women and men, between an aging workforce, a growing "retired" force, and opportunities for meaningful engagement, between family paths and occupational paths, between the myth and the realities of "good" jobs and safety nets?

The first step is to become more **mindful** of the gap between two fundamental institutions: the family and the economy. This is a **moving gap**, shifting in tandem with social forces, but also with the disjunctures between what families and family members offer and need at various ages and life stages and what jobs offer and require at various ages and life stages (Moen & Chesley, 2008).

Americans are more adept at fostering technological inventions than social ones, but can be creative in times of unprecedented dislocations and transformations. One such example: the invention of Social Security as a safety net and a way of moving older Americans out of the workforce during the Great Depression. Another: the invention of the G.I. Bill offering returning veterans of World War II and their families opportunities for reinventing their lives. "All" that is required for American society to move beyond the career mystique is **imagination** and the **will** to change.

References

Friedan, B. (1963). *The feminine mystique.* New York: Bantam Doubleday Dell.

Moen, P., & Roehling, P. (2005). *The career mystique: Cracks in the American dream.* Boulder: Rowman & Littlefield Publishers, Inc.

Moen, P., & Chesley, N. (2008). Toxic job ecologies, time convoys, and work-family conflict: Can families (re)gain control and life-course "fit"? In K. Korabik, D. S. Lero, & D. L. Whitehead (Eds.), *Handbook of work – family integration: Research, theory, and best practices* (pp. 95-122). New York: Elsevier.

About the Author

Phyllis Moen, Ph.D. holds a McKnight Presidential Endowed Chair and is Professor of Sociology at the University of Minnesota. She is a life course scholar, which means that she is interested in *time, investigating* women's and men's lives, family relationships, and careers at work and at home, and linking them to both policy and well-being over the life course. Professor Moen has published numerous books, such as *Women's Two Roles: a Contemporary Dilemma* (1992) and *It's about Time: Couples and Careers* (2003). Most recent is *The Career Mystique: Cracks in the American Dream*, with Patricia Roehling, named Best Publication in Sociology for 2005 by the Professional and Scholarly Publication section of the Association of American Publishers. She co-directs (with Erin Kelly) the Flexible Work and Well-Being Center, funded as part of a larger National Institutes of Health network to investigate ways to provide employees with greater flexibility and control over the time and timing of their work. Dr. Moen is recipient of the Families and Work Institute's *Work-Life Legacy Award* for 2008.

This article was originally published in the *NCFR Report*, 2006, *51*(2), and is reprinted with permission.

Promoting Work/Family Balance through Family Life Education

MICHAEL LANE MORRIS

The challenges of juggling the demands of work and family have become a paramount issue for employees, their families, and employers. As a result, over the past four decades, research about work and family topics has grown exponentially and involved a wide variety of scholarship areas such as family studies, management, economics, health, sociology and psychology. Research has shown that competing expectations and stressful tensions arising from the domains of work and family interfere with one's ability to function in life's important roles. As a result, this interference hinders the ability to relate in healthy ways at home and/or work (Morris & Madsen, 2007). Consider the following illustrative examples:

Janice is a 32-year old aerospace engineer and a single parent of two preschool children. She receives little child care support from her extended family because they live in Boston and she and her children live in Los Angeles. Recently, she was offered a promotion opportunity for the dream job that she has always wanted. Janice has mixed feelings about accepting the badly needed promotion. As the sole provider of her family, Janice needs the increased salary. However, she also knows the new position will require longer office hours, travel, and occasionally work at home on the weekends. If she accepts this new role, Janice worries if she will have enough time to also care for her young children.

Because of an interstate construction project, Anne's commute to work has increased from a 15-minute to a 35-minutes. Anne is resentful because her supervisor insists that she arrive promptly at 8am. In conversations with her friends who travel the same route, Anne has learned that interstate traffic flow is much better after 8:30am. Anne wishes her boss would be a little more flexible with her morning schedule.

Roger is a very successful senior IT executive. Lynn, Roger's wife, complains to Roger about his excessive work habits. When the couple goes on vacation, Roger spends much of his vacation time working via wireless technologies. When Lynn presents her complaints, Roger reminds Lynn that "climbing the corporate ladder in his company is not easy and requires this kind of work ethic to achieve success." Lynn feels very ignored and unappreciated.

As a foreman for his company, Mac works the late shift (11pm-7am) and his wife Joan works a standard work day (8am-5pm) as an administrative assistant at the university. Mac and Joan regularly fight over their personal finances (excessive credit card debt), their work schedules, and their desire to begin a family. Recently, the couple learned that pregnancy was not possible due to medical complications. With all of the conflict at home, Mac's supervisor has noticed that Mac seems more irritable, less focused, and is making a lot of mistakes on key assignments.

These vignettes clearly illustrate that work/family issues are extremely complex. Work/family issues impact all of us regardless of our educational level, gender, income level, family structure, occupation, race, age, job status, or religion. What are some facts about the prevalence and impact of work/family stress? (Galinsky & Bond, 1998; Bond, Galinsky, Kim, & Brownfield, 2005; Cascio, 2000; Lockwood, 2003; Miller, 2005; Tyler, 2006). Consider these research findings:

- 90% of employees want more time with their family
- 85% of employees have day-to-day family responsibilities
- 46% of working parents have children under age 18 living at home
- 33% of employees worry about child care daily
- 78% of married employees live in dual income or dual career work/family situations
- 25% of employees have eldercare responsibilities
- Absenteeism including work/family stress cost companies nearly $300 billion/year
- 79% of employees experience medium to high levels of work/family stress
- 70% of employees report no balance exists in their work/family situation
- Employees with work/family conflict are three times more likely to quit their job
- 50% of mistakes/errors made by employees is due to work/family conflict
- Every three months, 50% of employees experience at least one (1) significant stress-related work/family conflict
- 25% of employees go to work five or more days per year when they are too stressed to be effective while an additional 48% of employees go to work one to four days per year too stressed to be effective.

As Family Life Educators (FLEs), it is important for us to understand work/family challenges so that we can develop effective interventions to promote more productive and fulfilling outcomes for individuals, families, and organizations. Specifically, the expertise of family life educators is needed to create and implement solutions that will enable individuals to be more balanced, healthy, resilient, engaged and fulfilled in both spheres. (Rapoport, Bailyn, Fletcher, & Pruitt, 2002). Similarly, at the organizational level, FLEs are also needed to promote the acceptance of work cultures that support work/family balance and positively influence the health and well-being of employees, families and/or organizational contexts (Crooker, Smith, & Tabak, 2002).

To assist FLEs in their practice within the work/family domains, the purpose of this chapter is to (1) define work/family balance and other related work/family terms, (2) provide an overview of the predictive factors that influence work/family balance, (3) identify individual, family, and organizational outcomes associated with work/family balance, and (4) summarize work/family solutions that promote work/family balance for individuals, families and organizations.[1]

Work/Family Balance & Other Work/Family Terms

What does the phrase "work/family balance" mean? Within the academic and popular press, the "work/family balance" phrase has received considerable attention. Academics have been primarily interested in exploring the prevalence, predictors, and outcome indicators of "work/family balance" that impact the relational and occupational health, well-being, and performance of individuals, families, and organizations (Grzywacz & Carlson, 2007). Similarly, in the popular press, "work/family balance" aspirations are easily marketed to consumers who purchase self-help articles and books in order to learn "how to" achieve a more satisfying balance in their lives.

Finding a commonly accepted definition of the phrase "work/family balance" within the work/family literature is difficult (Frone, 2003). Pitt-Catsouphes, Kossek, and Sweet (2006) have called the "work/family balance" phrase an "almost taken for granted metaphor" (p. 9).

While a commonly accepted definition of the "work/family balance" phrase is not found in the literature, a number of definitions do exist and inform our understanding of the work/family balance concept. Early efforts to define work/family balance characterized it as the "absence of conflict" between the work and family domains. Work/family conflict is defined as the mutual incompatibility between work and family roles that originated from time-based, strain-based, and behavior-based

[1] Authors Note: Regarding purposes 2-4 above, due to space constraints and a desire to provide practice-oriented content to FLEs from the vast work/family research domain, it is the author's intent to identify and present an overview of the key content issues. Thus, a more general, rather than specific, approach to referencing and citations will be used in this chapter. Interested readers should consult the sources cited later in the chapter for more detailed referencing.

sources (Greenhaus & Beutell, 1985). *Time-based conflict* is defined as the time demands of one role that make it difficult or impossible to participate in another role. *Strain-based conflict* is defined as psychological strain that is created in one domain that spills-over into another domain, making it difficult to fulfill the responsibilities of both roles. *Behavior-based conflict* is when behaviors normally associated with or are appropriate for one domain are inappropriately applied in another domain. For example, competitiveness may be necessary in the workplace but counter-productive in the home.

As research on work/family conflict evolved over time, the term "work/family interference" was later introduced as a similar/substitute construct to measure new dimensions of work/family conflict. Research efforts utilizing the work/family interference term were broadened to include examinations of the frequency, prevalence, and/or intensity of the conflict phenomenon (Edwards & Rothbard, 2000). Historically speaking, the school of thought that examined work/family balance through the "absence of conflict" lens is the oldest, the most developed, and contains the largest body of research. In contrast to the conflict standpoint in defining work/family balance, more contemporary definitions have emerged and are beginning to examine the work/family balance concept in other ways that are useful to our development of theory, research, and practice. As representative examples of this new thinking, here are four additional definitions of work/family balance:

- "The extent to which individuals are equally engaged in and equally satisfied with work and family roles" (Greenhaus, Collins, & Shaw, 2003, p. 513).
- "A global assessment that work resources meet family demands, and family resources meet work demands such that participation is effective in both domains" (Voydanoff, 2005, p. 825).
- The extent to which an individual's effectiveness and satisfaction in work and family roles are compatible with the individual's life priorities (Greenhaus & Allen 2006).
- "The accomplishment of role-related expectations that are negotiated and shared between and individual and his or her role-related partners in work and family domains" (Grzywacz & Carlson, 2007, p. 458).

Careful reviews of both the older and newer definitions of work/family balance are useful for gleaning ideas that expand and shape our understanding of the concept. First, these definitions illustrate that "cross-domain effects" exist in the interface between work and family. Friedman and Greenhaus (2000) define cross-domain effects as those experiences and choices in one domain that influence outcomes in the other. This approach assumes a bidirectional influence of mutual and reciprocal effects between the work and family domains.

Figure 1

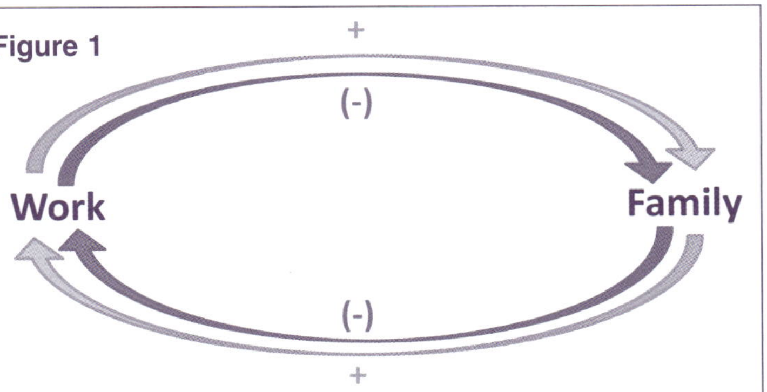

Second, these definitions also illustrate that the bi-directional influence of cross-domain effects is charged with either a positive or negative valence (Friedman & Greenhaus, 2000). As figure 1 depicts, at least four reciprocal influences exist between the domains of work and family.

Third, these definitions indicate that work/family balance is a dynamic and complex concept that includes cognitive, emotional, social, and behavioral dimensions. In terms of cognition, the definitions suggest that there are appraisal and attribution processes that individuals use to assess their levels of available resources in order to apply them to their work/family situations. In terms of emotion, feelings of satisfaction and fulfillment are important criteria in examining work/family experiences. Individuals, families, and organizations use these important criteria in reflecting on their values, priorities, beliefs, and expectations about work and family. In terms of social dimensions, work/family balance occurs within settings and cultures that involve the need for sharing relationships and partnerships with others. Also, these definitions reflect a behavioral component associated with work/family balance that includes efforts in negotiation, collaboration, effective engagement in multiple roles, and performance of work and/or family responsibilities.

Finally, these work/family balance definitions make us more keenly aware of and sensitive to the plethora of personalized/individualized meanings associated with the phrase "work/family balance." About work/life balance (WLB), Fleetwood (2007) noted: "It is unclear whether WLB refers to an objective state of affairs, a subjective experience, perception or feeling; an actuality or an aspiration; a discourse or a practice; a metaphor for flexible working; a metaphor for the gendered division of labor; or a metaphor for some other political agenda" (p.352). Clearly, the phrase work/life balance means different things to different people.

In addition to the work/family balance concept, there are a host of other work/family concepts that have begun to emerge in the work/family literature to describe the interface between the worlds of work and family (see Table 1). Concepts like *enrichment* (Greenhaus & Powell, 2006), *integration* (Bailyn, Drago, & Kochan, 2001), *facilitation* (Grzywacz, 2002), *spillover, resource drain, congruence, compensation, segmentation* (Edwards & Rothbard, 2000), and *enhancement* (Graves, Ohlott,

& Ruderman, 2007) are adding to our understanding of the work/family balance dynamic. For example, the concepts of enrichment and facilitation are receiving considerable attention by work/family scholars because they have the potential to describe the more positive qualities, connections, and benefits gained from the work and family interface for individuals, families, and organizations. However, this is an emerging area of research, and while the initial findings seem promising, no consistent conclusions can be drawn at this time. Further, preliminary research suggests that the processes and outcomes that are associated with work/family conflict are not necessarily the same processes and outcomes that relate to concepts such as work/family enrichment or work/family facilitation.

I close this section with a friendly professional reminder. The challenge for FLEs in working with familiar, everyday language phrases like "work/family balance," or other work/family-related terms, is that we must carefully define the key terms that powerfully impact our intervention efforts. As scholar practitioners, we must remember that definitions are extremely critical to our intervention efforts. They serve as a roadmap in developing the methods and content we will use to assist others in juggling the challenges between work and family. Thus, we must carefully select, define, and present our work/family concepts. Then, we must compare and synchronize our definitions with those with whom we work. This alignment will strengthen our efforts in being helpful to others.

Table 1. Other Work/Family Balance Concepts and Terms

Work/Family Concept	Definition
Enrichment	The degree to which experiences, resulting from either instrumental pathways (i.e., skills, abilities, values) or affective pathways (i.e., moods), in one domain (e.g. work) positively enhance the quality of life in the other domain (e.g., family) (Greenhaus & Powell, 2006).
Integration	A holistic strategy including effective and efficient coordination of strengths, efforts and energies from the work and family domains. Integration includes a healthy system of flexible and permeable boundaries that facilitates and encourages equal attentiveness and connection with priorities and valued activities originating in the work-life, family-life, and community-life domains (Bailyn, Drago, & Kochan, 2001).
Spillover	The shared similar effects (e.g., affect, values, skills, behaviors) of work and family. Spillover experiences can be either positive or negative, but the experiences of work and family are identical—either both are positive or both are negative (Edwards & Rothbard, 2000).
Facilitation	The extent to which participation in one domain fosters enhanced engagement or processes in another domain. Facilitation includes skills, experiences, resources, and knowledge interacting with individual and contextual circumstances that are portable and contribute to increased levels of organization and personal development (Grzywacz, 2002).
Resource Drain	The transfer or shift of a limited amount of available of resources (e.g., time, energy, attention) from one domain to another and thereby reducing the availability of the same resources for utilization in the domain originally owning the resource. When the remaining or unused resources become insufficient and/or are depleted, the potential for increased levels of stress, fatigue, and burnout ensues (Edwards & Rothbard, 2000).
Congruence	Involves the similarity between work and family by attributing the similarity to a third variable, like genetic factors or personality, which affects both domains. Congruence is very similar to spillover, except through congruence the similarity is mediated through the third variable. In contrast, spillover is a direct influence between work and family (Edwards & Rothbard, 2000).
Compensation	The efforts to offset negative experiences in one domain by increased efforts to seek positive experiences in the other domain. Efforts are pursued through one of two pathways. One pathway includes increased involvement in one domain reciprocated by decreased involvement in the other domain. The other pathway includes pursuing the domain offering greater rewards and fulfillment at the expense of the domain that offers little return (Edwards & Rothbard, 2000).
Segmentation	The complete compartmentalization or fragmentation of work and family systems. Segmentation includes a line of demarcation separating the world of work from family—and family from work (Edwards & Rothbard, 2000).
Enhancement	The facilitation that occurs when one domain increases an individual's energy and attitude and contributes to the development of skills in the other domain (Graves, Ohlott, & Ruderman, 2007).

Individual, Family, and Organizational Variables that Predict and/or Influence Work/Family Balance

Over the past 40 years, the body of research examining the predictors, criteria, and mediators of work/family balance has grown extensively. In preparing this section, I reviewed a number of meta-analytic literature reviews involving nearly 1000 research studies to formulate mega-themes and sub-themes of predictor variables that have been found to positively and/or negatively influence work/family balance and other work/family dynamics (e.g., conflict, integration, facilitation).[2]

Table 2 summarizes many of the individual-level, family-level, and organization-level variables identified in the empirical literature that positively and/or negatively influence the work/family interface (Eby, Casper, Lockwood, Bordeaux, & Brinley, 2005). When reviewing the broad array of variable mega-themes found in table 2, two general observations are in order.

First, although the work/family predictors and/or influences are presented under typological categories of individual, family, and organization, the sources of influence being presented can be unique to or shared by each of the three typological areas (i.e., individual, family, organization). For example, many researchers have examined identity characteristics such as motivation and dimensions of personality at each of the three levels as well as studied how these same identity characteristics originate in one typological area and cross over to influence another life dimension (e.g., how is an individual's personality at work influenced by marital stress?) (Wayne, Musisca, & Fleeson, 2004). Thus, because these predictors are listed under one typological category (i.e., individual-level), this does not limit the predictor's relevance to other typological areas (e.g., family-level or organization-level).

Second, research has suggested that the predictive sources of influence can differ in their magnitude of influence in terms of direction (i.e., work versus family). Comparatively speaking, research studies consistently show that while both work and family contexts are influenced by each other (i.e., bidirectional), the family context tends to be more strongly impacted by work stressors than family stressors impacting the work context (Frone, 2003).

While space limitations prohibit an in-depth discussion and presentation of research to support the inclusion of each of these mega-themes found in table 2, the following bulleted statements below provide a few examples from the research literature. It is hoped that these examples will illustrate many of the important research questions being addressed by work/family scholars, as well as, demonstrate how individual, family, and organizational variables have been shown to influence the work/family interface.

- The decision to adopt family-friendly practices is directly correlated to the proportion of women employed by the organization (Goodstein, 1994).
- Shift work requirements, working weekends and rotating schedules are positively related to increased levels of work/family conflict (Judge, Boudreau, & Bretz, 1994).
- Characteristics associated with the design of work (e.g., responsibilities, number of hours worked) influence an employee's ability to control and balance the demands of work and family (Batt & Valcour, 2003).
- Decreased job autonomy, increased schedule inflexibility, and increased unpredictability in jobs created more work/family imbalance (Bond, Thompson, Galinsky, & Prottas, 2003; Galinsky, Bond, & Friedman, 1996).
- Working fathers and men without children equally benefit from flexible schedules in reducing work/family conflict (Marshall & Barnett, 1994).
- When the needs, demands, and/or expectations of individual versus family versus work collide, most employees make adjustments in their personal lives or their family to accommodate the needs, demands, and/or expectations of work (Thomas & Ganster, 1995).

[2] Authors Note: For more detailed information on these meta-analytic studies, please see Allen, Herst, Bruck, & Sutton (2000); Byron, (2005); Eby, Casper, Lockwood, Bordeaux, & Brinley (2005); Ford, Heinen, & Langkamer (2007); Frone (2003); Gilboa, Shirom, Fried, & Cooper (2008); Kossek & Ozeki (1998); MacDermid & Harvey, (2006); Thompson, Beauvis, & Allen (2006); Quick, Quick, Nelson, & Hurrell (1997).

Table 2. Individual, Family and Organization Predictors of Work/Family Balance

Individual-Level Influences	Family-Level Influences	Organization-Level Influences
Background Characteristics • Demographics (e.g., age, sex, race) • Work history and experience • Education-level • Leisure behaviors/practices • Career lifecycle Phase (e.g., early-career/novice, mid-career, late-career, retirement)	**Family Characteristics** • Socio-economic status (e.g., standard of living) • Family Responsibility (e.g., number of kids, age of kids) • Marital status (e.g., single, married, divorced, remarried, cohabitating) • Marital Type (e.g., dual-earner versus single-earner) • Family life cycle stage • Division of Domestic Labor (e.g., equity)	**Organization Characteristics** • Settings (e.g., industry, location, sector) • Demographic Composition (e.g., proportions of men to women) • Non-family related benefits and compensation (e.g., pension benefits) • Structure (i.e., extent of centralization versus decentralization) Size (e.g., small, medium, and large)
Identity Characteristics • Personality (e.g., Big Five, Type A, Optimism, Hardiness,) • Emotions (e.g., mood, positive affect, negative affect, anxiety/ worry, anger, guilt) • Gender Role Orientation (e.g., masculinity versus femininity) • Motivational Traits (e.g., self-esteem, locus of control, needs/wants, value system)	**Family and Parenting Stress Demands** • Care giving Demands (e.g., child, elders) • Conflict (e.g., marital, parent/child) • Behavioral Outcomes (e.g., conduct problems, school performance) • Child well-being (e.g., mental and physical health) • Parenting Style (e.g., laissez faire)· Child's perceptions of job (e.g., safety, security) • Co-parent's work/non-work attitudes (e.g., involvement with children versus job)	**Job Characteristics** • Decision-making latitude Autonomy • Job demands (e.g., number of hours worked, pace, volume, repetitive routine, complexity) • Person/job fit (e.g., competence)· Job insecurity • Job design (e.g., skill variety, shift work, amount, frequency, mandatory nature of overtime) • Job attributes (e.g. prestige, authority) • Physical environment (e.g., air quality, temperature) • Pollution risk exposure (e.g., noise, toxic, hazardous materials) • Travel expectations (e.g., amount, frequency, duration of trips) • Scheduling (e.g. inflexible versus flexible)
Personal Attitudes about Work or Family • Family Satisfaction • Commitment/loyalty (e.g., affective and continuance) • Involvement (e.g., behavioral, psychological) • Withdrawal cognitions (e.g., thoughts about leaving the family) • Perceptions about family (e.g., family pride)	**Family/Spouse Attitudes** • Satisfaction (e.g., life, marriage, family, parenting) • Involvement/commitment (e.g., time spent together) • Leisure and recreation • Work attitudes (e.g., spouse's job satisfaction, spouse's view of employee's job) • Background (e.g., spouse income, education, gender, health condition)	**Organization's Culture of W/F Support** • Employer's responsiveness (e.g., adoption of family-friendly benefits) • Manager/supervisor support (e.g., attitudes about using family-friendly programs) • Coworker/peer support (e.g., attitudes about job-sharing, flex-time) • HR Policies and Practices (e.g., promotion practices, training) • Family-friendly benefits offering (e.g., flex-schedule, telecommuting)

Table 2. Individual, Family and Organization Predictors of Work/Family Balance

Individual-Level Influences	Family-Level Influences	Organization-Level Influences
Personal Attitudes about Job and Career· • Job/Career Satisfaction • Career Commitment • Career Salience/Involvement/Identity (e.g., a calling versus a job) • Career Satisfaction • Career Development Opportunities (e.g., hopes for advancement) • Withdrawal cognitions (e.g., turnover intentions, thoughts about being absent or late) • Perceptions about job/work (e.g., income, security) • Perceptions about the organization (e.g., employer of choice)	**Family Support System Network** • Spousal Support • Friendship Network (e.g., number, quality, time spent in friendships) • Community ties and support (e.g., church, schools) • Grandparent's Involvement (e.g., child-care, financial support)	**Role Stress** • Role Conflict • Role Ambiguity • Role Overload

Individual, Family, and Organizational Outcomes Associated with Work/Family Balance

Now that we have discussed a number of the predictor variables that influence the work/family balance interface, we now address the question: "In what ways?" Similar to the volumes of research examining predictors of work/family balance, efforts examining the positive and negative outcome effects associated with work/family balance for individuals, families, and organizations have also been extensive. Utilizing the same content analysis methodology described in the previous section, the author explored a number of research studies (Allen, Herst, Bruck, & Sutton, 2000; Eby, Casper, Lockwood, Bordeaux, & Brinley, 2005; Quick, Quick, Nelson, & Hurrell, 1997) to identify some of the outcomes that have been examined in the work/family balance literature. Using the same typology of individual-level, family-level, and organization-level as above, these outcomes are presented in Table 3.

When reviewing the broad array of potential work/family outcomes found in table 3, two general observations are in order. First, outcomes vary depending on the directional source of the predictor, and therefore, it is important to distinguish the direction of influence (i.e., work-to-family versus family-to-work) to determine how the outcome is influenced (Frone, 2003). For example, Frone (2003) noted this by suggesting, role-related outcomes stemming from work-to-family conflict reside in the family domain, whereas role-related outcomes stemming from family-to-work conflict reside in the work domain. In either case, the outcomes from the respective domains can differ and vary greatly. Frone further noted, in some cases, the predictor's direction of influence did not matter, as both work and family domains were equally impacted—either positively or negatively. Therefore, it is important to establish the direction of influence, as the outcomes may not be similar.

Second, because the outcomes generated from work/family stress sources vary, and potentially compete, there is an important need to monitor the influence of predictors as well as the impact of solutions (Frone, 2003). For example, some researchers have found that their intervention attempts to reduce work/family conflict and also promote work/family enrichment have yielded unexpected outcomes. Specifically, conflict was reduced, but surprisingly, enrichment was also reduced (Wayne, Musisca, & Fleeson, 2004). In addressing this issue, Grzywacz and Carlson, (2007) noted that work/family practitioners must be aware of and prepared to address the potential for competing outcomes.

The following examples illustrate some of the research questions explored by work/family scholars who have investigated the impact or outcomes of work/family balance.

- Levels of employee retention are higher in organizations that have effective family-friendly programs (Families and Work Institute, 1993).
- Family-supportive work cultures decrease turnover intention attitudes in employees (Allen, 2001).
- When compared to their competitors, firms that offer more extensive family-friendly policies and programs have a higher ability to recruit and retain better qualified employees, higher overall performance as measured by product quality, better manager/employee relationships, and higher financial indicators of corporate success like market share, profits, and sales growth (Perry-Smith & Blum, 2000).

- Employees with eldercare responsibilities experience higher levels of tardiness and absenteeism (Hepburn & Barling, 1996).
- The general health of children improves as a result of income produced from parental employment and access to better health and medical care (Friedman & Greenhaus, 2000).
- In general, all forms of work/family conflict (i.e., work-to-family, family-to-work) produce negative relationships with job satisfaction, career satisfaction, and life satisfaction (Kossek & Ozeki, 1998).

Table 3. Individual, Family and Organization Outcomes of Work/Family Balance

Individual-Level Outcomes	Family-Level Outcomes	Organization-Level Outcomes
Work/Career Attitudes • Job/career satisfaction • Commitment • Loyalty • Engagement • Organizational citizenship • Mobility (e.g., turnover intent) • Career Success	**Interaction Quality** • Adjustment • Satisfaction (e.g., marital, parenting, life) • Dissatisfaction (e.g., marital, family) • Strengths (e.g., marital, family) • Family functioning (e.g., communication, cohesion) • Conflict • Enrichment	**Employee Participation Behaviors** • Turnover/turnover intent • Absenteeism • Concentration • Tardiness • Employee retention • Strikes/work stoppages • Disruptive behavior (e.g. grievances/complaints filed)
Health & Wellness • Physical health (e.g., hypertension, fatigue) • Mental health (e.g., anxiety, depression, mood, hardiness, resiliency) • Behavioral health (e.g., sleeping disorders, substance abuse, eating disorders • Medical health (e.g., chronic illness) • Psychological wellness (e.g., burnout, vitality, motivation)	**Family Participation Behaviors** • Behavioral involvement (e.g., withdrawal, engagement) • Psychological investment (e.g., care) • Role investment (e.g., role salience) • Family performance • Leisure satisfaction • Spouse and family attitudes (e.g., support, encouragement) • Friendship network/support • Community support	**Organizational Well-being** • Health care costs (e.g., accidents, injuries, illness) • Financial performance (e.g., profits, market share) • Corporate Image (e.g., employer of choice) • Policy/program utilization (e.g., telecommuting policy, flex-schedule) • Supervisor/manager support • Strategic HR outcomes (e.g., employee recruitment, training transfer) • Highly productive teams
Quality of Work Relationships • Positive qualities (e.g., Trust, Respect) • Negative qualities (e.g., aggression, harassment, violence, verbal assault)	**Health & Wellness** • Family member wellness (e.g., child health, spouse) • Medical consequences (e.g., sexual dysfunctions) • Family stress • Holistic coping behaviors	**Employee Job Performance** • Quality of productivity (e.g., error rates, mistakes) • Quantity of productivity • Work effort (e.g., employee engagement)

Individual, Family, and Organizational Interventions Promoting Work/Family Balance

Work/family interventions are activities, policies, programs, and practices that are designed to promote healthy integration and balance in the interface between work and family for individuals, families, and organizations. They also alleviate stressful conflict and tensions between the work and family (Arthur & Cook, 2003; Lobel & Kossek, 1996; Morris & Madsen, 2007).

The volume and variety of work/family interventions that are available to FLEs for assisting individuals, families, and organizations seem almost endless. For example, within organizational context alone, The Society for Human Resource Management (Fegley, 2007) provides a listing of 224 employee benefits divided among the following eight benefit categories: Family-friendly benefits, housing and relocation, personal services, financial and compensation, business travel, health care and wellness, leave, and other/miscellaneous.

In defining the concept of "intervention," Argyris (1970) defined intervention as "entering into an ongoing system of relationships to come between or among persons, groups, or objects for the purpose of helping them" (p.15). According to Argyris (1970), while interventions are intended to help others, they should be designed to promote autonomy and empowerment, differentiate healthy boundaries, and provide all systemic members (i.e., individual, family, organization) opportunities to enhance their competence and effectiveness. Coping is fostered by interventions that enable individuals, families, and organizations to mobilize their existing and expanded resources in order to effectively manage and modify stressful events (Lazarus & Folkman, 1984).

Consistent with the format used in the previous two sections, in tabular form (see Table 4), we will highlight intervention tools that can be incorporated into work/family programs (e.g., training), policies, and practices. These interventions are considered useful in coping with the negative influences and consequential outcomes associated with work and family as well as promoting the positive influences and outcomes of work/family balance for individuals, families, and organizations (Frone, 2003; Quick et al., 1997). Additionally, these interventions are effective in directly addressing or modifying work/family demands (primary prevention), modifying the responses to work/family demands (secondary prevention), and managing the symptomatic outcomes of work/family demands (tertiary prevention) (Quick et al., 1997).

According to Friedman, DeGroot, and Christensen (1998), effective work/family interventions should assist individuals, families, and organizations clarify priorities and make purposeful choices, communicate, listen, and negotiate competing needs, respectfully behave in ways that are consistent with values systems, build healthy interactions, and foster and reward productivity, manage boundaries appropriately, examine competing priorities, be flexible, creative, and synergistic in meeting needs. The interventions presented in Table 4 meet Friedman's et al. criteria.

Table 4. Individual, Family and Organization Interventions Promoting Work/Family Balance

Individual-Level Interventions	Family-Level Interventions	Organization-Level Interventions
• Lifestyle/leisure management (examining lifestyle choices and creating healthy decision-making filters) • Role training and management (developing time management skills, building social support) • Perception management (building positive self-concept traits like optimism and hope, controlling cognitive distortions) • Constructive self-talk (altering irrational beliefs and messages with rational views) • Transformational Coping (reframing events by viewing them in a broader life perspective) • Selective ignoring (cognitive anchoring oneself to more positive aspects of a troublesome situation) • Changing personality-based behaviors (altering or reengineering noxious personality traits into more productive behaviors) • Relaxation training (variety of methods designed to achieve muscular, physical, mental relaxation and peace) • Communication outlets (ventilating through written journals, spoken, action-oriented means)· Fitness routines (improve physical endurance, flexibility, and stamina with exercise and nutrition) • Individual counseling/therapy (symptom-specific programs)	• Role sensitivity training (using role play activities to enable others to understand other viewpoints) • Role analysis (examining domestic roles, role expectations, role labor, etc.) • Family group discussions (identifying and discussing major W/F challenges impeding family balance) • Marriage/parenting/family enrichment (fostering closeness, communication, problem-solving, decision-making) • W/F life planning (examining W/F history, identifying W/F goals, developing W/F action plans) • Reading and learning (building awareness and skills through books, mentors, video) • W/F demand/control assessment (introspective examination of key W/F demands versus controls) • W/F resource management (consistent with family values, inventory and allocate all available resources to meet goals) • Family counseling/therapy (family symptom-specific programs) • Caregiving system analysis (assessing family strengths, weaknesses, opportunities, and threats in care-giving system for children and elders)	• Job redesign/enrichment (restructure core job dimensions) • Participative management (empower autonomy and/or employee voice in job-related W/F decision-making) • Flexible work schedules (increasing individual control and discretion of when and where work occurs) • Career development planning (structuring career paths for personal growth and development) • Wellness centers (creation of growth-oriented environments like fitness centers) • Role analysis (clarifying confusion and conflicts of "expected" work role from "enacted role.") • Goal setting (establishing clear objectives and mapping areas of work responsibility and performance expectations) • Social support (providing enriching relationships and culture that provide emotional, informational, informational support) • Training programs (providing learning opportunities that debunk W/F myths and build supervisory W/F leadership competencies) • HR policies/programs/practices (adopting organizational strategies to address time-based, information-based, financial-based, and service-based employee needs)

Unfortunately, the amount of research examining the *effectiveness* of work/family interventions is sparse. More research is needed, as many unanswered questions exist. According to MacDermid and Harvey (2006), within the work/family research domain, few studies exist examining how coping interventions are selected, if the chosen intervention selections are appropriate, how effective or successful the interventions are in promoting balance, the order of preference (i.e., first or last attempt), how personal or contextual circumstances influence the suitability, success, or improve control over work/family demands.

However, of the research that is available, most involves examining the availability, awareness, accessibility, affordability, utilization, and satisfaction of family-friendly benefits (Morris, 2008). The following examples provide evidence of this research.

- The mere presence or offering of family-friendly support services does not guarantee that employees will utilize them. Nor, does it guarantee that employee's lives will be affected in reducing work/family stress. Supportive workplace attitudes and people (e.g., supervisors, peers/colleagues) must also be present (Thompson, Beauvais, & Allen, 2006).
- Effective family-friendly policies and programs are useful in helping all employees, regardless of gender, experience work/family balance enabling them to enjoy productive and successful careers (Kirchmeyer, 1998).
- Telecommuting more than 2.5 days a week decreased the level of work/family conflict, but increased the conflict with co-workers (Gajendran & Harrison, 2007).
- In general, employees possess limited and vague awareness of the work/family policies and programs that their organizations provide (Pitt-Catsouphes, 1999).
- Work/family initiatives have the greatest potential for impact when the family-friendly benefits are geographically located nearby or on-site, when the family-friendly resource (e.g., daycare) are conducive to employee work schedules, and when eligibility for participation by all employees is evenly distributed and fair (Batt & Valcour, 2003; Kossek & Friede, 2006).
- Family-friendly benefits must be consistent with the employee's ability to exchange time and financial resources to access and utilize the benefit (Connelly, Degraff, & Willis, 2004).
- Presently, U.S. companies offer an average of eight or more work/family programs, with and they are anticipated to grow in the years ahead as companies strategically use family-friendly benefits to achieve competitive advantage over their competitors (Bond, Galinsky, Kim, & Brownfield, 2005; Lockwood, 2003).
- A suite or bundle of family-friendly benefits are most frequently utilized and appreciated by employees when they are perceived as economical and relevant to the employee's immediate needs (Creed & Scully, 1999; Lambert, 1999).
- Forty-six percent of employers perceive a positive return on their corporate financial investments in flexible work arrangements; 42% a positive return on leave programs; and 21% a positive return on eldercare programs (Galinsky & Bond (1998).

Summary & Closing Thoughts for Practitioners

In this chapter, I attempted to explore the definition of work/family balance and other important work/family concepts. I also highlighted the positive and negative predictive influences and outcomes that have been associated with the work/family balance interface. Furthermore, I presented a number of useful interventions for promoting work/family balance for individuals, families, and organizations. Additionally, I noted that the role of FLEs in supporting work/family balance is paramount, especially when the benefits of balance are so great for individuals, their families, and organizations.

As closing thoughts for FLE practitioners, there are a few useful tips that our experience in promoting work/family balance has taught us. Those useful tips include:

1. ***Effective work/family interventions are built on solid theory and research.*** Most work/family researchers and FLE scholars/practitioners have not based their studies or interventions on strong conceptual frameworks and theories (Grandey & Cropanzano, 1999; Powell & Cassidy, 2001). Effective FLE practice requires a good theoretical/research base, not good intentions, interesting ideas, or endorsements from popular culture (Duncan & Goddard, 2005).
2. ***Be holistic: Work and family can be allies, not enemies.*** In daily practice, the relationships between work and family are often treated as separate worlds, with clear biases that favor the importance of work over family. Under rigid circumstances, this separation approach to work and family produces unnecessary stress, pressure, and conflict for individuals, families, and organizations. This zero-sum game of competing priorities causes considerable tensions between the domains of work and family making them enemies rather than allies (Friedman & Greenhaus, 2000). The worlds of work and family don't have to be enemies—instead, they can be allies with complimentary priorities. As FLEs, our efforts must address the artificial separation found in work and family life by helping individuals, families, and organizations understand that everyone can win through a healthy balance between work and family.

3. ***Carefully select work/family interventions to avoid intervention backlash***. In working with work/family issues, effective practice requires a thorough understanding of the influences, outcomes, and solutions associated with work/family balance. As the tables above illustrate, across individuals, families, and organizations, there are multiple domains of influence, many possible outcomes, and a vast array of intervention solutions connected with work/family balance. Because of this diversity, FLEs must carefully select and implement balance-promoting interventions that are considerate to the immediate needs of the individual, family, and/or organization. In an effort to promote work/family balance, it is not wise to assume that all work/family interventions are created equal. In this author's experience, a "one size fits all intervention approach" will not be effective in addressing the specialized needs of the diverse audiences seeking ways to improve their work/family situations. Special attention will be needed to address key issues like gender, family life cycle, career life cycle, organizational context, etc. To ignore these customized needs invites considerable backlash.

4. ***Market work/family interventions effectively***. Effective marketing of work/family interventions requires the development of a "business case" that demonstrates the value-added benefits of work/family balance to individuals, families, and organizations (Apgar, 1982; Duncan & Goddard, 2005). As with other FLE interventions, the development of a "business case" involves demonstrating tangible evidence that interventions are good for the relational, physical, mental, and emotional health of employees and their families, while also demonstrating that it is good for the financial health of the employer's bottom line—a win-win solution for everyone (Berg, Kalleberg, & Applebaum, 2003; Halpern & Murphy, 2005). To promote work/family initiatives, FLEs marketing messages should be advertised as doing something more than offering a "luxurious perk," or is a "nice thing to do for employees," or demands that it is "a corporate responsibility." Instead, FLEs need to communicate how work/family interventions can be an important strategic tool contributing to the successful achievement of individual, family, and organizational goals (Arthur & Cook, 2003, 2004).

References

Allen, T. D., Herst, D. E. L., Bruck, C. S., & Sutton, M. (2000). Consequences associated with work-to-family conflict: A review and agenda for future research. *Journal of Occupational Health Psychology, 5*(2), 278-308.

Allen, T. D. (2001). Family-supportive work environments: The role of organizational perceptions. *Journal of Vocational Behavior, 58,* 414-435.

Apgar, K. (1982). *Life education in the workplace: How to design, lead, and market employee seminars.* New York: Family Service Association of America.

Argyris, C. (1970). *Intervention theory and method.* Reading, MA: Addison-Wesley.

Arthur, M. M., & Cook, A. (2003). The relationship between work-family human resource practices and firm profitability: A multi-theoretical perspective. *Research in Personnel and Human Resources Management, 22*, 219-252.

Arthur, M. M., & Cook, A. (2004). Taking stock of work-family initiatives: How announcements of family-friendly human resource decision affect shareholder value. *Industrial and Labor Relations Review, 57*(4), 599-613.

Bailyn, L., Drago, R., & Kochan, T. (2001). *Integrating work and family life: A holistic approach* (Sloan Work-Family Policy Network report). Cambridge, MA: MIT Sloan School of Management.

Batt, R., & Valcour, P. (2003). Human resources practices as predictors of work-family outcomes and employee turnover. *Industrial Relations, 42*(2), 189-220.

Berg, P., Kalleberg, A., & Applebaum, E. (2003). Balancing work and family: The role of high-commitment environments. *Industrial Relations, 42*(2), 168-188.

Bond, J. T., Galinsky, E., Kim, S. S, & Brownfield, E. (2005). *2005 National study of employers.* New York: Families and Work Institute.

Bond, J. T., Thompson, C. A., Galinsky, E., & Prottas, D. (2003). *Highlights of the 2002 national study of the changing workforce.* New York: Families and Work Institute.

Byron, K. (2005). A meta-analytic review of work-family conflict and its antecedents. *Journal of Vocational Behavior, 67,* 168-198.

Cascio, W. F. (2000). *Costing human resources: The financial impact of behavior in organizations* (4th ed.). Cincinnati, OH: South-Western College Publications.

Connelly, R., Degraff, D., & Willis, R. (2004). The value of employer-sponsored childcare to employees. *Industrial Relations, 43*(4), 759-792.

Creed, D., & Scully, M. (1999). Analyzing availability and utilization. In M. Pitt-Catsouphes (Ed.), *Metrics manual: Ten approaches to measuring work/life initiatives*. Chestnut Hill, MA: Boston College Center for Work and Family.

Crooker, K. J., Smith, F. L., & Tabak, F. (2002). Creating work-life balance: A model of pluralism across life domains. *Human Resource Development Review, 1*, 387-419.

Duncan, S. F., & Goddard, H. W. (2005). *Family life education: Principles and practices for effective outreach.* Thousand Oaks, CA: Sage Publishing.

Eby, L. T., Casper, W. J., Lockwood, A., Bordeaux, C., & Brinley, A. (2005). Work and family research in IO/OB: Content analysis and review of the literature (1980-2002). *Journal of Vocational Behavior, 66,* 124-197.

Edwards, J. R., & Rothbard, N. P. (2000). Mechanisms linking work and family: Clarifying the relationship between work and family constructs. *Academy of Management Review, 25*, 178-199.

Families & Work Institute (1993). *An evaluation of Johnson & Johnson's work-family initiative.* New York: Author.

Fegley, S. (2007). *2007 Benefits.* Alexandria, VA: The Society of Human Resource Management.

Fleetwood, S. (2007). Rethinking work-life balance: Editor's introduction. *International Journal of Human Resource Management, 18*(3), 351-359.

Ford, M. T., Heinen, B. A., & Langkamer, K. L. (2007). Work and family satisfaction and conflict: A meta-analysis of cross-domain relations. *Journal of Applied Psychology, 92*(1), 57-80.

Friedman, S., & Greenhaus, J. (2000). *Work and family – Allies or enemies: What happens when business professionals confront life choices?* New York: Oxford.

Friedman, S. D., Degroot, J., Christensen, P. M. (1998). Introduction. In S. D. Friedman, J. Degroot, & P. M. Christensen (Eds.), *Integrating work and life: The Wharton resource guide* (pp. 1-18). San Francisco, CA: Jossey-Bass/Pfeiffer.

Frone, M. R. (2003). Work-family balance. In J. C. Quick & L. E. Tetrick (Eds.), *Handbook of occupational health psychology* (pp. 143-162). Washington, DC: American Psychological Association.

Gajendran, R. S., & Harrison, D. A. (2007). The good, the bad, and the unknown about telecommuting: Meta-analysis of psychological mediators and individual consequences. *Journal of Applied Psychology, 92,* 1524-1541.

Galinsky, E., & Bond, J. T. (1998). *Executive summary: The 1998 business work/life study: A sourcebook.* New York: Families and Work Institute.

Galinsky, E., Bond, J. T., & Friedman, D.E. (1996).The role of employers in addressing the needs of employed parents. *Journal of Social Issues, 52,* 111-136.

Gilboa, S., Shirom, A., Fried, Y., & Cooper, C. (2008). A meta-analysis of work demand stressors and job performance: Examining main and moderating effects. *Personnel Psychology, 61,* 227-271.

Goodstein, J. D. (1994). Institutional pressures and strategic responsiveness: Employer involvement in work-family issues. *Academy of Management Journal, 37,* 350-382.

Grandey, A. A., & Cropanzano, R. (1999). The conservation of resources model applied to work family conflict and strain. *Journal of Vocational Behavior, 54*(2), 350-370.

Graves, L. M., Ohlott, P. J., & Ruderman, M. N. (2007). Commitment to family roles: Effects on managers' attitudes and performance. *Journal of Applied Psychology, 92*, 44-56.

Greenhaus, J. H., & Beutell, N. J. (1985). Sources of conflict between work and family roles. *The Academy of Management Review, 10*, 76-88.

Greenhaus, J. H., & Powell, G. N. (2006). When work and family are allies: A theory of work-family enrichment. *Academy of Management Review, 31*, 72-92.

Greenhaus, J. H., & Allen, T. D. (2006). *Work-family balance: Exploration of a concept.* Paper presented at the Families and Work Conference, Provo, UT.

Greenhaus, J. H., Collins, K. M., & Shaw, J. D. (2003). The relation between work-family balance and quality of life. *Journal of Vocational Behavior, 63*, 510-531.

Grzywacz, J. G. (2002, February). *Toward a theory of work-family facilitation.* Paper presented at the 2002 Persons, Processes, and Places: Research on Families, Workplaces, and Communities Conference, San Francisco, CA.

Grzywacz, J. G., & Carlson, D. S. (2007). Conceptualizing work-family balance: Implications for practice and research. *Advances in Developing Human Resources, 9,* 455-471.

Halpern D. F., & Murphy, S. E. (2005). From balance to interaction: Why the metaphor is important. In D. F. Halpern & S. E. Murphy (Eds.), *From work-family balance to work-family interaction* (pp. 3-10). Mahwah, NJ: Lawrence Erlbaum Associates.

Hepburn, C.G., & Barling, J. (1996). Eldercare responsibilities, interrole conflict, and employee absence: A daily study. *Journal of Occupational Health Psychology, 1*, 311-318.

Judge, T. A., Boudreau, J. W., & Bretz, R. D. (1994). Job and life attitudes of male executives. *Journal of Applied Psychology, 79,* 767-782.

Kirchmeyer, C. (1998). Determinants of managerial career success: Evidence and explanation of male/female differences. *Journal of Management, 24,* 673-692.

Kossek, E. E., & Friede, A. (2006). The business case: Managerial perspectives on work and the family. In M. Pitt-Catsouphes, E. E. Kossek & S. Sweet (Eds.), *The work and family handbook: Multi-disciplinary perspectives and approaches* (pp. 611-626). Mahwah, NJ: Lawrence Erlbaum Associates.

Kossek, E. E., & Ozeki, C. (1998). Work-family conflict, policies, and the job-life satisfaction relationship: A review and directions for organizational behavior-human resources research. *Journal of Applied Psychology, 83,* 139-149.

Lambert, S. J. (1999). Establishing the link with business strategies: The value-added approach. In M. Pitt-Catsouphes (Ed.), *Metrics manual: Ten approaches to measuring work/life initiatives* (pp. 117-142). Chestnut Hill, MA: Boston College Center for Work and Family.

Lazarus, R. S., & Folkman, S. (1984). *Stress, appraisal, and coping.* New York: Springer.

Lobel, S. A., & Kossek, E. E., (1996). Human resource strategies to support diversity in work and personal lifestyles: Beyond the "family friendly" organization. In E. E. Kossek & S. Lobel (Eds.), *Managing diversity: Human resource strategies for transforming the workplace* (pp. 221-244). Cambridge, MA: Blackwell Publishers.

Lockwood, N. R. (2003). Work/life balance: Challenges and solutions. *SHRM Knowledge Center.* Retrieved April 4, 2006, from http://www.shrm.org/research/quarterly/ 0302worklife_ essay.asp

MacDermid, S. M., & Harvey, A. (2006). The work-family conflict construct: Methodological implications. In M. Pitt-Catsouphes, E. E. Kossek, & S. Sweet (Eds.), *The work and family handbook* (pp. 567-586). Mahwah, NJ: Lawrence Erlbaum Associates, Publishers.

Marshall, N. L., & Barnett, R. C., (1994). Family-friendly workplaces, work-family interface, and worker health. In G. P. Keita & J. J. Harrell (Eds.), *Job stress in a changing workforce* (pp. 253-264). Washington, D.C: American Psychological Association.

Miller, S. (2005). Work/life programs tackle unscheduled absenteeism: Improve the bottom line. *SHRM Compensation & Benefits Focus Area.* Retrieved January 9, 2008 from http://www.shrm.org/rewards/library_published/benefits/nonIC/CMS_014387.asp

Morris, M. L., & Madsen, S. R. (2007). Advancing work-life integration in individuals, organizations, and communities. *Advances in Developing Human Resources, 9*(4), 1-6.

Morris, M. L. (2008). Combating workplace stressors: Using work/life initiatives as an OD intervention. *Human Resource Development Quarterly, 19,* 95-105.

Perry-Smith, J. E., & Blum, T. C. (2000). Work-family human resource bundles and perceived organizational performance. *Academy of Management Journal, 43*(5), 1107-1117.

Pitt-Catsouphes, M. (1999). Needs assessments. In M. Pitt-Catsouphes (Ed.), *Metrics manual: Ten approaches to measuring work/life initiatives* (pp. 63-94). Chestnut Hill, MA: Boston College Center for Work and Family.

Pitt-Catsouphes, M., Kossek, E. E., & Sweet, S. (2006). Charting new territory: Advancing multi-disciplinary perspectives, methods, and approaches in the study of work and family. In M. Pitt-Catsouphes, E. E. Kossek, & S. Sweet (Eds.), *The work and family handbook* (pp. 1-16). Mahwah, NJ: Lawrence Erlbaum Associates, Publishers.

Powell, L., & Cassidy, D. (2001). *Family life education: An introduction.* Mountain View, CA: Mayfield.

Quick, J. C., Quick, J. D., Nelson, D. L., & Hurrell, Jr. J. J. (1997). *Preventive stress management in organizations.* Washington, DC: American Psychological Association.

Rapoport, R., Bailyn, L., Fletcher, J. K., & Pruitt, B. H. (2002). *Beyond work-family balance: Advancing gender equity and workplace performance.* San Francisco: Jossey Bass.

Thomas, L.T., & Ganster, D. C., (1995). Impact of family-supportive work variables on work-family conflict and strain: A control perspective. *Journal of Applied Psychology, 80,* 6-15.

Thompson, C. A., Beauvis, L. L., & Allen, T. D. (2006). Work and family from an industrial/organizational psychology perspective. In M. Pitt-Catsouphes, E. E. Kossek, & S. Sweet (Eds.), *The work and family handbook* (pp. 283-307). Mahwah, NJ: Lawrence Erlbaum Associates, Publishers.

Tyler, K. (2006). Stress management. *HR Magazine, 51*(9), 78-83.

Voydanoff, P. (2005). The effects of community demands, resources, and strategies on the nature and consequence of the work-family interface: An agenda for future research. *Family Relations, 54,* 583-595.

Wayne, J. H., Musisca, N., & Fleeson, W. (2004). Considering the role of personality in the work-family experience: Relationships of the big five to work-family conflict and facilitation. *Journal of Vocational Behavior, 64,* 108-130.

About the Author

Michael "Lane" Morris, Ph.D., CFLE, is the program director of Human Resource Development in the College of Business of Administration at the University of Tennessee. Currently, Dr. Morris is the President of the Academy of Human Resource Development (AHRD), which is the preeminent academic organization for the Human Resource Development discipline. He also serves as a core faculty member and leadership development coach on many of the EMBA programs in the College of Business. As a Certified Family Life Educator, Dr. Morris serves as an individual and organization development consultant and executive coach on multiple topics like occupational stress/health/wellness consultant, work/life balance, performance assessment and metrics, leadership development, and interpersonal dynamics and change.

Marketing Family Life Education Programs by Helping, Not Selling*

Jody Johnston Pawel

The first thing you need to know about marketing family life education (FLE) programs is that you don't have to *sell anything.* Marketing is about building relationships and an awareness about who you are, what you do, for whom, and why. You can exchange the words "your program" for "you" so you are clear that we won't be talking about self-promotion or tooting your own horn.

The second thing I want to assure you is that you don't need a large budget to market your programs. I'm fondly known as "*The Queen of Free*" because I find free or inexpensive resources to reach my goals. Because of my small budget I've also become a "*do-it-yourselfer*" who has learned how to do every task mentioned in this chapter. Most are not too difficult. You just need moderate computer skills, persistence, and a willingness to learn by doing.

This chapter will show you how to build relationships and awareness for your program using free and inexpensive marketing strategies that will give you the best "*bang for your buck.*"

Marketing is Critical to Your Program's Survival

As a Family Life Educator, you provide valuable programs that improve people's lives. There are many people, however, who need your services but either have no knowledge of or simply aren't using them. If you aren't *actively and consistently* marketing your programs, you are remaining invisible to the people who need them. Furthermore, by serving too-few clients, you will either not get the income you need to sustain your programs or be unable to justify continued support from grant funders.

You are the *Best* Person to Market Your Service

If you don't want to market, it's probably because you are turned off by "selling." You love helping people, but don't feel comfortable tooting your own horn or making cheesy commercial plugs. Good, because hard sells turn off *everyone!* The *most effective* marketing uses a "Helpful Marketing" approach (Pawel, 2006).

* For the purposes of modeling, this chapter has been written in a language, tone, and style of effective marketing and article writing rather than in an academic style.

- "Hard sell" marketing is *impersonal* and focuses on *us*, by *talking* about what *we* have to offer and *convincing* clients that they need it — whether they do or not!
- "Helpful" marketing is *personal* and focuses on *clients*, by *listening* to *their* needs and *helping* them find solutions — whether we have the resources or refer them to someone who does!

You already do the latter every day, so you are actually better suited to market your programs than commercial marketers because you understand your clients' needs, and know how to solve their problems. You just need to learn how to market your services in ways that feel comfortable and authentic to you.

What to Do *Before* You Begin Marketing

Have a Great Service

Before you do *anything*, your program must be top-quality in every way: how it's delivered, the quality of the training, and the ongoing support clients receive. It must be remarkable with proven results, or you won't get clients or referrals (Port, 2006).

Establish Your Niche

The broader your audiences, the greater chance your marketing messages will sound like you are trying to meet everyone's needs. When people hear vague, general messages they are more likely to discard or disregard them.

By selecting a highly specific niche market and targeting your messages to *those* people, your messages will be clear, compelling, and speak to *them* in ways that help them understand how you offer something that specifically meets their needs (Abraham, 2000).

To identify your "Niche Target Market," describe the demographics (marital status, parents, age, education, geographic location) or psychographics (personality, values, attitudes, interests, or lifestyles) of the people you serve (Port & Meyerson, 2005).

Consider the following questions: Are your services universally useful? Do they meet a wide range of needs? Then segment your market into several narrowly defined sub-markets, customizing your marketing efforts and messages to speak specifically to the needs of each target market. For example, I offer parenting classes to the general public, to court-mandated parents through the protective service agency, and to foster parents, caseworkers and family-service professionals through continuing education workshops. Although the programs I offer each niche population are quite similar, I market my services to each in different ways using different messages.

Identify your Ideal Client

Within your niche target market there are people who are either *more* or *less* ideal for you to work with. "Ideal clients" energize and inspire you while others drain your energy and passion. You want to identify who your ideal client is and screen potential clients against this criterion, to determine if you would be a good fit to work with each other. Then refer the others elsewhere (Port, 2006).

You are still serving the challenging clients by helping them find a similar service, but you won't be draining your energy resources by serving them directly. Your energy and motivation will stay high and you now have space for another ideal client.

If you have more than one target market, identify the ideal clients for each. For example, I listed four very different target niche markets in my example, I seek *almost* the same ideal clients for all of my programs: voluntary, self-motivated clients who want to be good parents (or professionals), and are open to learning and recognize the value of getting professional guidance to achieve their goals.

"How," you might ask, "can you serve 'mandated' clients if your ideal client is 'voluntary' and 'self-motivated'?" For those clients that I cannot pre-screen, I have an "orientation session" in which I help them shift from being there because they "have to" to staying because they "want to." I also help them see that their parenting goals and intentions are on track but there might be "more effective" ways of achieving them. This motivates them to learn new ideas.

What is your U.S.P.?

Your USP is your Unique Selling Position (Abraham, 2000). Every service is *somehow* unique. Communicating *how* you are unique is a critical factor in helping people choose *your* service. It is one crystal-clear, compelling paragraph — or less — that highlights a benefit your clients get from *you* but *cannot* get from others. Your USP must be a consistent theme in all of your marketing efforts. You can have more than one USP for different products/service lines of your business. For example, *The Parent's Toolshop's* USP is its "Universal Blueprint® Parenting Success Formula" which offers a step-by-step decision-making and problem-solving *system* that empowers people to find *individualized* effective responses to *any* relationship challenge — with children of any age and even with adults!

Know the Answers to Who, What and Why

When you meet someone, they often ask, "What do you do?" (Port, 2006). The typical response is, "I'm a Family Life Educator" to which the other person will probably think, "Huh?" and then change the subject. If you've taken a traditional marketing course, you will start reciting your scripted and rehearsed "elevator speech," which probably gives far more information than the person wants to know. This causes them to either change the subject or walk away! Instead, you want to have a short (only 10-20 seconds long) "Who and Do What, and Why" statement that *clearly and concisely* tells people:

- Whom you serve (Target Market),
- What you do (Niche),
- How it's unique (USP)
- Whom you love to serve (ideal client)
- Why you serve (your motivation and passion)
- How it helps or benefits people

Your "Who and Do What" statement is *planned but not canned*, and is so intriguing that the person will *ask you, "How do you do this?"* You will then engage people in a *two-way dialogue* that answers the questions they ask in ways that help them better understand what your USP is, and who are your ideal clients. If your service is not a good match for them, they might know other people who are and will tell them about your service.

Here are a few examples of "Who and Do What" statements:

- A parent educator could say, "I teach parents the skills they need to prevent and resolve parenting challenges."
- A stress management trainer could say, "I work with parents who are literally sick and tired from juggling a stressful life and help them become healthy and energetic."
- A family therapist could say, "I help parents with troubled teens to regain order and have a peaceful, loving family."
- A marriage workshop presenter could say, "I help couples rediscover their love and passion for each other."

Now seriously, aren't these more interesting answers than "I'm a parent educator," or "I'm a family therapist"? After reading each statement, weren't you intrigued enough to want to know more? Did you have at least one question you wanted to ask? Such as, "How do you do that?"

Your "Who and Do What" statement is the basis of *all* your other marketing messages; therefore it is *the most important message* for you to craft carefully. Actually, you want to plan a short "Who and Do What" statement and some dialogue-engaging responses to the most common "tell me more" requests you might get. These messages are *so* important that you may spend weeks or months planning and testing the response in a variety of settings until you say them in the most compelling, clear, passionate, authentic, heartfelt, and *concise* way possible.

Create Compelling Marketing Messages

Unlike tangible products, which people can see, touch and compare to similar products, services are intangible — essentially invisible! As a result, every message you send must make your service more tangible, concrete and easier to understand and compare, so others can determine which service will best meet their needs (Beckwith, 1997).

Most people start their marketing efforts by spending hundreds of dollars printing and mailing pretty brochures and flyers, but these materials are often so poorly-written they go straight to the trash can. Let's look at what marketing messages need to say to engage people and help them decide if they would be an ideal client for your service.

Help Potential Clients Evaluate and Choose *Your* Program

Your marketing message must help your ideal client see that your program is a perfect match for their needs at whatever stage of the decision-making process they are at (Silverman, 2001). Do this by:

- Describing in visual, emotional terms the compelling benefits they will receive if they use your service.
- Listing specific results you can promise with outcome statistics to back up your claims.
- Providing clear, objective, credible information. Don't make over-the-top claims, even if you can prove them, because people will doubt them and postpone their decision.
- Pointing out what is unique, different, or superior about your program (your USP.)
- Providing a low- or no-risk way to try your service.
- Include believable testimonials and endorsements.

If you do all this, people will more quickly assess whether your program is a good match for their needs.

Answer W.I.I.F.M?

Typical service publicity says, "We provide..." followed by a list of *what* the organization or service offers. The person reading the publicity reads this and asks himself, "So what? Who cares? What's in it for me (W.I.I.F.M.)?" (Hunt, 2005). If *every* piece of your publicity materials does not answer these three questions, throw it in the trash *now*, because that's what its recipients will likely do.

All of your publicity materials must include benefit statements, which describe the following:

- The *features* of your service, which are facts about *what* your service offers.
- The *benefits* of your service, which are what people experience as a result of the feature. They answer the three critical W.I.I.F.M. questions.
- The *bridge,* which connects the feature to the benefit. *Always* use the word "you." For example: "*Feature*...allows you to...*Benefit*" or "*Feature*...gives you...*Benefit*."
- This will give you a *good* benefit statement. To get a *compelling* benefit statement, go deeper. Keep saying, "so that..." (or "So what!?) Describe, in sensual terms, what their life will be like when they achieve this goal or get this solution. What will they see, feel, hear, or do then?

Exercise
Using your current publicity materials answer the WIIFM questions for each feature. Identify the benefits your service provides. Then create benefit statements for each using the template in Figure 1 (Pawel, 2007).

Figure 1

Feature = WHAT you do	+	Bridge	+	Benefit = HOW it helps
	+	*"...so that..."* *"...allows you to..."* *"...gives you..."*	+	
Benefit Statement:				
Go deeper! So that...so what?!:				

Produce Dynamite Publicity Materials

Publicity materials are often very pretty...but pretty ineffective in their wording. That's why you want to do the writing exercise outlined in Figure 1 first. Depending on your marketing strategy, you will be mixing and matching some of the different messages you've written. For example, a well-written website is essential for internet marketing, while a catchy flyer is important for speaker marketing. Almost all FLEs have flyers, brochures, and business cards, so let's review them to see if they meet good marketing criteria (Pawel. 2004).

Flyers Should Stress BENEFITS
Flyers describe a particular event or service. In addition to important information about when, where and how to register, your flyer must describe benefits people receive from your service. You need to spell out how their lives or problems will improve as a result of attending — be specific!

Brochures Should Be TECHNICAL
A brochure explains your organization and all its products/services. It needs to include more information than a flyer, so pay close attention to the content. Of all publicity materials, your brochure needs to be *the* most professionally produced. Your brochure should stress benefits, but must also back up any claims with facts. Describe your staff's credentials, history or experience in the field, and statistical support for your effectiveness. Avoid vague generalizations and using too many adjectives. Make a number of short, concise, powerful points in simple language.

Business Cards Need More Than Basics
In addition to your name, title and contact information:

- Include a clear, ***benefit-focused line*** or two that states your USP.
- Include your ***email*** address and website ***URL***.
- Use inexpensive ***full-color*** professional printing, not blurry homemade inkjet cards.
- Unless you are a celebrity or big-name speaker, ***don't use your photo***. Use the space to state your USP or benefits.

Get More Program Sponsors and Gigs

If you are a Family Life Educator, you are probably already a skillful public speaker and group facilitator (if not, see the training resources at the end). You have a great program that offers *solutions* to people's problems and delivers results. What you really need are more programs and better attendance at them. Here are places and ways to promote your program (Pawel, 2005).

Speak at conferences
Unfortunately, our conferences are different from many other professional conferences because only conference keynote speakers get paid. Workshop speakers do not get paid *and* must pay their own travel and conference fees. For high-quality speakers whose expenses aren't reimbursed, this results in a very unequal value exchange.

You may ask for exhibit booth space in exchange for presenting one or more workshops. This can maximize your attendance at the conference and give you more visibility and time to interact with participants. If a trade is not a possibility, speaking for free may be worth the visibility, credibility, networking and practice you receive. Only you can weigh this.

Join a local speaker's bureau or professional training organization
For example, every state has a staff of trainers for their protective service professionals and foster parents. Ask how you can apply.

Offer your <u>own</u> continuing education workshops
This involves getting continuing education unit (CEU) approval, buying mailing lists, printing, postage, renting meeting space and CEU record-keeping. You can handle the logistics yourself or hire a company like those listed in the resource section to do it for you.

Provide employee education programs through corporations
Corporations usually have funding for trainers. The challenge is getting your foot in the door to talk to a decision-maker. If all you do is send a flyer or brochure with a letter, forget it. Here are other options to try:

- Go in the front door: To succeed at this approach, you need extremely savvy skills to get past the gatekeeper, and a compelling way to present your workshop idea in less than thirty seconds. You can do this by phone and have a scripted voice mail message to leave, or send an attention-grabbing package that will get opened and read.
- Go in the back door: Have a current employee approach the event planners and give a glowing review about your abilities, along with your contact information.

Be willing to do one free program to prove yourself. Get evaluations of the program, then quote the testimonials from that program when approaching the decision maker about offering a more extensive or paid offering through the corporation.

Arrange trades with potential sponsors
Community organizations are always looking for programs for their clientele. While they usually can't afford to hire you, you can often arrange a nice win/win trade agreement, such as:

- They provide you with free meeting space, advertise your program to their clientele (students, parishioners, etc.) and allow you to open the program to the public, and
- You provide your program to their clients at a substantial discount (if the client can afford to pay something) or at no charge. The public's tuition payments cover your time. The sponsor's in-kind trade covers your other expenses, like meeting space.

There are several advantages to this approach. You can have programs at multiple sites, which is convenient for your clients. If the organization is large, they will be advertising your programs internally. This usually costs them very little, but exposes your service to hundreds or thousands of potential clients you would have never reached, and at no cost to you!

Setting fees
It is important that there be *some* value exchange for your services. You do not have to receive money, just *value,* as in the win/win trade example above. Here are two good reasons:

- People need to make a commitment when attending. Otherwise you can get participants whose attitude and behavior can be detrimental to those who pay to attend.
- If there is no value exchange, it sends the implied message your service has no value.

When setting your fees, conduct market research on similar programs in your area. Don't price yourself below the norm or people will believe you offer less value. If you ask for higher fees, show *why* you or your program is worth it. Have a "standard" fee that you will negotiate for trades, such as discounts to non-profit organizations or the following exchanges (Walters, 1986):

- A *professional* videotape of the presentation (offer to donate a percentage of the profits if it is a non-profit organization);
- You get a percentage of the participants' fees;

- They buy your book for every person or let you sell resources; or
- They agree to book a paid program or offer ongoing program for an extended period of time if you provide a free or discounted program initially.

Use Mail Ethically To Stay In Touch

The most persuasive and effective way to share your resources is face to face, which usually takes 2-5 contacts for people to act. Phone calls are the next most effective means. Mail contacts usually take 3-7 contacts to see results. Sending a letter with a follow-up phone call increases its effectiveness 1,000 percent (Abraham, 2000).

To whom can you send mail?
The most important asset you can have is an active, current mailing list of people who are potential ideal clients. Start a list with referral sources listed in the phone book and send them schedules of programs that would be of value to their clients.

If you buy lists, there's a different process you need to learn to screen and choose ideal clients (Sorkin, 2008). Instead, get names from legitimate free sources, such as:

- people who attend conferences where you speak,
- membership associations your clients are likely to belong to, and
- internet discussion groups your ideal clients might join.

Ultimately, the recipient decides whether your mail/email is junk/spam. You want potential clients to *voluntarily* join your mail list so you can start building a relationship. The most effective way to do this is by having people *request* your information or gifts. Then ask their permission to send them the gift and other information in the future (see "Step 2" of the Internet Marketing section for more details about spam laws).

How often to send mail?
Multiple contacts are the secret to a successful mail campaign. The first letter will probably only net a 5% - 6% response. After three weeks, if you haven't received a response, send a second notice. If they don't respond after another ten days, send a third and final notice. The second and third mailings usually get another 5%-7% response. If you stop at just one mailing, you will likely recruit half the new clients (Abraham, 2000)! Generally speaking, you want to communicate no *less* than once a month and no *more* than once a week unless people know they are opting in for a daily communication.

What is best to send?
With the proliferation of junk mail, post-9/11 anthrax scares, and the habit most people have of opening their mail over the trash can, direct mail is the riskiest and most expensive marketing strategy.

The power of postcards
Postcards are the least expensive hard-copy mail piece to produce and send. Also, up to 95 percent of recipients will read them, because they fall out of mail stacks. This means most people will at least glance at the message as they pick it up. Although postcards have space limitations, they can also direct people to your website, where you can provide more details. Print a higher volume of postcards with your logo, contact information, and space for customized messages. Then reuse these for several mailings. The U.S. Postal Service has regulations regarding placement of text on the backside of a postcard; use the resource list for a link to these directions.

No cost email
Most people send their letters and newsletters by email these days because it is a *fast and free* form of communication. Just follow the anti-spam guidelines mentioned above and in "Step 2" of the Internet Marketing section.

Your subject line is *the* most important part of your email message, because it determines whether it will get deleted or read. Your message needs to be short with bullet points or benefits that are easy to scan, with a link to more information online. The next most-important section of your email is your signature and P.S. Believe it or not, the P.S. is the most read part of any letter (Silver, 2000)! Your signature is a regular opportunity to tell people who you are and what you do. In addition to your contact information, make an offer (preferably a freebie) that will send people to your website. If you use Microsoft Outlook you can automatically add a signature to every email you send, reply to, or forward.

Automating the process
The most effective message is one that is personalized to the recipient. For both hard mail and email, this involves having a mailing list in a database format (with tables or fields) and a mail merge software. Hard mailings involve a significant amount of manual labor. While merge programs and folding machines can automate some of these tasks, these projects are still time consuming. There are some services that will do large mailings with your letter and inserts. There are automated greeting card services you can access online to send greeting cards (glossy Hallmark-type cards) and postcards *by mail* with your own

personalized message, sometimes in your own handwriting font! You can either send a personalized card one at a time or to each person on your list! You can even send sequential campaigns that send a card every few days!

Track your results
You want to test and track the results of every campaign you plan to reuse. Consider the quality of the response versus the quantity of response. How many people inquired, and how many followed through? To do this make two test messages with one element different between them, such as the subject line or headline. Then send each test message to half the list. Use a code to track the results, like coupon codes or different contact numbers. Determine which message got the better results and use that one the next time with one *additional* element changed. Keep the winner and the test results. If you use "ad tracker" campaigns like those in the resource section, it will track the results for you.

Inform and Educate the Public through the Media

Use the media to announce an event, get a feature story about your program, educate the public on a special topic or be interviewed as an expert. Just observe the following simple guidelines (DePalma & Dushinski, 1998) and your program will get great visibility while you become a resource the media repeatedly calls.

When to call: Never call *radio & TV media* within one hour before a newscast or during airtime. For *print media*, ask when their deadlines are.

How often to call: Don't leave multiple messages. Instead, leave one message and keep trying to reach them.

What to send: Your press release must tie in with a news event unless it is newsworthy in itself. Give the media a story that will interest, inform and entertain their readers/listeners/viewers, and bring you to their attention as an expert in your field.

Stimulate Word-of-Mouth Referrals

The average person is exposed to about 200-1000 sales communications a day, but only acts on 1 in 15,000 ads. In contrast, the average person acts on 1 in 3 *personal* recommendations. That makes word-of-mouth marketing *the* most powerful and inexpensive marketing tool available (Silverman, 2001). Most people think word-of-mouth marketing is out of their control. Nothing could be further from the truth. Here's what to do to get people to try your program, and then tell others about it.

How to get people to spread the word
A few simple actions can make word-of-mouth marketing an effortless success strategy:

- Ask your clients to send others your way. Even if their friends don't attend your program, give them good service by connecting them with a service they *can* use. They will remember that you helped them and still send others your way.
- Offer a gift for referrals. For example, support and recommend their service (if it's relevant for your clients), donate money to their favorite charity, or give them a discount, or a free gift.
- Make it easy to refer others. Give clients something with your name on it that they can pass on, such as tip sheets, business cards, or imprinted pens or mugs.
- Send a thank you note to those who refer someone to you.
- Keep yours clients in mind by sending them information, articles, and books about their areas of interest. They'll keep you in mind when talking to others.

Reactivate past clients
Clients stop using services for three reasons (Abraham, 2000). Here's why and what you can do:

- Out of sight, out of mind; *regularly follow-up* with clients to stay connected.
- They were dissatisfied; *listen* to their concerns and needs. Apologize. Make amends.
- Their situation changed; if they no longer need your service, *ask them to consider recommending it to others.*

Actively network
Anyone might know *someone* who could use your service. *Intentionally* network at relevant events, but be *ready* to network anytime, anywhere (Sukenick, 1995). Here are some ideas:

- Be a visible presence where potential clients work, worship, learn and shop.
- Professional experts who serve your clients are your most valuable connections. Attend or give a presentation of your service at their networking meetings.
- Ask not how others can help you; ask how you can help others.
- Follow up with potential clients or referral sources. Your success depends on it.

Get testimonials and expert endorsements
Don't like "tooting your own horn?" Then let potential sponsors and clients hear other people's praises of you. Someone's unsolicited comments will always carry more weight than any self-promoting statement you make. Plus, hearing their opinions is a critical step in the evaluation and decision-making process.

How do you get testimonials? Just ask and say "Thank you":

- When someone compliments your program, ask if you can quote them. A quote with a real name is always more credible than a partial name, which is more credible than an anonymous endorsement, which is better than no testimonial at all!
- Ask experts to review your materials and comment, with permission to quote them.
- Ask referral sources to give a written recommendation you can use.
- Include a clause in your speaking contract that the program sponsor will provide a testimonial you can use for future publicity.

Internet Marketing Basics

Who needs a website?
A website is available 24 hours a day, 7 days a week to people who are *already looking* for your services. If your clients don't have computers, think about the people who find resources *for* them, including their friends or relatives and professional referral sources. If you don't have a website, you are "virtually" invisible to these potential clients and referral sources. Websites are inexpensive and easy to set up these days. *Every* family life education program should have a website, if only to offer contact information, program descriptions *and* details about how their services benefit the client.

The internet surfing cycle
An effective website guides visitors through four steps of the Internet surfing cycle (Port & Meyerson, 2006):

- *It is "optimized,"* so people find it quickly and easily when using search engines like Google.
- *It has an appealing design* that engages visitors, so they stay and explore the site.
- *It converts visitors to clients,* by developing a relationship and meeting their needs.
- *It receives regular, active marketing,* so there are always new visitors ... which restarts the cycle.

You want to get steps 2 and 3 in place *before* visitors arrive, so next we look at these two strategies first.

Step #1: Design an Engaging, Effective Website
A professional-looking design is the first step in getting visitors to stay and explore your website. It must be simple, professional, and highly effective, by including the following four ingredients (Port & Myerson, 2006).

- A *Descriptive Domain Name* that contains keywords that relate to the services you offer, so your site will rank higher in the search results. Avoid hyphens and words that are difficult to spell.
- An *Attractive Design* that loads quickly (not big graphic files), has a uniform theme, pleasant color choices and uses fonts that are easy on the eyes.
- *Easy Navigation* with menus on every page, simple, clear "take action" directions, and secure ordering options.
- *Compelling Content* that follows three basic rules:
    - The homepage gives a snapshot of the entire site and tells visitors, in 30 seconds, what you can do for them; the focus is not about you or the service, but the benefits the client receives from the service;
    - It is written in an informal, conversational tone to your client, using "you" and "your"; focus on recruiting your "ideal" client, instead of trying to get lots of unqualified prospects;
    - The content is easy to scan.

Step #2: The Five Factors That Convert Visitors to Clients
Conversion techniques offer multiple opportunities to connect with, support, educate and help visitors, so they are more likely to become clients later. Here are five conversion strategies that are both ethical and effective (Port & Myerson, 2005; Port & Myerson, 2006):

- While visitors are at your site, start building a relationship with them. Get them involved, engaged and connected by using interactive features such as:
    - Assessments, surveys, quizzes, contests, and information request forms.

- Ways for visitors to interact with others, by contributing articles, reviews, success stories, and ask or answer questions.
- Provide articles or interviews by experts in your field.

- Offer no-risk ways to start a relationship with you, such as giving away free resources (e.g., tip sheets, e-courses, articles, e-books, PowerPoint presentations, e-newsletters, audio recordings, or free tele-seminars).
- Have people request gifts and give permission to receive them. The most effective way to get more contact opportunities is by having visitors opt-in to receive gifts, in exchange for their name and email address. For this process to be effective and ethical it must:
  - Offer something of value, so people will share their contact information
  - Be voluntary. People shouldn't have to give contact information to get into your site, only to request information.
  - Protect their privacy. Next to the opt-in box, state that you will not share their information with anyone and put a link to your privacy statement.
  - Be a double-opt-in, permission-based offer. This prevents spamming and email fraud.
  - Be clear about what they are getting, before they opt-in. If you plan to automatically subscribe every gift recipient to your e-newsletter or mailing list, clearly state this.
  - Comply with best email practices, by providing unsubscribe directions on every email.
- Follow up with people who request free sample resources so they get the most value from them. Continue offering relevant, useful information that will deepen your relationship with them.
- Have a "Call to Action" or opt-in offer on almost every page. You never know from which page people will enter your site, so tell people what they can get while they are there and how to get it. They aren't obligated to opt-in, but if you don't even ask, you might miss your only chance to start a relationship. Fortunately, you can automate all of these processes with an email auto-responder and/or shopping cart system.

Now your site is ready for visitors! Once you get your website designed and your conversion strategies in place, list your catchy website address in the online yellow pages and add it to your business cards, email signature, workshop handouts, articles, business letterhead, company brochures, exhibit booth display...*everything you can!*

Step #3. Optimize Your Site So Your Ideal Clients Find You First!

Optimizing your site is extremely rewarding, as you track your results and see your website listed higher in the search engine rankings. It's also more technical, so we are only going learn about this strategy, why it's important, and a few basics about the main ways visitors learn about your site:

- *Entering key words into search engines like Google.* Most people only click on the first 10-30 results. By "optimizing" your site, you "rank" higher in these top positions.
- Direct referrals from other websites who link to your website.

Conduct search engine optimization

Search engines "rank" a site based on the *number* of times a word or phrase is used in a website as well as *where* the word or phrase is located on the page. To do this, search engines look at three "tags":

- The *Title* tag is displayed first in the search results list, at the top of that page's browser window and when someone bookmarks that page.
- The *Description* tag summarizes the contents of that page. It appears below the title in search results. People read this to decide if they want to visit that site.
- The *Keywords* are the words on the web page that most closely match the words in the search request. The search results page highlights these words in the section below the description. If your page is missing the keywords tag, your page won't be found!

It's easy to add key words to the file properties, but it's trickier to know *what* the key words should be. You can guess by asking, "If I were looking for my website or page, what words would I type into Google to find it?" This isn't the most scientifically accurate way to choose your key words, but that process is time-consuming, expensive and confusing unless you have some free or inexpensive tools that will do it for you. Just be sure to have *something* in these three tags, if only "logical guesses."

Increase and improve your site's links

Most search engines, like Google, consider the number of links pointing to and from related sites *the most important* element in deciding a site's ranking in the search results. It is actually possible to achieve a top ranking almost entirely on link popularity alone. To increase the link popularity and ranking of your site, you want to have:

- Internal links within the site, so search engines can index the pages quickly.
- Incoming links from related sites, which tell the search engine, "This site is popular!"
- Outgoing links to related sites. Search engines check the content of the linked sites to see if it's related. If so, it improves both sites' rankings.
- Keywords in the visible text of the links get the website a higher ranking.
- Quality links from major search engines. So register the site with the top 7-10 search engines.
- No broken links, because they decrease the ranking.

Link exchanges are a win-win situation for both website owners, because they improve each site's search results rankings. Never use link exchange sites or link farms, because many search engines consider them unethical and could ban you from their listings. Instead, search related sites. Add a link in your site to those you'd recommend to your visitors. Then send an email to each site owner informing them that you have linked to their site and politely ask for a link to your site. Personalize your request and give them the exact link, title and description you want them to use.

Step #4. Market Your Site So People Find You Without Searching!
While optimization is technical, internet *marketing* can be fun! Here are the best, least expensive, easiest strategies you can use:

- *Submit Articles* to share helpful information, gain credibility and expertise in your field, and boost visibility for you and your program. You can post free articles on your site and submit them to article "banks."
- *Participate in Discussion Groups and Forums* where your ideal clients and referral sources gather. *Never* directly plug your business unless the group asks for such recommendations. You could alienate the group or get banned from participating. Instead, respond to questions or requests and mention what you do in the context of sharing knowledge and resources. Then include your email signature, which should have your website address and a *short* 20-50 word description of your program.
- *Start and Join Affiliate Programs*. By *setting up* an affiliate program for *your* resources, others will send you *new referrals* for a percentage of any profits. By joining *other people's* affiliate programs, *you make passive income* by recommending resources that help others. Simply insert your affiliate link into your articles, testimonials, newsletters, or as a free bonus for new clients. If you would recommend a resource anyway and your clients are charged the same or less, then it's a win/win/win for everyone!
- *Submit Online Press Releases* when you start a new program or release a new resource. The media interviews you get will boost your credibility and expert status.
- *Cross Promotions and Joint Ventures Bring More Traffic*. "Cross promotions" are when you and another provider recommend each other's resources to your own lists. Joint Ventures involve jointly creating a resource and then promoting it to your own lists (Abraham, 2000). It's half the work for twice the exposure! Here are a few possibilities:
    - Arrange discounts on resources your clients *want* that others provide. The partner gets new clients or sales, your clients get discounted resources they want, and you get happy clients and a cut of the profits.
    - Offer discounts or gifts to someone else's clients. Create an offer for someone who already serves your target market. Have the clients claim the gift from you, so you get exposure to potential clients to add to your list, the clients get gifts they *want*, and the partner gets happy clients.
    - You and another company jointly create a new resource that meets the needs of all your clients. You both endorse it, offer it to your own clients and split the fees and profits.
- *Blogging for Traffic*. A "blog" is short for a web-log, where you can share ideas, information, news or opinions. Most blogs allow others to reply to your posts. Reporters now look to blogs for the latest announcements, breaking news and hot trends. Blogs are easy to set up.

In *every* case, partners contact their *own* clients, so there are no privacy violations. The offers are permission-based opt-ins, so there's no spamming or obligation to buy anything. But, if they do, *everyone* "wins."

The time and money you invest in building awareness for your program will pay off tenfold if you use these strategies skillfully and with integrity.

References

Abraham, J. (2000). *Getting everything you can out of all you've got.* New York: St. Martin's Press.

Beckwith, H. (1997). *Selling the invisible: A field guide to modern marketing.* New York: Warner Books, Inc.

DePalma, T., & Dushinski, K. (1998). *Maximum exposure.* Arvada, CO: MarketAbility.

Hunt, J. (2005). *Writing benefit statements* [audio recording of radio show]. Bob Summers, Recognized Expert Marketing Show.

Pawel, J. J. (2003). *Marketing magic: Secret tricks for increasing your visibility and success.* Springboro, OH: Ambris Publishing.

Pawel, J. J. (2004, Spring). Direct mail campaigns. *CFLE Network, 16*(2), 5,9. Minneapolis, MN: National Council on Family Relations.

Pawel, J. J. (2004, Summer). Six secrets of writing dynamite publicity materials. *CFLE Network, 16*(3), 5, 9. Minneapolis, MN: National Council on Family Relations.

Pawel, J. J. (2004, Fall). Informing and educating the public through the media. *CFLE Network, 16*(4), 6, 13. Minneapolis, MN: National Council on Family Relations.

Pawel, J. J. (2005, Winter). Becoming a professional speaker. *CFLE Network, 17*(1), 6, 8. Minneapolis, MN: National Council on Family Relations.

Pawel, J. J. (2006, Winter). Helping, not selling: The key to marketing with integrity. *CFLE Network, 18*(1), 4, 10. Minneapolis, MN: National Council on Family Relations.

Pawel, J.J. (2006, Spring). Six success strategies for getting more clients. *CFLE Network, 18*(2), 4, 7. Minneapolis, MN: National Council on Family Relations.

Pawel, J.J. (2006, Summer). Internet basics for family life educators: four factors for getting your ideal clients to flock to your website (part 1). *CFLE Network, 18*(3), 10–11. Minneapolis, MN: National Council on Family Relations.

Pawel, J.J. (2006, Fall). Internet basics for family life educators: four factors for getting your ideal clients to flock to your website (part 2). *CFLE Network, 18*(4), 9, 15. Minneapolis, MN: National Council on Family Relations.

Pawel, J.J. (2007). "Writing Compelling Benefit Statements." Workshop worksheet. Springboro, OH: Author.

Port, M. (2006). *Book yourself solid: the fastest, easiest, and most reliable system for getting more clients than you can handle even if you hate marketing and selling.* Hoboken, NJ: John Wiley & Son.

Port, M., & Meyerson, M. (2005). *90-day product factory.* Retrieved from http://snipurl.com/ProductFactory90day

Port, M., & Meyerson, M. (2006). *Traffic school: the ultimate web traffic and conversion system.* [Manual for on-line training program]. Retrieved from http://snipurl.com/trafficschoolprogram

Silver, Y. (2000). *Ultimate sales letter toolbox: all the openings, bullets, selling words, phrases, copy-connectors, guarantees, closers, p.s.'s you'll ever need to create killer sales letters.* Silver Spring, MD: Surefire Marketing, Inc.

Silverman, G. (2001). *The secrets of word-of-mouth marketing.* Saranac Lake, NY: AMA Publications.

Sukenick, R. (1995). *Networking your way to success: a proven method for building, developing, and implementing a network of your own key contacts.* Dubuque, IA: Kendall/Hunt Publishing.

Sorkin, D (2008). *Direct Marketing Association (DMA): Guidelines for commercial solicitations online.* Retrieved from www.SpamLaws.com

Walters, D. (1986). *How to enter the world of paid speaking* [Cassette]. Peoria, IL: Royal Publishing.

Key Resources

Samples:

Postcards: claim your free trial, which includes a fill-in-the-blank postcard sized email (sample in chapter) here: http://www.instantmarketingtoolbox.com/freetrial

Press release from Marketability.com: http://www.integritymarketing.org/resources/pressreleasesamplema.bmp

Publicity:

TU-VETS Corporation: Affordable full-color printing www.tu-vets.com

VistaPrint.com: FREE four-color business cards www.vistaprint.com

Writing benefit statements, audio by Julie Hunt: www.IntegrityMarketing.org/audio/WritingBenefits-JulieHunt.mp3

Writing benefit statements, audio by Jody Pawel for NEPI bonus teleseminar for parent educators: www.IntegrityMarketing.org/audio/WritingBenefits.mp3

Speaking

Become a six-figure a year professional speaker, Teleseminar Training Series, Lori Giovannoni: www.lorigiovannoni.com/professionalspeaker.htm

Group facilitator certification training: www.Parents Toolshop.com/HTML/teach.htm

National Speakers Association: http://www.nsaspeaker.org/

Susan Kendrick, speakers' kits, audiotape and video covers, book back covers: http://www.writetoyourmarket.com

Toastmasters: http://www.toastmasters.org/

CEU Workshop Resources

AMEDCO/American Continuing Education, Inc., in Minneapolis, MN. For one fee per participant they'll secure CEU approval, coordinate mailing lists, printing, mailing, registration and CEU documentation. You pay all actual expenses. http://www.cmehelp.com/Index.htm Call Norm Skog at 1-800-314-1921

Speedy CEUs: http://www.speedyceus.com/

Mail /Email

ACT! Mailing list database software for personalized merged mail campaigns: http://act.com

Amazing Mail: Type your sales message and upload your image and mailing list. They assemble the art, print the cards and mail them. Large print runs http://www.AmazingMail.com

Constant Contact. E-mail and e-newsletters: http://www.constantcontact.com/index.jsp

Duncan, G. (1999, February 23). *What does it cost to do a mailing?* Retrieved from http://www.duncandirect.com/articles/library/costmail.html

How to sell to associations: http://parapub.com/

List of associations: http://www.AssociationCentral.com

Mailloop software for email, newsletters, autoresponses & more: http://www.mailloop.com/

Send Out Cards: Greeting cards and postcards with personalized message in your handwriting, even automated sequential mail campaign. http://www.SendOutCards.com Member sponsor number: 19586.

Spam laws: To check the laws regarding spam state-by-state, visit: http://www.spamlaws.com/federal/108s877.html

USPS: Instructions and downloadable templates for postcards, brochures, letters and envelopes are at http://www.usps.gov

Media

Yearbook of Experts, Authorities & Spokespersons: http://www.expertclick.com/

Radio-TV Interview Report: Get ad: http://www.rtir.com

Register with services that match you with journalists and other individuals seeking information in your area of expertise:

- http://www.profnet.com
- http://www.allexperts.com
- http://www.authorinterviews.com/?dl=1
- http://www.GuestFinder.com

Internet

90 Day Product Factory: #1 Product Creation, Marketing a d Sales Resource on the Internet, co-created by Mitch Meyerson and Michael Port http://snipurl.com/ProductFactory90day

Article submission service: http://www.mastersyndicator.com

Creating Free Digital Resources: http://www.IntegrityMarketing.org/resources/createdigitalresources.htm

DreamHost. Inexpensive website hosting with maximum speed and space: www.DreamHost.com

"Easy-Bake Web Blogs" http://snipurl.com/easyweblogs

Easy Web Automation. Basic level provides database and e-mail management including anti-spam double-opt-in functions, merged or broadcast e-mails, and automated sequential email campaigns and e-courses (auto-responders). Mid-level offers user-friendly shopping cart with secure on-line credit card processing that interfaces with Quick Books. Top level offers affiliate programs, ad trackers, coupon discounts, bundle offers and digital resource distribution like e-books, audios and video files. http://snipurl.com/EasyWebAutomation

Free Link Checking Tools: Xenu: http://home.snafu.de/tilman/xenulink.html

Free press release submission site: www.free-press-release.com. For more information, read an article by Mark Harty - http://www.strategictraffic.com/7sins

GoDaddy.com. Inexpensive website hosting with shopping cart options. www.GoDaddy.com

Pay-Per-Click information: "Pay Per Click Search Engines – The Basics," by Halstatt Pires at http://www.selfseo.com/story-2613.php

Search Engine Optimization Tool: http://snipurl.com/SearchEngineTool

Traffic School: The Ultimate Web Traffic and Conversion System, on-line training program co-created by Mitch Meyerson and Michael Port http://snipurl.com/trafficschoolprogram

Related Websites

Integrity Marketing for Helping Professionals	www.IntegrityMarketing.org
90 Day Product Factory	http://snipurl.com/ProductFactory90day
Traffic. School	http://snipurl.com/trafficschoolprogram
Book Yourself Solid	http://snipurl.com/BookYourselfSolidNOW
MarketAbility 1-888-55-TWIST	www.MarketAbility.com

About the Author

Jody Johnston Pawel, LSW, CFLE is a second-generation parent educator, award-winning parenting author, President of Parent's Toolshop® Consulting and Integrity Marketing for Helping Professionals, and a Certified Book Yourself Solid Coach. She has more than twenty-five years' experience training parents and professionals, starting and coordinating nonprofit programs and serving as a parenting expert to the media. See www.ParentsToolshop.com and www.IntegrityMarketing.org.

Preparing for your Profession

Nancy Gonzalez*

In your search for employment or other opportunities, there are ways to present what you have to offer in the best possible light. Your resume or curriculum vitae (CV) is your written smile and handshake—but you'll need the other kind of smile and handshake, too! Much of this information is available in the abundant supply of job search handbooks in bookstores everywhere. What may not be covered in other resources is the kind of advising that is not only technical, but supportive and thought-provoking in the psychosocial sense—the kind of coaching you would get from a good mentor who wants you to succeed. This is what I hope to provide here. First I'll cover your job search documents. Then I'll offer some ideas about the interviewing process.

As a former academic adviser, I have met in "interviews" with thousands of college students and have seen hundreds of resumes and vitae. In my experience I've seen two "gotchas" that can "get you" in the process. The two most avoidable problems are:

1) writing a resume/vitae that's too long, boring or with too many errors, and
2) having something too peculiar or distracting in your interpersonal approach.

But first, let's start with the basics.

What is the difference between a resume and a curriculum vitae?

A resume is a short summary of your professional life. It's primarily a list of positions you have held, your schooling, and your related credentialing. It is usually one or two pages. A curriculum vitae is as its Latin meaning translates: it's the course of your life. A CV is longer, and it lists every achievement in your academic life. Sometimes, in an effort to list everything—but to stick to two pages—resume writers will try to shoehorn in all the information they can, with densely-packed copy in a smaller font. Don't. Less is more. You are more likely to engage your reader if your resume is readable and interesting. Wherever possible, stick to the active rather than passive voice in your narrations, except for a sprinkling to vary your sentence structure. It's human nature to be drawn to printed pages that have clear headings and pleasing open spaces. No one likes to wade through dense text. Sometimes exacting detail and "too much information" can leave its own impression too! In contrast, a CV is a comprehensive inventory of just about every employment experience, every publication, every membership in an association, every grant you've been awarded, every award you've received and, of course, your academic degrees and any credentialing, certifications or licensures. For full professors or established researchers, a CV can be several pages long.

Why does a resume have to be short and a CV can be long? Why can't I have a five-page resume if a CV is typically longer? Because that's just the way it is. Whether it's arbitrary, historical accident, or tradition, the customary format of the resume is well-worn, and there's not much you can do about it. Unless you're applying for something related to academia or research—where a CV is the norm—a resume is shorter.

* *The author gratefully acknowledges the helpful review of this chapter by colleagues Charles Cheesebrough, Diane Cushman and Lu Kaiser.*

When do I use which?

Sometimes the application instructions will specify which to send. Don't automatically assume that a CV is the best. For corporate or non-academic positions, a CV may be "overkill" or give the impression that you are "overqualified." Employers may set it aside, thinking that they can't afford to pay you!

If you are applying for a position in academia, a CV is always appropriate and usually requested. For a research appointment, a teaching job at the college-level or a grant application, a CV is standard practice. Those procuring your services at these levels want all of this detail. Sample resumes and CVs are abundant on the internet.

Someone once said "the only person whose resume should be longer than one page is the President of the United States." While this is an exaggeration, it contains an important truth: a resume is supposed to be a calling card listing the highlights. Its function is to get you an interview! You want to pique the interest of your reader. Those who are fielding resumes will tell you that they frequently receive dozens for each opening. They need to sift through the pile and decide whom to call, and that can be a mind-numbing process. New college graduates should rarely have a resume longer than one page. Only those in established careers can use a two-pager and get away with it. For any supplementary information, you can place it in your cover letter or attach an addendum at the end. For example, my husband is an accomplished software engineer. His resume is two pages, but in his specific career, there is a list of software programs and computer languages that is extremely long and would be overwhelming on a resume. Employers in his field wish to know the exhaustive list of programs, databases and languages that he knows. But by the time he's listed his Pascals, Javas, and Pythons, he needs another page. In this case, on his resume he can write "accomplished in several programming languages (see addendum)." This enables him to have a two-page resume that is readable, but it also directs the employers to vital information that they need to know.

The typical resume is relatively short, but this said, don't say too little. If you give merely your title and the dates you held the position, it might give the impression that you didn't accomplish much there either. Under each job listed—or job category—you should have three or four sentences that highlight your accomplishments. Below are three examples from my own career. Each description is technically accurate, but note different impressions they leave.

Position held: Academic Adviser

1. Advised college students on their major requirements for graduation. (Too little).
2. Advised and counseled college students in behavioral sciences, business, accounting, management and technology-related and information systems programs. Received recognition for individual advising enhancement models and career development programs, enabling forthcoming graduates to take advantage of the university's rich academic opportunities and prepare themselves in the most advantageous way for their entry into their professional endeavors. (Your eyes are beginning to glaze-over here, right?) Through a competitive process, and by recommendation of my immediate supervisor, the department director and the college Dean, I received the organization's Sustained Outstanding Service Award. (Are you still awake?)
3. Provided academic and career advising to college students in Liberal Arts, Management and Technology majors. Devised innovative advising tools and publications. Facilitated career information groups and job search coaching sessions. Received college-wide award for Sustained Outstanding Service Award. (Just right.)

The last description hits all the salient points. Nobody cares one bit that my award passed through three levels of management. From this description, they can tell that I've worked with different personalities (majors), that I can facilitate groups and teach, and that I've stood out among my peers.

Anything over two pages should have an addendum or be in curriculum vitae format and titled as such. Ironically, a CV can be almost as long as you like and *does* typically contain an extensive account of all of your accomplishments, education, awards and publications. But even a CV can be too foggy and ponderous. Use the active voice and good economy with your verbiage.

Writing a Curriculum Vitae

First of all, refer to it in your cover letter as a "curriculum vitae." "Curricula Vitae" is plural.

A curriculum vitae is an important part of an application for an academic and research position or a grant proposal. CVs are also standard fare with your application for tenure, with a proposal for a speaking engagement and the like. Although more comprehensive, many of the same rules for writing a resume apply.

A CV begins as a resume does, with your name and contact information. Thereafter, list all of your achievements, usually in order of importance. Nobel Laureates, Rhodes or Fulbright Scholars, or MacArthur Foundation "Genius Grant" Fellows should note this straight off the bat. (Although if you hold any of these distinctions, quit reading. I have nothing to offer you!) If you are applying for a research position, you may wish to highlight your research first. For a faculty appointment, your academic positions should figure prominently, followed by any academic awards and honors.

Newly-graduated applicants usually list their academic degrees first, along with related information such as any postgraduate work, thesis/dissertation titles and any academic awards, undergraduate degrees, majors and minors, etc. List any professional licenses and certifications as well. Those applying for positions that involve teaching should consider placing teaching experience and any teaching awards toward the beginning of your CV. Also helpful are the titles of courses you have taught, any special teaching methods or innovations, and any positive teaching evaluations.

Sometimes in the teaching vs. research status wars, teaching skills get short shrift. This is changing. Don't be sheepish about being a good teacher! Depending on whether you are applying as an instructor in a large research university or at a small liberal arts college, teaching and research will take-on different levels of importance based on the institutional missions. Even research universities are becoming more sensitive to customer service. Include skills such as fluencies in other languages or other competencies. If you are applying for a grant, your audience will be interested in seeing a list of other grants you've been awarded. These are usually listed in reverse chronological order.

On a CV, always list published, peer-reviewed research, scholarly articles, conference speeches, books, and then any writing you've done for a non-scientific audience. Be sure to include any works in progress. Toward the end, you can add community service, such as university committees, professional association participation, volunteer work and the like. Provide references if requested, although many times "available upon request" is most appropriate, especially since your choice as a reference may vary depending on the nature of your application.

Finally, when laying-out your CV, be sure to use consistent formatting: indent similar paragraphs the same way, etc. If there are standard ways of formatting in your field—many professionals in the social sciences use APA format—be sure to follow these rules when listing your publications. Bold or italicize the headings of your categories, and be sure to include open spaces for a pleasing, readable appearance.

Remember that the person reviewing your CV or resume initially may not be an expert in your field. Knowledge of "string theory" might sound like you're a violin virtuoso rather than a theoretical physicist. Knowing how to create a "clean room" can mean expertise in high-tech manufacturing or hotel housekeeping. Check for overuse of jargon, field-specific abbreviations and the like by asking someone outside of your discipline to look-it-over and point out anything that isn't clear. However, if you know your CV is going directly to a peer, the field-specific nomenclature is preferred.

A Dozen Job Search Suggestions

1. Proofread carefully for typos or spelling/grammatical mistakes.

This point appears in all articles on resume tips for good reason: it is obvious, but often overlooked. In my experience, about two thirds of all the documents I've reviewed have at least one error. If grammar and spelling are not your strengths, find help from someone who writes well. Then always have it proofread by someone else. You can have an impressive list of accomplishments only to trash your chances at a job that specifically asks for "attention to detail." Don't just rely on you're spell Czech. As ewe can sea, it dozen find all foe paws.

2. No Fudging.

Tell the absolute truth. While you want to highlight everything good, and not accentuate the bad, make sure everything you say is truthful. Ethical conduct is crucial in all careers. Furthermore, hiring officials are fact-checking these things more often. Where you specify specialized knowledge, degrees, licensures or certifications, offer to provide proof. Fudging in interviews can be a disaster.

An acquaintance of mine was interviewing candidates for a computer programming job in the mid-1980s. About that time, computing went from mainframes to PCs to networked work stations within just a couple of years. Middle-aged programmers who didn't have the foresight to keep up their skills were laid-off by the zillion. They all had to develop PC savvy fast—or claim that they had—to get an interview.

My friend interviewed a guy who claimed that he had "30 years' experience with 'US-CD' Pascal," a programming language. This wasn't just a typo on his resume, which would be forgivable. He said it multiple times in the interview. First of all, it's *UC-SD* Pascal, named for the University of California—San Diego. Secondly, UC-SD Pascal had been developed just a few years before the interview. There's no way he had 30 years of experience, because it hadn't been invented yet! Interview is over.

3. Watch for red flags.

Stay away from facts that might work against you. For example, let's say you've owned your own business and you've been selected as "Entrepreneur of the Year" with the local business community. Now you've applied for an Executive Director position in a non-profit organization with a governing board that makes the major decisions.

Entrepreneurship demonstrates achievement and energy, but it also may be scary to an organization that functions on group consensus. Those hiring for this position will be looking for evidence that you are not a loose cannon. In addition to describing these successes, make sure to highlight evidence that you can work effectively on teams and within an existing organization's structure. You may wish to emphasize this in your cover letter.

Avoid revealing religious, political or any other involvement in activities that might alienate your reader. It may be something you are very proud of, but you cannot be sure that your reader will not have prejudices. Unless you're applying for a chaplaincy, a Congressional staff position, or seeking a goal that is closely aligned with these values, it's safer to withhold this, at least in the resume phase.

If asked for your salary expectations, always write "negotiable," even if you believe the position pays less than you can handle. You never know what's possible. There may be another pot of money available that you don't know about. If they interview you and decide they can't live without you, they may combine the salary with the salary of an unfilled position they can eliminate.

4. Break the "rules" ... a little.

You don't have to list the exact dates of employment down to the minute. It's not a police blotter. Let's say that you quit a job before landing the next one, and there is a three-month gap. There are plenty of life circumstances that can bring on legitimate reasons for short gaps in employment—a death in the family or layoff are two examples. Back in my early career, a layoff carried some stigma with it—many assumed it was an employer's way of firing someone politely. This has changed. Layoffs are now so commonplace; we all know a friend, a neighbor or a relative who's experienced one. If one of your jobs ran from August 2000 through February 2002 and your current job began in May 2002, leave off the missing months and just write:

Position 1: 2000 – 2002, and

Position 2: 2002 – present.

It's not inaccurate. If you are asked for exact dates, you will of course provide them. But there's a good chance you will never be asked!

Regarding this point, one—or even two—lengthy gaps in employment are no longer the red flag they used to be. In fact, a long gap can be less of a concern than numerous short ones. There is now widespread recognition that many people stop-out to care for their families. And since asking about your family is an illegal question, they will probably just assume this is the case. Employers know that families are a part of almost everyone's life and that employees with families are a strong part of our stable workforce.

Most people list their previous jobs in reverse chronological order, but this is not sacrosanct. You can list the one that is more important or most closely-related first. You do not have to list every job you've ever held. For example, let's consider someone who's been a Certified Public Accountant at a major firm, left to raise a family, and did bookkeeping for a gift shop on the side while parenting. She can list the large firm—and leave-off the gift shop. If you're concerned with age-bias, omit your graduation dates and include only the years of job history that are most related. Sometimes a volunteer position speaks louder than paid employment. If you have a choice between listing your work with Habitat for Humanity or Big Brothers/Big Sisters and a summer job mowing greens at a golf course, choose your volunteer position.

You don't have to use the same resume for every job you apply for. In fact, each resume should be "tweaked" slightly with each application to speak to the exact qualifications requested on the job posting or ad. Read the position description carefully and be sure to tailor it to *their* requested needs—not what *you* need in a job. That comes after the offer!

5. Control your Message.

A few jobs will give you the option of applying via resume or by filling out the organization's pre-fabricated application. Choose the resume! Sometimes writing a resume can be intimidating, and it's tempting to take the path of least resistance. But applying by resume makes you look motivated. And it gives you more control over the message. Typically, company applications ask for things—such as exact dates of employment—that can be irrelevant red flags. If you apply by resume, it is quite possible that you could be hired first—and then asked to fill out the generic application as a formality thereafter.

6. Use Standard Fonts, Formatting and Paper.

Use a standard font such as Times or another font in common usage and modest-looking paper. Stick to standard appearances, nothing too slick or elaborate. The one exception to standard-looking resumes applies to those seeking creative work, such as design, commercial art and the like. These applicants can venture a bit into avant-garde territory.

7. Have a "Cover Story" Ready.

Your resume is drafted! Now have a knowledgeable friend read it to look for anything that might look off-putting or that might elicit questions. For example, if it took you seven years to finish your master's or if you have a 10-year gap in employment, have a prepared answer. If you're comfortable with your answer, they will be too.

8. Regarding advice: Listen to all of it, but implement it carefully.

When recruiting friends or relatives for resume preparation or interviewing advice, you may be referred to Uncle George who "once worked in HR." Use caution. Your friend who is a great talker in your book club might be a pompous bore at work. Your cousin might be a great mid-level retail manager, but he will not be much help if you are applying for a tenure-track professorship at a university. The person in your circle who is more reserved might be the one with the best interviewing skills. The one who looks like a space cadet might be the one whose resumes are a slam-dunk and who gets every job she applies for. Uncle George might have worked in personnel, but it was back when resumes still listed your height and weight. You get the idea. Parents—and spouses—are the worst. Bless their hearts, but most of them can't be objective. Back in my advising days, if I had a nickel for every bad resume I'd seen co-written by a parent, I'd be in Nassau right now, sipping fruit drinks festooned with miniature umbrellas.

There's another important consideration in "networking." When we list references or find an employer via personal contacts, we are essentially tapping the social capital that others have accumulated. Excellent references are career gold. Someone I know recently served as a professional (and personal) reference for a colleague who ultimately got the job despite considerable competition. The woman who acted as reference had worked with this man for 10 years. He was so competent and trustworthy, she was able to tell the employer to "hire him before he gets away!" After she told the employer about his work that she had seen, she said, "You know, I worked with this guy for 10 years. Nobody can hide bad character for that length of time. If there were any problems, I would have seen them. There are only 3 or 4 people in my whole career whom I would endorse with my own reputation—he is one of them." When this happens, it is magic.

However, using personal contacts carries its risks when the referral comes from someone who is not credible or someone whose reputation in that organization is iffy. Let's say you're applying for a job that you heard about from a friend of your cousin. "Drop my name in the interview," he says, "Tell them I sent you." If he's a star performer, you have a real edge. If he's a problem employee, that's a connection you don't need. Discerning who is a good reference and whom you should bypass isn't easy. Unless you know your reference very well, proceed with caution.

9. Write a good cover letter.

Every application needs a cover letter to introduce your resume or CV. Again, less is more. One page with four or five paragraphs is probably enough; two pages is the max. Make sure your cover letter does not rehash everything that's already on the resume—the cover letter should enhance your resume. There are entire books written on letter writing that can help you. In the cover letter, you can explain anything that is not apparent on the resume and help them draw any conclusions that they may not think about unless you point it out. For example: let's say the job ad asks for the "ability to multitask." This is your chance to point out that you managed to complete graduate school while serving as the lead teaching assistant in your department and handling an advising load of undergraduates—at the same time.

Your cover letter serves another purpose: *It's a writing sample!* While your resume or CV is a basic list, your cover letter is your chance to demonstrate your writing ability. When I read long paragraphs of bulky text, passive voice and unnecessary "50-dollar words," I wonder if the person is more interested in getting their information across than in learning about the organization's needs.

10. Now that your resume is done, get ready to interview!

Your library or local bookstore will have scores of "how to interview" books to coach you through those difficult interview questions. They can provide guidance on many special issues, such as negotiating your salary, disclosing disabilities or addressing an unusual situation. All of this expertise will not be duplicated here. However, one preparation tip is not usually available in a book, but it's an important one: make sure your appearance and demeanor make a good impression! Yes, it's shallow and shouldn't matter. But it often does.

Obviously, there are individual differences affecting appearance that are unchangeable or due to disability and the like. This is *not* what I'm referring to. Any employer who would evaluate someone negatively based on these criteria isn't worthy of you anyway. But there are many distractions that can be fixed with shoe polish or a dandruff shampoo!

When you're ready, practice with a few mock interviews. Ask a few people you respect for some feedback on your personal style and presentation. Non-family help is best. Sometimes you can ask a friend of a friend, which might make the process less awkward. If you have lots of extra cash, there are "image consultants" and career coaches you can hire who do this. People are reluctant to say unflattering things to people they like, so you will have to give them permission to be ruthless! Tell them they will be doing you a great service if they would take a few minutes and be your mirror. One person's opinion might just be a fluke. But if two or three tell you the same thing—listen. You can't change everything—and you may not change anything—but awareness never hurts.

This preparation takes great maturity on your part. Resolve in advance to be grateful for even painful and embarrassing input. Those who can listen and integrate this information are almost always glad they did. Questions you might ask to prime the pump and put them at ease are:

- **Do I have any strange mannerisms?**
  One of my advisees pushed up her glasses every 30 seconds. This doesn't reveal a character flaw; it's just distracting. After about three minutes, I felt an unbearable urge to reach over and push them up for her. You want the

interviewer to be paying attention to *you*—not your glasses! A simple adjustment at an optometrist could solve it. Do I laugh like a horse? This is what I was told. Now when I interview, I leave Seabiscuit at home!

- **Jewelry, make-up or ornamentation: Do I have too much?**
  Few career books address this issue in depth, because it's uncomfortable to discuss. Body piercings, tattoos, unusual clothing, hair colors that do not occur naturally in the human populations and such are personal choices that make fashion statements, establish your individuality or communicate your value system. If your appearance reflects some ethnic, religious or cultural message that is central to your identity—well, then you must hold fast to your values. I admire your integrity. But be aware that there may be some conservative workplaces and some hiring personnel who may pass you by. In many educational, non-profit and creative workplaces, individuality is the norm. A good way to conduct some reconnaissance is to visit the workplace if you can do so with anonymity—or check out their website. In a busy public reception area, it's easy to pick up some organizational brochures and glance at the workers. What are they wearing? A rule of thumb for interview dress: wear an outfit that is one notch more formal than daily office dress.

  But if shelving your personal style means "selling-out" or if some aspect of your appearance is terribly important to you—and you'd refuse to work for a place that had a problem with it—it might work as an asset in another way. It will act as a good filter, identifying only those places that can accept your appearance.

- **Is my wardrobe, hairstyle or eyewear unflattering or 15 years out of date?**
  For older applicants who are worried about age-bias, this is especially important. Sometimes your hairdo or your outfit will date-you in spite of a resume carefully checked to be vague in this area. Update your look, but look authentic. For help, ask a fashionable friend or a dapper dresser for recommendations.

- **How's my grooming?**
  Nails? Stray hairs? Breath? Use adequate anti-perspirant, but no colognes. What smells great to you might smell like mosquito repellant to someone else. With asthma increasing in prevalence, this is especially important as scents can trigger an asthma attack. On your way into the interview site, stop by the restroom to remove the spinach from your teeth. Even if you haven't eaten spinach in months, the evidence always reappears just before an interview. Make sure your clothing is neat and that your shoes are polished. I used to work with someone whose wardrobe was magazine-worthy perfection. However, I don't think she ever polished her shoes. They were always scuffed and, on the back of the accelerator-pedal shoe, the heel always looked as if it had tangled with a belt sander.

- **How are my table manners?**
  Interviews are occasionally conducted over meals. Do I know which fork to use? One tip: let your interviewer order first. You can say, "Please go first, I'm just about ready." Then make your choice comparable. If your interviewer orders a chef salad, don't get the filet mignon. Leave the impression, an accurate one, that you can be responsible with an expense account. Table manners are obvious, but not everyone remembers the importance of treating waiters as politely as the interviewer. Don't order alcohol, even if your interviewer imbibes. Unless you are applying for a job as a taste-tester in a winery, it will work against you. You don't know how the interviewer will perceive it, and it could cloud your thinking.

- **Are any of my behaviors out of the ordinary?**
  Am I a blabbermouth? Do I interrupt people?
  Do I look nervous? Do I bite my nails or say "um" too often?
  How is my grammar? Is my speaking voice too soft?
  Do I make good eye-contact?
  Is my handshake OK? The "limp fish" is bad. The Chuck Norris grip is painful.

In most of the United States (U.S.) culture, there still seems to be a bias toward conversational eye-contact and moderate extroversion. Some people are soft-spoken and reserved. Others are extroverted and engaging. If you tend to gravitate toward either extreme, adjust accordingly—the meek may inherit the earth, but embarking on a job in sales would be challenging. Extroversion is great, as long as it's not boisterous.

This input from others is not easy to listen to, but it is a great gift to yourself. I have tried to console people who have gone on interview after interview and couldn't figure out why no offers were forthcoming. They had one of the attributes listed above—or one like it—and the problem was obvious to me. But without assurance that the person wanted and could handle this feedback, I wouldn't risk making matters worse.

People have lost-out on job offers due to something simple that could have easily been changed. Don't let pride cost you a job! After your friends have been kind enough to be honest, be sure to thank them and adopt any recommendations you agree with. Then congratulate yourself. It takes a strong, confident person to listen to critique and make changes where necessary.

However, allow me to add a special note here to those who would find this feedback exercise too frightening. If you feel too fragile, you can skip this step if you think it may dash your self-confidence just when you need it most. Situational anxiety is very common and almost universal in job interviews. It's an oft-cited maxim that people are more afraid of public speaking than death! However, if the thought of interviewing is truly terrifying, you may have a medical disability: Social Anxiety. Please see your doctor right away. According to the National Institutes of Mental Health, 16% of the U.S. population (1 in 6!) suffers from an anxiety disorder.

Social Anxiety is a tragedy for our national productivity. I have no statistics to prove it, but it's my experience that anxiety sufferers can be the most thoughtful, hard-working, productive, and enjoyable colleagues of all. Who knows how many "good catches" are passed-over by employers who hire an over-confident personality by mistake? It's also a tragedy because it's usually correctable.

I recall one college student I worked with who was so fearful, that I advised him by phone for some time before he could manage an in-person meeting. As my advisee found out, anxiety disorders are remarkably treatable. With a good doctor and intervention, he responded very, very well. In a matter of weeks, he went from a guy who couldn't face a supportive adviser to a confident, young man who was able to explain his disability to his professors, ask for incompletes, and negotiate a timetable to complete his classes. He knew I was willing to advocate for him if needed, but he did it himself! It was amazing! Many clinically-anxious people are reluctant to seek help. But if you suspect this may be an issue, I urge you to see your doctor. If you are able to interview comfortably and talk about your qualifications confidently, you may not only get hired sooner, you might be offered more money!

Now here's a quick note about interview structure. Back when I started out, it seemed that every interview was basically the same—they had the traditional questions and answers were pretty predictable and preparing was much easier. There are still many interviews that follow this format. However, since then, a new interview style has emerged called the "behavioral interview." These are the interviews that "throw you a curve ball" and ask a question that is truly bizarre. For example, they could show you a Swiss Army Knife and ask: "if you could be one of these tools, which would you be?" (Swiss Army Knives are those multi-purpose pocket implements that look like a jackknife, only it has a scissors, a file, a fork, a corkscrew, or the like.) These questions are agonizing, because you have no idea what's coming. There are examples of behavioral interview questions on the internet, so type "behavioral interview" into your favorite search engine. The most important thing to remember here is that they are probably not looking for a specific answer as much as they are trying to see how you can handle the unexpected. Take a breath, smile, and remain calm—choose an answer that makes sense to you. For the aforementioned, if you were a human services advocate, you might say "I would be a scissors, because clients need an advocate to cut through 'red tape'." Have a generic answer ready in case you become just totally bewildered. You might smile and say, "I presume that with this question, you are probably trying to find out how I would handle the unexpected. I will be honest. I can't think of a response at this moment, but maybe that is because I am not impulsive. When I am faced with a choice, I prefer not to go with my knee-jerk response. I would be likely to consult with a colleague or my manager." This is my favorite because, for me, it's not evasive—it's true. Get some sample questions and practice!

11. Do due diligence.

No single source of advice or information is enough. Some people buy one job search manual and follow everything to the letter—big mistake. I have provided some suggested readings at the end of this article, but I encourage you to look for information from a broad array of sources. Implement what best fits you. Use the internet to find resume and CV writing tips and interviewing advice. For information on the institution, firm or organization that interests you, always make sure to read their website and do an internet search to find out about the mission, culture and well-being of the organization. This information can help you ask intelligent questions and let your interviewer know that you've done your homework.

Always use your home computer for email and writing your resume. Sometimes you will be applying for jobs and you don't want your current employer to know. If you will be leaving work to go directly to an interview in dressier attire than is customary on your current job, leave your interview clothes in the car and change at a fast food restroom on the way. (It's been done. You want fries with that?)

Lastly, to anyone who interviews you or helps you in the process, be sure to send a note of thanks. This is so obvious but, in my experience, the majority of job seekers don't do this. When I review a resume for a new professional, I typically get a thank you only 10% of the time!

12. Special tips for family professionals.

This article is being written with family professionals, particularly family life educators, as the audience. Jobs in the human services field tend to be very competitive—there were 85 applicants for the position I hold now. During economic downturns, it's particularly gloomy. I graduated with my bachelor's degree in 1982 during one of the worst recessions in years—I started as a receptionist in a human services setting and there were over 60 applicants for that job. You might have to start at a pre-entry level. However, as we used to say on the farm, "cream always rises to the top." If you are a diligent worker, you can move up by promotion.

For family life educators, there is another challenge—explaining to employers who you are and what you can offer their organization. Family life educators have been around throughout history—but we've been called different things. One hundred years ago, families received instruction on marriage, parenting, eldercare and the like, but it came from clergy, midwives, family and neighbors. I have an old book on etiquette from the 1880s, and it is full of parenting advice in the form of teaching manners to children. Our profession—Family Life Education—in the formal sense, is not yet the household word that the fields of nursing or accounting are. Often, when you see a job advertisement or announcement, employers will ask for a social worker or a therapist when what would serve them best is a family life educator. In these instances, apply for these positions! Use your cover letter to explain that while you are not a social worker or counselor, you believe your training as a family life educator may be ideal for their needs. The National Council on Family Relations (NCFR) offers a certification in our field called the Certified Family Life Educator (CFLE). Check NCFR's website for more information at www.ncfr.org .

The positive aspect of working in human services, however, is that by definition, these jobs are not going to be among those that can be "off-shored" to global competition. Working with families usually means being there in person. There is place for you in the workforce in a job that's a good fit for you. But it may be three or four jobs and several years into the future. I went back for my master's and took some time out for motherhood—both took several years. Keep at it. I finally got my dream job, but I was 43.

Finally, I'd like to say a few words about mentoring. If you can find some colleagues along the way who can help you develop your potential, they can save you time and even heartache. There may be some who come into your life via formal mentoring programs, but for me, they just appeared. How do you spot them? Look around you for older, smart people who are a little farther down the pike and whose personality meshes well with yours. Then:

- Listen for those who can admit mistakes and who can talk about their course corrections.
- Look for people who have the respect of their peers.
- Look around you for people who know their strengths yet laugh at their weaknesses.
- Look for someone who can speak the truth, even if it's not pleasant.
- Look around you for people who care in general, whom you might be able to coax into caring about you.
- And finally, once you've found them, tell them you want their shaping even if it hurts.

Being a mentor isn't easy and there is little motivation for anyone to do it. Influencing the future of another human being is a serious responsibility. It requires risk, and who needs that? But it's one way in which altruistic people find meaning in their own lives; Erik Erikson called it "generativity." I've had many people who have helped me here and there, but I have had two mentors in adulthood and one in adolescence without whom I would not be where I am today. Two of them shared all of their wisdom with me through much active coaching. The other one spoke fewer words but instead acted as a mirror that helped me discover wisdom within myself that I didn't know I had. Mentors are one of life's greatest gifts. There is a catch, however. If you accept mentoring, you have a duty to give back someday. Once you're an established professional, the universe will send you a mentee who needs *your* help.

Now that you have some tips from me, and you have consulted many other people and resources, sift through them all and use only what makes sense to you. Never substitute anyone else's judgment for your own, including mine. You're the only one who knows where you've been and where you're going. Thank you for allowing me the privilege to be a part of your journey!

Suggested Readings

Bolles, R. N. (2008). *What color is your parachute? 2008: A practical manual for job-hunters and career-changers.* Berkeley, CA: Ten Speed Press.

Kennedy, J. L. (2007). *Resumes for dummies* (5th ed.). Indianapolis, IN: Wiley Publishing.

Goleman, D. (2006). *Social intelligence: The revolutionary new science of human relationships.* NY: Bantam Books.

Goleman, D. (1998). *Working with emotional intelligence.* NY: Bantam Books.

Moses, B. (1998). *Career intelligence: The 12 new rules for work and life success.* San Francisco, CA: Berrett-Koehler Publishers.

Pink, D. H. (2006). *A whole new mind: Why right-brainers will rule the future.* NY: Berkeley Publishing.

Yate, M. (2006). *Knock 'em dead 2008: The ultimate job search guide.* Avon, MA: Adams Media.

About the Author

Nancy Gonzalez, M.Ed., CFLE is on staff at the National Council on Family Relations and serves as the editor of the organization's member magazine, *NCFR Report*, and as NCFR's staff blogger. She is an adjunct instructor of Family Law and Public Policy at Concordia University—St. Paul, MN. Nancy's first career was as an Academic Adviser at the University of Minnesota for 15 years, helping literally thousands of college students prepare for their careers.

Integrating Family Life Education Content Areas into Practice

Section II

Families and Individuals in Societal Contexts

KEVIN M. ROY AND
SHELLEY M. MACDERMID

Think back to the turn of the last century. Members of your family typically expected to live into their forties – seeing their fiftieth birthday would have been an accomplishment. However, you, at the turn of this century, expect to live well into your seventies. How is it that we are living longer, healthier lives in this new century? Is it because of personal choices or because of changes in public institutions, such as health care? And how do those additional years change society's notion of how life should be lived?

In this chapter, we consider links between the characteristics of societies and the daily lives of their members, with the goal of generating ideas that can be applied in family life education settings. The chapter was designed to address the points of view of a variety of audiences, holding the interest of a class of high school students or providing useful information for a community group of parents to consider.

The chapter begins with a summary of concepts from some of the theories that have influenced scholars' thoughts about families and society. These concepts are then applied to specific issues related to each of four major segments of the life span: childhood, adolescence and emerging adulthood, adulthood, and later adulthood. Finally, we offer resources and tips that family life educators might find useful.

Although it seems obvious that the characteristics of a society affect its members, it can be difficult to make the connection compelling for family life education audiences. If society is a forest, the daily lives of individuals and families are like the blades of grass on the forest floor – it is very hard to get a clear understanding of the forest from the vantage point of the grass. But there are at least two very important lessons about the blades of grass. First, the blades of grass are not only influenced by the trees, but also exert their own influence in return. For example, they compete with the trees for nutrients in the soil, protect the roots of the trees from heat, and attract beneficial organisms. Second, although each blade of grass interacts with only its most proximal environment – air, soil, nutrients – it is also affected by much more distal factors. Over the past decade, families have grown increasingly aware of the impact of global warming on their daily routines. They have begun to consider new fuel alternatives and perhaps changes in their daily routines, which in turn would shape the pace of climatic change. In effect, individuals and families affect societies, not just the reverse, and that large-scale societal factors influence individuals in ways of which they are not always aware.

Many people are often uncomfortable with the notion that policies shape family life – the dominant culture in the United States maintains a public stance of governmental "non-intervention" in family decisions. However, even though social institutions may be invisible at times, it is important to consider how institutions shape family life, and in turn, how families

CURRICULUM GUIDELINES: FAMILIES & INDIVIDUALS IN SOCIETAL CONTEXTS

An understanding of families and their relationships to other institutions, such as the educational, governmental, religious, and occupational institutions in society. Based on knowledge of:

1. various family structures and functions;
2. cultural variations among families (family heritage), including social class, geography, ethnicity, race, and religion;
3. dating, courtship, and marital choice;
4. kinship (inter-generational) relations;
5. cross-cultural understanding of the life-styles of minority families (including Blacks, Hispanics, American Indians, and Asian-Americans) and the life-styles of families in various societies around the world;
6. changing gender roles, including role expectations and behaviors of courtship partners, marital partners, parents and children, siblings, and extended kin;
7. present and future demographic trends among families;
8. families as they have developed through history;
9. the reciprocal influence between the occupational work place and family members; and
10. the reciprocal influence of the major social institutions and families, i.e., governmental, religious, educational, and economic.

shape social institutions. In the following sections, we describe two theoretical perspectives that can be used as lenses for examining connections between societies and daily life.

Ecological Perspective

According to the *Merriam-Webster Online Dictionary* (society, n.d.), a society is "a community, nation, or broad grouping of people having common traditions, institutions, and collective activities and interests." One way to examine societies is to think of them as comprising interconnected settings or contexts within which each of us grows and develops. Within this ecological framework, (Bronfenbrenner, 1988), the smallest or most immediate setting we experience is labeled the "microsystem." Examples of microsystems are the home or children's school classrooms. Microsystems are linked by mesosystems. The relationships between home and school or home and workplace are examples of mesosystems – these can vary in strength depending upon the degree to which activities in one setting support those in another. When the developing individual is affected by but does not participate in a particular setting, we use the term "exosystem." For example, links between their parents' workplaces and the family are exosystems for children.

Macrosystems are the institutions of a society: "significant practices, relationships, or organizations" (*macrosystem*, n.d.). Religion, health care, education, the economy, and government are examples, but families are perhaps the most common of all societal institutions. All over the world and throughout history, cultures rely on families to nurture their members, prepare them for participation as citizens, and support them throughout life (Goode, 1982). Families thus are mediators between social change and individual lives, and because of that, have been targets for social policy, media, and other efforts to change human behavior.

> *Families are not isolated, self-enclosed social systems; and the other institutions of society, such as the military, the church, or the school system, continually rediscover that they are not dealing with individuals, but with members of families. Even in the most industrialized and urban of societies, where it is sometimes supposed that people lead rootless and anonymous lives, most people are in continual interaction with other family members.* (Goode, 1982, p. 3)

Life Course Perspective

Alternatively, a focus on time may help family life educators understand the interaction of families and social institutions. The life course perspective on family life (Bengtson & Allen, 1993) suggests that individual family members move through a succession of roles over the course of their lives, such as parent, spouse, worker, or student. Family members work together to build these roles. However, each role is played out in unique ways due to the historical moment. For example, in 1900, male breadwinning was at the heart of American fatherhood (Griswold, 1993). Today, social expectations of fathers are shifting: Are fathers more than breadwinners? Do we, as a society, expect and support fathers as caregivers as well?

Social institutions are woven from the experiences of groups of men and women born at the same time, such as the Baby Boomers. The sheer size, amount of resources, and increased longevity of this birth cohort has reshaped society. The life course of individual Baby Boomers has been age-structured, so that the transitions from school to work to retirement are socially created, socially recognized and shared (Hagestad & Neugarten, 1985; Riley & Riley, 1994). The collective experiences of Baby Boomers have also loosened the age structure of the life course, encouraging a return to education for older adults, later childbirth, flexible retirement, and multiple phases of family formation. In other words, social changes affect different birth cohorts in different ways, and cohort experiences in turn create new social changes.

Social institutions also fit together with families in unique ways to manage the flexibility of the life course. The typical school-day schedule of 9 a.m. - 3 p.m., with three months of summer vacation, reflects the concerns of a primarily agricultural economy that relied on the support of children during tending seasons. Recent local moves to around-the-year schooling are efforts to "update" social institutions to changed post-industrial rhythms. The typical workday schedule of 9 a.m. – 5 p.m. likewise reflects the needs of a mostly white, mostly married, and mostly male work force. In the global economy, flexible scheduling, temporary hires, and rapid readjustments to market forces have revolutionized family members' experiences with work. However, workday expectations still govern many of our lives, reflecting a time lag needed for social institutions to reform themselves in sync with family life.

Social institutions appear invisible in part because we experience these issues so individually. We hold intense discussions with partners over when a working mother should go back to work, who should pick up the children, and whether or not to move and take a better job offer. These late night debates are not necessarily private – they echo debates held across hundreds of dinner tables every night. In part, changing family roles reflect shifting expectations in social institutions. When the life course of family members is shaped so intimately by institutions in today's society, private issues become public concerns, as C. Wright Mills suggested over forty years ago (1959). In the following sections, we explore these theoretical perspectives by looking at four distinct periods of the life span. In each period, we identify an issue that is shaped distinctively by institutions in society.

Demographic Change and Children's Experiences

In this section, we bring together concepts related to the curriculum guideline of families in society and the life span framework concept of childhood. To accomplish our purpose, we explore the connections between a demographic trend – changes in mothers' employment – and the daily lives of children.

Demographic changes occur at the level of the society or the macrosystem. One well-known macro-level change is the increase in women's participation in the labor force. Like many others, this change is actually more complex than first meets the eye. Overall, women's participation began to increase more than a century ago (Rubin & Riney, 1994; U.S. Bureau of the Census, 1975, 1993), but women of color and poor and unmarried women had always participated in large numbers. The biggest recent change is that the participation of mothers of preschool children has increased substantially in the past 40 years (U.S. Bureau of the Census, 2001).

This macro-level change is made up of the decisions of millions of individual women to enter the labor force while their children are young, in response to financial pressures in the economy, personal fulfillment goals, or other reasons. These individual decisions have changed children's microsystems, specifically where and with

CHILDHOOD — *Within the context of the family system*

Families and Individuals in Societal Contexts

- Jobs, money, and the family
- Programs that support individuals and families
- Importance of families, neighborhood, and the community
- Families and schools working together
- Differing spiritual beliefs and practices

Multicultural • Gender Fair • Special Needs Aware

Reciprocal interactions between family and ecosystem

ADOLESCENCE — *Within the context of the family system*

Families and Individuals in Societal Contexts

- Families and the workplace
- Reciprocal influences of the economy and families
- School as preparation for the future
- Functioning in the school system
- Education throughout the life span
- Individual and family responsibility in the community
- Influence of religion and spirituality on families
- Support for families with special needs and problems
- Reciprocal influences of technology and families
- Population issues and resource allocation
- Role of family in society
- Supportive networks - family, peers, religious institutions, community

Multicultural • Gender Fair • Special Needs Aware

Reciprocal interactions between family and ecosystem

ADULTHOOD — *Within the context of the family system*

Families and Individuals in Societal Contexts

- Family participation in the education of children
- Utilizing the education system
- Influence of religion and spirituality on families
- Supportive networks - family, peers, religious institutions, community
- Understanding and obtaining community support services
- Life-long learning
- Population issues and resource allocation
- Reciprocal influences of technology and families
- Economic fluctuations and their impact on families
- Interrelationship of families, work, and society
- Individual and family responsibility in the community
- Role of the family in society

Multicultural • Gender Fair • Special Needs Aware

Reciprocal interactions between family and ecosystem

LATER ADULTHOOD — *Within the context of the family system*

Families and Individuals in Societal Contexts

- Life-long learning
- Supporting the educational system
- Influence of religion and spirituality on families
- Supportive networks - family, peers, religious institutions, community
- Understanding and obtaining community support services
- Reciprocal influences of technology and aging families
- Economic fluctuations and their impact on aging families
- Population issues and resource allocation - health care, transportation, housing
- Social issues - age discrimination, elder abuse prevention, caregiving
- Role of family in society

Multicultural • Gender Fair • Special Needs Aware

Reciprocal interactions between family and ecosystem

whom they spend their time. Children today spend more time in the care of people other than their parents than in the past. This applies to children regardless of whether or not their mothers are employed: In 1997, 52% and 44% of the children of employed and nonemployed mothers, respectively, were enrolled in "preprimary educational programs," compared to 8% and 5% 40 years earlier (Bianchi, 2000).

Another micro-level change is that mothers and fathers have begun to reallocate "carework" – the work of nurturing family members. For example, both employed and nonemployed women have substantially reduced their involvement in housework (Bianchi, Robinson, & Milkie, 2006). Parents today – both mothers and fathers – are spending more time with their children than was the case 40 years ago (Bianchi, Robinson, & Milkie, 2006). Fathers in families where mothers are employed tend to be more knowledgeable about their children's whereabouts and activities (Crouter, 2002). Scholars also have begun to pay more attention to the "invisible" carework of planning and coordination that keeps families running (DeVault, 1994).

As a result of these microsystem changes, workers quite different from their predecessors now populate workplaces. Women now comprise almost half of the labor force. Most employed mothers and fathers are now in families with two paid jobs, not just one. Parents' workplaces are exosystems for children because children do not participate directly in but are affected by them. Workers – particularly those who are highly skilled and highly paid – have become increasingly vocal about their desire for work arrangements that facilitate effectiveness both at home and at work (Campbell & Koblenz, 1997; Galinsky, Bond, & Friedman, 1993). In ecological terms, workers are asking for a stronger work-family mesosystem. Macro-level changes led to the implementation of the Family and Medical Leave Act of 1993, which provides job-protected unpaid leave for serious family needs. Some employers have instituted a wide variety of "family-friendly" policies and parental leave programs, although the overall percentage of workers with access is still very small. The important gains from maternal employment (for some preschool children in particular) may be limited without access to these policies that make employment manageable for families (Brooks-Gunn, Han, & Waldfogel, 2002).

When learners are studying the connections between societies and individual families, educators face the challenge of helping them to avoid "social address" explanations for differences among groups. This occurs when a person is assigned a label, which is then assumed to explain their behavior (Bronfenbrenner, 1988). For example, a social address explanation would assume that all differences between the children of employed and homemaker mothers are a function of their mothers' employment status. Similar reasoning has been used for differences between groups defined by ethnicity or social class. Such explanations ignore the processes through which settings affect individuals. To be complete and accurate, explanations must take into account the characteristics of persons (such as children's temperament), the larger environment (such as the family's need for the mother's income), the structure and content of the settings involved (such as mothers' and fathers' work conditions), and the way those interact (Parcel & Menaghan, 1994). For example, the shift of low-income mothers from welfare to work has complicated consequences, depending on the age of children (Chase-Lansdale et al., 2003). Work had little positive or negative effect on preschool age children's behavior and well-being. However, mothers' entry into work improved adolescents' mental health, and exit from work increased adolescent behavior problems.

Family life educators may find it useful to have learners find out where and by whom they were cared for as children, why those arrangements were made, and how their parents feel about those choices now. Learners also can check out the local employee policies (by investigating company websites, annual reports, or company news articles), or read the most recent article about the Best 100 Companies in an October issue of *Working Mother* magazine to identify company similarities and differences (check NAEYC and NAFCC in the Related Websites section for definitions of quality child care).

Adolescence, Emerging Adulthood, and the Experience of Family Poverty

Adolescence emerged fifty years ago as its own distinct stage of life. In recent years, we have noted another new stage of the life span: emerging adulthood, for young adults between the ages of 18-30 (Arnett, 2004). In a way, social institutions create these stages. Full-time educational institutions isolate students, who become adult workers when participating in full-time employment (Furstenberg, 2000). The period of isolation in preparation for adult roles tends to benefit adolescents and young adults with resource-rich institutions and families. In resource-poor educational institutions, isolation harms young people's chances to become successful adults. Adolescents in disadvantaged families can find few "time outs" for secondary and higher education, away from adult roles of work and caregiving. Poverty leaves them with few difficult options when making the multiple transitions required in a short span of years: fertility, school leaving, employment, migration, and marriage/cohabitation.

During these transitions, young people navigate between available resources and their own interests. They make decisions independently of the family, with the goal of avoiding risky behavior and embracing behavior that signals successful adulthood, such as timely completion of education and succinct movement into the labor force. However, the majority of young men and women follow transition patterns that are disorderly and influenced by many social factors (Rindfuss, 1991). Transitions of adolescents in poor families are shaped, for example, by the timing of the onset of poverty within their family.

For example, Elder (1999) found that pre-school age children who were impoverished during the Great Depression coped with long-term cumulative disadvantages during the transition to adulthood, whereas those who were impoverished in adolescence proved to be more resilient from their losses. Other historical and social changes may promote prominent effects during adolescence. Under welfare reform, for example, adolescents are more susceptible to school leaving and are more likely to work long hours to recoup lost income when their mothers enter the labor market (Gennetian et al., 2002).

Emerging adulthood is a period in which young women and men establish identities and move into the larger social world with a second family of peers. Young adults may struggle with leaving and returning the family household repeatedly (Goldscheider, 1999). They develop divergent views of family life and success (Larson & Richards, 1994). In recently-immigrated or poor families, young adults may become acculturated to social expectations in middle-class American society and remain distrustful of advice on "how to make it" from adults who resist social institutions (Purkayastha, 2002). Aside from promoting a period of isolation, social institutions may also send confusing messages about who is responsible for decision-making. Recent state laws hold parents responsible for teens' decisions to commit crimes or skip school. Welfare reform in particular has shaped parent/child relations in poor households. Six states (Delaware, New Jersey, Ohio, West Virginia, Wisconsin, and Wyoming) have explicitly regulated that adolescent parents under the age of 21 must live with their parents in order to receive public assistance, with sixteen other states enacting non-explicit rules with the same effect. Options for higher education for adolescents, in place of mandatory work requirements, have been slow to develop from many state welfare plans.

Although other countries, such as Germany and Japan, have invested in public systems to ease all adolescents through the school to work transition with vocational training and apprenticeship programs, social institutions in the United States primarily rely on parents to socialize their children to work (Rosenbaum, 2001). Institutional support is aimed at poor adolescents only indirectly, during childhood (through Head Start and Women, Infants and Children Special Supplemental Nutrition (WIC) programs, for example), or through "making work pay" (with the benefits of policies such as the Earned Income Tax Credit trickling down to young people in poor families). Resource gaps between rich and poor school systems, the lack of supportive physical infrastructure in poor communities, and under-developed vocational programs lead many young adults to aspire to college and good jobs, only to find barriers to their success (Newman, 1999). With the increasing need for advanced educational degrees for good jobs, social institutions may push young adults to delay significant life transitions until the third decade of life. As the authors of an edited volume (Edelman & Ladner, 1991) suggested a decade ago, adolescence and poverty were key issues for the coming century (see Key Resource section for examples of books dealing with this and other significant adolescent issues).

Adulthood and Marriage

In this section we focus on marriage, which offers another opportunity to examine curriculum concepts related to the intersection of societies and the lives of individuals. In particular, we can illustrate the reciprocal influence of institutions, and family structures and functions.

Rules, customs, and expectations about marriage are one of the most pervasive ways that societies influence adults — well over 90% of whom eventually marry (Kain, 1990; U.S. Bureau of the Census, 1999). Planning to marry is one of the most personal and private decisions individuals make, but when they actually marry, they enter a very public legal, religious and social institution. Laws in most states, for example, restrict who may marry based on sex, age, and family status (i.e., not legally married to someone else; not related too closely by blood), and in some states, health. States require candidates for marriage to be licensed and often to wait for a period of time between obtaining the license and marrying. Once married, individuals enter a new legal status with many implications. Consider the following vignette:

> *Amanda married in her twenties and gave birth to a daughter. After 15 years of marriage, Amanda and her husband divorced. Eventually Amanda met and fell in love with Chris. After their wedding, they lived together with Amanda's daughter. They bought a house and enjoyed social activities with a large network of shared friends. After several years, Amanda and Chris decided to have a child of their own. A healthy baby boy was born. The demands of the new baby put quite a bit of strain on the household, however, and Amanda and Chris's relationship began to suffer. Despite Amanda's efforts, Chris decided to end their relationship and move away, taking the baby. Chris won't let Amanda see the child. Amanda is again without a partner and has no access to her child. Her daughter is devastated to be denied any contact with her brother. Amanda may lose the house because Chris is no longer contributing to the expenses of the mortgage. Amanda recently learned that Chris concealed a considerable amount of wealth during their relationship.*

In this vignette, if Chris was short for "Christopher," he and Amanda could be legally married. Amanda and her daughter could receive health insurance coverage through Chris's employer. If Chris were to die, probate laws would ensure that Amanda received a large share of the estate. Divorce laws would ensure that Amanda received consideration in the division of marital property and visitation with her son. If Chris was short for "Christine," however, Amanda would have no legal guarantee of access to any of these resources in most states. She and Chris would not be legally permitted to marry. Amanda and her daughter could not be covered under Chris's health care coverage at work. Laws governing the disposition of assets after death or divorce would not apply to Amanda. Amanda would have no legal relationship to Chris's biological child (Wilcox & Allen, 2000). Currently, Massachusetts permits same-sex partners to marry, six additional states grant the full equivalent of spousal rights to same-sex partners, and four states grant partial equivalent of spousal rights to same-sex partners (Human Rights Campaign, 2008).

For many people who marry, it is much more than just a legal act. Marriage has a long history as a religious tradition, with a visible role in texts such as the Bible, the Koran, and the Talmud, for example. One recent example of an intersection of legal and religious institutions around the issue of marriage is the creation of "covenant marriage," which is currently codified in the laws of Arkansas, Louisiana, and Arizona. When entering into a covenant marriage, the partners agree to limit the grounds on which they can divorce to adultery, abuse, or a felony with jail time and may promise solutions to marital problems through counseling, not the courts (Chapman, 2003). A "Covenant Marriage Movement" has now joined these state legislatures; it is made up of associations, organizations, and educational groups, most of which have religious affiliations or are themselves denominations or churches (Covenant Marriage Movement, 2008).

Marriage plays a large role in family structures and functions. According to the glossary for the 2000 Census, a family is "a group of two or more people who reside together and who are related by birth, marriage, or adoption" (U.S. Bureau of the Census, n.d.). Using this definition, Amanda, Christine, and their children would not be considered a family. They are not alone. There are many groups of individuals who consider themselves families but are not defined as such by others. In particular, it is not unusual for members of minority cultures to live in diverse arrangements including members of multiple generations and/or multiple branches of an extended family (see Key Resource section books dealing with these issues). Although these arrangements may not fit technical definitions of family and sometimes preclude access to financial and other resources, they may be examples of healthy flexibility in role arrangements that enable families to surmount challenges (McAdoo, 1993). In addition, there is great variation in how families are defined around the world and even across institutions within individual countries.

Late Adulthood and the Effects of Changing Age Structures on Families

The traditional age structure of most societies is pyramid-shaped, with few older adults and many children at the top and bottom of the pyramid, respectively. Recent demographic changes, including declines in both mortality and fertility, have dramatically reshaped family life. The family pyramid has stretched and thinned out into a "bean pole", with fewer children in each generation and more shared years between parents, children, and grandchildren (Bengtson, Rosenthal, & Burton, 1990). In this way, aging shapes entire families and societies, not just individuals.

One family member's transitions cause ripples that affect other family members' lives. For older men and women, the transition to grandparenthood depends upon when their adult children have children. The passage of adult children in and out of marriage, and the stepfamilies that result, places older adults in a complex network of blended families. Illnesses of elderly parents require "sandwich generation" adults, mostly women, to maintain both employment and caregiving duties, more substantially than adult women in previous decades (Moen, Robison, & Fields, 1994). Social institutions are often unable to "catch up" with the demands of changing family structures. For example, the United States, unlike countries like Norway, has not developed a policy to allow adult women to accumulate pension benefits while they are on leave caring for family members. The U.S. has, however, expanded the Medicare health insurance program for seniors to cover prescription drugs, which has reduced the number of elderly individuals to fail to take some or all of their prescribed medications (Neuman et al., 2007).

As family structures change, social expectations for late adulthood are sometimes unclear. Older adults may seek new ways to integrate themselves into schools, jobs, and families. Grandparents may get much more involved in caregiving than was the case in past decades. Family members spend more years as mothers, daughters, and granddaughters, and this may mean that intergenerational relationships will grow stronger, more diverse, and more important than nuclear family bonds in contemporary American society (Bengtson, 2001).

Few policies exist, however, to promote social integration of older adults into volunteer, paid work, or even religious roles. In the past, for example, specific laws set the age of 65 as mandatory retirement from the workforce. Social policies, in this way, standardized the life course of working families. With improvements in the health of older Americans, and the need for financial resources well into old age, retirement has become more flexible. Workers often maintain part-time jobs to supplement Social Security income in their later years. Some innovative intergenerational programs, such as Generations of Hope in Illinois, offer models for tapping into the expertise of older adults as they provide guidance and support to young boys and girls in disadvantaged families and foster care.

How are social institutions to provide resources to reshaped families? Popular debates in the media pit children against older adults in a scramble for public support. Less visible is the gap in health and financial support between older African

Americans and European Americans. This chapter suggests that we should acknowledge how the well-being of family members of different ages affects the well-being of other family members. Social institutions may promote more flexibility in life decisions by taking a family focus and recognizing, and supporting, interdependence among family members.

Educators can focus program participants on the topics of changing family structure and social institutions by asking them to think about the notion of "shared years" and "sandwich generation." What are the implications for being a parent and a child for twenty years? How have social institutions, like churches, the labor force, schools, or the military, responded to this common family situation? Are institutions "flexible" to allow adults to care for two other generations, or if not, how can they be more flexible? (see Related Websites for more information on later adulthood families).

Tips for Family Life Educators

When thinking about social institutions and families across the life span, it is important for educators to keep three points in mind: life experiences redefine opportunities in social institutions; lives and social institutions are moving targets; and systems interact with each other, with families, and with individuals in important ways.

Life experiences redefine opportunities in social institutions.
Coping with poverty as a young child will undoubtedly impact an adolescent's ability to become a successfully educated and employed adult. Also, the ability of grandparents to caregive for younger generations will shape the ability for parents to obtain and maintain good jobs. In this way, families shape society, just as society shapes families.

Lives and social institutions are moving targets.
The same public school system will not offer an identical educational experience to two siblings or to a parent and a child. An undereducated adolescent may fail to find a secure job, but after a college degree or an economic upturn, opportunities may open up. After a long illness or the loss of a spouse, an older adult can take on a new role and find purpose in life. Change is constant, regardless of the stage of life, and we cannot assume that a relationship between an individual and an institution – an adult and the work force, for example – cannot change over time.

Systems interact with each other, with families, and with individuals in important ways.
With dynamic family life and changing social institutions, our focus should be on how systems fit with each other. If a family experiences setbacks, we need to examine both the family itself, and the demands and supports that emerge from family interaction with social systems. We also need to promote the flexibility of social institutions that are discordant with the needs of contemporary, dynamic family life.

References

Arnett, J. (2004). *Emerging adulthood: The winding road from the late teens through the twenties.* New York: Oxford University Press.

Bengston, V. (2001). Beyond the nuclear family: The increasing importance of multigenerational bonds. *Journal of Marriage and Family, 63*, 1-16.

Bengston, V., & Allen, K. (1993). The life course perspective applied to families over time. In P. Boss, W. Doherty, R. LaRossa, W. Schumm & S. Steinmetz (Eds.), *Sourcebook of family theories and methods: A contextual approach* (pp. 469-498). New York: Plenum Press.

Bengston, V., Rosenthal, C., & Burton, L. (1990). Families and aging: Diversity and heterogeneity. In R. Binstock & L. George (Eds.), *Handbook on aging and the social sciences* (3rd ed.) (pp. 263-287). New York: Academic Press.

Bianchi, S. (2000). Maternal employment and time with children: Dramatic change or surprising continuity? *Demography, 37*, 401-414.

Bianchi, S., Robinson, J., & Milkie, M. (2006). *Changing rhythms of American family life.* New York: Russell Sage.

Bronfenbrenner, U. (1988). Interacting systems in human development. Research paradigms present and future. In N. Bolger, A. Caspi, G. Downey & M. Moorehouse (Eds.), *Persons in context: Developmental processes* (pp. 25-49). Cambridge, UK: Cambridge University Press.

Brooks-Gunn, J., Han, W., & Waldfogel, J. (2002). Maternal employment and child cognitive outcomes in the first three years of life: The NICHD study of early child care. *Child Development, 73*, 1052-1072.

Campbell, A., & Koblenz, M. (1997). *The work and life pyramid of needs.* Evanston and Deerfield, IL: Baxter Healthcare Corporation and MK Consulting.

Chase-Lansdale, L., Moffitt, R., Lohman, B., Cherlin, A., Coley, R.L., Pittman, L., Roff, J., et al. (2003). Mothers' transitions from welfare to work and the well-being of preschoolers and adolescents. *Science, 299*(5612), 1548-1552.

Chapman, G. (2003). *Covenant marriage: Building communication and intimacy*. Nashville, TN: Broadman & Holman Publishers.

Covenant Marriage Movement. (2008). Retrieved February 28, 2008 from http://www.covenantmarriage.com/

Crouter, A. C. (2002, May). *Parents' knowledge of children's daily activities in dual-earner families*. Paper presented at the first annual Work-family Journalism Conference, Boston, MA.

DeVault, M. L. (1994). Constructing the family. In G. Handel & G. Whitchurch (Eds.), *The psychosocial interior of the family* (4th ed.) (pp. 299-312). Hawthorne, NY: Aldine de Gruyter.

Edelman, P., & Ladner, J. (1991). *Adolescence and poverty: Challenge for the 1990s*. Washington, DC: Center for National Policy Press.

Elder, G. H., Jr. (1999). *Children of the great depression: Social change in life experience* (25th anniversary edition). Boulder, CO: Westview Press.

Furstenberg, F. (2000). The sociology of adolescence and youth in the 1990s: A critical commentary. *Journal of Marriage and the Family, 62*(4), 896-910.

Galinsky, E., Bond, J. T., & Friedman, D. E. (1993). *Highlights of the national study of the changing workforce*. New York: Families and Work Institute.

Gennetian, L., Duncan, G., Knox, V., Vargas, W., Clark-Kaufman, E., & London, A. (2002). *How welfare and work policies for parents affect adolescents: A synthesis of research*. New York, NY: Manpower Demonstration Research Corporation.

Goldscheider, F. (1999). *The changing transition to adulthood: Leaving and returning home*. Thousand Oaks, CA: Sage.

Goode, W. J. (1982). *The family*. Englewood Cliffs, NJ: Prentice-Hall.

Griswold, R. (1993). *Fatherhood in America: A history*. New York: Basic Books.

Hagestad, G., & Neugarten, B. (1985). Age and the life course. In E. Shanas & R. Binstock (Eds.), *Handbook of aging and the social sciences* (2nd ed.) (pp. 35-61). New York: Springer Press.

Human Rights Campaign. (2008). Human rights campaign: Relationship recognition in the U.S. Retrieved February 1, 2008, from http://www.hrc.org/documents/Relationship_Recognition_Laws_Map.pdf

Kain, E. S. (1990). *The myth of family decline: Understanding families in a world of rapid social change*. Lexington, MA: D.C. Heath and Co.

Larson, R., & Richards, M. (1994). *Divergent realities: The emotional lives of mothers, fathers and adolescents*. New York: Basic Books.

Macrosystem. (n.d.). In Merriam-Webster's online dictionary. Retrieved October 19, 2002, from www.merriam-webster.com/

McAdoo, H. P. (Ed.). (1993). *Family ethnicity: Strength in diversity*. Thousand Oaks, CA: Sage Publications.

Mills, C.W. (1959). *The sociological imagination*. New York: Oxford.

Moen, P., Robison, J., & Fields, V. (1994). Women's work and caregiving roles: A life course approach. *Journals of Gerontology Series B: Psychological Sciences and Social Sciences, 49*, 176-186.

Newman, K. (1999). *No shame in my game: The working poor in the inner city*. New York: Vintage/Russell Sage Foundation.

Neuman, P., Strollo, M. K., Guterman, W., Rogers, W. H., Li, A., Rodday, A. M. C., et al. (2007). Medicare prescription drug benefit progress report: Findings from a 2006 national survey of seniors. *Health Affairs, 5*. Retrieved August 21, 2007, from http:/ /content.healthaffairs.org/cgi/reprint/hlthaff.26.5.w630v1?ijkey=wpOorB7zwSX6c&keytype=ref&siteid=healthaff

Parcel, T. L., & Menaghan, E. G. (1994). *Parents' jobs and children's lives*. New York: Aldine de Gruyter.

Purkayastha, B. (2002). Rules, roles and realities: Indo-American families in the United States. In R. Taylor (Ed.), *Minority families in the United States: A multicultural perspective* (3rd ed.), (pp. 212-224). Upper Saddle River, NJ: Prentice Hall.

Riley, M. W., & Riley, J. W., Jr. (1994). Structural lag: Past and future. In M. W. Riley, R. L. Kahn & A. Foner (Eds.), *Age and structural lag: Society's failure to provide meaningful opportunities in work, family, and leisure*. New York: John Wiley & Sons.

Rindfuss, R. (1991). The young adult years: Diversity, structural change, and fertility. *Demography 28*(4), 493-512.

Rosenbaum, J. (2001). *Beyond college for all: Career paths for the forgotten half*. New York, NY: Russell Sage Foundation.

Rubin, R. M., & Riney, B. J. (1994). *Working wives and dual-earner families*. Westport, CT: Praeger.

Society. (n.d.). In Merriam-Webster's online dictionary. Retrieved October 19, 2002, from http://www.merriam-webster.com/

U.S. Bureau of the Census (n.d.). *Glossary to the 2000 census.* Retrieved October 19, 2002, from http://www.census.gov/main/www/cen2000.html

U.S. Bureau of the Census. (2001). *Statistical abstract of the United States* (121st ed.). Washington, DC: U.S. Government Printing Office.

U.S. Bureau of the Census. (1999). *Statistical abstract of the United States* (119th ed.). Washington, DC: U.S. Government Printing Office.

U.S. Bureau of the Census. (1993). *Statistical abstract of the United States* (113th ed.). Washington, DC: U.S. Government Printing Office.

U.S. Bureau of the Census. (1975). *Historical statistics of the United States, colonial times to 1970,* (Bicentennial ed., Part 2). Washington, DC: U.S. Government Printing Office.

Wilcox, K. L., & Allen, K. R. (2000). Families and the gay community: Stressors and strengths. In P. C. McKenry & S. J. Price (Eds), *Families and change: Coping with stressful events and transitions* (pp. 378-400). Thousand Oaks, CA: Sage.

Key Resources

Allison, D. (1993). *Bastard out of Carolina.* New York: Penguin.

Bengtson, V. L., Acock, A. C., Allen, K. R., Dilworth-Anderson, P., & Klein, D. M. (2006).

Sourcebook of family theory and research. Thousand Oaks, CA: Sage.

Brooks, D. (2007, October 9). The odyssey years. *The New York Times.* Retrieved from http://www.nytimes.com

Coleman, M., & Ganong, L. (2003). *Points & counterpoints: Controversial relationship and family issues in the 21st century.* Los Angeles, CA: Roxbury.

Coles, R., Testa, R., & Coles, M. (2001). *Growing up poor: A literary anthology.* New York: New Press.

Jones, L., & Newman, L. (1997a). *Our America: Life and death on the south side of Chicago.* New York, NY: Washington Square Press.

Jones, L., & Newman, L. (1997b). *Ghetto life 101 and remorse.* Audio CD. Chicago, IL: Sound Portraits Productions.

Kleiner, H. S., Hertzog, J., & Targ, D. B. (1998). Grandparents acting as parents: Background information for educators. In G. R. Williams, V. L. Murphy, C. Sheriff, J. Millspaugh & C. Mertensmeyer (Eds.), *Grandparents raising grandchildren: A resource guide for professionals* (pp.35-44). Columbia, MO: ParentLink.

Study Guide for Bastard Out of Carolina. (2002). Novels for students series. Foster City, CA: Gale Group.

Targ, D. B., Brintnall-Peterson, M., & Hollidge, M. (2001). *Grandparents raising grandchildren educational program* (Notebook and Video). Washington, D.C.: AARP.

White, J. M. & Klein, D. M. (2007). *Family theories* (3rd ed.). Thousand Oaks, CA: Sage.

Related Websites

Active Living Coalition for Older Adults: www.alcoa.ca/e/index.htm

Adolescence Change and Continuity: www.oberlin.edu/faculty/ndarling/adolesce.htm

Alternatives to Marriage Project: www.unmarried.org/

Americans for Divorce Reform: www.divorcereform.org/cov.html

Boston College Sloan Work and Family Research Network: wfnetwork.bc.edu/index.php

Catalyst: www.catalystwomen.org/

Center for Adolescent and Family Studies (Indiana University): site.educ.indiana.edu/cafs/

Child and Family Canada: www.cfc-efc.ca/

Children's Defense Fund: www.childrensdefense.org/

Department of Labor Women's Bureau: www.dol.gov/wb/

Economic Success Clearinghouse: www.financeproject.org/index.cfm?page=24

Families and Work Institute: www.familiesandwork.org/

Generations of Hope: www.generationsofhope.org/

National Association for the Education of Young Children: www.naeyc.org/

Network on Transitions to Adulthood: www.transad.pop.upenn.edu

ParentLink: www.parentlink.net/

Senior Net: www.seniornet.org/

Smart Marriages: www.smartmarriages.com/

United Nations Population Fund, Supporting the Next Generation: www.unfpa.org/adolescents/index.htm

U.S. Administration on Aging Elder Page: www.aoa.gov/eldfam/eldfam.asp

About the Authors

Kevin M. Roy, Ph.D., is Associate Professor of Family Science at the University of Maryland, College Park School of Public Health. His research examines the intersection of social policy and lives, particularly the life course of men and young adults on the margins of family life and employment. E-mail: kroy@umd.edu.

Shelley M. MacDermid, Ph.D., CFLE is Professor of Family Studies, Director of the Center for Families, and Co-Director of the Military Family Research Institute at Purdue University, West Lafayette, IN. She served as editor of the Families in Society sections of two previous teaching resources published by the National Council on Family Relations. E-mail: shelley@purdue.edu.

Internal Dynamics of Families

MICHAEL J. WALCHESKI AND
DAVID J. BREDEHOFT

What time is it? A quick glance at your watch indicates that it is 3:30 p.m. The internal dynamics of a family are very much like the inner-workings of your watch. Without much thought we frequently glance at our wristwatch. However, knowing the time of day does not imply we are aware of, or understand the "movements" behind the face. We refer to watch movements as "innards, guts, or works." For many, a casual observation of the family is a lot like looking at our watch for the time, the specific movements are out of sight, but nonetheless present. Similar to the watch, families have internal processes called internal family dynamics. A watchmaker must understand the dynamics of the movements to be successful in working with watches; likewise a family life educator must understand the internal dynamics of families to be effective in working with families.

Connecting the Dots between the Curriculum Guidelines... the Framework for Family Life Education...and Internal Dynamics of Families

Understanding the internal dynamics of families across the life span is essential in the preparation of family life educators. An understanding of the primary tenets of family systems (Gale & Long, 1996) provides a foundation for conceptualizing the internal movements of the family. It informs the process of planning, executing, and evaluating family life education (FLE) programs. Furthermore, helping family members understand specific dynamics is an essential component in assisting families in anticipating the internal processes across the life span. Integrating theory and practice involve two essential tools that assist the family life educator: the *Curriculum Guidelines* (NCFR, 1984) and the *Framework for Family Life Education* (Bredehoft, 1997, 2001). When brought together these two tools provide a context for understanding the internal dynamics of families.

The *Internal Dynamics of Families* section of the *Curriculum Guidelines* (NCFR, 1984) outline the significance of the social processes present in families, specifically those related to cooperation and conflict. These processes emphasize communication patterns and problems in the various sub-systems within the family, specifically around stress and conflict management. Decision-making and goal-setting reflect processes needed during times of normal stress and crisis by responding to family members' particular needs (Allen & Blaisure, 2009).

Objectives for understanding the internal dynamics of families are outlined in the *Framework for Family Life Education* (Bredehoft, 1997, 2001), and are intentionally applied to families across the life span. This Framework draws the family life educator's attention to:

- individual development of family members and their relationships;
- family composition, history, traditions, and celebrations;

CURRICULUM GUIDELINES:
INTERNAL DYNAMICS OF FAMILIES

An understanding of family strengths and weaknesses and how family members relate to each other. Based on knowledge of:

1. internal social processes including cooperation and conflict;
2. communication patterns and problems, in husband-wife relationships and in parent-child relationships, including stress and conflict management;
3. conflict management;
4. decision-making and goal-setting;
5. "normal" stress in families: such as, transition periods in the family life cycle, three-generation households, caring for the elderly, and dual careers;
6. family stress/crises, such as divorce, remarriage, death, economic uncertainty and hardship, violence, substance abuse;
7. families with special needs, including adoptive, foster, migrant, low income, military, and blended families, as well as those with disabled members.

- family change and transitions; different needs and expectations of family members;
- sources of stress and coping with stress;
- family rules and roles;
- lifestyle choices and changes;
- family communication and expression of feelings;
- intergenerational dynamics; and
- families as sources of protection, guidance, affection and support.

Together, the *Curriculum Guidelines* and the *Framework for Family Life Education* strengthens the preparation of family life educators and informs the process of conducting family life education by telegraphing and normalizing what families can anticipate across the life span.

What's Behind the Face?

Contemporary films are a rich resource for exploring the internal dynamics of families (Hesley & Hesley, 2001; Shepard & Brew, 2005; Stinchfield, 2006). Using films such as *Life as a House* (Winkler, 2002), *Proof* (Stern, Weinstein, Weinstein, Goldstein, & Madden, 2006) and *The Joy Luck Club* (Wang, 1993) are a way to bridge theory with practice. Observing family dynamics within a film accomplishes an important objective. The film becomes the common experience to study and discuss family dynamics. First, family life education students can use a film to identify common internal social processes and patterns. Second, family life educators can use film with families to explore their own family dynamics, providing a common ground to discuss shared experiences.

For example, in the movie *Parenthood* (Caracciolo & Howard, 1989) we meet Gil and Karen Buckman who have three children and are expecting their fourth. We see the Buckman family attempting to bring up their children in the context of estranged relatives, the "black sheep" of the family, family secrets, and their work and family pressure. Their story is told in the swirling dynamic of both their extended family and other influencing social systems.

Parenthood illustrates what family life is like for a couple with young children. While challenging, the Buckmans are experiencing the stressors of a predictable stage (Carter & McGoldrick, 2005) in the family life cycle (parents with young children). As the story unfolds, the movie illustrates several internal family dynamics. Karen and Gil have to successfully manage their conflict by communicating, making decisions, and setting goals for themselves and their children after unexpectedly becoming pregnant with their fourth child (for a discussion on decision-making and goal-setting as resource management, see Rettig, 2009).

Why focus on the internal dynamics in families? It provides an explanation for the movements within the family and an appropriate level of involvement by family life educators (Doherty, 1995). We present the internal dynamics of families in light of the preparation of family life educators and the practice of family life education in the next section.

Internal Dynamics of Families on Two Levels

The focus on the internal dynamics in families is important on two levels: (1) the pre-professional family life educator and (2) the practicing family life educator.

The Pre-professional Level

First, for the pre-professional level internal dynamics of families is the conceptual foundation for thinking about families. It provides understanding of internal family dynamics, a lens through which we view the family. This lens has changed and evolved into a clearer picture of the family over the past several decades (Nichols and Schwartz, 2001).

In order to understand the complexity of movement in families, it is essential to have a fundamental understanding of primary theories and processes related to families. The content area of *Internal Dynamics of Families* addresses one of the primary assumptions of FLE, learning about marriage and family patterns and processes (Arcus, Schvaneveldt & Moss, 1993; Powell & Cassidy, 2007). Perhaps more subtle than other content areas in the *Curriculum Guidelines*, understanding the internal dynamics of families is essential to effective practice with families in family life education. An in-depth discussion of theoretical underpinnings is beyond the scope of this work (for additional resources on these and other theoretical underpinnings see "Key Resources" in this chapter). Instead, we selected three theories because of their ability to inform family life educators about the internal dynamics of families: family systems theory, human ecology theory, and family development theory. After we highlight each theory, we will provide an example and direct application for the family life educator.

CHILDHOOD — *Within the context of the family system*

Internal Dynamics of Families

- Family members as individuals
- Individuality and importance of all family members
- Getting along in the family
- Expressing feelings in families
- Personal family history
- Family similarities and differences
- Impact of change on families
- Responsibilities, rights, interdependence of family members
- Family rules
- Families as sources of protection, guidance, affection, support
- Families as possible sources of anger and violence
- Family problems

Multicultural • Gender Fair • Special Needs Aware

Reciprocal interactions between family and ecosystem

ADOLESCENCE — *Within the context of the family system*

Internal Dynamics of Families

- Becoming an adult within the family
- Changes in family composition - births, divorce, deaths
- Managing and expressing feelings in families
- Coping with internal change and stress in the family
- Interaction of friends and family
- Personal and family decision-making
- Communicating in families
- Interaction between family members
- Different needs and expectations of family members
- Responsibilities, rights, interdependence of family members
- Family rules – overt and covert
- Intergenerational relationships
- Influence of family background
- Family history, traditions and celebrations
- Families as sources of protection, guidance, affection, support
- Families as possible sources of anger and violence
- Family differences - membership, economic level, role performance, values

Multicultural • Gender Fair • Special Needs Aware

Reciprocal interactions between family and ecosystem

Family Systems Theory

"Family systems theory views the family as a living organism operating within certain boundaries, rules, expectations, and interaction patterns across many generations" (Powell & Cassidy, 2007, p. 60). When change occurs in any part of the family, the entire family is affected and the family system must address the change (Burr, Day, & Bahr, 1993; Day, Gilbert, Settles, & Burr, 1995). The family system has a significant affect on each family member; concurrently each family member influences the family system, because family members are interconnected and operate as a whole.

Returning to the movie *Parenthood* for an example which highlights family systems, we see Gil, Karen and their three children. At first glance, we just see five people, but that is not the "family system." The family system is the interconnectedness and movements between the five family members. To view the family system then is to take your focus off individual family members and instead view the processes between them (e.g., boundaries, rules, roles, expectations, communication patterns).

Family life educators can take one major lesson from family systems theory: family is a whole. A change in one part of the family system affects all other parts. Attend to the interaction patterns within the family system.

Human Ecology Theory

Human ecology theory emphasizes the idea that families are not isolated systems in society (Powell & Cassidy, 2007). The ecological perspective suggests that families are just one system within a collection of many systems (Olson, DeFrain, & Skogrand, 2008). Families are constantly influencing and being influenced by the systemic movement of other systems (e.g., medical system, work system, school system, government system, and economic system) (Burr et al., 1993; Day et al., 1995).

The following is an example of two systems influencing the Buckman family in the movie *Parenthood*. The fulcrum in this example is around the parenting of Karen and Gil's oldest son Kevin. Kevin is acting-out in school and as a result Gil and Karen are called in to speak with the principal and school psychologist. Afraid of being stigmatized, Gil wants to pull Kevin out of the school. At the same time Gil also is feeling guilty about not spending time with Kevin and in some way feels responsible for his son's struggles in school. Compounding the problem is the pressure from work for Gil to spend 60, 70 even 80 hours a week at work. Gil's and Karen's dilemma is *more time at work - less time with Kevin* or *more time with Kevin - less time at work.*

Family life educators can take one major lesson from human ecology theory: families are part of a much larger whole. The family life educator must not only consider family members' needs, they also have to understand the influences of the ecosystem on their participants.

Family Development/Family Life Cycle Theory

Family development or family life cycle theory articulates the family's movement across the life span in specific stages (Carter & McGoldrick, 2005; Duvall & Miller, 1985; Powell & Cassidy, 2007; Rogers & White, 1993). These models are a

ADULTHOOD — *Within the context of the family system*

Internal Dynamics of Families
- Individual development in the family
- Individual and family roles
- Intimate relationships in the family
- Sources of stress and coping with stress
- Lifestyle choices
- Changing needs and expectations of family members
- Intergenerational dynamics throughout the life span
- Responsibilities, rights, interdependence of family members
- Family transitions - marriage, birth, divorce, remarriage, death
- Family history, traditions, and celebrations
- Factors affecting marital and family relationships
- Giving and receiving affection
- Power and authority in the family
- Effects of family on self-concepts of its members
- Family rules - overt and covert
- Families as sources of protection, guidance, affection, support
- Differences in families - membership, economic level, role performance, values
- Families as possible sources of anger and violence
- Varying influences on family interaction patterns - ethnic, racial, gender, social, cultural

Multicultural • Gender Fair • Special Needs Aware

Reciprocal interactions between family and ecosystem

LATER ADULTHOOD — *Within the context of the family system*

Internal Dynamics of Families
- Individual development in the family
- Individual and family roles
- Changing needs and expectations of family members
- Family transitions - marriage, divorce, remarriage, retirement of mate, death
- Responsibilities, rights, interdependence of family members and productivity
- Intimate relationships in the family
- Effects of family on self-concepts of its members
- Factors affecting marital and family relationships
- Giving and receiving affection
- Changes in power and authority in the family
- Sources of stress and coping with stress, diseases, disabilities
- Family rules - overt and covert
- Families as sources of protection, guidance, affection, support
- Lifestyle choices and changes - retirement planning, retirement
- Family history, traditions, and celebrations
- Intergenerational dynamics throughout the life span
- Varying influences on family interaction patterns - ethnic, racial, gender, social, cultural
- Families as possible sources of anger and violence
- Family differences - membership, economic level, role performance, values

Multicultural • Gender Fair • Special Needs Aware

Reciprocal interactions between family and ecosystem

blueprint for roles and tasks within the family (Olson, DeFrain, & Skogrand, 2008) as they move across the stages of the life cycle. These models view the family as a system of relationships moving through time. They telegraph normal predictable benchmarks for families as they transition from stage to stage. There is a word of caution found in many discussions of developmental approaches to the family. Family life educators should not assume that all families in a particular stage of family development experience or should experience the same patterns or processes (Powell & Cassidy, 2007; Carter & McGoldrick, 2005; Walsh, 2002, 2006).

An example of a family negotiating the roles and tasks of a life cycle stage comes at the end of the movie *Parenthood* when Grandma makes the following insightful comment to Gil who was frustrated with all of the family changes he and Karen were facing.

Grandma: You know, when I was nineteen, Grandpa took me on a rollercoaster.

Gil Buckman: Oh?

Grandma: Up, down, up, down. Oh, what a ride!

Gil Buckman: What a great story.

Grandma: I always wanted to go again. You know, it was just so interesting to me that a ride could make me so frightened, so scared, so sick, so excited, and so thrilled all together!

Grandma's description of riding the rollercoaster is typical of the ups-and-downs families experience as they move through the family life cycle.

Family life educators can take one major lesson from family development theory: families and family members traverse normal predictable stages along life's path. We can plan, anticipate, and educate for the roles and tasks (ups and downs) in these stages.

The Practicing Family Life Educator Level

At a practicing family life educator level, the internal dynamics of families provides specific content for families involved in family life education. The family life educator uses this content to design programs to meet family needs (for a discussion on planning and implementing family life education programs, see Clarke & Bredehoft, 2009). We see families "as agents in their own lives" (MCFR, 2000. p. 3). This content then has the potential to empower families with the knowledge of processes and patterns occurring at normative stages in the family. More specifically, teaching families about internal dynamics may include: communication patterns and problems across family sub-systems; stress and conflict management in couple, or parent-child relationship.

The *Curriculum Guidelines* draws our attention to the presence of normal family stress and crises and the *Framework for Family Life Education* illustrates them as predictable and unpredictable stressors across the family life span.

Predictable Stressors

Normalizing what families can anticipate across the life span is an important role for the practicing family life educator. By normalizing these benchmarks, the family life educator helps reduce family stress. While many stressors can be anticipated, knowing them helps, but does not alleviate their influence, particularly in the transition from one stage to another (Carter & McGoldrick, 2005). Often, predictable stressors are referred to as developmental transitions (McKenry & Price, 2005; Carter & McGoldrick, 2005). Common, predictable, or normative stressors include transition periods in the family life cycle: marriage, birth, parenting, aging, death and dying (McHenry & Price, 2005). Family life educators can work prescriptively to alleviate stress occurring from predictable stressors and empower families to change as agents of their own determination (MCFR, 2000; Morgaine, 1992). For example, the day-to-day parenting issues Karen and Gil struggle with in the movie *Parenthood.*

Unpredictable Stressors

While normative stress in families comes with the transition from one stage to another (Carter & McGoldrick, 2005; Walsh, 2002), unpredictable stress or crisis presents additional challenges to the family. Unpredictable stressors also influence the family across the life span. The unpredictable stressors change or are different from stage to stage. Often, unpredictable family stress or crises include: divorce, remarriage, death, economic uncertainty and hardship, violence, physical illness, mental illness, and substance abuse (McKenry & Price, 2005). For example, Gil and Karen are unexpectedly expecting their fourth child, which has a significant impact on their family's transition and adjustment and represents additional unpredictable stressors.

Family Life Educators Need To:

- understand that each family form has its own unique strengths and challenges when it comes to internal dynamics.
- continually be aware and sensitive to new family forms and their particular internal dynamics.
- appreciate the problems and contexts that accompany different family forms.
- step back from their family of origin and not use it to create a template for how families should be.
- develop a high degree of proficiency in one model of family systems and become very proficient in applying it to families. This will become a baseline for understanding the family dynamics you encounter in the future.
- learn how to access and critically evaluate information.
- walk the walk and talk the talk. Model the skills you teach in your everyday life. We believe as Socrates believed, "The unexamined life is not worth living."

What Makes Grandpa's Watch Work?

One day a long time ago, when I was five years old, I snuck into my parents' bedroom. I was fascinated with watches and I knew my dad kept one of my grandpa Bredehoft's watches in his top dresser drawer.

I remember this incident quite vividly because I wasn't supposed to be in mom's and dad's bedroom! Nevertheless, something drew me to grandpa's watch. Maybe it was because I had seen dad take it out and lovingly admire it. Or maybe it was because it was so gold, shiny, and pretty. As I was playing with this forbidden fruit, I became curious, curious about what made grandpa's watch work. So I pried off the back to get a look inside. All of the wheels and cogs of grandpa's watch moving in perfect harmony mesmerized me. Seeing the movements behind the face brought me closer to answering the question, "What makes grandpa's watch work?"

The question, "What makes watches work?" is very much like the question, "What makes families work?" As a watchmaker understands the dynamic movements of a watch so too a family life educator must understand the internal dynamics of families.

References

Allen, W., & Blaisure, K. R. (2009). Family life educators and the development of cultural competency. In D. J. Bredehoft & M. J. Walcheski (Eds.), *Family life education: Integrating theory and practice* (pp. 209-219). Minneapolis, MN: National Council on Family Relations.

Arcus, M. E., Schvaneveldt, J. D., & Moss, J.J. (1993). The nature of family life education. In M. E. Arcus, J. D. Schvaneveldt & J. J. Moss (Eds.), *Handbook of family life education: Vol. 1.* (pp. 1-25). Newbury Park: Sage.

Bredehoft, D. J. (Ed.). (1997). *The framework for life span family life education* (2nd ed.) [Poster]. Minneapolis: National Council on Family Relations.

Bredehoft, D. J. (2001). The framework for life span family life education revised and revisited. *The Family Journal*, *9*(2), 134-139.

Burr, W. R., Day, R. D., & Bahr, K. S. (1993). *Family science*. Pacific Grove, CA: Brooks/Cole.

Caracciolo, J. M. (Producer), & Howard, R. (Director). (1989). *Parenthood* [Motion picture]. United States: Universal Pictures.

Carter, B., & McGoldrick, M. (2005). *The expanded family life cycle: Individual, family, and social perspectives* (3rd ed.). Boston: Allyn and Bacon.

Clarke, J. I., & Bredehoft, D. J. (2009). Family life education methodology. In D. J. Bredehoft & M. J. Walcheski (Eds.), *Family life education: Integrating theory and practice* (2nd ed.) (pp. 199-206). Minneapolis, MN: National Council on Family Relations.

Day, R. D., Gilbert, K. R., Settles, B. H., & Burr, W. R. (1995). *Research and theory in family science.* Pacific Grove, CA: Brooks/Cole.

Doherty, W. J. (1995). Boundaries between parent and family education and family therapy. *Family Relations*, *44*, 353-358.

Duvall, E. M., & Miller, B. C. (1985). *Marriage and family development* (6th ed.). New York: Harper & Row.

Gale, J. E., & Long, J. K. (1996). Theoretical foundations of family therapy. In F. P. Piercy, D. H. Sprenkle, J. L. Wetchler, and Associates (Eds.), *Family therapy sourcebook* (2nd ed.) (pp. 1-24). New York: Guilford.

Hesley, J. W., & Hesley, J. G. (2001). *Rent two films and let's talk in the morning: Using popular movies in psychotherapy* (2nd ed.). New York: John Wiley & Sons.

Minnesota Council on Family Relations. (2000). Ethical thinking in practice for parent and family educators. Minneapolis, MN: Author.

McKenry, P. C., & Price, S. J. (2005). *Families & change: Coping with stressful events and transitions* (2nd ed.). Thousand Oaks: Sage Publications.

Morgaine, C. A. (1992). Alternative paradigms for helping families change themselves. *Family Relations*, *41,* 12-17.

National Council on Family Relations. (1984). *Standards and criteria for certification of family life educators, college/university curriculum guidelines, and content guidelines for family life education: A framework for planning programs over the life span.* Minneapolis: Author.

Nichols, M.P., & and Schwartz, R. C. (2001). *Family therapy: Concepts and methods* (5th ed.). Boston: Allyn & Bacon

Olson, D. H., DeFrain, J., Skogrand, L. (2008). *Marriage and the family: Diversity and strengths* (6th ed.). Boston: McGraw Hill.

Powell, L. H., & Cassidy, D. (2007). *Family life education: Working with families across the life span* (2nd ed.). Long Grove: IL: Waveland Press, Inc.

Rettig, K. D. (2009). Family resource management. In D. J. Bredehoft & M. J. Walcheski (Eds.), *Family life education: Integrating theory and practice* (2nd ed.) (pp. 163-172). Minneapolis, MN: National Council on Family Relations.

Rogers, R. H., & White, J. M. (1993). Family development theory. In P. G. Boss, W. J. Doherty, R. LaRossa, W. R. Schumm & S. K. Steinmetz (Eds.), *Sourcebook of family theories and methods* (pp. 99-116). New York: Plenum.

Stern, J. D. (Executive Producer), Weinstein, B. (Executive Producer), Weinstein, H. (Executive Producer), Goldstein, J. (Executive Producer), & Madden, J. (Director). (2006). *Proof* [Motion picture]. United States: Hart-Sharp Entertainment.

Shepard, D. S., & Brew, L. (2005). Teaching theories of couples counseling: The use of popular movies. *The Family Journal*, *13*(4), 406 - 415.

Stinchfield, T. A. (2006). Using popular films to teach systems thinking. *The Family Journal*, *14*(2), 123-128.

Walsh, F. (2002). Conceptualization of normal family processes. In F. Walsh (Ed.), *Normal family processes* (2nd ed.) (pp. 3-69) New York: The Guilford Press.

Walsh, F. (2006). *Strengthening family resilience* (2nd ed.). New York: The Guilford Press.

Wang, W. (Director). (1993). *The joy luck club* [Motion picture]. United States: Hollywood Pictures.

Winkler, I. (Director/Producer). (2002). *Life as a house* [Motion picture]. United States: Winkler Films.

Key Resources

Carter, B., & McGoldrick, M. (2005). *The expanded family life cycle: Individual, family, and social perspectives* (3rd ed.). Boston: Allyn and Bacon.

Fanning, P., & Mckay, M. (Eds.). (2000). *Family guide to emotional wellness: Proven self-help techniques and exercises for dealing with common problems and building crucial life skills*. Oakland, CA: New Harbinger Publishers.

Hawkins, A. J., Carroll, J. S., Doherty, W. J., & Willoughby, B. (2009). A comprehensive framework for marriage education. In D. J. Bredehoft & M. J. Walcheski (Eds.), *Family life education: Integrating theory and practice* (2nd ed.) (pp. 43-58). Minneapolis, MN: National Council on Family Relations.

Hesley, J. W., & Hesley, J. G. (2001). *Rent two films and let's talk in the morning: Using popular movies in psychotherapy* (2nd ed.). New York: John Wiley & Sons.

Larson, J. H. (2009). Innovations in marriage education: Current status and challenges for the future. In D. J. Bredehoft & M. J. Walcheski (Eds.), *Family life education: Integrating theory and practice* (2nd ed.) (pp. 59-64). Minneapolis, MN: National Council on Family Relations.

Markman, H. J., Stanley, S. M., & Blumberg, S. L. (2001). *Fighting for your marriage: Positive steps for preventing divorce and preserving a lasting love* (revised ed.). San Francisco, CA: Jossey-Bass.

Morris, V., & Butler, R. (1996). *How to care for aging parents*. New York: Workman Publishing Company.

Neuman, G. M., & Romanowski, R. (1999). *Helping your kids cope with divorce the sandcastles way*. New York: Random House.

Olson, D. H., & Olson, A. K. (2000). *Empowering couples: Building on your strengths* (2nd ed.). Minneapolis, MN: Life Innovations, Inc.

Stinnett, N., Stinnett, N., DeFrain, J., & DeFrain, N. (1999). *Creating a strong family*. West Monroe, LA: Howard.

Visher, E. B., & Visher, J. S. (1991). *How to win as a stepfamily*. New York: Brunner/Mazel Trade.

Related Websites

Answers 4 Families: www.answers4families.org

American Association of Marriage and Family Therapy: www.aamft.org

Children, Youth and Family Consortium: www.cyfc.umn.edu

Divorce Support: www.divorcesupport.com

Families Illustrated: www.familiesillustrated.org

Head Start: www2.acf.dhhs.gov/programs/hsb

Internet Movie Data Base: www.us.imdb.com

Life Innovations, Inc.: www.lifeinnovations.com

National Council on Family Relations: www.ncfr.org

Parent Soup: www.parentsoup.com/teens

Parent's Toolshop Consulting, Ltd.: www.parentstoolshop.com

Practical Parenting Partnerships: www.pppctr.org

Special Needs Network: www.mfrc.calib.com/snn

About the Authors

Michael J. Walcheski, Ph.D., CFLE is Professor of Psychology and Family Studies and Chair, Department of Graduate Studies in the College of Education at Concordia University, St. Paul, MN. He is co-editor of *Family Life Education: Integrating Theory and Practice*. E-mail: Walcheski@csp.edu.

David J. Bredehoft, Ph.D., CFLE is Professor of Psychology and Family Studies and Chair, Department of Social and Behavioral Sciences at Concordia University, St. Paul, MN. He is the editor of *The Framework for Life Span Family Life Education (2nd ed.)*, coeditor of *Family Life Education: Integrating Theory and Practice*, and coauthor of *How much is enough? Everything you need to know to steer clear of overindulgence and raise likeable, responsible, and respectful children*. E-mail: bredehoft@csp.edu.

Human Growth and Development across the Life Span

David J. Bredehoft,
Deborah Eckhoff and
Carole Gesme

The required theoretical and practical understandings for family life educators (FLEs) are continually expanding. Among these is the knowledge of human growth and development. Human development is the scientific study of *human change over time* (Papalia & Olds, 1996). This course of study "seeks to understand how and why people–all kinds of people–change and how they stay the same as they grow older" (Berger, 2003, p. 1). Because they work with family members of all ages, family life educators need to have a thorough understanding of the stages of human development across the life span (childhood, adolescence, adulthood, and later adulthood). Effective family life educators need to fully grasp the basic tenet of development: *people change and grow as long as they live*.

Consider the following three stories:

A father arrives at the child care center to pick up his two-year-old daughter. The director asks to speak with him. He is informed that his daughter has bitten a little boy. Dad is too shocked to reply. The director hands him the incident report and they quickly leave. Once home, Dad relates the story to Mom who listens in disbelief. They begin to discuss what could have happened to cause their sweet daughter to react this way. The parents sign up for a workshop called Toddler Trouble offered through a community center. The distressed parents tell their story at the fist session. The family life educator appears unalarmed. When they question his reaction, he shares that this is fairly normal for a two-year-old. This type of behavior would be viewed very differently if she were a nine-year-old.

The parents of a twelve-year-old daughter seem uncomfortable as they sit in the crowded, parent-filled school's gym. The school sent a brochure home encouraging parents to attend an informal discussion group about teenagers. The facilitator asks parents to get into small groups and discuss what teenage behaviors are frustrating to them. The parents learn about and share the group's concern about their daughters' chasing boys. They confess they are embarrassed by such behavior, and are worried about it leading to promiscuity. The couple is relieved to know that other parents of twelve-year-olds are having similar concerns. The information the family life educator provides is comforting to them.

An elderly couple seems out of place as they wander around looking at the art work displayed by students in the fourth grade. They have been invited to this open house by their grandson who lives with them full-time. In the past year, there have been serious changes. Their son and daughter-in-law were killed in a car accident, and accepting their death has

CURRICULUM GUIDELINES: HUMAN GROWTH & DEVELOPMENT ACROSS THE LIFE SPAN

An understanding of the developmental changes of individuals in families throughout the life span (including prenatal, infancy, early and middle childhood, adolescence, adult, and aging) to meet their changing needs. Based on knowledge of:

1. physical;
2. emotional;
3. cognitive;
4. social;
5. moral; and
6. personality.

been hard for all three of them, and having their grandson live with them means raising another child. They have far less energy than they used to, and they were just starting to look into the possibility of retirement. They are thankful for the parent educator who has been leading this support group that focuses on grief and loss.

These stories illustrate the need for family life educators to be firmly grounded in the science of human growth and development. Knowing *what is* and *what is not* within normative development is crucial in interpreting the developmental journey of life.

The Developmental Journey of Life

Human development can be thought of as a journey. The journey begins at conception with a genetic roadmap to guide the way. As this journey continues through predictable stages of birth, infancy, childhood, adolescence, adulthood and later adulthood , each traveler is uniquely shaped by the environments in which she or he navigates. How does the science of human growth and development support family life education? What do family life educators need to know of if they are going to assist families traveling along the developmental life journey?

Development Basics for Family Life Educators

A firm understanding of human development is necessary!

To be effective, an FLE has to have a firm understanding of the human growth and development process. Developmental theory advocates that every human develops in a predictable way over time (e.g., childhood, adolescence, adulthood, and later adulthood). When we combine the human growth and development section of the *Curriculum Guidelines* (National Council on Family Relations, 1984) and the *Framework for Family Life Education* (Bredehoft, 1997, 2001) it provides family life educators with a basic primer on physical, emotional, cognitive, social, moral, and personality development patterns. Specific developmental theories will be referred to in this article however; an in-depth discussion outlining specific developmental theories (e.g., Erikson, 1950, 1994, 1998; Freud, 1938; Levinson, 1978, 1997; Loevinger, 1976; Kohlberg, 1975, 1981; Piaget, 2000, and Whitbourne, 1986) is beyond the scope of this work. For resources on specific developmental theories, see "Key Resources and Related Websites" in this chapter.

What to expect along the journey

Family life educators equipped with developmental background can provide families with a roadmap for *what* to expect, called "developmental milestones." Developmental milestones are normal human life patterns (e.g., body and brain). Examples of the physical milestones for a four-month-old child are:

- weight: 10-18 pounds
- length: 23-27 inches
- sleeps about 6 hours before waking during the night
- averages 14-17 hours of sleep daily
- lifts head and chest when lying on stomach
- holds both eyes in a fixed position
- follows a moving object or person with eyes
- grasps rattle or finger
- wiggles and kicks with arms and legs
- rolls over (stomach to back)
- sits with support (Oesterreich, 1995, ¶ 3)

Most of the developmental theories have not changed significantly in the last decade. However, the knowledge base in one developmental area has changed radically in the last decade: physical development – brain research to be specific (Kotulak, 1997). This has created a developmental knowledge gap for many family life educators. Thanks to new technologies and research, scientists have made new discoveries in brain development:

- brain development before the age of one is more rapid and extensive than previously realized

- brain development is much more vulnerable than has ever been suspected
- the influence of early environment on brain development is long-lasting
- the environment affects not only the number of brain cells and connections among them, but the way in which these connections are "wired" as well
- scientific evidence shows a negative impact from early stress on brain function
- the brain goes through crucial periods in which brain cells must have certain kinds of stimulation to develop such powers as vision, smell, muscle control, language, and reasoning. (Briscoe, 1999, pp. 21-22)

These new brain discoveries underscore the importance of continuing to learn about development. Parents should know that behavior toward a baby deeply affects the wiring of the infant's brain, and that repeated positive experiences like singing, cooing, and holding a baby close is an important expression of love which directly affects the way a child's brain forms connections.

Families find comfort in knowing what is coming down the road. Further, it is also comforting to know if something is within the normal range. Examples of additional milestones (e.g., physical, social, emotional, cognitive) can be found in *Touchpoints the Essential Reference: Your Child's Emotional and Behavioral Development* (Brazelton, 1992), *Touchpoints - Birth to Three* (Brazelton & Sparrow, 2006), and *Touchpoints Three to Six* (Brazelton & Sparrow, 2001).

When to expect it along the journey

Remember, everyone goes through the trip at about the same time. Family life educators equipped with developmental knowledge will be able to provide families with a timetable for *when* to expect a milestone. For example, we know that most children start walking between eight and fourteen months and start talking between one and two years (Miller, 1985). Family life educators can help families to anticipate and prepare for new developmental stages if they know when the developmental milestones typically occur. However, it is also important to remember that there will be some variation in the timetable (the inevitable variability around the average or normative course of development and the uniqueness of each person, Sroufe, Cooper, & DeHart, 1992). Not every family member is on the *same timeline* for the journey.

Remember, essentially everyone makes the same trip

In other words, everyone goes through developmental stages in the same sequence - developmental stages are systematic. As Papalia and Olds (1996) say, "Each human being is like other people in some ways but

CHILDHOOD — *Within the context of the family system*

Human Growth & Development Across the Life Span

- Emotional and social development
- Responsibility for keeping healthy - nutrition, personal hygiene
- Uniqueness of each person
- Similarities and differences in individual development
- Understanding people with special needs
- Perceptions about older people - adolescents, adults, elderly
- Social and environmental conditions affecting growth and development

Multicultural • Gender Fair • Special Needs Aware

Reciprocal interactions between family and ecosystem

ADOLESCENCE — *Within the context of the family system*

Human Growth & Development Across the Life Span

- Accepting individual differences in development
- Responsibility for personal health - nutrition, personal hygiene, exercise
- Effects of chemical substances on physical health and development
- Types of development - physical, cognitive, affective, moral, personality, social, sexual
- Interaction among types of development
- Patterns of development across the life span - conception to death
- Stereotypes and realities about adulthood and aging
- Developmental disabilities
- Social and environmental conditions affecting growth and development

Multicultural • Gender Fair • Special Needs Aware

Reciprocal interactions between family and ecosystem

ADULTHOOD — *Within the context of the family system*

Human Growth & Development Across the Life Span

- Factors influencing individual differences in development
- Types of development: physical, cognitive, affective, moral, personality, social, sexual
- Interaction among types of development
- Responsibility for personal and family health
- Promoting development in self and others
- Patterns of development across the life span - conception to death
- Myths and realities of adulthood and aging
- Adjusting to disabilities
- Social and environmental conditions affecting growth and development

Multicultural • Gender Fair • Special Needs Aware

Reciprocal interactions between family and ecosystem

LATER ADULTHOOD — *Within the context of the family system*

Human Growth & Development Across the Life Span

- Factors influencing individual differences in development
- Types of development: physical, cognitive, affective, moral, personality, social, sexual
- Interaction among types of development
- Adjusting to disabilities
- Patterns of development over the life span - conception to death
- Adapting to and coping with physical changes in later adulthood
- Responsibility for personal health and safety
- Grieving and adjusting to loss
- Myths and realities of aging
- Social and environmental conditions affecting growth and development

Multicultural • Gender Fair • Special Needs Aware

Reciprocal interactions between family and ecosystem

unique in others" (p. 2). Using Piagets' stages of cognitive development as an example, children start at the *sensorimotor* stage of cognitive development, proceed to the *preoperational* stage, *concrete operations*, and then to *formal operations* (Cowan, 1978). "Only when children [adolescents, adults, later adults] deviate drastically from the norm is there cause for considering them exceptionally advanced or delayed. The important point to remember is that normal children generally go through the same sequence of events" (Papalia & Olds, 1996, p. 7).

Successful completion of one leg of the trip is a prerequisite for the next
The process of development is a building block process. Successful completion of one stage becomes a prerequisite for the next. Loevinger's (1976) eight stages of ego development is an example of this building block process in adult development. She contends that the *Individualistic* level (recognizing that the process of acting is more important than the outcome) builds on the previous *Conscientious* level (the development of self-evaluated standards). Knowing and understanding this developmental principle underscores how important it is that family life educators be able to assess where each family member is on their developmental journey, and to develop an appropriate educational plan if successful completion of a developmental stage is not occurring.

Remember, arriving at the final destination is not a foregone conclusion
Not every person reaches the highest level of development automatically (Duska & Whelan, 1975). This is true in the case of both cognitive and moral development. Not every adolescent automatically becomes *formal operational* and is able think in the abstract simply because she is 18-years-old. Not every middle-aged adult automatically functions at Kohlberg's (1975, 1981) *post-conventional level* (social contract orientation/universal ethical principal orientation) simply because he is 50 years old. This means that in some cases, FLEs will have to devise a strategy to help family members accept their own limitations.

Ready or not – here it comes!
In some areas of human developmental, individuals are pushed ahead to the next stage of development, whether they are ready for it or not (e.g., physical development and psychosocial development). Your body's physical development is on a schedule, as in the case of puberty. There is nothing you can do to speed it up or slow it down. Ready or not – here it comes! Such is the case with entering puberty early for girls. Early maturation increases girls' vulnerability to a variety of problems: "more likely to smoke, drink, be depressed, have an eating disorder, request earlier independence from their parents, and have older friends; and their bodies likely elicit responses from males that lead to earlier dating and earlier sexual experiences" (Santrock, 2003, p. 85). In the case of psychosocial development, Erikson (1950) points out that humans are "pushed on" to the next stage of development, whether or not they have resolved the previous stage. Even if adolescents' identity issues (*Identity vs. Role Confusion*) are not resolved at the conclusion of adolescence, they are still required to function at the next stage (*Intimacy vs. Isolation*). Further, not positively resolving a previous stage causes difficulty and even pain in the current stage.

A GPS for middle adulthood and beyond
Many vehicles today come with the option of a Global Positioning System (GPS). Plug in the address, and voila – a little magic voice tells you exactly where to go and how to get there. Wouldn't it be interesting to have a GPS that maps out your life – especially the long and somewhat uncharted road of middle and late adulthood?

One criticism of Erikson's (1950) developmental theory is that even though it covers the entire life span, his stages still are mainly focused on childhood and adolescence (ages 1-18). Only two stages (*Generativity vs. Stagnation* and *Integrity vs. Despair*) address middle and late adulthood, a span of fifty to sixty years. Levinson's *Seasons of a Man's Life* (1978) attempted to fill in some of the void Erikson missed in these adult stages, but his sample and theory have been criticized for gender bias. More recently, Cohen (2005), a student of Erikson, proposed an expanded theory of adult development predicated on the development of the mature mind.

Cohen believes that *developmental intelligence* is at the core of adult development. "Developmental Intelligence (DI) [is] the maturing of our individual capacities for cognition, judgment, emotional intelligence, social intelligence, life experience, and consciousness (includes spirituality) – further enhanced by their improved integration and synergy with another as we age. *DI shows itself as wisdom*" (Cohen, 2005, p. 35). DI is the greatest benefit of the aging brain - maturity and wisdom.

It should be noted that Cohen's phases (2005) are not truly "developmental" in the sense that he believes it is possible for people to experience them in a different order than the ones presented here, and the phases may overlap.

Cohen's Four Stages of Maturity (adapted from Cohen, 2005, pp. 52-53)

Phase I *– Midlife reevaluation, exploration, and transition (Midlife Reevaluation)* (mid-thirties to mid-sixties, usually occurs early forties to late fifties)

- seriously confront mortality for the first time
- a sense of quest shapes plans and action
- brain changes spur developmental intelligence (basis for wisdom)

Phase II – *Liberation, experimentation, and innovation (Liberation)* (mid-fifties to mid-seventies, usually occurs late fifties to early seventies)

- "if not now, when?" fosters new sense of inner liberation
- a new sense of personal freedom shapes plans and action
- desire for novelty is stimulated by new neuron formation in the information procession part of the brain
- retirement allows time to experiment with new experiences

Phase III – *Recapitulation, resolution, and contribution (Summing Up)* (late sixties to nineties, usually occurs late sixties to eighties)

- motivated to share personal wisdom
- the desire to find meaning in life shape plans and actions
- utilization of both sides of the brain foster autobiographical expression
- attend to unfinished business or unresolved conflicts

Phase IV – *Continuation, reflection, and celebration (Encore)* (late seventies to end of life)

- reaffirmation of major life themes shape plans and actions
- positive emotions and morale occur from changes to the amygdalae
- family and community benefit from the desire to live well

Be mindful that even if you have a GPS guiding you, you still have to negotiate life's potholes – it's not automatic.

Potholes along the Developmental Journey

No journey ever goes smoothly without a hitch. It is like driving down the highway after a long hard winter and before you know it - you hit a pothole! Some potholes are shallow and do not do much damage, while others are deep and dangerous and cause your car's axle to break. The developmental journey of life is no different. Families may encounter numerous potholes on their developmental journey. One job a family life educator has is to alert families. Warning! Potholes ahead! For example, FLEs should warn parents of the problems associated with overindulgence (Bredehoft, Mennicke, Potter, & Clarke, 1998; Bredehoft, 2006; Bredehoft & Leach, 2006; Walcheski, Bredehoft, & Leach, 2007) and what to do instead (Clarke, Dawson, & Bredehoft, 2004; Bredehoft & Armao, in press).

Some potholes are shallow, while others are deep and dangerous and it is good to know the difference. Note: there is a difference between an episodic crisis (a deep pothole that is potentially dangerous), a "simultaneous multigenerational developmental crisis" (a very complicated pothole), and a developmental milestone (a shallow pothole). Not every family experiences the same episodic crises. Mom becomes critically injured and dies following an auto accident or dad is downsized at work are examples of episodic crises. A simultaneous multigenerational developmental crisis on the other hand occurs when family members from two or more generations experience a developmental milestone at the same time.

Developmental Milestones

Developmental milestones are normal human and family life patterns. They are normal. They are expected. As previously discussed, there are individual developmental milestones (e.g., Erikson, 1950, 1994, 1998; Brazelton, 1992; Brazelton & Sparrow, 2001, 2006; Freud, 1938; Levinson, 1978, 1997; Loevinger, 1976; Kohlberg, 1975, 1981; Piaget & Inhelder, 2000, and Whitbourne, 1986) and family developmental milestones (Duvall & Milller, 1985; Rodgers & White, 1993). Each (individual or family milestones) has a set of developmental tasks to be accomplished. In addition, the fact that these milestones are normal and can be anticipated should not in any way diminish the fact that they can cause family stress (Olson et al., 1983). FLEs are in a position to educate families about both types of developmental milestones (individual and family) and because of this, they can help reduce family stresses and strains associated with these milestones.

Episodic Crises

An episodic crisis is a distinctive emotionally significant event in the life of an individual or family. An interesting thing about episodic crises is that since family members are at unique places on the developmental road they will view and interpret a crisis differently. For example, following up on the example of the mother who died in the car crash, a four year old's view and understanding of death is quite different from her ten-year-old brother and her forty-five-year-old father. They are different because one is at Piaget's (1969) *preoperational level* of thinking, while the other two are at the *concrete operational level* and *formal operational level* respectively. In addition, a family's ability to cope with the episodic crisis depends on the family's crisis meeting resources, family hardships, and prior strains (McCubbin & Patterson, 1982, 1983). Family life educators are in a position to develop specific programs for individuals and families going through these episodic crises (e.g., grief support groups) as well as assist with decision-making and resource management issues associate with them (for a discussion on decision making as resource management see Rettig, 2009).

Simultaneous Multigenerational Developmental Crises

One of the most informative things that the integration of the *Curriculum Guidelines* (NCFR, 1984) and the *Framework for Family Life Education* (Bredehoft, 1997, 2001) accomplishes for family life educators is to identify potential simultaneous multigenerational developmental crises (SMDC). What becomes very apparent is the list of developmental tasks spanning both individual and family life cycles. A SMDC occurs when two or more family members from different generations are experiencing a developmental milestone simultaneously. For example, an adolescent daughter is struggling with an identity crisis (*identity vs. role confusion*), while dad is experiencing a midlife crisis (*generativity vs. stagnation*), and grandpa is feeling like his life was a failure (*integrity vs. despair*). Understanding simultaneous multigenerational developmental crises adds to the sense of complexity that otherwise is lost when family life educators focus solely on individual development.

Picture it like a family road trip

Your extended family is on a road trip in your new minivan. Dad and mom are sitting in the front seats; you and your sibling are right behind them, with your grandparents sitting in the very back. As family life educators, most often we think about each family member's developmental course in isolation. In some ways, this is like asking the driver to stop the minivan and have one of the passengers get out of the vehicle while ignoring the influence of the other passengers and the effects of the journey (environment, culture, etc.) itself. For many situations that FLEs find themselves in, this is an entirely appropriate view. However, we challenge you not to stop there. We believe you should also take a more complex and perhaps, a more realistic view of this family road trip: begin to see the family system as a whole. Simultaneously, at any given point in the road trip, each family member is at a different developmental point: physically, emotionally, cognitively, socially, and morally. Growth and maturation in one family member both influences others, and is influenced by other family members on this road family trip. And remember, every family encounters potholes throughout the family life cycle.

Developmental Guidelines for Program Development

In conclusion, we would like to leave you with a set of principles that can guide you in future program development. The National Association for the Education of Young Children (NAEYC) has identified twelve "empirically-based" principles of child development and learning that all family life educators should use to guide decisions about developmentally appropriate practice (note these principles are essentially consistent across the life span and FLEs can be apply them to adolescents and adult development):

1. Domains of children's development – physical, social, emotional, and cognitive – are closely related. Development in one domain influences and is influenced by development in other domains.
2. Development occurs in a relatively orderly sequence, with later abilities, skills, and knowledge building on those already acquired.
3. Development proceeds at varying rates from child to child, as well as unevenly within different areas of each child's functioning.
4. Early experiences have both cumulative and delayed effects on individual children's development; optimal periods exist for certain types of development and learning.
5. Development proceeds in predictable directions toward greater complexity, organization, and internalization.
6. Development and learning occur in and are influenced by multiple social and cultural contexts.
7. Children are active learners, drawing on direct physical and social experience as well as on culturally transmitted knowledge to construct their own understandings of the world around them.
8. Development and learning result from the interaction of biological maturation and the environment, which includes both the physical and social worlds that children live in.
9. Play is an important vehicle for children's social, emotional, and cognitive development, as well as a reflection of their development.
10. Development advances when children have opportunities to practice newly acquired skills as well as when they experience a challenge just beyond the level of their present mastery.
11. Children demonstrate different modes of knowing and learning and different ways of representing what they know.
12. Children develop and learn best in the context of a community where they are safe and valued, their physical needs are met, and they feel psychologically secure. (NAEYC, 1997, pp. 1-7)

References

Berger, K. S. (2003). *The developing person: Through childhood and adolescence.* New York: Worth Publishers.

Brazelton, T. B. (1992). *Touchpoints the essential reference: Your child's emotional and behavioral development.* Reading, MA: Addison-Wesley.

Brazelton, T. B., & Sparrow, J. A. (2006). *Touchpoints - birth to three* (2nd ed.). Cambridge, MA: Da Capo Press.

Brazelton, T. B., & Sparrow, J. A. (2001). *Touchpoints three to six.* Cambridge, MA: Da Capo Press.

Bredehoft, D. J. (Ed.). (1997). *The framework for life span family life education* (2nd ed.) [Poster]. Minneapolis, MN: National Council on Family Relations.

Bredehoft, D. J. (2001). The framework for life span family life education revised and revisited. *The Family Journal, 9*(2), 134-139.

Bredehoft, D. J., Mennicke, S., Potter, A. M., & Clarke, J. I. (1998). Perceptions attributed by adults to parental overindulgence during childhood. *Journal of Family and Consumer Sciences Education, 16*(2), 3-17.

Bredehoft, D. J., & Leach, M. K. (2006). *Influence of childhood overindulgence on young adult dispositions – Executive summary: Study 2.* Retrieved from www.overindulgence.info/AboutOurResearch.htm

Bredehoft, D. J. (2006). *Becoming a parent after growing up overindulged: Executive summary - Study 3.* Retrieved from http://www.overindulgence.info/AboutOurResearch.htm

Bredehoft, D. J., & Armao, C. K. (2008). What teachers can do when overindulged children come to school. *Lutheran Education Journal, 142*(1), 25-35.

Briscoe, J. (1999, May). *Brain development & susceptibility to violence.* In Family information services professional resource materials (pp. 21-30). Minneapolis, MN: Family Information Services.

Cohen, G. D. (2005). *The mature mind: The positive power of the aging brain.* New York: Basic Books.

Cowan, P. A. (1978). *Piaget with feeling: Cognitive, social and emotional dimensions.* New York: Holt, Rinehart and Winston.

Clarke, J. I., Dawson, C., & Bredehoft, D. J. (2004). *How much is enough? Everything you need to know to steer clear of overindulgence and raise likeable, responsible, and respectful children.* New York: Marlowe & Company.

Duska, R., & Whelan, M. (1975). *Moral development: A guide to Piaget and Kohlberg.* New York: Paulist Press.

Duvall, E. M., & Miller, B. C. (1985). *Marriage and family development* (6th ed.). New York: Harper & Row Publishers, Inc.

Erikson, E. H. (1950). *Childhood and society.* New York: W.W. Norton & Company.

Erikson, E. H. (1994). *Identity and the life cycle.* New York: W.W. Norton & Company.

Erikson, E. H. (1998). *Life cycle completed.* New York: W.W. Norton & Company.

Freud, S. (1938). *The basic writings of Sigmund Freud.* (A. A. Brill, Ed. & Trans.). New York: Modern Library.

Kohlberg, L. (1975, June). The cognitive-developmental approach to moral education. *Phi Delta Kappan*, 670-678.

Kohlberg, L. (1981). *The philosophy of moral development.* New York: Harper & Row.

Kotulak, R. (1997). *Inside the brain: Revolutionary discoveries of how the mind works.* Kansas City: Andrews and McMeel Publishing.

Levinson, D. J. (1978). *The seasons of a man's life.* New York: Knopf.

Levinson, D. J. (1997). *Seasons of a woman's life.* New York, NY: Alfred A. Knopf.

Loevinger, J. (1976). *Ego development.* San Francisco: Jossey-Bass.

McCubbin, H. I., & Patterson, J. M. (1982). Family adaptation to crises. In H. McCubbin, A. Cauble & J. Patterson (Eds.), *Family stress, coping and social support.* Springfield, IL: Charles C. Thomas.

McCubbin, H. I., & Patterson, J. M. (1983). The family stress process: The double ABCX model of adjustment and adaptation. In H. I. McCubbin, M. B. Sussman & J. M. Patterson (Eds.), *Social stress and the family: Advances and developments in family stress theory and research.* Marriage and Family Review, Vol. 6. New York: Haworth.

Miller, K. *Ages and stages: Developmental descriptions & activities birth through eight years.* Marshfield, MA: Telshare Publishing Company, Inc.

National Association for the Education of Young Children. (1997). *Principles of child development and learning that inform developmentally appropriate practice.* Retrieved December 17, 2002, from the National Association for Education of Young Children web site: www.naeyc.org/resources/position_statements/dap3.htm

National Council on Family Relations. (1984). *Standards and criteria for certification of family life educators, college/university curriculum guidelines, and content guidelines for family life education: A framework for planning programs over the life span.* Minneapolis, MN: Author.

Oesterreich, L. (1995). *Ages & stages – newborn to 1 year.* Retrieved December 11, 2002, from the National Network for Child Care web site: www.nncc.org/Child.Dev/ages.stages.new.one.html

Olson, D. H., McCubbin, H., Barnes, H. L., Larsen, A. S., Muxen, M. J., & Wilson, M. A. (1983). *Families: What makes them work.* Beverly Hills, CA: Sage Publications.

Papalia, D. E., & Olds, S. W. (1996). *A child's world: Infancy through adolescence* (7th Ed.). New York: McGraw-Hill.

Piaget, J. (1969). *The mechanisms of perception.* London: Routledge.

Piaget, J., & Inhelder, B. (2000). *The psychology of the child.* New York: Basic Books.

Rettig, K. D. (2009). Family resource management. In D. J. Bredehoft & M. J. Walcheski (Eds.), *Family life education: Integrating theory and practice* (2nd ed.) (pp. 163-172). Minneapolis, MN: National Council on Family Relations.

Rodgers, R. H., & White, J. M. (1993). Family development theory. In P. G. Boss, W. J. Doherty, R. LaRossa, W. R. Schumm & S. K. Steinmetz (Eds.), *Sourcebook of family theories and methods* (pp. 99-116). New York: Plenum.

Santrock, J. W. (2003). *Adolescence* (9th ed.). Boston, MA: McGraw-Hill.

Sroufe, L. A., Cooper, R. G., & DeHart, G. B. (1992). *Child development: Its nature and course* (2d ed.). New York: Knopf.

Walcheski, M. J., Bredehoft, D. J., & Leach, M. K. (2007). *Overindulgence, parenting styles, and parent sense of competence: Executive summary: Study 4.* Retrieved from http://www.overindulgence.info/AboutOurResearch.htm

Whitbourne, S. K. (1986). *The me I know: A study of adult identity.* New York: Springer-Verlag.

Key Resources

The American Academy of Child and Adolescent Psychiatry. 3615 Wisconsin Ave., N.W., Washington, DC 20016-3007, Phone: 202-966-7300 or fax: 202-966-2891, website: www.aacap.org/web/aacap/.

American Psychological Association - Division 7 – Developmental Psychology. For Information Contact: Department of Psychology, University of Virginia, 102 Gilmer Hall, Charlottesville, VA 22904, Phone: 804-243-3577 or Fax 804- 982-4694, website: www.apa.org/about/division/div7.html.

Center for Early Education and Development. 215 Pattee Hall, 150 Pillsbury Dr. SE, Minneapolis, MN 55455; 612-625-2898, email: ceed@icimail.coled.umn.edu, website: www.education.umn.edu/ceed/.

National Association for the Education of Young Children, 1509 16th Street, N.W., Washington, DC 20036-1426, Phone: 202-232-8777 or 1-800-424-2460, Fax: 202-328-1846, email: naeyc@naeyc.org, website: www.naeyc.org/.

National Council on Family Relations, 3989 Central Avenue N.E., Suite 550, Minneapolis, MN 55421, Phone 888-781-9331, Fax: 763-781-9348, email: info@ncfr.org, website: www.ncfr.org .

Schubert Center for Child Development. Clark Hall, Room 310, 11130 Bellflower Road, Cleveland, Ohio 44106-7120, Phone: 216-368-2414 or Fax: 216-368-5241, email: schubert-ctr@po.cwru.edu, website: www.cwru.edu/artsci/schubert/.

Society for Research in Child Development. University of Michigan, 505 E. Huron, Suite 301, Ann Arbor, MI 48104-1567, Phone: 734-998-6569 or Fax 734-998-6569, email: srck@umich.edu, website: www.srcd.org.

Related Websites

The Children, Youth and Families Education Research Network: www.cyfernet.org/

Cognitive Development Society: www.cogdevsoc.org/

Erik Erikson: psychology.about.com/od/theoriesofpersonality/a/psychosocial.htm

Internet Resources for Special Children: orsaminore.dreamhosters.com/handy/links/uk_various.html

International Society for the Study of Behavioural Development: www.issbd.org/

International Society on Infant Studies: www.isisweb.org/

Jean Piaget: www.psychology.about.com/od/piagetstheory/a/keyconcepts.htm

Jean Piaget Society: www.piaget.org/

Lawrence Kohlberg: www.psychology.about.com/od/developmentalpsychology/a/kohlberg.htm

Overindulgence: www.overindulgence.info/

Sigmund Freud: www.psychology.about.com/od/sigmundfreud/p/sigmund_freud.htm

Society for Developmental & Behavioral Pediatrics: www.dbpeds.org/

About the Authors

David J. Bredehoft, Ph.D., CFLE is Professor of Psychology and Family Studies and Chair, Department of Social and Behavioral Sciences at Concordia University, St. Paul, MN. He is the editor of *The Framework for Life Span Family Life Education (2nd ed.)*, coeditor of *Family Life Education: Integrating Theory and Practice* (National Council on Family Relations, 2009), and coauthor of *How much is enough? Everything you need to know to steer clear of overindulgence and raise likeable, responsible, and respectful children* (Marlowe & Company, 2004). E-mail: bredehoft@csp.edu.

Deborah Eckhoff, M.A., CFLE is a graduate of the Human Development Program at Saint Mary's University, and is employed by Ceridian LifeWorks Services. E-mail: deborah.eckhoff@ceridian.com.

Carole Gesme, MA, CFLE is a parent educator, teacher, trainer, author and creator of several therapeutic and educational games and tools. Email: cgesme@compuserve.com.

Human Sexuality

CAROL ANDERSON DARLING AND
STACY HOWARD

Many individuals and families are struggling to sort out conflicting messages about sexuality. Whereas the influ ence of movies, music, and advertisements provides us with the allure and excitement of sexuality, the dangers and problems associated with sexual interactions are often conveyed to us through news programs, public policies, school messages, and parents. Thus, the youth in our culture must find their way in a world of contradictions. While the media scream, "always say yes," many adults admonish, "just say no," but the majority just say nothing (Brown & Taverner, 2001).

Sexuality education is a lifelong process of developing a strong foundation for sexual health by acquiring information and forming attitudes, beliefs, and values. While sexuality is quite complex, most adults agree on what is not healthy for teenagers. Sexuality educators, family professionals, and parents share a deep concern about coercive or violent sex, sexually-transmitted infections including HIV/AIDS, and unintended adolescent pregnancy. It is when sexuality is practiced irresponsibly, that sexual behaviors, attitudes, and beliefs can have dire consequences. What is healthy sexuality? Sex is an essential part of our lives and a critical element in our development. It not only carries the potential to create new life, but is also a part of how we see ourselves and can foster intimacy, bonding, and shared pleasures in relationships (Satcher, 2001). Sexual health is tied to both physical and mental health. This perception of health goes beyond absence of disease to include the ability of individuals to integrate sexuality into their lives, derive pleasure from it, and reproduce, if they so choose. However, it also includes the ability to understand the risks, responsibilities, outcomes, and impacts of sexual interaction.

Integrating Theory and Practice into Sexuality Education

Theories contribute to our understanding of sexual behavior by providing reasonable explanations of various phenomena. Although no single theory is intended to explain everything in the universe, scientific theory utilizes a certain set of concepts to explain a particular set of phenomena (Chibucos & Leite, 2005; White & Klein, 2007). Weiss's list of 25 classic works in sexual theory (1998b), along with his assessment of 39 theoretical perspectives that have been or could be used in sexuality research, depict the myriad of concepts pertaining to sexuality and the interdisciplinarity of the field (Weiss, 1998a). A special issue of *The Journal of Sex Research* was devoted to theory as it related to human sexuality and included comments on social constructivism (DeLameter & Hyde, 1998), sexual strategy theory (Buss, 1998), social exchange theory (Spreecher, 1998), symbolic interactionism (Longmore, 1998), social learning theory (Hogben & Byrne, 1998), and systems theory (Jurich & Myers-Bowman, 1998). Geer and O'Donohue's (1987) book on *Theories of Human Sexuality* provides a broad range of 14 approaches to the field of sexuality. Since we are affected by our childhood, familial, gendered, and socialization experiences along with our cultural beliefs, the integration of multiple theories is warranted.

CURRICULUM GUIDELINES: HUMAN SEXUALITY

An understanding of the physiological, psychological, and social aspects of sexual development throughout the life span, so as to achieve healthy sexual adjustment. Based on knowledge of:

1. reproductive physiology;
2. biological determinants;
3. emotional and psychological aspects of sexual involvement;
4. sexual behaviors;
5. sexual values and decision-making;
6. family planning;
7. physiological and psychological components of the sexual response;
8. sexual dysfunction; and
9. influence of sexual involvement on interpersonal relationships.

While sexuality can be analyzed from numerous theoretical frameworks, a few need to be highlighted as they provide a broad perspective for analyzing human sexuality. Using a holistic approach, such as an ecological perspective, is essential (Bronfenbrenner, 2005; Bubolz, Eicher, & Sontag, 1979; Bubolz & Sontag, 1993; Darling, 1987). By examining the organism, which could be the individual, family, or classroom, as it interacts with its multifaceted environments, including the human-behavioral, human-constructed, and natural environments along with various regulatory systems, the complexity of human sexuality within a cultural context can be more readily understood. When applying this framework to a topic such as contraception, students can gain multiple insights about physiological, relational, legal, educational, and socio-cultural dimensions of contraceptive decision-making.

Viewing the family as a system provides an important paradigm when analyzing human sexuality (White & Klein, 2007). Understanding "intergenerational communications" about sexuality, physical and psychological "boundaries" related to sexuality, and feedback in coupled relationships, as well as parent-child sexual communications, can be insightful when interpreting the complex relationships between individuals and their families. Theoretical clarifications can evolve from discussions of boundaries and distance regulation related to parental, sibling, relational or personal subsystems, i.e., what, when, and why are certain doors closed in the home and what boundaries do family members have related to their own bodies? A discussion of family stories, rituals, and rules related to sexuality can also provide understanding and meaning.

Incorporating a developmental framework, for both individuals and families, can be very helpful when trying to understand sexuality from a perspective of change (Serbin & Sprafkin, 1987; White & Klein, 2007). Whereas change is ever present, gradual, and a part of individual aging, families and society are changing at a faster rate. Along with media influences, alternate lifestyles, and advances in biotechnology, family life and sexuality have also evolved. In order to help students understand the idea of developmental influences in one's life; a teacher can use an analogy of baking chocolate chip cookies (J. Maddock, personal communication, January 15, 2002). Most students have made chocolate chip cookies and know the generic recipe. As the process of making these cookies is discussed, one can find that some people use different kinds of shortening, sugar, salt, nuts, chocolate chips, and eggs and may mix, bake, and store the cookies in a variety of ways. If each student were to bake a batch of chocolate chip cookies, they would all be tasty, but there would be similarities and differences in appearance, texture, and flavor. Using the cookie analogy, an educator can talk about prenatal development and sexual differentiation; early childhood experiences, adolescent changes, adult development, and family socialization experiences that can all influence the development of an individual's sexuality.

Sexuality throughout the Life Span

By utilizing the life span approach to address sexuality education (Bredehoft, 1997, 2001), it becomes clear that regardless of the decade or one's point in life, sexuality remains important throughout each stage and not only in our reproductive years, as some may believe (DeLamater & Friedrich, 2002; Satcher, 2001). Certain elements of sexuality come into focus at various times in life depending on one's environment, stage of the life cycle, and interpersonal relationships. Sexuality is a natural part of life from birth to death. Its impact can easily be seen in children when they begin to learn the norms surrounding their newly discovered bodies, when teens begin to struggle during puberty, when adults continue to seek and enjoy sexual relationships, and as we continue to age. Due to continuing changes in human, sexual, and relational development through the life span, some pertinent concepts and topics from human sexuality curriculum for children, adolescence, adulthood, and later adulthood will be addressed (Erikson, 1968).

Childhood

As family life educators dealing with sexuality, it is important for you and your students to understand the sexual learning of young children by thinking back to your own childhood and adolescent experiences with sexuality. How did you learn about sexuality and how did you feel about it? After thinking of your early experiences, consider what you would want your children or students to know or experience.

The capacity for sexual response is present from birth. Whereas male infants can get erections, female infants in the 24 hours after birth can experience vaginal lubrication (Masters, Johnson, & Kolodny, 1982). In addition, infants have also been observed fondling their genitals (Martinson, 1994). During early childhood, children form their gender identity, or sense of maleness or femaleness, and are socialized according to cultural norms for how they are supposed to act (Bussey & Bandura, 1999). Children engage in a variety of sexual play experiences when very young, but these experiences become increasingly covert. As children become aware of cultural norms, sexuality becomes segregated from the rest of their experiences. Because children are taught not to touch the bodies of others and not to talk about sex, they turn to peers for sexual information.

Early in life, children learn about sexuality through interactions with their environments and especially their parents. From the moment of birth, children learn about love, touch, relationships, and sexuality through parental communication, choice of dress, display of affection, as well as interaction and play. Often an attachment or bond between the infant and parents develops and is facilitated by positive physical contact (Bowlby, 1965). If this attachment is stable, secure, and satisfying, it can lead to positive emotional attachments in adulthood (Goldberg, Muir, & Kerr, 1995).

Sexuality education often seeks to assist children in understanding a positive view of sexuality, to provide information and skills about taking care of their sexual health, and to help them acquire the necessary skills to make decisions throughout their lives. At an early age, children have curiosities about how their bodies look and work, where babies come from, and why boys and girls are different (Montfort, Brick, & Blume, 1993). Thus, it is important for parents, teachers, and caregivers to deal with questions as they arise, never put off responding to children's questions, and tell the truth in a brief and factual manner. Answer as much as the child desires and no more, while checking on a child's understanding to determine if any misinterpretations occurred and clarifications are needed. By dealing with questions as they come forth in conversations, one becomes an "askable" parent or educator. This communication process becomes even more crucial when we remember that children become increasingly vulnerable to exploitation and abuse when they do not receive the necessary age-appropriate information about sexuality. Children need to learn that it is acceptable to talk about sexuality and to ask questions about it, develop positive feelings about their own bodies, feel good about themselves, and understand their body rights and responsibilities.

It is never easy for a parent or teacher to approach topics of sexuality with children. Therefore having

CHILDHOOD — *Within the context of the family system*

Human Sexuality

- Physical and sexual development
- Body privacy and protection against sexual abuse
- Uniqueness of each person
- Similarities and differences in individual sexual development
- Aspects of human reproduction - prenatal development, birth, puberty
- Children's perceptions about sexuality
- Social and environmental conditions affecting sexuality

Multicultural • Gender Fair • Special Needs Aware

Reciprocal interactions between family and ecosystem

ADOLESCENCE — *Within the context of the family system*

Human Sexuality

- Physical and sexual development
- Interaction among types of development
- Body privacy and protection against sexual abuse
- Communicating about sexuality - personal values and beliefs, shared decision-making
- Choices, consequences, responsibility of sexual behavior
- Prevention and transmission of sexually transmitted diseases
- Human reproduction and conception
- Normality of sexual feelings and sexual responses
- Stereotypes and realities about human sexuality
- Varying family and societal beliefs about sexuality

Multicultural • Gender Fair • Special Needs Aware

Reciprocal interactions between family and ecosystem

ADULTHOOD — *Within the context of the family system*

Human Sexuality

- Responsible sexual behavior - choices, consequences, shared decision-making
- Normality of sexual feelings and sexual responses
- Communicating about sexuality - personal values, beliefs, shared decision-making
- Prevention and transmission of sexually transmitted diseases
- Contraception, infertility, genetics
- Prevention of sexual abuse
- Varying societal beliefs about sexuality

Multicultural • Gender Fair • Special Needs Aware

Reciprocal interactions between family and ecosystem

LATER ADULTHOOD — *Within the context of the family system*

Human Sexuality

- Human sexual response and aging
- Normality of sexual feelings and sexual responses
- Body privacy and prevention of sexual abuse
- Communicating about sexuality - personal values, beliefs, shared decision-making
- Sexuality education about later adulthood
- Sexual expression and intimacy in later adulthood
- Awareness of sexuality needs in adult living situations
- Varying societal beliefs, myths, and realities about sexuality and aging

Multicultural • Gender Fair • Special Needs Aware

Reciprocal interactions between family and ecosystem

dolls, which are anatomically correct, and animals, such as guppies, frogs, cats, and dogs, may be ways to provide for "teachable moments." An array of children's books to show students or parents can also become a valuable vehicle to facilitate these special conversations. Children's books such as *Bellybuttons Are Navels* (Schoen & Quay, 1990), *How Babies are Made* (Andry & Schepp, 1984), *It's My Body: A Book to Teach Young Children How to Resist Uncomfortable Touch* (Freeman & Deach, 1995), *Amazing You* (Saltz, 2005) and *Changing You* (Saltz, 2007) can be very helpful. Finding children's picture books about these topics when traveling in other countries can be a meaningful resource about cultural differences in the sexual socialization of young children.

Adolescence

Whether or not adolescents become involved in any sexual interactions, they are still very sexual people. Unfortunately, many adults have a clear idea of what behaviors may be wrong, but little idea of what is right. Thus, when attempting to portray a positive paradigm of sexuality with students or parents, you might ask them to develop some "sex positive" statements about adolescent sexuality and sexual behavior. In other words, what would be a healthy and positive expression of sexuality during the teen years?

Puberty is a profound time in human development that includes dynamic changes in physical, social, and emotional states that occur at an unmatched speed. Adolescent sexual health is based on esteem and respect for the self and others of both genders, however the timing of sexual development for both sexes is highly variable and affected by genetic, health, nutritional, and life-experience factors. Understanding physical changes such as growth spurts, changes in body hair, first menstruation and ejaculation, voice changes, and the role of oil and sweat producing glands can be helpful to adolescents. The biological changes associated with puberty can also lead to a surge of sexual interest. By knowing what to expect in advance, they will not be frightened or confused by the changes they will experience in their bodies and feelings. For adolescents, issues surrounding puberty increasingly demand an endless amount of attention since many teens experience the onset of confusion, anxiety, turmoil, excitement, and an unavoidable dread (McCann & Petrich-Kelly, 1999).

During middle and late adolescence, a greater number of youth engage in heterosexual intercourse. According to the Centers for Disease Control and Prevention (2006), in 2005 approximately half of the students in grades 9 to 12 reported having had intercourse (45.7% females and 46.7% males). Not only did 6.2% of these high school students have their first sexual intercourse experience before age 13, but also 14.3% had sexual intercourse with more than four persons. During this period, adolescents experience some conflict between identity, especially gender identity, and role confusion. In addition, they are trying to learn how to manage physical and emotional intimacy. Using the sexual (social) scripting perspective to integrate the who, what, when, where and why of sexual relationships can provide insight to these changing elements in a teen's life (Gagnon & Simon, 1973; Krahe, Bieneck, & Scheinberger-Olwig, 2007; Simon & Gagnon, 1987). Scripting can become a conceptual tool to look at sexual and social conduct, which includes both the specific behaviors and multifaceted meanings associated with them.

One teaching strategy to deal with peer pressure and risk-taking, especially sexual risk-taking, is learning to use refusal skills. Refusal skills are techniques that can be used to reinforce decisions that are healthy, safe, legal, and show respect for yourself and others. After creating a panel of judges, one can divide the classroom into 3 to 5 competing groups. A series of sexuality pressure lines can be presented to each group such as, If you don't have sex, I'll find someone who will; If you love me, you'll have sex with me; Everyone is doing it; You can't get pregnant the first time; I don't want to do anything, I just want to lie next to you; or, Sex will help our relationship grow stronger. After each group gives a response or refusal to a pressure line, the panel judges it and a score for each group is recorded. Now ask the class to consider statements that could occur in "virtual" conversations. Given the widespread involvement of adolescents in Internet chat rooms, Myspace.com, and other on-line interactive sites, understanding that peer pressure might occur more often on-line than in person, is an important reality. By gaining some experience in handling difficult situations in a non-threatening environment, such as provided in this game-like activity, it is hoped that students will feel more comfortable when deflecting peer pressure in non-classroom environments.

Adolescence is a time that requires accurate information about a wide range of topics related to sexuality. Not only is sexual orientation usually determined by adolescence, if not earlier, but also there is no valid scientific evidence that sexual orientation can be changed (American Psychiatric Association, 2000; Haldeman, 1994). Due to dealing with anti-gay attitudes in our culture, gays may often experience stress that has an impact on their mental health and can result in a greater incidence of depression, suicide, lower self-acceptance, and a greater likelihood of hiding their sexual orientation (Remafedi, 1998, Russell & Joyner, 2001; Udry & Chantala, 2002). There are also developmental, sexual, and relational issues for those with cognitive, physical, or mental disabilities, but their needs are often ignored. During this time of change, youth need an opportunity to ask questions, explore, and assess their sexual attitudes and options in order to develop their own values concerning personal sexual health. Youth also need assistance from family life and sexuality educators in developing insights concerning interpersonal relationships and understanding their obligations and responsibilities to themselves and others.

Today, teens can be bombarded by the media (television, movies, music, and the Internet) that provides increasingly frequent portrayals of sexuality (Brown, 2002). By incorporating social learning theory (Bandura, 1994), students can analyze the role of popular teen media's influence on youth's opinions about what is supposedly acceptable sexual behavior. In other words, people who watch media content, which contains attractive characters who enjoy having sexual intercourse and rarely suffer any negative consequences, will be more likely to imitate that behavior. Although there is increasing public concern about the potential of health risks of early unprotected sexual activity, most of the mass media rarely depict the three C's of responsible sexual behavior: Commitment, Contraceptives, and consideration of Consequences (Kunkel, et al., 1999). Thus, the influence of media becomes a challenge for sexuality educators and parents.

Several family variables influence adolescent sexual and contraceptive behavior (Miller, 2002). When adults and teens talk about sexuality, teens are more likely to delay first intercourse and if they are sexually active, they are more likely to use contraceptives or have fewer partners (Jaccard, Dittus, & Gordon, 1996; Miller, 1998; Resnick et al., 1997; Upchurch, Aneshensel, Sucoff, & Levy-Storms, 1999). In comparison, parental control can be associated with negative effects if it is excessive or coercive (Miller, 1998). While young adults reported wishing their parents had shared more information with them about sexuality, parents are often unsure and uncomfortable with this role (Hutchinson & Coony, 1998). Since parents need to personalize their sexual communications to each child's needs, Miron and Miron's (2002) book on talking to teens about love, sex, and relationships can be of help with suggested exercises, real life examples, and factual information to assist parents with this dialogue. Similarly Haffner's books (2002, 2004, 2008) are designed to guide parents in dealing with their children in a sexually healthy manner.

It is the charge of family life and sexuality educators to understand that regardless if we agree with today's youths' actions, beliefs, or attitudes, it cannot be ignored that countless teens are engaging in a variety of sexual behaviors with a range of results and consequences. Youth need to be equipped with accurate information, values clarification, and parental guidance in order to help them in their decision-making responsibilities concerning their sexuality.

Adulthood

The primary task young adults face is the development of intimacy—forming committed, intimate, loving relationships. The process of sexual maturation continues in adulthood by addressing tasks such as learning effective communication with partners in intimate relationships and developing the ability to make informed decisions about reproduction and prevention of sexually-transmitted infections (DeLameter & Friedrich, 2002). Sexual lifestyles can vary, as some may choose to remain single, celibate, or cohabitate and/or participate in a long-term monogamous relationship or multiple relationships that are either serial or simultaneous. Couples also report engaging in a variety of sexual activities in addition to vaginal intercourse, including oral-genital sex, anal intercourse, and masturbation (Laumann, Gagnon, Michael, & Michaels, 1994).

Sexual satisfaction can become a focus of sexuality during the adult years. Satisfaction, which is an elusive concept, is the perceived discrepancy between level of aspiration and level of achievement, ranging from the perception of fulfillment to that of deprivation. It is therefore a highly personal experience heavily influenced by an individual's past experiences, current expectations, and future aspirations. As a result adults are interested in learning about a variety of topics related to the physiological and interpersonal dimensions of their sexual relationships. Such topics as orgasmic responsiveness involving male and female multiple orgasms, male and female ejaculation, types of orgasm, and timing of orgasm abound in the print media along with suggestions on how to enhance the love in your relationship. However, popular press articles are not always based on research. Thus, a potential learning experience could involve students reading a popular press article; critiquing its allure to readers along with its scholarship; and finding research articles to enhance, refute, or support its claims.

While there is a wide range of sexual activities that occur among consenting adults, discussing feelings about some of these activities and relationship issues can be meaningful to students studying adult development. Sexually healthy adults are persons who feel comfortable with their sexuality and feel free to choose whether or not they desire to engage in a variety of sexual behaviors. An individual can be sexually healthy and still say "no." While one should not feel pressured to engage in sexual behaviors, someone's attitudes about sex may be revealed by how that person regards his or her partner and their relationship. The *Guidelines for Comprehensive Sexuality Education* (National Guidelines Task Force, 2004) articulated four primary areas for sexuality education that focus on the promotion of adult sexual health: (1) information; (2) attitudes, values, and insights; (3) relationships and interpersonal skills; and (4) responsibility.

Later Adulthood

In addition to contemplating issues of sexuality during childhood and adolescence, you and your students may also want to think about one's sex life at around the age of 20. Then add 10, 20, 30, 40, or more years to this paradigm and contemplate what one's sex life was, is, and might be like. Will your sex life be getting better all the time, or do you look ahead to the future with trepidation about the fear of wrinkles, thinning or graying hair, and redistribution of body weight as gravity becomes an influential factor in your life? Not only are these physical and sexual changes often misunderstood, but also sexuality and aging can be very different experiences for different people. Often times the sexual interest and activity of older persons are two of the best-kept secrets in our society.

Most older people want and are able to lead an active and satisfying sexual life. While there are some changes in sexual capacity that occur, they are manageable and considered as part of "normal aging." Women generally experience little loss of sexual capacity with changes occurring mainly with the shape, flexibility, and lubrication of the vagina. These changes can be traced to lower levels of estrogen during and after menopause. As men age, they experience andropause or the decline of androgen and production of testosterone. Older men often notice more distinct changes in sexual functioning although these changes vary greatly from man to man. It may take a man a little longer to attain an erection, it may not be quite as firm, and may also take longer for a subsequent erection to occur. Moreover, the volume of ejaculate may be reduced and the ejaculation less forceful.

Although the incidence of illness and disability increases with age, even the most serious diseases rarely warrant stopping sexual activity. Understanding the role of heart disease, physical conditioning, diabetes, smoking, arthritis, hysterectomies, prostatctomies, and alcohol can be enlightening for older persons. A common emotional concern for older men is erectile disorder, but this can be caused by any number of reasons such as fatigue, tension, illness, alcohol, and the actual fear of impotence. Medicines should also be examined for their effects on sexuality, since doctors can prescribe alternate medicines, if available, to deal with high blood pressure, depression, and other health issues. While the use of Viagra and other similar drugs has made a recent impact on the culture of aging, care needs to be taken to examine when and how it is used and its role in a partnered relationship.

Floyd and Weiss (2001) discovered among a population of college students that although a group of young adults was optimistic about their continued sexual activity later in life, there was also a considerable amount of ageism found. The researchers uncovered that the college students' attitudes toward later adulthood sexuality were more conservative and restrictive than their present attitudes. There is a need for education and communication about later adulthood sexuality in order for such attitudes to be either avoided or lessened. Since these students are the children and grandchildren of older persons and potential future educators and caregivers, their ability to understand the sexual desires and needs of later adulthood is essential.

Many persons that are aging often misunderstand physical and sexual changes. Since they are part of the "secrecy generation," they do not talk to others about these issues. We know that sexual feelings, desires, and activities are present throughout the life cycle, but some people in our society assume that older persons do not need or are not interested in sexual education or enrichment. This discrepancy can pose a great risk to older adults who have a right to sexuality education, sexual health care, and opportunities for socializing and sexual expression. Education concerning the sexual feelings, attitudes, and behaviors of older adults should be available to them, their families, health care providers, and other caregivers (Brick & Lunquist, 2003). There is reason to believe that a majority of men and women can adapt to aging and maintain an interest in sex, continue to find it as a source of satisfaction, and make fresh discoveries to enrich their sexual lives.

Suggestions for New Practitioners

Although generally short-term abstinence or sexuality education programs do not have measurable impacts on teen behavior, the curricula of the most effective sex and HIV education programs share ten common characteristics. These programs:

- Focus on reducing one or more sexual behaviors that lead to unintended pregnancy or HIV/STD infection.
- Are based on theoretical approaches that have been demonstrated to influence other health- related behaviors and identify specific important sexual antecedents to be targeted.
- Deliver and consistently reinforce a clear message about abstaining from sexual activity and/or using condoms or other forms of contraception. This appears to be one of the most important characteristics that distinguishes effective from ineffective programs.
- Provide basic, accurate information about the risks of teen sexual activity and about ways to avoid intercourse or use methods of protection against pregnancy and STDs.
- Include activities that address social pressures that influence sexual behavior.
- Provide examples of and practice with communication, negotiation, and refusal skills.
- Employ teaching methods designed to involve participants and have them personalize the information.
- Incorporate behavioral goals, teaching methods, and materials that are appropriate to the age, sexual experience, and culture of the students.
- Last a sufficient length of time (more than a few hours).
- Select teachers or peer leaders who believe in the program and then provide them with adequate training (Kirby, 2001, p.10).

New practitioners must explore those methods and materials that demonstrate effective outcomes.

Certain qualifications are important for a sexuality educator, such as comfort with sexual communications; an ability to listen, understand questions, and assess needs; and appropriate education and knowledge about human sexuality. Nevertheless, frustration, anger, weariness, and sadness are all emotions that sexuality educators experience far too often in response to the realities of their students' lives and our limitations to assist them. To truly have an effect on a young person's life, it takes much more than time-limited instruction and skill building (Shelby, 1998). A sexuality educator needs competence, caring, communication, and commitment.

Future Issues and Challenges for Family Life Educators

One of the challenges for the future is to deal with the relative silence surrounding sexual issues in the community. Whereas sexuality is discussed in the entertainment industry, through community scandals, and within commercial sources, we are missing open dialogue about sexual health and the promotion of responsible sexual behaviors. The dangers of not discussing sexual health outweigh any possible advantages of silence. Some of the issues that challenge us include the prevalence of sexually-transmitted infections and HIV, infertility, cancer resulting from sexually-transmitted infections in women, the rate of sexual dysfunctions in the population, sexual abuse and discrimination on the basis of sexuality, and the level of unwanted pregnancy. The cost of our silence on these issues will be to elevate a health challenge to a health crisis (Ross, 2002).

In order for family life and sexuality educators to speak up for sexual health issues, they need to continually update their knowledge base, invigorate their instructional methods, and remind themselves just why they do what they do. According to Kirby (1997), research tells us that effective programs for sexuality education are being taught by teachers who believe in the program they are a part of and are trained to deliver and meet expectations. Training for teachers is crucial to the success of programs across the board and to the health of our society at large.

Future Program Needs to Equip Family Life Educators

A variety of experts in the field of family life and sexuality education offered their suggestions for future programming (Wilson, 1997).

- Focus on earlier education
- Link sexuality education with other kinds of education and services
- Examine situations in which students are living and do something about inadequate schools, unsupportive home environments, and unsafe neighborhoods
- Do a better job of training teachers
- Actively recruit educators who reflect the diversity of those they are educating
- Pay more attention to adult sexuality
- Focus on equipping parents to become more comfortable with issues related to sexuality
- Design better programs that are for parents and older adults
- Place more emphasis on reaching people outside the school setting
- Understand and use the media effectively, especially as it relates to sexual communications to our youth

While teaching about sexuality is a complex endeavor, there is a strong interest in this topic by all ages and critical needs to be met to facilitate the sexual health of individuals throughout the life span.

References

American Psychiatric Association. (2000). *Position statement on therapies focused on attempts to change sexual orientation (reparative or conversion therapies).* Washington DC: Author.

Andry, A., & Schepp, S. (1984). *How babies are made.* New York: Time-Life Books.

Bandura, A. (1994). Social cognitive theory of mass communication. In J. Bryant & D. Zillmann (Eds.), *Media effects: Advances in theory and research* (pp. 61-90). Hillsdale, NJ: Earlbaum.

Bowlby, J. (1965). Maternal care and mental health. In J. Bowlby (Ed.), *Child care and growth of love* (pp.18-32). London: Penguin.

Bredehoft, D. J. (Ed.). (1997). The *framework for life span family life education* (2nd ed.) [Poster]. Minneapolis, MN: National Council on Family Relations.

Bredehoft, D. J. (2001). The framework for life span family life education revised and revisited. *The Family Journal, 2,* 134-139.

Brick, P., & Lunquist, J. (2003). New expectations: Sexuality education for mid and later life. New York: Sex and Information Council of the United States.

Bronfenbrenner, U. (2005). *Making human beings human: Biological perspectives on human development.* Thousand Oaks, CA; Sage Publications.

Brown, J. (2002). Mass media influences on sexuality. *The Journal of Sex Research, 39*, 42-45.

Brown, S., & Taverner, B. (2001). *Streetwise to sex-wise: Sexuality education for high-risk youth.* Morristown, NJ: Planned Parenthood of Greater Northern New Jersey, Inc.

Bubolz, M., Eicher, J., & Sontag, M. (1979). The human ecosystem: A model. *Journal of Home Economics, 71*, 28-30.

Bubolz, M., & Sontag, M. (1993). Human ecology theory. In P. G. Boss, W. J. Doherty, R. LaRossa, W. R. Schumm & S. K. Steinmetz (Eds.), *Sourcebook of family theories and methods: A contextual approach* (pp. 419-448). New York: Plenum Press.

Buss, D. (1998). Sexual strategies theory: Historical origins and current status. *The Journal of Sex Research, 35*, 19-31.

Bussey, K., & Bandura, A. (1999). Social cognitive theory of gender development and differentiation. *Psychological Review, 106*, 676-713.

Chibucos, T., & Leite, R. (2005). *Readings in family theory.* Thousand Oaks, CA: Sage Publications.

Centers for Disease Control and Prevention. (2006). Youth risk behavior surveillance-United States, 2005. *Morbidity and Morality Weekly Report, 55*, SS-5.

Darling, C. (1987). Family life education. In M. B. Sussman & S. K. Steinmetz (Eds.), *Handbook of marriage and the family* (pp. 815-813). New York: Plenum Press.

DeLameter, J., & Friedrich, W. (2002). Human sexual development. *The Journal of Sex Research, 39*, 10-14.

DeLameter, J., & Hyde, J. (1998). Essential versus social constructivism in the study of human sexuality. *The Journal of Sex Research, 25*, 10-18.

Erikson, E. H. (1968). *Identity: Youth and crisis.* New York: Norton.

Floyd, M., & Weiss, L. (2001). Sex and aging: A survey of young adults. *Journal of Sex Education and Therapy, 26*, 133-139.

Freeman, L., & Deach, C. (1995). *It's my body: A book to teach young children how to resist uncomfortable touch.* Seattle, WA: Parenting Press, Inc.

Gagnon, J., & Simon, W. (1973). *Sexual conduct: The social sources of human sexuality.* Chicago: Aldine.

Geer, J., & O'Donohue, W. (1987). *Theories of human sexuality.* New York: Plenum Press.

Goldberg, S., Muir, R., & Kerr, J. (1995). *Attachment theory: Social development, and clinical perspectives.* Hillsdale, NJ: Analytic Press.

Haffner, D. (2002). *Beyond the big talk: Every parent's guide to raising sexually healthy teens from middle school to high school and beyond.* New York: New Market Press.

Haffner, D. (2004). *From diapers to dating: A parents guide to raising sexually healthy children from infancy to middle school* 2nd ed. New York: New Market Press.

Haffner, D. (2008). *What every 21st-century parent needs to know: Facing today's challenges with wisdom and heart.* New York: New Market Press.

Haldeman, D. C. (1994). The practice and the ethics of sexual orientation conversion therapy. *Journal of Consulting and Clinical Psychology, 62*, 221-227.

Hogben, M., & Byrne, D. (1998). Using social learning theory to explain individual differences in human sexuality. *The Journal of Sex Research, 35*, 58-71.

Hutchinson, M. K., & Cooney, T. M. (1998). Patterns of parent-teen sexual risk communication: Implications for intervention. *Family Relationships, 47*, 185-194.

Jaccard, J., Dittus, P. J., & Gordon, V. V. (1996). Maternal correlates of adolescent sexual and contraceptive behavior. *Family Planning Perspectives, 28*, 159-165.

Jurich, J. A., & Myers-Bowman, K. S. (1998). Systems theory and its application to research on human sexuality. *The Journal of Sex Research, 35*, 72-87.

Kirby, D. (1997). The impact of the postponing sexual involvement curriculum among youths in California. *Family Planning Perspectives, 29*, 100-108.

Kirby, D. (2001). *Emerging answers: Research findings on programs to reduce teen pregnancy (Summary).* Washington, DC: National Campaign to Prevent Teen Pregnancy.

Krahe, B., Bieneck, S., & Scheinberger-Olwig, R. (2007). Adolescents' sexual scripts: Schematic representations of consensual and nonconsensual heterosexual interactions. *Journal of Sex Research, 44*, 316-317.

Kunkel, D., Cope, S., Farinola, W., Biely, E., Rollin, E., & Donnerstein, E. (1999). *Sex on TV: A biennial report to the Kaiser Family Foundation, 1999*. Menlo Park, CA: The Henry Kaiser Family Foundation.

Laumann, E. O., Gagnon, J. H., Michael, R. T, & Michaels, S. (1994). *The social organization of sexuality: Sexual practices of the United States*. Chicago: The University of Chicago Press.

Longmore, M. (1998). Symbolic interactionism and the study of sexuality. *The Journal of Sex Research, 35*, 44-57.

McCann, F., & Petrich-Kelly, B. (1999). Learning to feel good about yourself: Public education reconsidered. *SIECUS Report, 27*, 24-27.

Martinson, F. M. (1994). *The sexual life of children*. Westport, CT: Bergin and Garvey.

Masters, W., Johnson, V., & Kolodny, R. C. (1982). *Human sexuality*. Boston: Little Brown.

Miller, B. (1998). *Families matter: A research synthesis of family influences of adolescent pregnancy*. Washington, DC: National Campaign to Prevent Teen Pregnancy.

Miller, B. (2002). Family influences on adolescent sexual and contraceptive behavior. *The Journal of Sex Research, 39*, 22-26.

Miron, A. G., & Miron, C. (2002). *How to talk with teens about love, relationships, & S-E-X: A guide for parents*. Minneapolis, MN: Free Spirit Publishing.

Montfort, S., Brick, P., & Blume, N. (1993). *Healthy foundations: The teacher's book: Responding to young children's questions and behaviors regarding sexuality*. Hackensack, NJ: Planned Parenthood of Greater Northern New Jersey, Inc.

National Guidelines Task Force. (2004). *Guidelines for comprehensive sexuality education* (2nd ed, Kindergarten-12th grade). New York: Sexuality Information and Education Council of the United States.

Resnick, M. D., Bearman, P. S., Blum, R. W., Badman, K. E., Harris, K. M., Jones, J., et al. (1997). Protecting adolescents from harm: Findings from the national longitudinal study on adolescent health. *Journal of the American Medical Association, 278*, 823-832.

Remafedi, G. (1998). The relationship between suicide risk and sexual orientation: Results of a population-based study. *American Journal of Public Health, 88*, 57-60.

Ross, M. W. (2002). Sexuality and health challenges: Responding to a public health imperative. *The Journal of Sex Research, 39*, 7-9.

Russell, S., & Joyner, K. (2001). Adolescent sexual orientation and suicide risk: Evidence from a national study. *American Journal of Public Health, 91*, 1276-1281.

Saltz, G. (2007). *Amazing you*. New York: Dutton Children's Books.

Saltz, G. (2007). *Changing you*. New York: Dutton Children's Books.

Satcher, D. (2001). *The Surgeon General's call to action to promote sexual health and responsible sexual behavior.* Retrieved November 29, 2002, from The Office of the Surgeon General's Web site: www.surgeongeneral.gov/library/calls.htm

Schoen, M., & Quay, M. (1990). *Bellybuttons are navels*. New York: Prometheus Books.

Serbin, L., & Sprafkin, C. (1987). A developmental approach: Sexuality from infancy through adolescence. In J. H. Geer & W. T. O'Donohue (Eds.), *Theories of human sexuality* (pp. 163-192). New York: Plenum Press.

Shelby, L. (1998). Youth first: A work in progress. *Educator's Update, 3*, 1-3.

Simon, W., & Gagnon, J. (1987). A sexual scripts approach. In J. H. Geer & W. T. O'Donohue (Eds.), *Theories of human sexuality* (pp. 363-383). New York: Plenum Press.

Sprecher, S. (1998). Social exchange theories and sexuality. *The Journal of Sex Research, 35*, 32-43.

Udry, J., & Chantala, K. (2002). Risk assessment of adolescents with same-sex relationships. *Journal of Adolescent Health, 31*, 84-92.

Upchurch, D. M., Aneshensel, C. S., Sucoff, C. A., & Levy-Storms, L. (1999). Neighborhood and family contexts of adolescent sexual activity. *Journal of Marriage and the Family, 61*, 920-933.

Weiss, D. (1998a). Conclusion: The state of sexual theory. *The Journal of Sex Research, 35*, 100-114.

Weiss, D. (1998b). The use of theory in sexuality research. *The Journal of Sex Research, 35*, 1-9.

White, J., & Klein, D. (2007). *Family Theories* (3rd ed.). Thousand Oaks, CA: Sage.

Wilson, S. (1997). The next 10 years. *Family Life Matters, 32*, 2.

Key Resources

Brown, S., & Taverner, B. (2001). *Streetwise to sex-wise: Sexuality education for high-risk youth* (2nd ed.). Morristown, NJ: Planned Parenthood of Greater Northern New Jersey, Inc.

Brick, P. (1998). *The new teaching safer sex.* Morristown, NJ: Planned Parenthood of Greater Northern New Jersey, Inc.

Brick, P., & Taverner, B. (2001). *Positive images: Teaching abstinence, contraception, and sexual health.* Morristown, NJ: Planned Parenthood of Greater Northern New Jersey, Inc.

Cooperman, C., & Rhodes, C. (1992). *New methods for puberty education.* Morristown, NJ: Planned Parenthood of Greater Northern New Jersey, Inc.

Jemmott, L. S., Jemmott, J. B. III, & McCaffree, K. A. (2001). *Making a difference.* New York: Select Media.

Jemmott, L. S., Jemmott, J. B. III, & McCaffree, K. A. (2001). *Making proud choices!* New York: Select Media.

Jemmott, L. S., Jemmott, J. B., III, & McCaffree, K. A. (1999). *Be proud! Be responsible! Strategies to empower youth to reduce their risks for AIDS* (5th ed.). New York: Select Media.

Loftus, M. (2001). The lost children of Rockdale County: Teenage Syphilis outbreak revisited. *SIECUS Report, 30*, 24-26.

Montfort, S., & Brick, P. (2000). *Unequal partners: Teaching about power and consent in adult-teen relationships.* Morristown, NJ: Planned Parenthood of Greater Northern New Jersey, Inc.

Vogelaar, A. (1999). *Talking one-to-one with teens about contraceptive and safer sex decisions.* Morristown, NJ: Planned Parenthood of Greater Northern New Jersey, Inc.

Related Websites

Alan Guttmacher Institute: www.guttmacher.org/

Advocates for Youth: www.advocatesforyouth.org

American Social Health Association: www.iwannaknow.org

Coalition for Positive Sexuality: www.positive.org

Go Ask Alice; www.health.columbia.edu/docs/services/alice/index.html

Kaiser Family Foundation: www.kff.org

Network for Family Life Education: www.sexetc.org/

Planned Parenthood Federation of America: hwww.plannedparenthood.org

Sexuality Information and Educational Council of the U.S. (SIECUS): www.siecus.org

Teenwire (Planned Parenthood Federation of America): www.teenwire.com

Films and Media Resources

As time goes by. Fanlight Productions, 4196 Washington Street, Suite 2, Boston, MA, 02131, (800-937-4113).

Bodies, birth, and babies. Planned Parenthood of Greater Northern New Jersey, 196 Speedwell Avenue, Morristown, NJ, 07960, (973-539-9580).

Condom talk. Planned Parenthood of Greater Northern New Jersey, 196 Speedwell Avenue, Morristown, NJ, 07960, (973-539-9580).

Conquering the media maze. United Learning, 1560 Sherman Ave., Suite 100, Evanston, IL, 60201, (800-323-9084).

Man to man: Exploring the myths of manhood. Human Resources Media, 175 Tompkins Ave., Pleasantville, NY, 10570-3156, (800-431-2050).

Men talk sex. Fanlight Productions, 4196 Washington Street, Suite 2, Boston, MA, 02131, (800-937-4113).

Safe sex: Girl chat. Pyramid Media, P.O. Box 1048, Santa Montica, CA, 90406, (800-421-2304).

Self image: The fantasy, the reality, in the mix: For teens by teens. Cambridge Parenting and Family Life, P.O. Box 2153, Dept. K11, Charleston, WV, 25328-2153, (800-468-4227).

Speaking of sex. Focus International, 1160 E. Jericho Turnpike, Huntington, NY, 11743, (800-843-0305).

Talking about sex: Am I normal. United Learning, 1560 Sherman Ave., Suite 100, Evanston, IL, 60201, (800-323-9084).

Tonight's the night: A video on intimacy, sexuality, and aging. Fanlight Productions, 4196 Washington Street, Suite 2, Boston, MA, 02131, (800-937-4113).

What is love? What is sex? Human Relations Media, 41 Kensico Drive, Mount Kisco, NY, 10549, (800-431-2050).

What works: Sexuality education. Media Works Inc., P.O. Box 15597 Kenmore Station, Boston, MA, 02215, (978-282-9550).

About the Authors

Carol Anderson Darling, Ph.D., CFLE, is the Margaret Sandels Professor of Human Sciences at Florida State University, has been involved with the CFLE program since its inception, and is a past NCFR President. She has been a sexuality researcher and educator for several years having taught human sexuality at the undergraduate and graduate levels at Florida State University and the University of Helsinki. She has also presented sexuality education workshops to teachers throughout the state of Florida and in South Korea. E-mail: cdarling@fsu.edu.

Stacy Howard, M.S., CFLE received her B.S. Degree in Sociology from the University of Louisville and her M.S. degree in Family Relations from Florida State University and is currently a doctoral candidate. She works for the Agency for Workforce Innovation's Office of Early Learning as the Consumer Affairs Manager. E-mail: taboot@comcast.net.

Interpersonal Relationships

AMY OLSON-SIGG AND
DAVID H. OLSON

Interpersonal relationships are the core of humans being human. As social beings, we cannot escape daily interactions with our spouse, friends, children, family members, neighbors and co-workers nor would we want to do so. Our personal relationships play a crucial role in the quality of our lives and of our society. We know that relationships play a fundamental role in the health and well-being of individuals, families, and communities. In fact, supportive interpersonal relationships and marriages have been linked to a variety of positive health outcomes from the reduction of cardiovascular responsivity to stress to increased psychological and personal well-being (Baker et al., 2000; Holt-Lunstad, Uchino, Smith & Hicks, 2007; Kirby, Baucom & Peterman, 2005; Lamb, Lee & DeMaris, 2003; Ryan & Willits, 2007; Waite & Gallagher, 2000).

Conversely, unhealthy (negative) relationships can contribute to our stress and ill health (Bland, Krogh, Winkelstein & Travisan, 1991; Newton & Sanford, 2003; Seeman & McEwen, 1996; Waite & Gallagher, 2000). While supportive marriages are associated with lower levels of cardiovascular disease and mortality, stressful (non-supportive) marriages heighten physiological stress correlating with a greater risk of death (Kimmel et al., 2000). Distressed marriages are also correlated with more depression (Beach, Katz, Sooyeon & Brody, 2003). In terms of power, inequality in relationships is associated with poorer psychological health in adults and in adolescent romantic relationships (Galliher, Rostosky, Welsh & Kawaguchi, 1999), and marital problems (Olson & Olson, 2000).

The quality of relationships within families impact individuals, and ultimately impact society. Quality parent-child relationships have been correlated with higher academic achievement (Luster, Bates, Vandenbelt & Nievar, 2004), a decrease in behavioral problems (Pearce, 2003), and less violence for adolescents (Knoester & Haynie, 2005). Lawrence Fisher found that healthy familial relationships improve the outcome of chronically ill patients (Fisher, 2000). Parental bonds as measured by feelings of closeness, communication, and involvement, are associated with a decrease in the likelihood that an adolescent will commit an act of violence (Knoester & Haynie, 2005).

In addition to the link between emotional support and physical and psychological health, social support also has a buffering effect from life events that threaten our health and well being (Fisher, 2000). How we interpret stressful events depends largely on our coping resources. And close interpersonal relationships are the main resource from which emotional support is derived.

Although healthy relationships are the goal of most individuals, why do they seem so difficult to attain? In a culture of massive technological and scientific change, human nature has remained pretty much the same. As evidence of this, the great Roman philosopher Cicero (106 B.C.- 43 B.C.) wrote *The Six Mistakes of Man* [*Humans*] over 2,000 years ago (Lenehan,1994). The timelessness of this writing is an amazing confirmation of the stagnation of human nature.

CURRICULUM GUIDELINES: INTERPERSONAL RELATIONSHIPS

An understanding of the development and maintenance of interpersonal relationships. Based on knowledge of:

1. understanding of self and others;
2. interpersonal communication skills, such as listening, empathy, self-disclosure,

   decision-making, problem-solving, and conflict resolution;
3. understanding of intimacy, love, and romance; and
4. relating to others with concern, respect, sincerity, and responsibility.

The Six Mistakes of Man [Humans]

Marcus Tullius Cicero

1. The delusion that personal gain is made by crushing others.
2. The tendency to worry about things that cannot be changed or corrected.
3. Insisting that a thing is impossible because we cannot accomplish it.
4. Refusal to set aside trivial preferences.
5. Neglecting development and refinement of the mind and not acquiring the habit of reading and studying.
6. Attempting to compel others to believe and live as we do.

Even though humans are making the same mistakes they made 2,000 years ago, we now seem to know what it is we need to do in order to live better lives. In the area of physical health for instance, why would anyone choose to smoke cigarettes when all the evidence demonstrates only negative health consequences?

We have also gained great insight into the key properties of healthy interpersonal relationships: Good communications skills such as attentive listening, good problem-solving and decision-making skills, assertiveness and flexibility are characteristics of happy marriages (Ridley, Wilhelm & Surra, 2001; Olson & Olson, 2000). Although the complexity of human nature may never allow a complete transformation, it is possible to build stronger and healthier relationships by family life education and relationships skill-building. This leads us to ask the question: How do family life educators deal with relevant interpersonal relationship issues over the life cycle (childhood, adolescence, adulthood, later adulthood)?

Childhood interpersonal relationship issues

For children, their family-of-origin is one of the most powerful sources of learning. If parents have not learned positive relationship skills, the chances are they will not teach through example and reinforce these skills in their children. This presents a challenge to family life educators to teach the parent(s) as well as the child. Programs that involve parents in learning and practicing skills such as active listening, decision-making, problem solving and conflict resolution are essential.

Studies consistently show the extent of parental involvement throughout childhood and adolescence is positively correlated with how well children learn as well as the trajectory of their social development and influences. For instance, children whose mothers were more securely attached to their children during the first few years of the child's life showed better social development at age three (McElwain, Cox, Burchinal & Macfie, 2003). One study found family communication and involvement to be a protective factor against urban African American children ages 9-15 being associated with gangs (Li, 2002). Other studies have shown relationships between more parental involvement (in the form of communicating and monitoring) with adolescents, with fewer behavioral problems and less association with deviant peers (Pearce, 2003; Roche, Ensminger, Chilcoat & Storr, 2003).

The earlier family involvement begins in a child's relationship skills educational process, the more powerful the effects will be. Fortunately, parental involvement is an important component in early childhood education (ECE) and Head Start programs.

Although healthy relationships skills modeled in the family environment certainly give a child an advantage, quality out-of-home early care and education (ECE) programs have also been shown to significantly improve a child's cognitive and social skills (Armor, 2003). While parent-focused home visiting/parent education programs provide benefits for parents, recent evaluations have revealed that child outcomes are best improved through high-quality out-of-home ECE programs which focus directly on the child (Gomby, Culross, & Behrman, 1999). In these evaluations, the chief factor in determining a quality environment was the existence of warm, sensitive and responsive interactions between caregiver and child. One may argue that these very factors must exist in all healthy interpersonal relationships and, therefore, are a goal for all interactions.

The Minnesota-based Early Childhood Family Education (ECFE) is an example of a program that provides supportive information and friendship with other parents. ECFE provides parenting programs, led by experienced, knowledgeable staff, for parents and their infants and school-age children. (For more information about ECFE, go to the Minnesota Department of Children Family and Learning web site listed in the related Web Site section). Some of the issues addressed are: self-esteem, development and behavior issues.

Head Start is a national ECE program providing developmental and social services for children ages 0-5 and their families. Some of the specific issues focus on: education, social-emotional development, physical and mental health and nutrition. Both Head Start and other ECE programs operate through organizations like school districts and community service organizations. Head Start is specifically for low-income families; both programs involve parent(s) and children and provide a great opportunity to model, nurture and support healthy relationships, such as parent/child relationship and friendships. Children in higher quality child care programs have been found to perform better on many dimensions, including language comprehension and short-term memory, compared to children in lower quality programs (NICHD, 2003). Participants in Early Head Start Programs were found to have a 2 point increase in verbal IQ scores (Armor, 2003).

Unfortunately, there seems to be a lack of programs available for children and their parents during the middle childhood years. The authors are not aware of any national programs aimed at improving interpersonal relationships for this age group.

CHILDHOOD — *Within the context of the family system*

Interpersonal Relationships

- Respecting self and others
- Sharing feelings constructively
- Expressing emotions
- Developing, maintaining, and ending relationships
- Building self-esteem and self-confidence
- Identifying and enhancing personal strengths
- Communicating with others
- Learning from and teaching others
- Sharing, friends, possessions, time
- Acting with consideration for self and others
- Handling problems with others

Reciprocal interactions between family and ecosystem

Multicultural • Gender Fair • Special Needs Aware

ADOLESCENCE — *Within the context of the family system*

Interpersonal Relationships

- Respecting self and others
- Changing and developing one's thoughts, attitudes, values
- Dealing with success and failure
- Accepting responsibility for one's actions
- Assessing and developing personal abilities and talents
- Communicating information, thoughts, and feelings
- Managing and expressing emotions
- Initiating, maintaining, and ending friendships
- Building self-esteem and self-confidence in self and others
- Assessing compatibility in interpersonal relationships
- Acting with consideration for self and others
- Understanding the basis for choosing a family lifestyle - values, heritage, religious beliefs
- Understanding the needs and motivations involved in dating
- Factors influencing mate selection - social, cultural, personal
- Understanding the dimensions of love and commitment
- Exploring the responsibilities of marriage

Reciprocal interactions between family and ecosystem

Multicultural • Gender Fair • Special Needs Aware

Adolescent interpersonal relationship issues

"Adolescence is the age of the final establishment of a dominant positive ego identity. It is then that a future within reach becomes part of the conscious life plan." (Erikson, 1963, p. 306)

Because adolescence is a time of great cognitive, physical, and emotional change, it is a critical period to reinforce positive self-image and respect for others. McKinley (2002) uses writings of various researchers and scholars (Erikson, Piaget, Turnbull, etc.) to point out how through teaching only intellectual development rather than inherent worth, we are missing the tremendous "teaching opportunities" that adolescence offers. Teaching youth that knowledge lies outside them represses the development of their own mind and instead demands only imitation of an external model. Perhaps the force to imitate plays a major role in the stagnation of human nature.

McKinley insightfully asserts that by reaching a deeper core within the adolescence (whether we call it spirit, soul, conscience or self-esteem) we can help them develop their own perceptions, priorities, and values instead of simply reacting to the environment that later evolves into autocratic styles of interaction. Another way to say this is to allow and encourage autonomy, rather than to expect obedience and conformity.

Programs for Youth

Historically, relationship skill development has been left to parents, trial-and-error or luck. There are now a variety of programs being offered around the country to teach youth the skills that are central in building and maintaining relationships. Armed with knowledge and relationship skills, youth can develop a sense of competence and confidence about marriage, as well as use these skills in all of their relationships including teachers, parents and friends. Some of the programs for youth available include: *Loving Well*, *BUILDING RELATIONSHIPS*, *CONNECTIONS*, and *PARTNERS*. Each will be briefly described.

The Art of Loving Well. A Character Education Curriculum for Today's Teenagers

The Art of Loving Well (Ellenwood, 1996*)* curriculum is composed of a text and teacher's guide. The curriculum uses literature revealing love and relationships to help teenagers develop responsible social and sexual values. *The Art of Loving Well* textbook includes 41 ethnically diverse literary selections, both time-honored classics and contemporary adolescent literature. Its three sections-"Early Loves and Losses", "Romance", and "Commitment and Marriage"-also contain activities that foster social

ADULTHOOD

Within the context of the family system

Interpersonal Relationships

- Establishing personal autonomy
- Building self-esteem and self-confidence in self and others
- Achieving constructive personal changes
- Communicating effectively
- Managing and expressing emotions
- Developing, maintaining, and ending relationships
- Exercising initiative in relationships
- Recognizing factors associated with quality relationships
- Taking responsibility and making commitments in relationships
- Evaluating choices and alternatives in relationships
- Acting in accordance with personal beliefs with consideration for others' best interest
- Understanding the effects of self-perceptions on relationships
- Varying influences on roles and relationships - ethnic, racial, gender, social, cultural
- Types of intimate relationships
- Creating and maintaining a family of one's own
- Changes in the marital relationship over time
- Dealing with crises

Multicultural • Gender Fair • Special Needs Aware

Reciprocal interactions between family and ecosystem

LATER ADULTHOOD

Within the context of the family system

Interpersonal Relationships

- Continuing personal autonomy
- Building self-esteem and self-confidence in self and others
- Understanding the effects of self-perceptions on relationships
- Exercising initiative in relationships
- Continuing intimate relationships
- Recognizing factors associated with quality relationships
- Taking responsibility and making commitments in relationships
- Evaluating choices and alternatives in relationships
- Acting in accordance with personal beliefs with consideration for others' best interest
- Changes in the marital relationship over time
- Maintaining relationships with one's own family
- Communicating effectively
- Managing and expressing emotions
- Dealing with crisis and loss
- Varying influences on roles and relationships - ethnic, racial, gender, social, cultural

Multicultural • Gender Fair • Special Needs Aware

Reciprocal interactions between family and ecosystem

and emotional skills, effective communication, critical thinking, decision making, conflict resolution and abstinence from premature sexual activity. The text reinforces the value of committed faithful friendship and marriage.

Developed at Boston University, *The Art of Loving Well* was field tested in 8th and 9th grade English and health classes with 10,000 students in Maine, Massachusetts and South Carolina. It has been used subsequently in 47 states in grades 7-12 in schools, community and church groups, and in homes. Independent evaluation of control and experimental groups confirms its positive impact on adolescent attitudes and behaviors. Teacher training is available (not mandatory) along with *The Art of Loving Well* text, *Teacher's Guide,* and accompanying videos (for more information, see Key Resource section).

BUILDING RELATIONSHIPS: Developing Skills for Life

BUILDING RELATIONSHIPS (Olson, DeFrain, & Olson, 1999) is designed to build awareness of dating and interpersonal relationships for teenagers ages 13 to 18. The *BUILDING RELATIONSHIPS* curriculum is composed of a student text, a teacher's manual and accompanying power point for each chapter (for information about how to obtain this program see Key Resource section).

The *BUILDING RELATIONSHIPS* text for students contains 13 chapters which focus on major issues for teenagers including: dating, communication problems, affection and sexuality, family of origin issues, financial issues and values and beliefs. The text engages students in learning by beginning each chapter with a ten-item quiz on the topic. The readers discover the embedded textual answers to the quiz as they read each chapter.

BUILDING RELATIONSHIPS is based on family systems theory (Goldenberg & Goldenberg, 2007) as well as communication (Whitchurch & Dickson, 1999) and conflict theory (Sprey, 1999), the program teaches the skills of assertiveness and active listening and constructive conflict resolution. Taught in schools, churches and community education courses, the course can vary in length. The *BUILDING RELATIONSHIPS* Program is used in over 500 locations in 31 states. Pre-testing and post-testing materials are included allowing for assessment of course effectiveness.

The CONNECTIONS Series

The *CONNECTIONS* Series (Kamper, 2004) consists of two programs that teach teenagers essential skills for healthy, happy relationships (Dating and Emotions; Relationships and Marriage). Concepts from the PREP marriage program such as relationship guidelines, myths, and expectations have recently been added to both programs.

CONNECTIONS: Dating and Emotions (ages 13-17)

This program helps younger teens understand the challenges that arise in early relationships and helps them establish a strong foundation for later life. Through a variety of exercises, teens learn how relationships develop, effective ways to communicate, spotting destructive patterns, dealing with emotions and other essential skills.

An Instructor's Kit includes lesson plans for 17 one-hour lessons, transparency and handout materials, activity cards, and one student workbook. Additional student workbooks may be purchased.

CONNECTIONS: Relationships and Marriage (ages 16-20)
Young adults face enormous-and conflicting-pressures in their relationships, especially their romantic ones. This program gives them practical tools for understanding, managing and making wise decisions about their relationships. The program covers topics like self-awareness, understanding relationships, communications and conflict…plus a Marriage Game.

An Instructor's Kit includes 18 one-hour lessons plans, transparency and handout masters, activity cards, and one student workbook. Additional student workbooks may be purchased. A Spanish supplement is available for the Relationships and Marriage program. Schools, youth programs, and youth organizations use this ready-to-teach program. *CONNECTIONS* programs are used in over 400 locations in 34 states. Instructor training is available however, teachers, youth workers and counselors can teach it, with a minimum of special preparation (for information on this program, see Key Resource section).

PARTNERS: A Curriculum for Preserving Marriages
This program is sponsored by the American Bar Association-Family Law Section and based on the work of the PAIRS Foundation (American Bar Association, 1999). The *PARTNERS* program is designed to teach students how to determine the qualities they prefer in a mate, communication and negotiation skills, how to manage stress in a relationship, and how the legal system impacts marriages, families and children. PARTNERS is a ten week course consisting of a DVD of five video segments and a CD-ROM Instructor's Manual to guide teachers through the course. The program video shows a young couple with a child facing a variety of common family problems. Ultimately their differences lead one partner to consider divorce and visit an attorney, learning what the hard realities of a marital breakup actually are.

Course instructors help students identify the real source of conflict and point out how conflict is fueled by existing communication patterns. They then teach alternative approaches which students practice through role-playing. Students are encouraged to utilize the communication skills they have learned in their daily lives. Additionally, students learn about family law and how it affects their lives.

Classroom teachers coordinate class discussions and homework outlined in the *PARTNERS* curriculum guide that accompanies the course. Local attorneys are encouraged to consult with classes to clarify how divorce, child custody, support and related family law issues are handled in their particular states.

PARTNERS is designed for a high school classroom setting (grades 11 and 12) using a video and instructor's guide. Student workbooks are not required. Local lawyers co-lead classroom discussions on alternate weeks during the ten-week curriculum. No teacher training is required (for more information on this program, see Key Resource section).

Adulthood interpersonal relationship issues

Adult relationships
The passage from adolescence to adulthood occurs in a gradual and more complex fashion than it did even thirty years ago. There are five traditional markers of reaching adulthood: finishing school, leaving home, financial independence, getting married and having a child. In 1960 70% of 25-year –old American woman and 65% of 30-year-old American men had attained all five of these benchmarks. By the year 2000, these numbers dropped dramatically to where only 25% of American women and 31% of American men had reached these benchmarks by the ages 25 and 30 respectively (Furstenberg, Kennedy, Mcloyd, Rumbaut, & Settersten, 2004).

This longer transition from adolescence to adulthood allows a variety of social institutions—such as colleges and universities, churches and church groups, military, and work settings—to be part of this transition into adulthood. Richard Settersten, Jr. in his book, "On the Frontier of Adulthood" discusses how the road to self-sufficiency is less about dependence as it is about learning interdependence (Settersten, Furstenberg, & Rumbaut, 2005). Interdependence lends itself well to current trends, where young adults experience a longer period of time where they rely on their families and others—relationships and social institutions—for support.

Marriage
Marriage preparation and marriage education are significant themes in the adulthood stage of life. Educational programs for premarital and marital couples are increasingly more available to couples nationally. These programs provide many opportunities for couples to learn and apply good relationship skills such as communicating effectively, managing and expressing emotions, taking responsibility for our actions, and problem-solving, to name a few. Premarital interventions have been shown to increase participants' communication skills, conflict management, and general relationship quality (Carroll & Doherty, 2003; Silliman & Schumm, 2000). A recent study found that a quality premarital program reduced divorce by 30% (Stanley, Amato, Johnson & Markman, 2006).

There are several premarital and marital programs available for couples to help increase the quality of their relationship. We will briefly describe five of the most established programs: *Couples Communication*, *Empowering Couples*, *PREP*, *PREPARE/ENRICH*, and *Relationship Enhancement*.

Couples Communication I & II

Miller and colleagues (Miller, Nunnally, Wachman, & Miller, 1991) developed Couples Communication Programs I and II. These two skill-building programs are designed to help premarital and married couples increase self and partner awareness, map their relationship, learn talking, listening and conflict resolution skills; align values, goals and manage anger. Based on communication systems theory (Whitechurch & Dickman, 1999), Couples Communication I and II have a moderate degree of structure with learning through experimental, didactic, and manuals (for more information, see the Key Resource section).

Empowering Couples Program

The Empowering Couples Program (Olson and Olson, 2000) contains a book and program for couples built on a strengths perspective and marriage research. The book and program are based on a national survey of 21,501 married couples to identify strengths of happy versus unhappy couples. The book includes 10 couple quizzes and couple discussion and exercises. Participants identify their couple strengths and build on these strengths through skill-building and planning (for more information, see Life Innovations in Key Resource section).

PREP Program

The PREP Program was built on the popular book, "Fighting for Your Marriage," by Markman, Stanley and Blumberg (2001). Based on social learning and cognitive-behavioral theories, PREP teaches communication, conflict-resolution, negotiation skills, restructuring expectations and fun enhancement through a variety of formats and facilitation models (for more information, see the Center for Marital and Family Studies in the related Web Site section).

PREPARE/ENRICH

The PREPARE/ENRICH Program was developed by Olson and colleagues (Olson & Olson, 1999) to help couples prepare for marriage and to strengthen their marriage. Empirically based, the premarital (PREPARE) and marital (ENRICH) programs are designed to help facilitate dialogue for couples about important issues in their relationship. The first step is taking a couple inventory (195 items covering 20 categories). Couples then complete six couple exercises where they will practice relationships skills such as assertiveness, active listening and conflict resolution on current issues as well as to prime them to resolve future issues (for more information, see Life Innovations in Key Resource section).

Relationship Enhancement Program

This couple program was developed by Gurney and colleagues (Cavedo & Guerney, 1999) to teach principles of education rooted in Rogerian and learning theories. It teaches couples nine practical skills: empathy, expression, problem discussing, problem solution, partner-facilitation, self-change, other-change, generalization and maintenance. This skill-building program provides learning through didactic, home study with phone coaching, experimental, audiotapes and text (for more information, contact the National Institute of Relationship Enhancement in Key Resource section).

Later adulthood interpersonal relationship issues

The importance of interpersonal relationships continues throughout the life span. Social support-having a network of relationships with other people-promotes positive mental and physical health and increases resistance to disease. Recent findings suggest providing social support may be even more beneficial than being the recipient of social support. Even after controlling for demographics, personality, health, mental health, and marital-relationship variables, older married individuals who provided instrumental support to friends, relatives, neighbors, as well as emotional support to their spouses, significantly reduced their mortality (Brown, Nesse, Vinokur, & Smith, 2003). Following retirement, people are often confronted with more free time than they ever remember having. Reconnecting with old friends and developing new friendships networks is important during this time to get the interpersonal support and stimulation that used to come from work.

Because aging occurs in a family context, family life educators will be called on to address the interpersonal issues of aging more than ever. In general, we are living longer and healthier lives (Recer, 2000). Currently, 12 percent of the U.S. population are 65 years of age or older and by the year 2030 that percentage is expected to reach twenty percent (Armas, 2003). Nearly 25% of American household families are providing care to older adult family members. In fact, overall, families spend as many years in eldercare as they spend caregiving for children (Flori, 2002). To add to the demands of caregiving, over 40 percent of caregivers are members of the "sandwich generation"-a term used to describe adults who are concurrently providing care for their own children while also helping support their parents (Flori, 2002).

Caregiving for the elderly can be a major strain for families-physically, mentally, and even financially (Schultz & Beach, 1999). Healthy interpersonal relationships can act as a buffer against these negative strains. Research has found caregivers who have strong and satisfying interpersonal relationships have less depression, more life satisfaction and fewer health problems than those with less satisfying relationships (Dunkin & Anderson-Hanley, 1998). Given the prevalence of caregiving families, family life educators should be familiar with caregiving phenomena, be able to recognize caregiver strain, and be able to reference community resources for both the elder and the caregiver.

Future Issues and Challenges for Family Life Educators

- **Teaching individuals to be proactive rather than reactive in their relationships.** Being proactive gets individuals invested in their relationships and empowers them with skills and a sense of responsibility. We need to help people learn how to more effectively deal with their current issues so they can lead more satisfying lives.
- **Relationship skills need to be an ongoing part of our formal and informal educational processes throughout the life cycle.**
- **Lack of programs and outreach for young adulthood and later adulthood.** Youth need programs to help them make a more successful transition into adulthood. Likewise, we have neglected older adults. While a variety of retirement programs exists, most are focused on financial planning for retirement. Many retirees could benefit from relationship courses that address changes at this developmental stage (decrease in social interaction due to retirement, more free time, and more time with partner).
- **Bridging relationship programs-teaching and bridging relationship skills across the life cycle.** An important challenge for FLEs is to encourage individuals to continue learning about interpersonal relationships. People need to understand that developing interpersonal relationship skills are an ongoing process. As people are growing, developing, and changing, their relationships will also change. While individuals and couples are attending one program, the impact would greatly increase if they attended a follow-up or sequential program. One example would to build a linkage between family life classes in the schools and taking premarital preparation. Another linkage would be between premarital counseling and marriage enrichment programs.

Interpersonal relationships are the portal and the arena in which we forge our self and social identities. Drs. Harville Hendrix and Helen Hunt encapsulated the significance of relational work when they said, "We are born in relationships, we are wounded in relationships, and we can be healed in relationships" (p.xix Hendrix, 1988). This work is an ongoing process, changing in feature, but never in importance, as human development is ongoing. It takes willingness, practice and insight to understand the intricacies of our feelings, and to learn the relationship skills that form the foundation of healthy individuals, families and communities. Human nature may be languishing behind technology, but we have enormous potential. If we put a fraction of the energies currently designated to technological advancement into improving interpersonal relationships, after 20 years we will look back at the change and it will be the equivalent of children today trying to imagine life without cell phones and personal computers. Relationship skills need to be an ongoing part of our formal and informal educational processes throughout the life cycle. The vitality of future society and its prospects for the future, rely on the quality of our human relationships.

References

American Bar Association. (1999). *Partners curriculum manual for teachers.* Chicago, IL: Family Law Section of the American Bar Association.

Armas, G. C. (2003). Worldwide population again. In *Annuals Editions: Aging* (Ed.) Cox, H. McGraw-Hill: Guilford, CT.

Armor, D. J. (2003). *Maximizing intelligence*. New Brunswick, NJ: Transaction Publishers.

Baker, B., Paquette, M., Szalai, J., Driver, H., Perger, T., Helmers, K., et al. (2000). The influence of marital adjustment on a 3-year left ventricle mass and ambulatory blood pressure in mild hypertension. *Archives of Internal Medicine, 160,* 3453-3458.

Beach, S. R. H., Katz, J., Sooyeon, K., & Brody, G. H. (2003). Prospective effects of marital satisfaction on depressive symptoms in established marriages: A dyadic model. *Journal of Social and Personal Relationships, 20*(3), 355-371.

Bland, S. H., Krogh, V., Winkelstein, W., & Trevisan, M. (1991). Social network and blood pressure: A population study. *Psychosom Med, 53*, 598-607.

Brown, S. L., Nesse, R. M., Vinokur, A. D., & Smith, D. M. (2003). Providing social support may be more beneficial than receiving it: Results from a prospective study of mortality. *Psychological Science, 14*(4), 320-327.

Carroll, J. S., & Doherty, W. J. (2003). Evaluating the effectiveness of premarital prevention programs: A meta-analytic review of outcome research. *Family Relations, 521*, 105-118.

Cavedo, C., & Guerney, B. G. (1999). Relationship enhancement enrichment and problem-prevention programs: Therapy-derived, powerful, versatile. In R. Berger & M.T. Hannah (Eds.), *Preventive approaches in couples therapy* (pp. 73-105). Lillington, NC: Edwards Brothers.

Dunkin, J. & Anderson-Hanley, C. (1998). Dementia caregiver burden: A review of the literature and guidelines for assessment and intervention. *Neurology, 51* (supplemental), S53-S60.

Ellenwood, S. (1996). *The art of loving well: A character education curriculum for today's teenagers.* Boston, MA: Boston University Press.

Erikson, E. H. (1963). *Childhood and society.* New York, NY: W. W. Norton & Company.

Flori, D. E. (2002 July/August). Clinical update: Caring for the elderly. *Family Therapy Magazine, 1*(4), 36-42.

Fisher, L. (2000). Can addressing family relationships improve outcomes in chronic disease? *Journal of Family Practice, 49*, 561-566.

Furstenberg, F. F. Jr., Kennedy, S., Mcloyd, V. C., Rumbaut, R. G., & Settersten, R. A. Jr. (2004). Growing up is harder to do. *Contexts, 3*, 33-41.

Galliher, R. V., Rostosky, S. S., Welsh, D. P., & Kawaguchi, M. C. (1999). Power and psychological well-being in late adolescent romantic relationships. *Sex Roles: A Journal of Research, 41*, 39-50.

Goldenberg, I., & Goldenberg, H. (2007). *Family therapy: An overview.* Pacific Grove, CA: Brooks/Cole.

Gomby, D., Culross, P. L., & Behrman, R. E. (1999). *Home visiting: Recent program evaluations - analysis and recommendations: Future of children*, (9, No.1). Packard Foundation.

Hendrix, H. (1988). *Getting the love you want: A guide for couples.* New York: Henry Holt.

Holt-Lunstad, J., Unchino, B. N., Smith, T. W., & Hicks, A. (2007). On the importance of relationship quality: The impact of ambivalence in friendships in cardiovascular functioning. *Annals of Behavioral Medicine, 33*(3), 278-290.

Kamper, C. (2004). *CONNECTIONS: Relationships and marriage,* Berkeley, CA: The Dibble Fund for Marriage Education.

Kimmel, P. L., Peterson, R. A., Weihs, K. L., Shidler, N., Simmens, S. J., Alleyne, S., et al. (2000). Dyadic relationship conflict, gender, and mortality in urban hemodialysis patients. *Journal of American Society of Nephrology, 11,* 1518-1525.

Kirby, J. S., Baucom, D. H., & Peterman, M. A. (2005). An investigation of unmet intimacy needs in marital relationships. *Journal of Marital and Family Therapy, 31*(4), 313-325.

Knoester, C., & Haynie, D. L. (2005). Community context, social integration into family and youth violence. *Journal of Marriage and Family, 67*(3), 767-780.

Lamb, K. A., Lee, G. R., & DeMaris, A. (2003). Union formation and depression: Selection and relationship effects. *Journal of Marriage and Family Therapy, 65*(4), 953-962.

Lenehan, A., Ed. (1994). *The best of "Bits & Pieces".* Fairfield, NJ: The Economics Press.

Li, X. (2002). Risk and protective factors associated with gang involvement among urban African-American adolescents. *Youth and Society, 34*(2), 172-194.

Luster, T., Bates, L., Vandenbelt, M., & Nievar, A. M. (2004). Family advocates' perspective on the early academic success of children born to low-income adolescent Mothers. *Family Relations, 53*(1), 68-77.

Markman, H. J., Stanley, S. M., & Blumberg, S. L. (2001). *Fighting for your marriage.* San Francisco: Jossey-Bass.

McElwain, N. L., Cox, M. J., Bruchinal, M. R., & Macfie, J. (2003). Differentiating among insecure mother-infant attachment classifications: A focus on child-friendly interactions and exploration during solitary play at 36 months. *Attachment and Human Development, 5*(2), 136-164.

McKinley, T. (2002). *The opportunity of adolescence.* Retrieved November 1, 2002 from www.winternet.com/~webpage/adolescencepaper.html

Miller, S. L., Nunnally, E. W., Wachman, D. B., & Miller, P. A. (2006). *Couple communication instructor manual.* Denver-Littleton, CO: Interpersonal Communication Programs.

NICHD, (2003). Does quality of child care affect child outcomes at age 4 and ½. Early Child Care Research Network, *Developmental Psychology, 39*(3), 451-469.

Newton, T. L., & Sanford, J. M. (2003). Conflict structure moderates associates between cardiovascular reactivity and negative marital interaction. *Healthy Psychology, 22,* 270-278.

Olson, D. H., DeFrain, J., & Olson, A. K. (1999). *Building relationships: Developing skills for life.* Minneapolis: Life Innovations, Inc.

Olson, D. H., & Olson, A. K. (1999). PREPARE/ENRICH program: Version 2000. In R. Berger & M. T. Hannah (Eds.), *Preventive approaches in couples therapy* (pp. 196-216). Lillington, NC: Edwards Brothers.

Olson, D. H., & Olson, A. K. (2000). *Empowering couples: Building on your strengths.* Minneapolis: Life Innovations, Inc.

Pearce, M. J. (2003). The protective effects of religiousness and parent involvement on the development on conduct problems among youth exposed to violence. *Child Development, 74*(6), 1682-1696.

Recer, P. (2000). Study: Elderly enjoying more vigorous old age. *In Annual Editions: Aging.* (Ed.) Cox, H. McGraw-Hill: Guilford, CT.

Ridley, C. A., Wilhelm, M. S., & Surra, C. A. (2001). Married couples' conflict responses and marital quality. *Journal of Social and Personal Relationships, 18*(4), 517-534.

Roche, K. M., Ensminger, M. E., Chilcoat, H., & Storr, C. (2003). Establishing independence in low-income urban areas: The relationship to adolescent aggressive behavior. *Journal of Marriage and Family, 65*(3), 668-680.

Ryan, A. K., & Willits, F. K. (2007). Family ties, physical health, and psychological well-being. *Journal of Aging and Health, 19*(6), 907-920.

Schulz, R., & Beach, S. (1999). Caregiving as a risk factor for mortality: The caregiver health effects study. *Journal of the American Medical Association, 282*, 2215-2219.

Seeman, T. E., & McEwen, B. S. (1996). Impact of social environment: Characteristics in neuroendocrine function. *Psychosom Med, 58*, 450-471.

Settersten, R.A. Jr., Furstenberg, F. F. Jr., & Rumbaut, R. G. (2005). *On the frontier of adulthood: Theory, research and public policy.* Chicago, IL: University of Chicago Press.

Silliman, B., & Schumm, W. R. (2000). Marriage preparation programs: Literature review. *The Family Journal, 8,* 128-137.

Sprey, J. (1999). Family dynamics: An essay on conflict and power. In M. B. Sussman, S. K. Steinmetz & G. W. Peterson (Eds.), (pp. 667-686). *Handbook of marriage and the family* (2nd Ed.), New York: Plenum Press.

Stanley, S. M., Amato, P. R., Johnson, C. A., & Markman, H. J. (2006). Premarital education, marital quality, and marital stability: Findings from a large, random household survey. *Journal of Family Psychology, 20*(1), 117-126.

Waite, L. J., & Gallagher, M. (2000). *The case for marriage: Why married people are happier, healthier and better off financially.* New York: NY: Doubleday.

Whitchurch, G. G., & Dickson, F. C. (1999). Family communication. In M. B. Sussman, S. K. Steinmetz & G. W. Peterson (Eds.), (pp. 687-704). *Handbook of marriage and the family* (2nd ed.), New York: Plenum Press.

Key Resources

The American Bar Association Section of Family Law, 750 N. Lake Shore Drive, Chicago, IL 60611 (312-988-5145 or www.abanet.org/family/partners/).

Brophy, E. H., & Honig, A. S. (1996). *Talking with your baby: Family as the first school.* Syracuse, NY: Syracuse University Press.

Kamper, C. (2004). *CONNECTIONS: Relationships and marriage*. Berkely, CA: The Dibble Fund for Marriage Education.

Interpersonal Communication Programs, Inc., 30772 Southview Drive, Suite 200, Evergreen, CO 80439, USA. For more information: (800-328-5099 or www.couplecommunication.com).

Edinberg, M. (1987). *Talking with your aging parent.* Boston, MA: Shambhala.

Furman, E. (1998). *Relationships in early childhood: Helping young children grow.* Madison, CT: International Universities Press.

Life Innovations, Inc. P.O. Box 190, Minneapolis, MN 55440-0190 (800-331-1661 or www.prepare-enrich.com/).

The Loving Well Project. Nancy McLaren, Boston University, School of Education, 605 Commonwealth Ave., Boston, MA 02215 (617-353-4088 or www.bu.edu/education/lovingwell/).

The National Institute of Relationship Enhancement. 4400 East-West Hwy., Suite 28, Bethesda, MD 20814-4501 (800-432-6454 or www.nire.org/).

Oberlander, J. R. (2000). *Slow and steady, get me ready: A parent's handbook for children from birth to age 5.* Fairfax Station, VA: Bio-Alpha, Inc.

Shames, S., Wolf, G., Wolf, K. G., & Rosenblatt, R. (1997). *Pursuing the dream: What helps children and their families succeed.* New York, NY: Aperture.

Siegler, A. (1998). *The essential guide to the new adolescence: How to raise an emotionally healthy teenager.* New York: Plume.

Unell, B. C., & Wyckoff, J. L. (2000). *The eight seasons of parenthood: How the stages of parenting constantly reshape our adult identities.* New York, NY: Times Books.

Wycott, J. L., & Unell, B. C. (1995). *20 teachable virtues.* New York: Perigee Press.

Related Web Sites

The American Psychological Association Help Center: www.apahelpcenter.org

Administration on Aging: www.aoa.dhhs.gov

Center for Research on Families and Relationships: www.crfr.ac.uk

The Coalition for Marriage, Family and Couples Education: www.smartmarriages.com

Family Caregiver Alliance: www.caregiver.org

Family Support America: www.familysupportamerica.org

Head Start: www.acf.hhs.gov/programs/hsb

Parenthood.com: www.parenthoodweb.com

Search Institute: www.search-institute.org

Well Spouse Foundation: www.wellspouse.org

About the Authors

Amy Olson-Sigg, MFT Trainee, is Research Associate at Life Innovations, Inc. She is co-author of *The Couple Checkup* (2008), *Empowering Couples: Building on Your Strengths* (2nd ed, 2000), and *Building Relationships: Developing Skills for Life*. Email: aolson@prepare-enrich.com.

David H. Olson, Ph.D., is Professor Emeritus, Family Social Science, University of Minnesota and President of Life Innovations, Inc., Minneapolis, MN. He has authored over 100 journal articles 20 books including *Marriage & Family: Diversity and Strengths* (6th Edition, 2008). Email: dolson@prepare-enrich.com.

Family Resource Management

Kathryn D. Rettig

What Is Family Resource Management?[1]

Family resource management involves assuming shared leadership in the family for envisioning a desirable and possible future; taking initiative for coordinating the problem-solving, decision-making, and actions that will move family members toward that future; and adjusting to constantly changing family members and environmental opportunities and demands. These dynamic managerial processes involve identifying and facing the practical problems of everyday life; thinking about alternative strategies for resolving them; and mobilizing a combination of personal, social, economic, and natural resources that can assist in accomplishing the intended changes.

A problem is a challenge rather than something negative. A problem can be defined as a discrepancy between the actual situation and our image of the ideal situation (Tallman, 1993), an image that is shaped by our values, goals, and standards. A practical problem is a value-based question about what should be done, or what is best in a particular situation that has unique conditions, people, and resource opportunities, and constraints. Practical problems arise repeatedly from generation to generation because they are fundamentally connected to our human nature (Brown & Paolucci, 1979).

Facing the Practical Problems of Everyday Life

Practical problems involve challenges, such as: Should we marry? Should we have or raise children? How should we educate our children for an unknown future? What is the best way to provide protective surveillance for our adolescents? How should we balance time and effort among work, rest, leisure, and family? What is the best way to assist or care for our elderly parents? How can we best provide for our future retirement and also meet our current financial needs? How do we want to use the leisure time of our lives? What kinds of contributions do we hope to make to society? What kinds of assets do we want to develop in our lifetimes? What kind of balances do we want among our different kinds of wealth in money, things, and people (financial, physical, human, social, and cultural capital)? And, what is the best way to transfer our financial, physical, and cultural assets to the next generation (University of Minnesota Extension Service, 2001)?

Families, compared to other small groups, are unique because of the diverse kinds of challenges that arise in everyday life, the frequency with which they arise, the number of problems existing simultaneously, the number that continuously remain

[1] Management is the conscious creation of opportunities in life, and the thoughtful adaptation to internal changes and environmental demands, through problem-solving and decision making, in order to mobilize resources in ways that will meet human needs, realize values, reach important goals, and enhance life quality. *Family* resource management requires using the above mental processes in coordinating several people, who may have competing values and goals, and making many decisions about how to create and use human and non human resources to realize conflicting ideas of the good life. It is a huge challenge for any visionary leader.

> **CURRICULUM GUIDELINES:**
> **FAMILY RESOURCE MANAGEMENT**
>
> An understanding of the decisions individuals and families make about developing and allocating resources (e.g., time, money, material assets, energy, friends, neighbors, and space) to meet their goals. Based on knowledge of:
>
> 1. an understanding of concepts such as goals, resources, planning, decision-making, implementing; and
> 2. an understanding of changing family resource management concerns over the life cycle and of various concerns for different family structures.

unresolved, and the multiple approaches to facing the issues (Rettig, 1998; Weick, 1971). The sources of family problems are both external and internal, and they vary by their orientations (growth, preventive, remedial), comprehensiveness (technical, elemental, integrative), and their content (organization, allocation, policy, interaction) (Liston, 1966). Tallman (1988, 1993) used a different taxonomy for family problems and suggested that in addition to classifying problems by source (external or internal), problems could be organized by their task requirements and outcome control, which resulted in 144 types of problems relevant to family life. Many of the practical problems of family life are also ethical issues and/or and moral dilemmas (Leichtentritt & Rettig, 1999) that are not classified in these earlier taxonomies.

Resolving the Practical Problems

The thinking processes of practical reasoning (Thomas & Laster, 1998) cannot be accomplished without many kinds of resources, especially the human resources of time, motivation, concentration, and energy. Practical reasoning requires several *alternating and simultaneous processes* (Knippel, 1998). The reasoning involves: (a) interpreting the context of the situation (environmental and personal demands); (b) formulating the valued ends that are desirable to seek (values, goals, standards); (c) finding information about possible means and strategies to reach the valued ends (resources); (d) considering the consequences of alternative actions and making a judgment (decision-making); and (e) taking actions based on judgments (decision implementation) (Fedje, 1998). In other words, practical reasoning processes require perceiving the needed or wanted changes (feeling), deciding on a response for oneself or with others (thinking), and actuating the decisions (acting) (Rettig, 1993). Practical reasoning processes require an ecological perspective (Bubolz, Eicher & Sontag, 1979; Bubolz & Sontag, 1993; Darling, 1987) because one must pay attention to whether environmental changes require a response, what alternatives are possible, and how the actions will change the environments.

Mobilizing Resources

The feeling, thinking, acting behaviors of problem-solving and decision-making in families are always about resources: their production, consumption, conservation, allocation, distribution, substitution, investment, exchange, transfer, and management. Resources are the means to make a desired outcome a reality. In order for a resource to be helpful, it has to be accessible (possession utility) at the time it is needed (time utility), at the place it is needed (place utility), and in a useful form (form utility) for working toward the intended outcome (Rettig, Rossmann & Hogan, 1993).

Human resources are the most important component in any problem-solving situation and include individual, *affective* qualities like motivation and enthusiasm; *cognitive* qualities of creativity and concentration; *psychomotor* qualities, such as communication and computer competencies; and *temporal* qualities such as time orientation (Rice & Tucker, 1986). Family members further provide *services* that other members need and enjoy, which is called service utility (Fitzsimmons, 1951). Family *groups* also have additional resources, such as trust and cooperation. The health and comfort of individuals and the quality of family life also depend very much on natural resources, such as the quality of air, water, and food supplies; and the availability of electrical and fossil fuel energy. For example, a fifteen-day power failure changes the activities of every family member and also the role relationships.

Making Many Kinds of Decisions

Solving any one practical problem may lead to making several kinds of decisions, having *varying decision processes*, (technical, economic, social-ethical, legal, and political processes) (Diesing, 1962), depending upon the presenting value conflicts and particular resource demands. Each of these decision situations emphasizes particular values and requires unique human resources. Each decision type involves a unique definition of a rational decision, or in other words, there are many different definitions of a rational decision (Diesing, 1962; Rettig, 1993), depending upon the presenting challenges and needed resources. All of these types of decisions are present in everyday family life. Parents mediate disputes between siblings (a legal decision situation) and adults often develop coalitions of family members in order to establish and maintain power (a political decision situation).

Economic decision situations involve the presenting problem of too many goals and too few resources to accomplish them (Diesing, 1962). The decision processes require prioritizing goals and deciding which of them can be maintained and which ones must be sacrificed, then allocating the scarce resources among the most important goals. The challenge of planning the use of family income for the next year or trying to figure out how time can be used for several different activities are examples of economic decision situations. The value of maximization is emphasized when deciding the best way to allocate the scarce resources.

Social (integrative, ethical) decisions (Diesing, 1962) arise because two or more people, who must make a decision together, have conflicts in values, goals, standards, or roles and must find ways to reframe the problem in new ways, agree on universal values (Kidder, 1994), or find new goals. These decision processes require reframing the way we look at the situation, and collaboration and cooperation in order to reach a creative solution that meets the needs of all parties. A study of interpersonal conflicts in everyday decision-making was reported by Kirchler, Rodler, Holzl and Meier (2001).

Using Multiple Managerial Approaches

The processes of resource management in families have been historically described as the intentional and conscious thinking and actions of individuals, and the explicit deliberations of two or more people (Deacon & Firebaugh, 1988; Fitzsimmons, 1951; Goldsmith, 2005; Gross, Crandall & Knoll, 1980; Melson, 1980; Moore & Asay, 2008; Paolucci, Hall & Axinn, 1977; Rice & Tucker, 1986). However, research has revealed a diversity of managerial patterns. The decision-making processes are distinctly different in open, closed, random, and synchronous family systems (Constantine, 1986). Goal-seeking actions in family systems are complicated, and may be beyond the conscious awareness of participants, or there may be few or no shared goals (Broderick, 1993).

The kind of problem that is faced may influence the kind of individual thinking style needed (Rettig, 1998; Rettig & Schulz, 1991) and the human resources that are involved (Pecchioni, 2001; Tam & Rettig, 1999). Sillars and Kalbflesch reported that couple decision styles varied on "a continuum from direct, explicit, organized, and proactive, to indirect, implicit impulsive, and incremental" (1989, p. 180). Couples with direct, explicit, decision-making styles, had more: prospective, rather than retrospective, awareness of problems; mastery orientation of facing problems, rather than the stoicism of accepting undesirable situations; conflict engagement than avoidance; explicit agreements than silent arrangements; proactive than incremental planning; and explicit communication with elaborated language that conveyed accurate meanings. In other words, couples with explicit decision-making styles had different kinds of human resources that facilitated the managerial processes in their lives.

CHILDHOOD — *Within the context of the family system*

Family Resource Management

- Taking care of possessions
- Helping with family tasks
- Learning about time and schedules
- Learning to choose
- Earning, spending and saving money
- Understanding space and privacy
- Developing talents and abilities
- Selecting and consuming - food, clothing, recreation
- Using and saving human and non-human resources
- Influences on consumer decisions – personal values, costs, media, peers

Reciprocal interactions between family and ecosystem

Multicultural • Gender Fair • Special Needs Aware

ADOLESCENCE — *Within the context of the family system*

Family Resource Management

- Allocating time for work, school, leisure
- Negotiating privacy and independence
- Selection of resources to meet personal needs - food, clothing, recreation
- Using personal resources
- Earning, spending, and saving money
- Responsibility for decisions
- Developing leisure interests
- Values as basis for choices
- Choosing long- and short-term goals
- Exploring career choices
- Assessment of and changes in personal and family resources
- Influences on consumer decisions - personal values, costs, media, peers

Reciprocal interactions between family and ecosystem

Multicultural • Gender Fair • Special Needs Aware

Why is Family Resource Management Important?[2]

Family resource management is an essential activity of daily life in families. The quality of resource management in families also has an impact on communities and the larger society. Family resource management is the essence of family life education because it is a way of thinking about everyday life that involves, according to Arcus (1993), "dealing with problems, preventing problems, and developing potentials," the three rationales that have been influential in the development of family life education (p. 230). Resource management and family life education are the means through which families strengthen and enrich individual and family well-being by making rational decisions (Arcus, Schvaneveldt & Moss, 1993).

Educators are involved in resource management education any time they are assisting others in thinking about life with greater mindfulness and lesser mindlessness (Langer, 1989). This education involves assisting others in taking initiative for facing problems; identifying the implicit values underlying their beliefs in ethical decision situations (Leichtentritt & Rettig, 2001); and verbalizing their value, goal, and role conflicts in social decision situations (Leichtentritt & Rettig, 2000). We can encourage others to engage in the perspective taking that is an important process in moral problem solving when prioritizing values (Leichtentritt & Rettig, 1999).

[2] For Society: Families create human resources and make substantial investments in human capital, creating workers who are capable and productive, and have the capacity for effective leadership. For Families: Thoughtful problem-solving can make life more satisfying by bringing about less disruptive changes, reducing tensions, resolving conflicts among members, and maintaining strength and synergy of the family group. For Individuals: Values can be realized, goals accomplished, and quality of life can be enhanced when by thinking about what it means, and how to allocate one's time.

ADULTHOOD

Within the context of the family system

Family Resource Management

- Expendability of human energy
- Developing personal resources
- Development of personal resources through career choices
- Values as a bases for choices
- Developing leisure interests
- Varying needs of family members for privacy and independence
- Using resources to meet basic needs of family - food, clothing, shelter
- Differing views about uses of family resources
- Establishing long- and short-term goals
- Financial planning
- Resource consumption and conservation - material and non-material
- Balancing family and work roles
- Influences on consumer decisions - personal values, costs, media, peers
- Retirement planning

Multicultural • Gender Fair • Special Needs Aware

Reciprocal interactions between family and ecosystem

LATER ADULTHOOD

Within the context of the family system

Family Resource Management

- Values as bases for choices
- Establishing a plan for the distribution of resources and management if incompetent - will, living will
- Using personal resources
- Expanding leisure interests
- Balancing life patterns of retirees with work roles of children
- Varying needs of family members for privacy and independence
- Resource consumption and conservation - material and non-material
- Using resources to meet basic needs of family - food, clothing, shelter
- Differing views about uses of family resources
- Establishing long- and short-term goals
- Managing financial resources in retirement
- Influences on consumer decisions - personal values, costs, media, peers

Multicultural • Gender Fair • Special Needs Aware

Reciprocal interactions between family and ecosystem

Prioritizing goals is important in economic decision situations because the economic resources of time, money, human energy, and natural resources are often insufficient for accomplishing all of the goals (Tam & Rettig, 1999). Educators can actively contribute to increasing resource awareness, brainstorming ideas that will modify our wasteful consumption patterns, and encourage conservation of natural resources (Cerna & Davis, 1997). Most of all, educators can model the explicit thinking processes as they teach in the other family education content areas. The result will hopefully lead to assisting learners in making problem-solving and decision-making competencies more proactive and intentional in everyday life.

Family resource management is especially important in life span family education because it is an *integrative* subject matter that is necessary for education in all of the content areas and across all life stages (Arcus, 1987). Problem-solving, decision-making, and communication, are the central processes of everyday life that have already been incorporated into all content areas of the life span family education framework (Bredehoft, 2001). Family resource management adds to the social-psychological and philosophical emphases of many family educators, the reminder that the economic perspective is simultaneously important in studying family life. Each decision, and its accompanying actions, requires the resource of time, the ultimate scarce resource. Economics is concerned with decision-making under conditions of scarcity (Blau, Ferber & Winkler, 2006).

What Ideas May be Helpful For New Practitioners[3]

The following paragraphs may provide ideas for new professionals who wish to make explicit the family resource management processes and content while teaching in other content areas of the life span family education framework. Special emphasis is given to human, rather than time and money resources, because human resources are typically not as easily visible (Fox & Bartholomae, 2000; Muske & Winter, 2001).

Families and Individuals in Societal Contexts

The most important purpose of resource management in families is the production of capable people and the maintenance of their physical and mental health (Rettig, 1993). Families are the most important *economic units* (institution) in society. An economic unit is one that can hold together a set of goals, a common good for its members (Diesing, 1962). Families engage in all of the economic activities of economic units, including production, consumption, conservation, allocation, distribution, substitution, investment, exchange, transfer, and management of human, economic, and natural resources.

Families are the only economic units in society that *produce* human resources by giving birth to children. Family socialization processes also greatly influence the quality of the future generation of people who will provide leadership and work in the labor force. In addition, families contribute to renewal of human resources through rest, leisure activities, emotional, and instrumental support. Many family textbooks portray families as consuming units and fail to recognize the most important production role of families in society, that of *resource creation in the form of capable people and supportive social groups.* These human and social resources, at a societal level, are referred to as human and social capital (Bubolz, 2001; Hogan, 2001).

---

[3] Make explicit the family resource management processes and content while teaching all other content areas of the life span family education framework.

Values can also be studied from a societal perspective as well as an individual perspective. The World Values Survey, conducted by the University of Michigan's Institute for Social Research, is a twenty-year examination of the attitudes, beliefs, and values of 65 societies (Inglehart & Baker, 2001). The results indicated that the worldview of people in low-income, compared to wealthy societies, differed systematically. Inglehart & Baker (2001) provide an interesting global map of values categorized as traditional vs. secular-rational values, and survival vs. self-expression values.

Parent Education and Guidance

There are always costs when anything is produced, especially children. The creation of human resources is time, money, and labor intensive. It takes years of socialization, training, schooling, substantial direct costs of money, and indirect costs (of money lost) when adults miss work or financial opportunities due to responsibilities of caring for family members (Folbre, 2001). A resource management perspective can contribute to education about parenthood by assisting others in gaining a deeper understanding of parental expenditures on children (Lino, 2006), particularly the indirect costs of child rearing (Rettig & Leichtentritt, 2000). There are also educational curricula in several states that assist divorcing or separating parents in planning for meeting the financial needs of their children (University of Minnesota Extension Service, 2000).

Many parents of young children have to decide whether they will stay home and care for them or remain in the work force. Parents who have higher incomes may decide to make *resource substitutions* of money for time. They choose to use their money resources to purchase child care in the market place as a substitute for the time-intensive method of production that would be using their own time for home care. Economists would refer to this as a "substitution in production" (Peters, 1995). Other adults make "substitutions in consumption" by deciding not to have children [to enjoy] and gaining satisfactions in alternative ways, such as working with children, or enjoying the children of others (Bennetts, 2007; Peters, 1995).

Low-income parents have special challenges in meeting the needs of their children, despite their resourcefulness and effective managerial practices. *Making Ends Meet* (Edin & Lein, 1997) reports a qualitative analysis of personal interviews and effectively portrays the lives of low-income, single mothers and the ways in which they *find resources* to maintain a minimum subsistence level of living. Another book that demonstrates the resourcefulness of low-income families is *The Ditchdigger's daughters: A black family's astonishing success story* (Thornton & Coudert, 1996). These and other studies demonstrate the importance of values in guiding decision-making and action strategies in culturally diverse families (Dilworth-Anderson, Burton & Turner, 1993; Furstenberg, Cook, Eccles, Elder, Sameroff, 1999).

Internal Dynamics of Families

Immigrant parents may or may not be low-income families, but they do face many challenges, particularly in situations where the old and new cultural value orientations (Paolucci et al., 1977) are very different. Some of the dimensions of cultural value orientations are evident in the first half hour of the movie *Fiddler on the Roof.* There are contrasts in the values of tradition-stability with change-variety and contrasts in time orientations with emphases on the past-present more than the present-future (Rettig, 1993). There are also contrasts in family power dynamics when the tradition of hierarchical, authoritarian decision-making is threatened by demands of young adults for more democratic participation (Xiong, 2000; Xiong, Detzner & Rettig, 2001; Xiong, Rettig & Tuicompepee, 2006).

Ideas about the meanings of family strength and the dynamic efforts to maintain that unity in Somali families were outlined in a study by Heitritter (1999). The power dynamics of problem-solving were reported by Allen, Burnett, Epstein & Rankin-Esquer (2001) and at about the same time, Hmong-American families' problem-solving interactions were described by (Xiong, 2000). Yang (2001) documented family dynamics in Korean-American families when mothers were trying to realize the value of academic success for their adolescent children (Yang & Rettig 2004), especially within the value tensions of contrasting cultures (Yang & Rettig, 2003). Yang also reported family dynamics in Korean families where men had lost jobs and were describing face-saving efforts with family members (Yang, 2002). More recently, Danes (2006) examined non-immigrant families and the tensions within family business-owning couples over time. The above studies have outlined social decision-making processes and the substantial human resource commitments that were required to resolve the presenting value conflicts.

Interpersonal Relationships

Effective management can often reduce tensions in close relationships. Actions such as anticipating and planning for meeting hunger and sleep needs can contribute to more congenial conversations, social activities, and creative problem solving. The stress of last minute pressures and lack of supplies are also avoided in resource-sufficient family systems. In low-income families, it is more difficult to plan ahead and parents must focus more on daily existence. Freedom of choice, multiple alternatives, and long-term planning are more likely to be possible when resources are sufficient and there are no worries about finding food for today.

Resource theory (Foa & Foa, 1980) is an interesting way to think about management and interpersonal relationships. The theory recognizes that family is the group where the widest range of resource *exchanges* takes place and where there is the greatest potential for meeting personal needs. According to the theory, humans have needs for the resources of love and affection (love), respect and esteem (status), comfort and assistance (services), meaningful communication (information), ownership of personal things (goods), and money for personal use (money) (Rettig & Leichtentritt, 1999).

The theory hypothesized that the level of personal satisfaction resulting from interpersonal exchanges of the above resources between persons will vary with the category and properties of the resources (particular or universal value and symbolic or concrete expression). In addition, satisfaction varies with the people involved in the exchanges and their relationship (close and enduring or not); and whether the person is the giver, receiver, both, or neither. Highest levels of satisfaction are possible for the receiver of resources and for exchanges of the most particularistic resources of love, status, and services in an enduring relationship (Rettig, Danes & Bauer, 1993) where one becomes both giver and receiver. Resources that are substituted for the needed ones (providing services, but not unconditional love) lead to lowered levels of satisfaction.

What are Future Challenges for Family Life Educators?[4]

Family resource management, in some form and style, is a necessity of family life if the family system is to survive. Therefore, it will always have a future, whether or not educational institutions and programs provide the explicit and coherent content that will assist learners in thinking about life in more proactive and intentional ways. Some things will remain stable. The central concepts of problems, values, goals, standards, resources, decisions, and plans will always be important in everyday life, as will the processes of communication, problem-solving, decision-making, choice, and decision implementation (Rettig, 1993).

The problems faced by families and the resources available to them will be constantly changing, and probably at a faster rate in the future. Because of the rapid changes in technological development and medical research, family resource management in the future will be especially relevant in the family education content areas of *ethics*, and *family law and policy*, in addition to those previously discussed (Daniels, Rettig & delMas, 2006; Rettig, 2007; Folbre, 2008).

Ethical, Legal and Family Policy Issues

The research on cloning and stem cells (Weiss, 2008), and the potentials for the results to affect reproduction and medical treatments, has challenged the adequacy of our ethical standards and our personal value systems. In addition, the research has moved ahead more rapidly than our public policies and laws. The Hastings Center in New York and The Kennedy Institute of Ethics at Georgetown University are two centers that publish articles and bibliographies on bioethical issues, as well as offer conferences and short courses concerning value conflicts, decision making, ethics, and needed policies. Additional resources might be found in *Family Court Review or Family Law Quarterly.*

The ethical issues featured in these publications include many in which family decision-making is inevitable; those of mental illness, prolonging life, assisted death, end-of-life care (Stum, 2007) health care for embryos and fetuses, and donation/procurement of organs and tissues. A child can now have five potential parents. Which parent should have priority in a legal dispute—the two parents of genetic issue, the surrogate mother, or the two adoptive parents? Ethics, family law, and policy are disciplines that family life educators will need to study in greater depth in order to think about future programming needs.

Sometimes teaching about family resources is easier when there are visual diagrams and/or case study methods. The complexity in the family environments of children in paternity and support cases in 1999 led us to develop a visual portrayal of resource availability by combining genograms and eco-maps to help us understand the human, social, and financial resources for each child (Rickert & Rettig, 2006). Case studies have also been effective in teaching an economic approach to the issues of divorce (Rettig & Leichtentritt, 2000); and the consequences of child support orders (Rettig & Watters, 2006).

Resource Sufficiency

There are many other future concerns that affect family resources. The policies on health care, Social Security, and Medicare are extremely important for health and economic well being of the population, particularly in an age where our water supply is at risk and water quality is deteriorating. Brown, Gardner and Halweil (1999) discussed 16 consequences of global population growth that place our lives at risk: grain production, cropland, fresh water, oceanic fish catch, meat production, recreation areas, forests, biodiversity, climate change, energy, waste, jobs, income, housing, education, and urbanization. Energy-intensive lifestyles in North America produce excessive amounts of waste and hazardous waste. It is difficult to safely dispose of nuclear fuel residues, mercury thermometers, cell phones, and computers, which have components dangerous to humans. Family educators need to emphasize the resource conservation principles of rethink, reduce, reuse, recycle, and repair, so that each household can reduce waste.

Resource theory (Foa & Foa, 1980) would hypothesize that if humans could access more easily the particularistic resources of love, respect, and services (personal care), they would have fewer needs for goods and money. The resource substitutions they are making by using money to buy goods and services, instead of developing close relationships and supportive social groups, are diminishing human satisfactions and harming the natural environment that supports them. Humans would be unable to survive without the natural environment that supports life.

---

[4] The challenges for educators include: assisting family members in facing the interpersonal and ethical problems that arise; learning to participate in shared decision-making and getting to a workable collaborative solution; learning about the changing laws and policies that influence the lives of family members; and adjusting to the issues of global resource scarcity and sufficiency.

References

Allen, E. S., Burnett, C. K., Epstein, N., & Rankin-Esquer, L. A. (2001). Decision-making power, autonomy and communication in remarried spouses compared with first-married spouses. *Family Relations*, *50*, 326-334.

Arcus, M. E. (1987). A framework for life span family life education. *Family Relations*, *36*, 5-10.

Arcus, M. E. (1993). Looking ahead in family life education. In M. E. Arcus, J. D. Schvaneveldt & J. J. Moss (Eds.), *Handbook of family life education: Foundations of family life education, Vol. I* (pp. 229-246). Newbury Park, CA: Sage.

Arcus, M. E., Schvaneveldt, J. D., & Moss, J. J. (1993). The nature of family life education. In M. E. Arcus, J. D. Schvaneveldt & J. J. Moss (Eds.), *Handbook of family life education: Foundations of family life education, Vol. I* (pp. 1-12). Newbury Park, CA: Sage.

Bennetts, L. (2007). *The feminine mistake: Are we giving up too much?* New York: Hyperion.

Blau, F. D., Ferber, M. A., & Winkler, A. E. (2006). *The economics of women, men, and work* (5th ed.). Upper Saddle River, NJ: Prentice-Hall.

Bredehoft, D. J. (2001). The framework for life span family life education revised and revisited. *The family Journal*, *9*(2), 134-139.

Broderick, C. F. (1993). *Understanding family process: Basics of family systems theory.* Newbury Park: Sage.

Brown, L. R., Gardner, G., & Halweil, B. (1999, February). 16 Impacts of population growth. *The Futurist*, *33*(2), 36-41.

Brown, M. M., & Paolucci, B. (1979). *Home economics: A definition.* Washington, DC: American Home Economics Association.

Bubolz, M. M., Eicher, J. B., & Sontag, M. S. (1979). The human ecosystem: A model. *Journal of Home Economics*, *71*, 28-30.

Bubolz, M. M., & Sontag, M. S. (1993). Human ecology theory. In P. G. Boss, W. J. Doherty, R. LaRossa, W. R. Schumm & S. K. Steinmetz (Eds.), *Sourcebook of family theories and methods: A contextual approach* (pp. 419-448). New York: Plenum.

Bubolz, M. M. (2001). Family as source, user, and builder of social capital. *Journal of Socio-Economics*, *30*, 129-131.

Cerna, E., & Davis, D. (Executive Producers). (1997, September 15). *Affluenza: A medical alert* [Television broadcast]. KCTS/Seattle and Oregon Public Broadcasting.

Constantine, L. L. (1986). Family paradigms: *The practice of theory in family therapy*. New York: The Guilford Press.

Danes, S. M. (2006). Tensions within family business-owning couples over time. *Stress, Trauma, and Crisis*, *9*(3-4), 227-246.

Daniels, K. C., Rettig, K. D., & delMas, R. (2006). Alternative formulas for distributing parental incomes at divorce. *Journal of Family and Economic Issues*, *27*(1), 1-28.

Darling, C. A. (1987). Family life education. In M. B. Sussman & S. K. Steinmetz (Eds.), *Handbook of marriage and the family* (pp. 815-833). New York: Plenum.

Deacon, R. E., & Firebaugh, F. M. (1988). *Family resource management: Principles and applications* (2nd ed.). Boston, MA: Allyn & Bacon, Inc.

Diesing, P. (1962). *Reason in society: Five types of decisions and their social conditions.* Westport, CT: Greenwood Press.

Dilworth-Anderson, P., Burton, L., & Turner, W. L. (1993). The importance of values in the study of culturally diverse families. *Family Relations*, *42*, 238-242.

Edin, K., & Lein, L. (1997). *Making ends meet: How single mothers survive welfare and low-wage work.* New York: Russell Sage Foundation.

Fedje, C. G. (1998). Helping learners develop their practical reasoning capacities. In R.G. Thomas & J. F. Laster (Eds.), *Inquiry into thinking* (pp. 29-46). Peoria, IL: Glencoe/McGraw-Hill.

Fitzsimmons, C. (1951). *The management of family resources*. San Francisco: W. H. Freeman.

Foa, U. G., & Foa, E. B. (1980). Resource theory: Interpersonal behavior as exchange. In Gergen, M. S. Greenberg & R. Willis (Eds.), *Social exchange: Advances in theory and research* (pp. 77-94). New York: Plenum.

Folbre, N. (2001). *The invisible heart: Economics and family values.* New York: The New Press.

Folbre, N. (2008). *Valuing children: Rethinking the economics of the family*. Cambridge, MA: Harvard University Press.

Fox, J. J., & Bartholomae, S. (2000). Economic stress and families. In P. C. McKenry & S. J. Price (Eds.), *Families and change: Coping with stressful events and transitions* (pp. 250-278). Thousand Oaks, CA: Sage.

Furstenberg, F. F., Cook, T. D., Eccles, J., Elder, G. H., & Sameroff, A. (1999). *Managing to make it: Urban families and adolescent success.* Chicago: University of Chicago Press.

Goldsmith E. (2005). *Resource management for individuals and families* (2nd ed.). Minneapolis, MN: West Publishing.

Gross, I. H., Crandall, E. W., & Knoll, M. M. (1980). *Management for modern families* (4th ed.). Englewood Cliffs, NJ: Prentice-Hall, Inc.

Heitritter, D. L. (1999). *Meanings of family strength voiced by Somali immigrants: Reaching an inductive understanding.* Unpublished doctoral dissertation, University of Minnesota, St. Paul.

Hogan, M. J. (2001). Social capital: Potential in family social science. *Journal of Socio-Economics, 30,* 129-131.

Inglehart, R., & Baker, W. E. (2001, March-April). Modernization's challenge to traditional values: Who's afraid of Ronald McDonald? *The Futurist, 35,* 16-21.

Kidder, R. M. (1994, July-August). Universal human values: Finding an ethical common ground. *The Futurist, 28,* 8-13.

Kirchler, E., Rodler, C., Holzl, E., & Meier, K. (2001). *Conflict and decision-making in close relationships: Love, money, and daily routines* (European Monographs in Social Psychology). Philadelphia, PA: Taylor & Francis, Inc.

Knippel, C. (1998). Practical reasoning in the family context. In R. G. Thomas & J. F. Laster (Eds.). *Inquiry into thinking* (pp. 16-28). Peoria, IL: Glencoe/McGraw-Hill.

Langer, E. J. (1989). *Mindfulness.* New York: Addison-Wesley Publishing Company.

Leichtentritt, R. D., & Rettig, K. D. (1999). My parent's dignified death is different from mine: Moral problem solving about euthanasia. *Journal of Social and Personal Relationships, 16,* 385-406.

Leichtentritt, R. D., & Rettig, K. D. (2000). Elderly Israelis and the family members meanings toward euthanasia. *Families, Systems & Health, 18,* 61-78.

Leichtentritt, R. D., & Rettig, K. D. (2001). Values underlying end-of-life decisions. *Health and Social Work, 26,* 150-159.

Lino, M. (2006). Expenditures on children by families, 2000. *Family Economics and Nutrition Review, 14*(1), 25-42.

Liston, M. I. (1966). *Management in the family group, syllabus and sourcebook.* Unpublished manuscript, Iowa State University at Ames, Iowa.

Melson, G. F. (1980). *Family and environment: An ecosystem perspective.* Minneapolis, MN: Burgess Publishing Company.

Moore, T. J., & Asay, S. M. (2008). *Family resource management.* Thousand Oaks, CA: Sage.

Muske, G., & Winter, M. (2001). An in-depth look at family cash-flow management practices. *Journal of Family and Economic Issues, 22,* 353-372.

Paolucci, B., Hall, O. A., & Axinn, N. W. (1977). *Family decision-making: An ecosystem approach.* New York: John Wiley & Sons.

Pecchioni, L. L. (2001). Implicit decision-making in family caregiving. *Journal of Social and Personal Relationships, 18,* 219-237.

Peters, H. E. (1995). An economic approach to the study of child well-being: Gary Becker on altruism and household production. *Journal of Family Issues, 16,* 587-608.

Rettig, K. D. (1993). Problem-solving and decision-making as central processes of family life: An ecological framework for family relations and family resource management. *Marriage and Family Review, 18,* 187-222.

Rettig, K. D. (1998). Families as contexts for thinking. In R. G. Thomas & J. F. Laster (Eds.), *Inquiry into thinking* (pp. 101-121). Peoria, IL: Glencoe/McGraw-Hill.

Rettig, K. D. (2007). Divorce injustices: Perceptions of formerly wealthy women of the stressors, crises and traumas. *Journal of Loss and Trauma, 12*(3), 175-198.

Rettig, K. D., & Leichtentritt, R. D. (1999). A general theory for perceptual indicators of family life quality. *Social Indicators Research, 47,* 307-342.

Rettig, K. D., & Leichtentritt, R. D. (2000). Family economic issues across time. In S. J. Price, P. C. McKenry & M. J. Murphy (Eds.), *Families across time: A life course perspective* (pp. 160-172). Los Angeles, CA: Roxbury Press.

Rettig, K. D., Danes, S. M., & Bauer, J. W. (1993). Gender differences in perceived family life quality among economically stressed farm families. In U. G. Foa, J. M. Converse, Jr. & E. B. Foa (Eds.), *Resource theory: Explorations and applications* (pp. 123-155). San Diego: Academic Press.

Rettig, K. D., Rossmann, M. M., & Hogan, M. J. (1993). Educating for family resource management. In M. E. Arcus, J. D. Schvaneveldt & J. J. Moss (Eds.), *Handbook of family life education: the practice of family life education, Vol. II* (pp. 115-154). Newbury Park, CA: Sage.

Rettig, K. D., & Schulz, C. (1991). Cognitive style preferences and financial management decision styles. *Financial Counseling and Planning, 2,* 25-54.

Rettig, K. D., & Watters, S. C. (2006). The consequences of child support policy for family financial well being. *Journal of Divorce and Remarriage*, *44*(1/2) 1-28.

Rice, A. S., & Tucker, S. M. (1986). *Family life management* (6th ed.). New York: Macmillan.

Rickert, D., & Rettig, K. D. (2006). Family support eco maps: Visual portrayals of resources for children. *Journal of Divorce and Remarriage*, *26*(1/2), 86-106.

Stum, M. S. (2007). Financing long-term care: Risk management intentions and behaviors of couples. *Financial Counseling and Planning*, *17*, 79-89.

Sillars, A. L,. & Kalbflesch, P. J. (1989). Implicit and explicit decision-making styles in couples. In D. Brinberg & J. Jaccard (Eds.), *Dyadic decision making* (pp. 179-215). New York: Springer-Verlag.

Tallman, I. (1988). Problem solving in families: A revisionist view. In D. M. Klein & J. Aldous (Eds.), *Social stress and family development* (pp. 102-126). New York: The Guilford Press.

Tallman, I. (1993). Theoretical issues in researching problem solving in families. *Marriage and Family Review*, *18*, 155-186.

Tam, V. C., & Rettig, K. D. (1999). Decision making of mothers in Hong Kong on the occasional use of alternative child-care arrangements. *Journal of Family and Economic Issues*, *20*, 163-190.

Thomas, R., & Laster, J. (Eds.). (1998) *Inquiry into thinking: Family and consumer sciences teacher education Yearbook 18*. Peoria, IL: American Association of Family and Consumer Sciences and Glencoe/McGraw-Hill.

Thornton, Y. S., & Coudert, J. (1996). *The ditchdigger's daughters: A black family's astonishing success story.* New York, NY: A Plume Book.

University of Minnesota Extension Service (2000). *Parents forever: A curriculum for divorcing and separating parents.* St. Paul, Minnesota: Minnesota Extension Service Distribution Center.

University of Minnesota Extension. (2001). *Who gets grandma's yellow pie plate? A guide to passing on personal possessions.* Retrieved October 10, 2002 from http://www.yellowpieplate.umn.edu/indexB.html

Weick, K. (1971). Group processes, family processes and problem solving. In J. Aldous, T. Condon, R. Hill, M. Straus & I. Tallman (Eds.). *Family problem solving: A symposium on theoretical, methodological, and substantive concerns* (pp. 3-32). Hinsdale, IL: Dryden Press.

Weiss, R. (2008, January 18). Scientists clone human embryos from adult cells. *Saint Paul Pioneer Press,* p. 1A.

Xiong, Z. B. (2000*). Hmong-American parent-adolescent problem-solving interactions: An analytic induction analysis.* Unpublished doctoral dissertation, University of Minnesota, St. Paul.

Xiong, Z. B., Detzner, D., & Rettig, K. (2001). Southeast Asian immigrant parenting practices and perceptions of parent-adolescent conflicts. *Journal of Teaching in Marriage and Family, 1*(1), 27-48.

Xiong, Z. B., Rettig, K., & Tuicompepee, A. (2006). Parent adolescent conflicts and adolescent adjustments in Hmong immigrant families in the United States. In D. M. Devore (Ed.), *Parent-child relations: New resear*ch (pp. 65-82). Nova Science Publishers, Inc.

Yang, S. (2001). *Korean-American mothers' meanings of academic success and their experiences with children in American schools*. Unpublished doctoral dissertation, University of Minnesota, St. Paul.

Yang, S. (2002). "Chaemyoun-saving (face saving)" due to Korean job loss: Listening to men's voices. *Journal of Comparative Family Studies*, *33*(1), 73-95.

Yang, S., & Rettig, K. (2003). The value tensions in Korean-American mother-child relationships while facilitating academic success. *Personal relationships*, *10*(3), 349-369.

Yang, S., & Rettig, K. (2004). Korean American mothers' experiences in facilitating academic success for their adolescents. *Marriage and Family Review*, *36*(3/4), 53-74.

Key Resources

Brown, L. R. (2002, March-April). The eco-economic revolution: Getting the market in sync with nature. *The Futurist*, *36*(2),23-32.

Cetron, M. J., & Davies, O. (2001, March-April). Trends now changing the world: Technology, the workplace, management, and institutions. *The Futurist*, *35*(2), 27-42.

Related Websites

American Association of Family and Consumer Sciences: www.aafcs.org

American Council on Consumer Interests: www.consumerinterests.org

Association for Financial Counseling and Planning Education: www.afcpe.org

Consumer Expenditures: www.bls.gov/cex

Consumer Price Index: www.bls.gov/cpi

Joint Center for Poverty Research: www.jcpr.org

About the Author

Kathryn Rettig, Ph.D., CFLE, is a Professor in the Department of Family Social Science at The University of Minnesota Twin Cities. She teaches Family Economics and Resource Management, Legal-Economic Controversies in Family Life, Integrative Research Seminar, and Ethical Issues and Moral Dilemmas in Family Life. She has published articles on related topics in a variety of professional journals and is the principal investigator for two research projects "Impact of Court Decisions on Minnesota Families" and the" Changing Landscape for Women in America: Work, Family, and Personal Issues." E-mail: krettig@umn.edu.

Parent Education and Guidance

ARMINTA L. JACOBSON

As parents assume responsibility for their children and adolescents' development, they often need guidance and support through parent education in assuming this role. Parent education has been defined as programs, support services and resources offered to parents and caregivers and designed to support them or increase their capacity and confidence in raising healthy children (Carter, 1996). Strengthening parenting is the focus of a variety of models, with group and individual approaches, across a wide range of settings. Parenting education is concerned with the larger picture of parenting within the family system and larger ecosystem while addressing specialized needs and concerns of parents (see National Council on Family Relations (NCFR) Curriculum Guidelines, 1984). Interests and needs related to parenting change across the family life span (see the Framework for Family Life Education, Bredehoft, 1997). As families develop through the life span, issues become more complex, and concerns about guidance change. Guidance and other issues vary across the life span, within individual families, and across the diversity of cultures and environments. In families with infants and children, basic issues of protection, caregiving, and socialization highlight concerns. As children enter school age and adolescence, parenting begins to focus on encouraging and guiding children as they learn to make decisions for themselves as they enter into relationships apart from the family (Hamner & Turner, 2001).

The body of knowledge needed for effective parent education and guidance includes a knowledge of the parenting process (parent roles and parent-child relationships across the life span), effective parenting and guidance, human development across the life span, the dynamics of family development and relationships, knowledge of diverse cultures and special needs of families, and learning processes across the life span (Jacobson & Hirschy, 2000).

Behaviors of parent educators vary depending upon their own experiences with parenting and their experiences and knowledge of the teaching/learning process. Parent educators who nurture, respectfully encourage, and motivate others to learn and develop build upon individual and family strengths. They involve parents as active participants and partners in their own learning, and develop a sense of trust and empowerment while providing a model for parents as they subsequently teach, guide, and influence their children and adolescents (Dunst, Trivette, & Johanson, 1994). Skillful reciprocal, two-way communication and conflict resolution techniques demonstrated and taught to parents form the basis for applying these techniques to parenting as well as teaching them to their own children.

Assumptions and attitudes parent educators hold about human development, relationships, parenting, and variations within parenting practices are the key to empowering and strengthening parents in their roles. The basis of these assumptions and attitudes are a commitment to strengthening parenting, knowledge, experience, sensitivity to others (Jacobson & Hirschy, 2001), and the practice of self-reflection and examination.

CURRICULUM GUIDELINES: PARENT EDUCATION & GUIDANCE

An understanding of how parents teach, guide, and influence children and adolescents. Based on knowledge of:

1. parenting as a process;
2. parental rights and responsibilities;
3. parental roles over the life cycle, and
4. variations in parenting practices.

The NCFR *Framework for Life Span Family Life Education* (Bredehoft, 1997, 2001) conceptualizes family life education as a life-long process from childhood to later adulthood. Key concepts in the Curriculum Guidelines (NCFR, 1984) for parent education and guidance include an understanding of how parents teach, guide, and influence children and adolescents based on knowledge of (a) parenting as a process; (2) parental rights and responsibilities; (c) parental roles over the life cycle: and (d) variations in parenting practices. Through experience and direct teaching, children, adolescents, and adults can gain basic knowledge and understanding about parenting and nurture the development of others.

Children learn about responsibilities of family members, caregiving, and different approaches to parenting by being parented. Programs such as Heath's (1995) *Learning How to Care: Education for Parenting* curriculum teach children parenting and caregiving through direct teaching and the experience of observing parents and infants who visit their classrooms. Children learn about needs of infants and toddlers while learning about parental responsibilities and differing styles. Teaching parenting to children and adolescents has been the goal of *The Parenting Project: Preparing Tomorrow's Parents Today*, a national effort, as well as *Parents Under Construction* (for more about these programs see related websites), developed and taught in Houston, Texas. This program, taught K-12 in the public schools, combines knowledge and skill-building through interactive learning, reinforcing the concept that learning to parent is a process. Babysitting classes offered through youth organizations, such as 4-H Clubs and Girl Scouts, provide opportunities to teach children and adolescents about parenting (caregiving) responsibilities and roles, safety, and meeting needs of children at different ages. Learning when and how to seek help are key features of babysitting classes.

Family and Consumer Science courses taught in secondary schools across the country provide both classroom instruction and guided hands-on experiences in child development, parenting, and childcare. Programs in public schools for adolescent parents (primarily mothers) teach parenting and provide support and resources. Parenting education needs of adolescents are also met through community organizations such as health clinics, YWCA, and family resource centers. Adolescent fathers, often overlooked in parenting education, are the focus of local programs across the nation as well as national fathering organizations. All family life education with adolescents should incorporate the development and incorporation of an ethical code into relationships and decision-making practice based upon ethical values and principles.

Parent-child communications, conflict-resolution, meeting developmental needs of children, and child-rearing practices are important topics to include in parent education for adults. Integrating the Curriculum Guidelines and concepts from the Framework for Life Span Family Life Education requires a process by which parent educators focus on assessing parenting needs; program and curriculum planning; implementation of parent education through groups, home-visits, and media; and evaluation.

Adults who are parents, or about to become parents, enter the parenting education experience having made the decision to parent. They vary in their commitment and perception of their need for parenting education. They enter parent education programs with a wide range of knowledge and understanding of their roles and responsibilities related to the care and nurturance of child and adolescent development. Parenting situations, environmental influences on parenting, education level and learning preferences are other examples of differences in parents. Assessments of child and parent development, parenting goals, needs for information and resources, and family strengths are examples of approaches for family life educators to follow in planning parenting education. Such approaches acknowledge parenting as a process entered into as a partnership with the family life educator through shared understanding (for further discussion on FLE methodology see Clarke and Bredehoft, 2009).

Choosing a curriculum which fits program goals and objectives and participant needs requires (a) assessment of local program and participant needs and interests, (b) sensitivity to regional and cultural uniqueness, (c) requirements for teacher/facilitator knowledge and skills or training, and (d) availability of funding. Other considerations in choosing a curriculum include the content, quality of teaching plans, and appropriateness of instructional processes (Duncan & Goddard, 2005).

Curriculum designed around ages and stages of children acknowledges children and parents move concurrently through predictable stages of development (Galinsky, 1987), creating changes in the family system. Examples of curriculum and programs designed for beginning developmental stages in the family life cycle include *Birth to Three*, and *Parents as Teachers*. Early Childhood *STEP (Systematic Training for Effective Parenting)*, and *Home Instruction for Parents of Preschool Youngsters (HIPPY)* are examples of curriculum and programs targeting parents of preschoolers (find more information about these programs on-line by using the related websites at the conclusion of this article). The knowledge of biosocial dimensions of interactions between parents and their children through the life span has had a major influence on parent education curriculum, especially with current emphases on attachment, temperament, and brain development (Kuczynski, 2003).

Programs and curriculum designed for parenting school-age children include topics such as parenting, communications, and behavioral management. Programs may be developed locally or through state-wide public school or other organizations such as Practical Parent Education, first developed locally in Texas, and Practical Parenting Partnerships, a family resource/parent education program offered through school districts in Missouri. Families and Schools Together (FAST) is designed for the purpose of family strengthening and parent involvement to help kids succeed in school and in life. Commercial curriculum is available which focuses on school success. Active Parenting's *Parents on Board* is an example. Local program efforts may include "Family Learning Nights" with parents and children engaged together in learning activities or "how to" sessions about helping children learn at home. *STEP/Teen* and *Active Parenting of Teens* are examples of curriculum focusing on parenting adolescents (find more information about these programs on-line by using the related websites at the conclusion of this article). Churches and other community organizations sponsor local programs with parents and their adolescent children attending workshops together to practice communications skills or learn about sexuality.

Different approaches to childrearing are explained by what individuals bring to parenting (e.g. experiences, mental health, culture), characteristics of children, and the environments in which childrearing takes place (Luster & Okagaki, 2003). Curriculum is designed for parents at work (e.g. *Lunch & Learn* video-based program by Active Parenting), parenting for divorcing parents (e.g. Practical Parent Education's *For Kids Sake* and University of Minnesota Extension's *Parents Forever*), for prevention and intervention of child abuse and neglect (e.g. *The Nurturing Program* and Hawaii's *Healthy Start* program). These are examples of curriculum which focus on individual issues and needs of parents and children as they relate to environment and circumstances within the environment.

Ethnic, racial, gender, social, and cultural influences on parenting are acknowledged with a variety of approaches and specialized curriculum such as Avance's program for Hispanic parents, and translated materials by *STEP* (find more information about these programs on-line by using the related websites at the conclusion of this article). But success depends upon sensitivity and commitment by family life educators. Basic knowledge and skills for strengthening parenting can be taught with an approach that provides dialogue and respect for differences in parenting values and practices. Team approaches to facilitating parent education with representative gender, social background, and ethnicity/culture/language helps build trust and a more effective educational process.

Programs which meet the needs and interests of teen and adult fathers and focus on the challenges of father involvement include Cooperative Extension models such

CHILDHOOD — *Within the context of the family system*

Parent Education and Guidance

- Safety for children
- Responsibilities of parents
- Different types of caregivers
- Parents who live away from children
- Rewards and demands of parenthood
- Meeting children needs at different stages of development
- Differing parenting styles and behavior
- Responsibilities of children
- Sources of help for parents - family, neighborhood, community
- Problems of family violence, abuse, neglect

Multicultural • Gender Fair • Special Needs Aware

Reciprocal interactions between family and ecosystem

ADOLESCENCE — *Within the context of the family system*

Parent Education and Guidance

- Parent-child communication
- Meeting children's needs at different stages of development
- Responding to individual differences in children
- Rewards and demands of parenthood
- Understanding marital and parenting roles
- Factors to consider in deciding if and when to become a parent
- Child-rearing practices
- Teaching life skills to children - self sufficiency, safety, decision-making
- Family conflict and conflict resolution
- Problems of family violence, abuse, neglect
- Sources of help for parents - family, neighborhood, community
- Varied parenting situations - single parenting, step-parenting, adoption caretaking of disabled children
- Influences on parenting styles - ethnic, racial, gender, social, cultural

Multicultural • Gender Fair • Special Needs Aware

Reciprocal interactions between family and ecosystem

ADULTHOOD — *Within the context of the family system*

Parent Education and Guidance

- Factors to consider in deciding if and when to become a parent
- Preparation for birth and parenthood
- Changing parental responsibilities as children become independent
- Parent-child communication
- Child-rearing practices, guidance, and parenting strategies
- Changing parent-child relationships across the life span
- Importance of parental communication regarding child-rearing practices
- Providing a safe environment for children
- Teaching life skills to children - self sufficiency, safety, decision-making
- Rewards and demands of parenthood
- Varied parenting situations - single parenting, step-parenting, adoption, caretaking of disabled child, elderly parent
- Sources of help for parents - family, neighborhood, community
- Problems of family violence, abuse, neglect
- Influences on parenting styles - ethnic, racial, gender, social, cultural

Multicultural • Gender Fair • Special Needs Aware

Reciprocal interactions between family and ecosystem

LATER ADULTHOOD

Within the context of the family system

Parent Education and Guidance

- Changing parent-child relationships in later life - negotiating adult relationships with adult children
- Demands and rewards of grandparenthood, including the possibility of rearing and caring for grandchildren
- Importance of parental communication regarding differences in parenting styles and values between parents and grandparents
- Grandparent-child communication
- Sources of help for grandparents - family, neighborhood, community
- Family conflict and conflict resolution
- Problems of family violence, elder abuse, neglect
- Adapting to the complexities of varied parenting situations - blended families, single parenting, step-parenting, care-taking of disabled children, return of adult children to the household

Multicultural • Gender Fair • Special Needs Aware

Reciprocal interactions between family and ecosystem

as Minnesota's *Dads Make a Difference* and *Fathers Reading Every Day (FRED)* in Texas. Examples of local efforts are *"Play Days"* for fathers and their children led by representatives from the Center for Successful Fathering in Austin, Texas, and Dads and Donuts breakfast gatherings at schools.

As grandparents in later adulthood assume primary roles for childcare and support of their adult children's parenting, efforts have proliferated to address the parenting knowledge and support needs of later adulthood. Changing roles and relationships, intergenerational communications and conflict resolution are examples of parenting concepts which can be addressed in family life education. The need for education and support are particularly acute with first generation immigrant grandparents and families with disabled children.

Tips for New Practitioners

Assessment & Evaluation Tips

The goal of assessment is better understanding of parenting interests and needs, cultural and ecological context, and learning needs and preferences. Involve partners– – parents, adolescents, teachers, social service professionals– – actively in this process (for further discussion of family life education assessment and evaluation see Treichel, 2009). Do not limit the evaluation process to "parent's perceptions" as recorded on an evaluation form at the close of a program. To determine appropriateness and effectiveness of work with parents use a variety of methods, such as nonverbal reactions of parents, to measure changes in parent and child behaviors and relationships. Standardized measurements of child development, parenting, and family functioning are valuable in program and participant assessment and evaluation (see Reppucci, Britner & Woolard, 1997, for list; or Buros Mental Measurements Yearbooks, available online through libraries).

Diversity Tips

The assumptions you hold about parents influence your success or failure (Curran, 1989). Seek to understand the beliefs and functions underlying these differences rather than making assumptions about parenting in families with backgrounds and characteristics different from your own. Purposively observe and listen and respectfully ask questions, developing cultural competence through increased understanding. When encountering perceptions of parenting roles and responsibilities and guidance different than your own, be flexible and open (for additional thoughts on family life education and diversity see Allen & Blaisure, 2009).

Integration Tips

Help parents understand parenting as a multigenerational developmental process. Developing and/or encouraging individuals in adulthood and later adulthood to serve as mentors and support systems for parents reinforces this concept. Including extended family members in classes and events promotes intergenerational continuity and support. Use hands-on, interactive learning strategies with a lot of feedback and support that help parents integrate their own experiences and knowledge as well as developmental and situational needs and issues. Practice skills with parents they can use to help their children and adolescence better understand parenting roles and responsibilities.

Future Issues and Challenges for Family Life Education

Approaches to parent education are varied – theoretical assumptions, models and strategies, objectives, and length and intensiveness of programs or interventions. Emphases range from specific guidance models to parent involvement in early literacy. While there is a need for specialized parent education, for example "parenting at a distance," efforts are needed to further define overall competencies of parenting based upon findings of research.

Public identity and professional recognition are challenges of family life educators. State licensing offered for Early Childhood Family Education in Minnesota and infusion of statewide efforts for educating and supporting parents in Missouri (see Parents as Teachers, Practical Parenting Partnership, and ParentLink in related web site section) are examples of successful efforts in recognizing family life education and its role in parent education. NCFR and the American Association of Family and Consumer Science are examples of professional associations which focus on family life education as a profession. Further growth in this area is evidenced by the development of collaborations and networks such as the National Parent Education Network, the Texas Registry of Parent Educator Networks, and the Center for Parenting at the University of Tennessee. The accompanying issue is the continuing need for standards for training, practice, and supervision of family life and parent educators.

Research studies, mostly correlational in nature, have primarily been delimited to particular program models with small samples. While there are studies showing the efficacy of parent education (Knapp & Deluty, 1989; Webster-Stratton, 1992), studies examining the reciprocal effects and causal influences of change in parental behavior with child outcomes are needed to better understand the process of parenting and parent education. The scientific committee (National Research Council & Institute of Medicine, 2000) contributing to *From Neurons to Neighborhoods* asked, "What does it take to change parenting behavior in ways sufficient to produce improved child outcomes, especially for high-risk parents and diverse families?" Within diversity of parenting, what aspects generalize across cultures and environments as key parental determinants of optimal child and adolescent development? Research is also needed which studies the application of theory to transmission of parenting competencies and motivation and support of parents in their development.

Parents seek information on childrearing. Parents often have difficulties finding information they need; it is not always understood or fully explained, and confidence may be undermined (Goodnow, 1995). It is the responsibility of parent educators to identify and help parents to overcome such barriers to learning about parenting. Concepts identified as opportunities, constraints, and challenges for early childhood intervention in the report *From Neurons to Neighborhoods* (NRCIM, 2000) also apply to parent education: (a) increasing access & participation through reduction of barriers, (b) ensuring greater quality control, (c) achieving cultural competence, (d) identifying and responding to distinctive subgroups, (e) influencing the impact of post-intervention (parent education) environments, and (f) strengthening the infrastructure for funding and delivering parent education.

Future Program Needs

Future program needs for family life educators include the development of curriculum and programs which (a) integrate a life span approach, (b) include self-assessment and evaluation of parent and family life educator competencies, (c) utilize the latest scientific knowledge and educational processes, and (d) integrate self-learning. Such programs would present parenting as a shared and developmental process across the life span and build in assessment to be used by parents and caregivers to determine the appropriate entry point into curriculum and programs. Curriculum development should involve parents as partners in planning, e.g. focus groups (Lengua et al., 1992), and systematically include peer review according to widely recognized professional standards of criteria for quality curriculum. Criteria for quality curriculum would include content and resources for parenting across a broad range of parent and life span development and include information about teaching children and adolescents the basics of parenting rights, responsibilities, and roles. Evaluation strategies would be an integral part of all curricula and would evaluate process and standards of family life educator knowledge and performance as well as changes in parenting knowledge, attitudes, and skills. Based upon pre-professional and on-going professional assessment, evaluation, and guided reflection, family life educators would follow decision points to determine their need to seek more knowledge or skills training. For effective use of curriculum, program development would include pre-training for family life educators and up-to-date online resources and on-going training opportunities. Ideally, this system of curriculum/program development and delivery would be within a professional system that included mentors that are more experienced as well as supervisors for novice family life educators.

Summary

The goal of parenting education and guidance is to foster mentally healthy, well-developed children and adolescents and strong resourceful families. Family life educators are supported in integration of the Curriculum Guidelines and concepts from the Framework for Family Life Education by their knowledge of children, adolescents, and parenting in diverse families as well as through collaboration, networking and sharing of ideas with other professionals. The joys and challenges of parent education are best met through careful planning, preparation, and openness to new resources and ideas and dynamic changes in parent education.

References

Allen, W., & Blaisure, K. R. (2009). Family life educators and the development of cultural competency. In D. J. Bredehoft & M. J. Walcheski (Eds.), *Family life education: Integrating theory and practice* (2nd ed.) (pp. 209-219). Minneapolis, MN: National Council on Family Relations.

Bredehoft, D. J. (Ed.). (1997). *The framework for life span family life education* (2nd ed.) [Poster]. Minneapolis: National Council on Family Relations.

Bredehoft, D. J. (2001). The framework for life span family life education revised and revisited. *The Family Journal*, 9(2), 134-139.

Carter, N. (1996). *See how we grow: A report on the status of parenting education in the United States*. Philadelphia: Pew Charitable Trusts.

Clarke, J. I., & Bredehoft, D. J. (2009). Family life education methodology. In D. J. Bredehoft & M. J. Walcheski (Eds.), *Family life education: Integrating theory and practice* (2nd ed.) (pp. 199-206). Minneapolis, MN: National Council on Family Relations.

Curran, D. (1989). *Working with parents: A guide to successful parent groups.* Circle Pines, MN: American Guidance Service.

Duncan, S. F., & Goddard, H. W. (2005). *Family life education: Principles and practices for effective outreach.* Thousand Oaks, CA: Sage.

Dunst, C. J., Trivette, C. M., & Johanson, C. (1994). Parent-professional collaboration and partnerships. In C. J. Dunst, C. M. Trivette & A. G. Deal (Eds.), *Supporting & strengthening families: Methods, strategies & practices* (pp. 197-211). Cambridge, MA: Brookline.

Galinsky, E. (1987). *Six stages of parenthood.* Reading, MA: Addison Wesley.

Goodnow, J. J. (1995). Parents' knowledge & expectations. In M. H. Bornstein (Ed.), *Handbook of parenting: Status & social conditions of parenting, Vol. 3* (pp. 305-332). Mahwah, NJ: Erlbaum.

Hamner, T. J., & Turner, P. H. (2001). *Parenting in contemporary society* (4th ed.). Boston: Allyn & Bacon.

Heath, H. (1995). *Learning how to care: Education for parenting.* Haverford, PA: Conrow Publishing.

Jacobson, A. L., & Hirschy, S. (2000). *Core knowledge for parent educators and professionals who work with families* [Brochure]. Denton, TX: University of North Texas, Center for Parent Education.

Jacobson, A. L., & Hirschy, S. (2001). *Choosing a parent educator* [Brochure]. Denton, TX: University of North Texas, Center for Parent Education.

Knapp, P. A., & Deluty, R. H. (1989). Relative effectiveness of two behavioral parent training programs. *Journal of Clinical Child Psychology, 18*(4), 314-322.

Kuczynski, L. (Ed.). (2003). *Handbook of dynamics in parent-child relations.* Thousand Oaks, CA.: Sage.

Lengua, J. L, Roosa, M. W., Schupak-Neuberg, E., Michaels, M. L., Berg, C. N., & Weschler, L. F. (1992). Using focus groups to guide the development of a parenting program for difficult-to-reach, high-risk families. *Family Relations, 41*, 163-168.

Luster, T., & Okagaki, L. (2003). Multiple influences on parenting: Ecological and life-course perspectives. In T. Luster & L. Okagaki, L. (Eds.), *Parenting: An ecological perspective* (pp. 227-250). Hillsdale, NJ: Erlbaum.

National Council on Family Relations. (1984). *College and university curriculum guidelines. NCFR Committee on Standards and Criteria for Certification of Family Life Educators.* Minneapolis: Author.

National Research Council & Institute of Medicine. (2000). *From neurons to neighborhoods: The science of early childhood development.* Washington, DC: National Academy Press.

Reppucci, N. D., Britner, P. A., & Woolard, J. L. (1997). *Preventing child abuse & neglect through parent education.* Baltimore, MD: Brookes.

Treichel, C. (2009). In the best interests of children and their families: Merging program development and program evaluation. In D. J. Bredehoft & M. J. Walcheski (Eds.), *Family life education: Integrating theory and practice* (pp. 221-231). Minneapolis, MN: National Council on Family Relations.

Webster-Stratton, C. (1992). Individually administered videotape parent training: "Who benefits?" *Cognitive Therapy & Research, 16*(1), 31-52.

Key Resources

Arcus, M. E., Schvaneveldt, J. D., & Moss, J. J. (Eds.). (1993). *Handbook of family life education (Vols. 1-2).* Newbury Park, CA: Sage

Baumrind, D. (1971). Harmonious parents and their preschool children. *Developmental Psychology, 4*(1), 99-102.

Belsky, J. (1984). The determinants of parenting: A process model. *Child Development, 55*, 83-96.

Bornstein, M. H. (Ed.). (2002). *Handbook of parenting: Vols. 1-5* (2nd ed.). Mahwah, NJ: Erlbaum.

Buss, A. H., Chess, S., Goldsmith, H. H., Hinde, R. A., McCall, R. B., Plomin, R., Rothbart, M. K., & Thomas, A. (1987). What is temperament: Four approaches. *Child Development, 66*, 55-68.

Bronfenbrenner, U. (1994). *Ecological models of human development. In International encyclopedia of education: Vol. 3* (2nd ed., pp. 1643-1647). Oxford, England: Elsevier Sciences.

Campbell, D., & Palm, G. F. (2004). *Group parent education: Promoting parent learning and support.* Thousand Oaks, CA: Sage.

Family Support America. (2001). *Guidelines for family support practice* (2nd ed.). Chicago: Author.

Fox, G. L., Bruce, C., & Combs-Orme, T. (2000). Parenting expectations and concerns of fathers and mothers of newborn infants. *Family Relations, 49*, 123-131.

Hitch, E. J., & Youatt, J. P. (2002). *Communicating family and consumer sciences: A guidebook for professionals*. Tinley Park, ILL: Goodheart-Wilcox Publisher.

Holden, G., & Miller, P. (1999). Enduring and different: A meta-analysis of the similarity in parents' child rearing. *Psychological Bulletin*, *125*(2), 223-254.

Isabella, R. A. (1993). Origins of attachment: Maternal interactive behavior across the first year. *Child Development* (64), 605-621.

Kramer, J. M., Arbuthnot, J., Gordon, D. A., Rousis, N. J., & Hoza, J. (1998). Effects of skill-based versus information-based divorce education programs on domestic violence and parental communication. *Family & Conciliation Courts Review*, *36*(1), 9-31.

Maccoby, E. E. (1992). The role of parents in the socialization of children: An historical overview. *Developmental Psychology*, *28*, 1006-1016.

McDermott, D., Heath, H., & Palm, G. (Eds.). (2006). Parenting Education and Support: Advances in Theories, Research, and Practice [Special Issue]. *Child Welfare*, *85*(5).

Powell, L. H., & Cassidy, D. (2007). *Family life education: Working with families across the life span* (2nd ed.). Mountain View, CA: Mayfield.

Roberts, T. W. (1994). *A systems perspective of parenting: The individual, the family, and the social network*. Pacific Grove, CA: Brooks/Cole.

Scarr, S. (1992). Developmental theories for the 1990s: Development and individual differences. *Child Development*, *63*, 1-19.

Seitz, V., Rosenbaum, L. I., & Apfel, N. H. (1985). Effects of family support intervention: A ten-year follow-up. *Child Development*, *56*, 376-391.

Smith, C. A. (Ed.). (1999). *The encyclopedia of parenting theory and research*. Westport, CT: Greenwood.

Smith, C. A., Cudaback, D., Goddard, H. W., & Myers-Walls, J. A. (1994). *National extension parent education model of critical parenting practices*. Manhattan, KS: Kansas State University.

Stafford, L., & Bayer, C. L. (1993). *Interaction between parents and children*. Newbury Park: Sage.

Thomas, R. (1996). Reflective dialogue parent education design: Focus on parent development. *Family Relations*, *45*, 189-200.

Related Web Sites

Active Parenting: www.activeparenting.com

Avance: www.avance.org

Birth to Three: www.birthto3.org

Boys Town Press: www.girlsandboystown.org/scripts/default.asp

Cooperative Extension System's National Network for Child Care: www.nncc.org/Guidance/guide.disc.page.html

CYFERnet: www.cyfernet.org/

Dads Make a Difference program: www.dadsmakeadifference.org/

Families and Work Institute: www.familiesandwork.org

Families and Schools Together: www.familiesandschools.org

Film Ideas Inc.: www.filmideas.com

Hawaii's Healthy Start: hawaii.gov/health/family-child-health/mchb/programs/hs.html

Home Instruction Program for Preschool Youngsters: www.hippyusa.org.

Injoy Videos: www.injoyvideos.com

Insight Media: www.insight-media.com

Learning Seed: www.learningseed.com

National Parenting Education Network: www.npen.org

The Nurturing Parenting Programs, Family Development Resources: www.nurturingparenting.com/

ParentLink: www.outreach.missouri.edu/parentlink

Parents as Teachers National Center: parentsasteachers.org

Parents Under Construction: www.childbuilders.org

Practical Parent Education: www.practicalparent.org

STEP: www.agsnet.com

Theory and Practice Database: www.gwu.edu./~tip/theories.html

The Parenting Project: www.parentingproject.org

Practical Parenting Partnerships: www.pppctr.org.

The University of North Texas Center for Parent Education: www.cpe.unt.edu

University of Minnesota Extension www.parenting.umn.edu

About the Author

Arminta L. Jacobson, Ph.D., CFLE, CFCS is a Professor of Development and Family Studies and Director of the Center for Parent Education at the University of North Texas. Email: arminta.jacobson@unt.edu.

Family Law and Public Policy*

Karen Bogenschneider

What role does public policy play in supporting the important functions families perform for their members and society? How important is it for family life educators to know how policy influences families and what they can do to influence family policy?

To illustrate the significance of these questions, this chapter begins with several true stories from families whose everyday lives have been impacted by policy, and real-life examples from family life educators about how policy can support or thwart their efforts to support families. As background for the reader, the chapter defines family policy and examines the character of policymaking in America—whether it focuses more on individuals or families, and how effective family-focused approaches are. Then the chapter addresses whether policy is the responsibility of family life educators and, if so, what roles they can play. Finally, for those interested in teaching about or becoming active in family policy pursuits, the chapter concludes with a listing of resources for family life educators.

In the summer of 1998, two e-mail messages arrived in my inbox, both from friends who had recently given birth—one in this country and one in Europe. My American friend returned to work following a two-month maternity leave. Immediately, she was placed on mandatory overtime, despite having two preschoolers at home and a husband who was working two jobs to make ends meet. This experience contrasts sharply with that of my Austrian friend during her pregnancy and birth. She received 16 weeks of leave during which she was forbidden to work; if found doing so, she could have been fined. Following her maternity leave, she was eligible for an additional 18 months of parental leave.

Cassie had finished her first two months as a freshman in high school. Her parents, Mary and Steve, were looking forward to parent-teacher conferences to see how Cassie was adjusting and what kinds of support they could provide at home. Conferences were scheduled once each year, and only one evening session was offered from 5 to 8 p.m. Mary and Steve both arranged to leave work early and arrived promptly at 5 p.m. Long lines were already forming outside the teacher's classrooms, so they divided up the list of Cassie's teachers. Despite this and despite having only one child, they were unable to meet with each teacher before the doors closed.

Irene was a 72-year-old grandmother who was raising her grandson in a public housing project in inner-city Philadelphia. When her grandson was involved in a drug deal, Irene was notified that she would be evicted from her apartment. Pro

* This article is based on and uses excerpts from a September 2007 article, "Policy—No Better Way to Spend a Life," published in *Report*, a newsletter of the National Council on Family Relations.

CURRICULUM GUIDELINES:
FAMILY LAW & PUBLIC POLICY

An understanding of the legal issues, policies, and laws influencing the well-being of families. Based on knowledge of:

1. the historical development of such laws;
2. laws relating to marriage, divorce, family support, child custody, child protection and rights, and family planning; and
3. public policy as it affects the family, including tax, civil rights, social security, economic support laws, and regulations.

bono legal counsel helped her keep her home on a technicality—the drug deal occurred over two miles from the housing project, just beyond the legal limit of the law.

These true stories attest to the undeniable power of policy in the lives of families—the power to create the conditions for families to do their best in what they do best—instilling the responsibility and commitment on which our country was built and its future depends. Examples abound of how policy shapes the ecology in which families operate. For example, without policy, we would not have Head Start, which since 1965, has promoted school readiness among 22 million children. Without policy, there would be no State Children's Health Insurance Program (SCHIP), which served 6.6 million children across the country in 2006. Without policy, 22.4 million families would not have received the Earned Income Tax Credit in 2004, which averaged $2,200 for a family with children. All families do better in a supportive policy environment–one in which, for example, schools actively seek parent involvement; employers recognize that workers are also family members; agencies and organizations are family-centered in their philosophy and operation; and laws support family members' roles as workers, parents, partners, and caregivers. As these examples illustrate, policy shapes the environment in which families function and, in so doing, shapes human and family development as surely as other professional endeavors.

Just as policy shapes the environment in which families function, it shapes the environment in which family life educators' operate. Whether or not family life educators decide to seek a career in which they can shape policy, it is likely that their career will be shaped by policy. Try to put yourself in the situations below that family educators often find themselves in:

- Imagine that you are a family life education teacher and you notice that some of your students are coming to school hungry. No matter how hard you try, you are unable to engage your class in any serious learning during the hour before lunch. Would you continue to do the best you can in an impossible situation, or would you venture into the policy arena to take the actions needed to feed children who are too hungry to learn?
- Imagine that you are working in a family resource center in Everytown, U.S.A. and you encounter several instances of families being disadvantaged by existing policies. For example, families with a special needs child divulge to you the difficulty of navigating the maze of programs that provide the social services their child needs. You encounter families who cannot afford health insurance, but your hands are tied because your State Children's Health Insurance Program (SCHIP) provides coverage for children, but not for their parents. You work with elderly clients who are caregivers for a loved one, but do not have access to the service they need most—respite care to give them a break from the strain of round-the-clock caregiving.

Would you shrug off these policy constraints that families face as too complex, controversial, and circumspect to get involved in? Would you wade into the policy arena or would you weigh the role that money and influence play and shy away from the political fray? Could you lead an effort to encourage policymakers to examine the effect of policies on family well being or could you take the initiative to teach others about how to bring a family impact perspective to policymaking? The first step in considering what role family life educators can play in the family policy world is knowing what family policy is, what it is not, and what a family perspective in policymaking can achieve (Bogenschneider, 2006).

What Is Family Policy? What Is a Family Perspective in Policymaking?

This chapter focuses primarily on family policy (i.e., how legislation affecting families is developed and adopted) rather than family law (i.e., how statutes are interpreted and applied). Returning to the roots of the field, Kamerman and Kahn (1978) made a clear distinction between explicit policies that are designed to achieve specific goals regarding families, and implicit policies that are not specifically or primarily intended to affect families but which nonetheless have indirect consequences for them. Paralleling this distinction, family policy is defined below using explicit and implicit terms, both of which build on a broad definition of policy as the development, enactment, and implementation of a plan or course of action carried out through a law, rule, code, or other mechanism in the public or private sectors.

The explicit term *family policy* focuses on four main family functions: (a) family creation (e.g., to marry or divorce, to bear or adopt children, to provide foster care), (b) economic support (e.g., to provide for members' basic needs), (c) childrearing (e.g., to socialize the next generation), and (d) family caregiving (e.g., to provide assistance for the disabled, ill, frail, and elderly). Obviously, families also provide members with love and transmit cultural and religious values, but these intimate functions matter to policy only when they interfere with these four main functions (Ooms, 1990).

A companion implicit term, *a family perspective in policymaking*, acknowledges that family considerations can play an important role in a broad range of policy issues (Kamerman & Kahn, 1978; Ooms, 1990). A family perspective in policymaking analyzes the consequences of any policy or program, regardless of whether it is explicitly aimed at families, for its impact on family well being (e.g., family stability, family relationships, and the family's ability to carry out its responsibilities). To clarify these terms, family policy includes issues encompassed under the four family functions, such as child care, child support, earned income tax credit (EITC), divorce, family violence, juvenile crime, long-term care, and teenage pregnancy (Ooms, 1990). Tax provisions that create a child care tax credit or decrease the marriage penalty would be classified as family policy. However, a tax reform law that lowers taxes for individuals, many of whom happen to live in families, would not be considered family policy. Other issues such as health care, housing, poverty, substance abuse, and unemployment would not be considered family policies because they are not aimed specifically at families. Nevertheless, these issues would certainly benefit from a family perspective that examines in what ways families contribute to problems, how families are affected by problems, and whether they need to be involved in solutions.

At the heart of both the explicit and implicit definitions is the critical family element, which moves beyond the individual to a relationship between two or more individuals tied together by blood, legal bonds, or the performance of family functions. This is a fundamental distinction that is often overlooked in policy circles. For example, children's policy or women's policy is often falsely equated with family policy even though the target is an individual, not a family relationship. Families, when mentioned in policy debate, typically represent some but not all relationships in families. For example, *family* can be a code word for mother and child, with little or no attention to the father (Blum, 1993) or grandparent (Henderson, 2004). The commonly used term *single-parent family* masks the role that unmarried partners and noncustodial parents play in the lives of children (McLanahan, Garfinkel, & Mincy, 2001; Walsh, 1995). Family resource centers deal primarily with parent-child relationships and often ignore marital or partner relationships, despite their documented influence on the quality of parenting. Courts have guarded the rights of biological and adoptive parents to raise their children as they see fit and have granted few rights to grandparents, even though they are commonly considered to be members of the extended family (Henderson, 2004).

Conceptualizing policy from a family perspective would bring some unique qualities to U.S. policymaking. For example, family policy inherently brings a life span orientation to policymaking because families encompass relationships from the cradle to the grave (see Life Span

CHILDHOOD — *Within the context of the family system*

Family Law and Public Policy

- Understanding and respecting the law
- Laws and policies affecting families
- Children's legal rights
- Public policy as it affects families with children, including taxes, civil rights, social security, economic support laws, and regulations

Multicultural • Gender Fair • Special Needs Aware

Reciprocal interactions between family and ecosystem

ADOLESCENCE — *Within the context of the family system*

Family Law and Public Policy

- Respecting civil rights of all people
- Understanding legal definitions and laws affecting families
- Individual and family legal protection, rights and responsibilities
- Laws relating to marriage, divorce, family support, child custody, child protection and rights, family planning
- Family conflict and legal protection of family members
- Families and the justice system
- Impact of laws and policies on families
- Public policy as it affects families with adolescent children, including taxes, civil rights, social security, economic support laws, regulations

Multicultural • Gender Fair • Special Needs Aware

Reciprocal interactions between family and ecosystem

ADULTHOOD — *Within the context of the family system*

Family Law and Public Policy

- Transmitting values regarding education, justice and the law
- Understanding and affecting laws and policies
- Laws relating to marriage, divorce, family support, child custody, child protection and rights, family planning
- Family conflict and legal protection of family members
- Public policy as it affects families including taxes, civil rights, social security, economic support laws, regulations

Multicultural • Gender Fair • Special Needs Aware

Reciprocal interactions between family and ecosystem

LATER ADULTHOOD — *Within the context of the family system*

Family Law and Public Policy

- Transmitting values regarding education, justice and the law
- Understanding and affecting laws and policies
- Protecting the civil rights of all people
- Laws relating to marriage, divorce, family support, protection and rights of vulnerable individuals, property, wills, estate planning, and living wills
- Family conflict and legal protection of family members
- Public policy as it affects families including taxes, civil rights, social security, economic support laws, and regulations

Multicultural • Gender Fair • Special Needs Aware

Reciprocal interactions between family and ecosystem

concepts in sidebar). A family focus also brings a perspective to American policymaking that no other institution or interest group does as well—commitment to others. Families teach the powerful moral lesson of commitment and connectedness to others, even when such actions exact a personal cost. The family perspective in policymaking has the potential to counter the narrow, self-serving, individualistic agendas forwarded by advocates, special interest groups, and political action committees. In a society that is often focused on getting more, the family perspective reshifts the focus to giving more. In a nation built on the premise that every person is endowed with certain inalienable rights, the family perspective serves as a reminder that these rights come with responsibilities. In a culture that often uses money and material possessions as a sign of worth, worthiness in families comes from actions difficult to ascribe a dollar value to such as commitment and self-sacrifice by each for the other.

This family message is important in all human societies, but may be particularly important in countries like the United States to help counter the self-interest of an individualistic culture, the materialistic pressures of market economies, and the meager government assistance of a small social safety net (Bogenschneider, 2000). Ironically, these very conditions that make family commitment so important also constitute some of the most entrenched barriers to enacting policies that strengthen and support families across the life span, the topic I turn to next.

Is U.S. Policymaking Focused More on Individuals or Families?

From a historical perspective, the United States is one of the only countries in the world that does not mention *family* in its constitution. This silence on families (Rice, 1977) was not accidental, but a deliberate attempt by the founding fathers to avoid a patronage system based on wealth or lineage as existed in the English monarchy against which they were rebelling. In contrast, the U.S. government was built on individualistic principles that have pervaded policymaking in ways the founding fathers might not have anticipated or intended. For example, it was not until 1981 that the word *family* was used in a subcommittee of the U.S. Congress (Jacobs, Little, & Almeida, 1993). Even today, the United States—with all its agencies advancing such national interests as agriculture, defense, energy, health, labor, and transportation—has no single federal agency that oversees family issues and devotes its attention exclusively to families (Eshleman, 1991). At the state level, slightly more than half of state legislatures have a specific committee or commission that deals with family issues, but many do not (State Legislative Leaders Foundation, 1995).

Neither the federal nor state governments have an explicit family policy, so policymakers pass piecemeal legislation that responds to specific individual needs but seldom acknowledges family considerations or provides a comprehensive vision for families (Elrod, 1999). Four examples are cited here that illustrate the family void in workplace policies as well as state and federal laws.

- In a recent experimental study of hiring prospects for women, employers were asked to pick applicants from their resumes. Even though their resumes were identical in every other respect, mothers were 47% less likely to land an interview than nonmothers (Correll, Benard, & Paik, 2007).
- Eligibility criteria for programs like the State Children's Health Insurance Program (SCHIP) send signals about what constitutes socially acceptable behavior (Marshall & Sawhill, 2004). For example, in Wisconsin if a mother and father live with their child, they are eligible for health insurance through SCHIP whether or not they are married. If a parent and partner (not the other parent) live with the child, the partner is not eligible for coverage unless they marry; however, if they marry, their joint earnings may raise them above the income cutoffs for the program (Normandin & Bogenschneider, 2005).
- Nannies are eligible for Social Security credits and workers' compensation, but mothers are not unless they have a job outside the home (Crittenden, 2001).
- The Earned Income Tax Credit (EITC), one of the country's most effective anti-poverty programs, can penalize marriage when both partners work. Some EITC reforms that will be implemented by 2008 will remove marriage penalties for cohabitating couples who earn below 200% of the poverty level. However, for cohabitating couples with incomes between \$20,000 and \$30,000, there is a substantial marriage penalty—a loss of an average \$1,700 in tax credits each year (Berlin, 2007).

Granted, government is not totally uninvolved in or neutral toward families. A number of policies support such family functions as education, health care, and caregiving for the young, aged, and disabled. Yet a careful scrutiny of American policies illustrates that policymakers' image of their client is disproportionately the individual—children, youth, women, veterans, the elderly, disabled, and poor—with families relegated to the periphery of policy development, implementation, and evaluation (Moen & Schorr, 1987). So, if policymakers acknowledged and took family considerations into account in policy decisions, would it matter? Would policies be more effective if they focused on families rather than individuals?

How Effective Are Family-Centered Approaches in Policymaking?

No definitive answer to this question exists. The best evidence for a family-focused approach to policymaking emerges from experimental studies that focus on family-based interventions compared to interventions that focus on the individual. Two streams of research are especially illustrative: one focuses on a social problem, juvenile crime, and one focuses on a method of family support, home visiting.

Juvenile Crime

In a recent meta-analysis, the Washington State Institute for Public Policy conducted a cost-benefit review of corrections programs aimed at preventing crime and reducing recidivism. The corrections programs that yielded the greatest return on investment targeted juveniles (Aos, Miller, & Drake, 2006); of these, the five most cost-effective rehabilitation programs and the single most cost-effective prevention program intentionally worked with families. The effectiveness of these family approaches should come as no surprise given that one of the strongest predictors of juvenile crime is ineffective parenting. Obviously, the approach these evidence-based programs use—recreating the powerful socialization forces of functional family life—is a sound one (Anderson & Bogenschneider, 2007).

Home Visiting

Home visiting has attracted considerable attention from policymakers despite inconclusive evaluations (Gomby, Culross, & Behrman, 1999). Promising results have emerged, however, from the methodologically sound, longitudinal studies of Old's program of nurse home visiting. Nurses visited low-income mothers, many of whom were unmarried teenagers, prenatally and during the first 2 years of the child's life. Compared with families that received only transportation and developmental screening, nurse home visiting resulted in benefits to children's behavior and the mother's life course that can be detected as long as 15 years later. In follow-up studies, the 15-year-olds born to low-income, nurse-visited mothers had 46% fewer verified reports of child abuse and neglect and also 56% fewer arrests. The nurse-visited mothers had an average of 69% fewer arrests, 37 fewer months on food stamps, 30 fewer months on Aid to Families with Dependent Children (AFDC), 23 fewer months on Medicaid, one-fifth fewer subsequent births, and a spacing of 28 months more between first and second children (Olds et al., 1997, 1998).

Summary

Taken together, these studies provide compelling examples of the potential of family-focused approaches. Not all family approaches have been this encouraging, however, as shown by evaluations of teenage pregnancy prevention (Kirby, 1997) and two-generation welfare programs (St. Pierre, Layzer, & Barnes, 1996). Exaggerating the effectiveness of family programs to policymakers is counterproductive, yet ignoring their demonstrated potential seems shortsighted.

Is Family Policy the Responsibility of Family Life Educators?

If we asked families whether policy should be on the plate of family life educators, the short answer would be *yes*. In polls, only 6% of parents said that government currently *was* doing a great deal to help them, but 47% said that government *could* do a great deal to help them (Hewlett & West, 1998). Families clearly recognize the need. It has been said that families are "everybody's concern, but nobody's responsibility" (Ooms, 1990, p. 77). Thus, it may fall to us, as family life educators, to speak up for families because few groups consistently represent family interests, and there are seldom sustained efforts to analyze policy from a family perspective.

The need is obvious. The benefits for families are apparent. My hope is that policy is not abandoned by family life educators because of its reputation for being "dirty"—a corrupt, influence-peddling, money-driven process. Of course, there are instances where politics have trumped the science, yet science also has swayed policy decisions when the right information is provided to the right policymakers at the right time in the political process. We will never be able to take the politics out of policymaking, nor should we. Our political system is one intentionally designed for decisions to be made, not by experts, but through civilized debate in public settings by those elected to represent diverse interests with divergent views (Weiss, 1999).

Based on my 25 years of policy experience, I have found elected officials to be bright, hard-working, and committed to making a difference. I have come to view politics much like the meaning of the Greek word polis (city) from which it was derived—working with others toward a common purpose. Family life educators need to become involved to monitor whether this common purpose privileges individual self-interest and greed at the expense of family well-being and the public good.

What Policy Roles Can Family Life Educators Play?

Policy work is not limited to what happens in state houses or the nation's Capitol; important policy decisions are also made in such settings as board rooms, city halls, courthouses, city halls, and social service programs. Moreover, policy roles do not necessarily entail direct contact with policymakers. Family life educators can generate and disseminate policy-relevant, family-sensitive research and evaluations. Family life educators can conduct family impact analyses as policies are developed and implemented to examine the impact on family well-being. Family life educators can educate the next generation of family policy professionals, engage community citizens in family policymaking, and encourage universities to become involved in family policy outreach. Bogenschneider (2006) reviews nine roles that family professionals can play, illustrated with 26 case studies that attempt to capture the excitement of getting involved in the policy arena along with some of the challenges it entails.

Put simply, two types of family life educators are needed: the policy wise and the policy wonk (Bogenschneider, 2007). Some family life educators devote themselves to the honorable and important career of making change one student or one family at a time; however, their effectiveness may well depend on how policy-wise they are. For example, the scenarios this article began with were not trumped up to prove a point, but actual situations that family life educators faced in the real world. When one family studies graduate student who was in graduate school became aware of hungry school children, she took time away from her studies to pull together a coalition that successfully lobbied for $820,000 in state funds to provide a morning milk break for poor children. An Extension Family Living Educator working in one of the most economically disadvantaged counties in her state conducted a survey of school children 6 to 13 years old to assess their nutritional needs. Confronted with data that 45% of children were coming to school hungry, she worked with a group of concerned citizens to conduct a policy education program for the local school board that eventually resulted in the establishment of the county's first school breakfast program (Bogenschneider, 2006). Faced with several instances of policies and programs that superseded rather than strengthened families, family professionals at the University of Minnesota taught the public why it is important to view policy through a family lens and how to conduct family impact analyses of policies and programs (Bogenschneider, 2006). These professionals were policy-wise—when they saw a family need that policy could address, they departed from business as usual and incorporated a policy component into their work with families.

We also need a new generation of family policy wonks whose job it is to change policy in ways that can benefit countless families across a community, state, or nation. Because most policy courses and prevention programs focus on individuals rather than families, we need family policy wonks who make policy a top priority in their work in institutions such as colleges and universities, Cooperative Extension, the nonprofit and private sectors, philanthropic organizations, and prevention and intervention programs. Because family policy does not have the status or legitimacy of economic or environmental policy, we need family life educators to inject the family perspective into settings committed to informing policy such as advocacy organizations, evaluation firms, government trade organizations, nonpartisan legislative service agencies, policy-oriented organizations, public policy schools, research and evaluation firms, and think tanks. Because policymakers routinely consider economic or environmental impacts of legislation and seldom consider its impact on families, we need family life educators well-versed in family impact analysis wherever policy is made, not only in state capitols and the U.S. Congress, but also in the countless cities, counties, schools, and other local jurisdictions across the country. The family policy wise and family policy wonk work in a wide range of venues performing an array of policy-related activities, four of which are described here.

Conducting family impact analysis

Family impact analysis critically examines the past, present, or probable future effects of a policy, program, or service on family stability, family relationships, and family members' ability to carry out their responsibilities (Ooms & Preister, 1988). Whereas evaluation research typically focuses on whether the stated goals or objectives of a program are being met, family impact analysis examines whether program goals may be counterproductive by producing negative consequences for families, sometimes in unintended ways. Family impact analysis can be used to review rules, legislation, or laws; to evaluate programs, services, and operating procedures of agencies or organizations; and to help prepare questions or testimony for hearings, board meetings, or public forums (Ooms & Preister, 1988).

Several tools have been developed for determining whether policies, programs, or institutions help or hurt, strengthen or weaken family life. For example, one general checklist can be used to assess the family impact of any policy, program, or service. Other specialized checklists are designed to diagnose the family impact of specific settings (e.g., communities and schools) and services (e.g., adolescent treatment centers, early care and education programs, and state child and family services plans). Tools and procedures for conducting family impact analysis can be found at http://www.familyimpactseminars.org/index.asp?p=2&page=impact.

Because family impact analysis, like environmental impact analysis, is a technical exercise, it is best conducted by professionals with family training and expertise. Thus, family life educators are well-prepared to help agencies or organizations conduct a self-assessment of the impact their philosophy, programs, services, and procedures are having on families; evaluating such efforts can be as simple as tracking the changes the organization makes to become more sensitive to and supportive of families.

Engaging citizens in family policymaking

Another role for family life educators is engaging families in policymaking and, in so doing, expanding policy beyond something that government is solely responsible for to include public problem-solving where citizens work together on behalf of families. A compelling example emerges from a group of parents and community leaders in Wayzata, Minnesota, who are fighting for influence over their children's lives against other forces more powerful than most individual parents (Doherty, 2000). These parents organized when they found themselves competing for time with their own children in an over-busy, over-scheduled, over-commercialized society. For example, they believe that active marketing of clothing to preteens has preempted parental influence on the clothing choices of children as young as age seven. The emphasis on athletics at the expense of family time is another example. Parents complained of coaches who threatened to bench athletes for missing practices even on holidays such as Mother's Day or Thanksgiving.

To make family life a priority in this Minnesota community, parents have generated and sustained a grassroots movement, Family Life 1st (Doherty, 2000). Family Life 1st is acquiring political clout by publicly recognizing local supporters of family life and generating media attention for their efforts. A Family Life 1st Seal of Approval has been created to acknowledge those individuals and organizations that support parents' attempts to create a better balance between time spent on activities outside the family and on relationships inside the family. For further information on how family life educators can help communities start their own Family Life 1st initiative, see Doherty's chapter in this volume and http://www.puttingfamilyfirst.org.

Building peer assistance networks

Another potential policy role for family life educators is family policy implementation, because how policies are implemented may be as important as what kinds of policies are enacted. For example, the Welfare Peer Assistance Network (WELPAN) was funded by the Joyce Foundation to bring together high-ranking welfare officials from seven Midwest states to share their experiences in implementing the 1996 welfare reform law. According to facilitators Tom Corbett and Jennifer Noyes, this peer mentoring technique is quite simple. Instead of a top-down approach that disseminates research from experts to those in the field, WELPAN employs a horizontal strategy of bringing together similarly situated peers who face mutual challenges to discuss their experiences and share what has worked in their respective settings (see http://www.irp.wisc.edu/initiatives/outreach/welpan.htm). From this networking emerges some common solutions to shared problems as well as new insights and perspectives that might be more readily apparent to those doing welfare reform than those studying or teaching about it. For example, in the 2004 debate over reauthorization of federal welfare legislation, WELPAN voiced the need for states to have more latitude to provide coordinated and coherent family services; a provision that granted state flexibility for cross-system collaboration was included in the Administration's proposal and the House bill.

The implications of this peer mentoring strategy extend well beyond welfare reform. For example, how often do child care providers in your locale have opportunities to interact with each other? What opportunities for dialogue exist among the personnel of family support centers? Do any conversations occur among employers and human resource managers interested in developing family-friendly benefits in the workplace? Family life educators can bring together family service-providers, facilitate the discussion, and record innovative ideas that can be used to improve family services, either within individual organizations or collaboratively across organizations.

Organizing Family Impact Seminars

Policymakers would not think of passing a bill without asking about its economic or environmental impacts. Family life educators can organize local or state Family Impact Seminars that encourage policymakers to routinely inquire how a policy might affect families and whether policies would be more effective if families were involved in the solution. Family Impact Seminars are a series of presentations, discussion sessions, and briefing reports for state policymakers including legislators, legislative aides, governor's office staff, nonpartisan legislative research staff, and state agency representatives. The Seminars provide high-quality, nonpartisan research on family issues such as corrections policy, early childhood care and education, health care, and Medicaid.

The format of the seminars consists of presentations by a panel of premier researchers, program directors, and policy analysts, accompanied by a background briefing report that summarizes policy-relevant research on the issue in a succinct, easy-to-understand format.

To date, 135 seminars have been conducted for state policymakers by Family Impact Seminar organizations in 24 state capitols and the District of Columbia (see http://www.familyimpactseminars.org/index.asp?p=2&page=site). In addition, over 30 seminars have been conducted for local policymakers by county Extension family living educators in Wisconsin. In evaluations, policymakers report that past Seminars have increased their knowledge of research on family issues and changed their attitudes about the value of research and the family perspective in ways that have shaped the development and enactment of public policies. State legislators report using this information to draft new legislation, evaluate pending legislation, incorporate into speeches, make voting decisions, and share with colleagues and constituents (Bogenschneider, Olson, Linney, & Mills, 2000).

Conclusion

Families are inherently private, yet inevitably affected by public policy. One important contribution that family life educators can make in the public sphere is helping policymakers see family issues as needing public policy responses to produce change. Family life educators are uniquely positioned to transfer to policymaking the family message of *commitment to others*—a powerful conceptual distinction that has the potential to temper the forces of self-interest and greed by raising up the responsibility each citizen bears to the larger society and the collective good.

Those of us involved in family policy are not naïve. Policy work takes patience and persistence. Policy work is often frustrating, sometimes irrational, and comes with no guarantee that the time invested will pay off. Only rarely do one's efforts lead to a major policy change. Yet family life educators are inspired by the times the random political events do line up right and they are able to contribute to the passage of a policy that keeps on giving to countless families for years to come. Family life educators possess the knowledge and skills to build more supportive policy environments for families in a number of ways such as:

- engaging our colleagues and clientele in examining policies and programs in regard to their impact on family well-being;
- empowering families to band together to develop shared solutions to common problems;
- motivating service providers to discuss ways to implement more family-centered policies and practices; and
- informing policymakers that family problems are often not just individual concerns but also societal responsibilities.

Family life educators know how to build family policy, but in the words of Goethe, it takes more than knowledge.

Knowing is not enough, we must apply.

Willing is not enough, we must do.

References

Anderson, C., & Bogenschneider, K. (2007). A policymaker's guide to effective juvenile justice programs: How important are family approaches? In K. Bogenschneider & H. Normandin (Eds.), *Cost-effective approaches in juvenile and adult corrections: What works? What doesn't?* (Wisconsin Family Impact Seminar Briefing Report No. 25, pp. 25-33). Retrieved February 23, 2008, from http://www.familyimpactseminars.org/s_wifis25report.pdf

Aos, S., Miller, M., & Drake, E. (2006). *Evidence-based public policy options to reduce future prison construction, criminal justice costs, and crime rates.* Olympia, WA: Washington State Institute for Public Policy.

Berlin, G. L. (2007, May). *Investing in parents to invest in children.* Paper presented at the National Summit on America's Children, Washington DC.

Blum, R. (1993). Critical issues for the family research agenda and their use in policy formulation. In G. E. Hendershot & F. B. LeClere (Eds.), *Family health: From data to policy* (pp. 110-112). Minneapolis, MN: National Council on Family Relations.

Bogenschneider, K. (2000). Has family policy come of age? A decade review of the state of U.S. family policy in the 1990s. *Journal of Marriage and the Family, 62*(4), 1136 - 1159.

Bogenschneider, K. (2006). *Family policy matters: How policymaking affects families and what professionals can do* (2nd ed.). Mahwah, NJ: Erlbaum.

Bogenschneider, K. (2007, September). Policy—No better way to spend a life. *NCFR Report, 52*(3), F11-F12.

Bogenschneider, K., Olson, J. R., Linney, K. D., & Mills, J. (2000). Connecting research and policymaking: Implications for theory and practice from the Family Impact Seminars. *Family Relations, 49*(3), 327-339.

Correll, S. J., Benard, S., & Paik, I. (2007). Getting a job: Is there a motherhood penalty? *American Journal of Sociology, 112*(5), 1297-1338.

Crittenden, A. (2001). *The price of motherhood: Why the most important job in the world is still the least valued.* New York: Henry Holt.

Doherty, W. J. (2000). Family science and family citizenship: Towards a model of community partnership with families. *Family Relations, 49*(3), 319-325.

Elrod, L. D. (1999). Epilogue: Of families, federalism, and a quest for policy. *Family Law Quarterly, 33*(3), 843-863.

Eshleman, R. (1991). *The family: An introduction.* Boston: Allyn Bacon.

Gomby, D. S., Culross, C. L., & Behrman, R. E. (1999). Home visiting: Recent program evaluations—analysis and recommendations. *The Future of Children, 9*(1), 4-26.

Henderson, T. L. (2004). Grandparent visitation rights: Successful acquisition of court-ordered visitation. *Journal of Family Issues, 20*(3), 1-31.

Hewlett, S. A., & West, C. (1998). *The war against parents: What we can do for America's beleaguered moms and dads.* New York: Houghton-Mifflin.

Jacobs, F. H., Little, P., & Almeida, C. (1993). Supporting family life: A survey of homeless shelters. *Journal of Social Distress and the Homeless, 2*(4), 269-288.

Kamerman, S. B., & Kahn, A. J. (1978). Families and the idea of family policy. In S. B. Kamerman & A. J. Kahn (Eds.), *Family policy: Government and families in fourteen countries* (pp. 1-16). New York: Columbia University Press.

Kirby, D. (1997, March). *No easy answers: Research findings on programs to reduce teen pregnancy* [Summary]. Washington, DC: National Campaign to Prevent Teen Pregnancy.

Marshall, W., & Sawhill, I. V. (2004). Progressive family policy in the twenty-first century. In D. P. Moynihan, T. M. Smeeding, & L. Rainwater (Eds.), *The future of the family* (pp. 198-230). New York: Russell Sage Foundation.

McLanahan, S., Garfinkel, I., & Mincy, R. B. (2001, December). *Fragile families, welfare reform, and marriage* (Welfare Reform and Beyond Brief No.10). Washington, DC: The Brookings Institution

Moen, P., & Schorr, A. L. (1987). Families and social policy. In M. B. Sussman & S. K. Steinmetz (Eds.), *Handbook of marriage and the family* (pp. 795-813). New York: Plenum Press.

Normandin, H., & Bogenschneider, K. (Eds.). (2005, October). *Medicaid: Who benefits, how expensive is it, and what are states doing to control costs?* (Wisconsin Family Impact Seminar Briefing Report No. 22). Retrieved Feb. 23, 2008, from http://www.familyimpactseminars.org/s_wifis22report.pdf

Olds, D., Eckenrode, J., Henderson, C. R., Jr, Kitzman, H., Powers, J., Cole, R., et al. (1997). Long-term effects of home visitation on maternal life course and child abuse and neglect: 15-year follow-up of a randomized trial. *Journal of the American Medical Association, 278,* 637-643.

Olds, D., Henderson, C. R., Jr., Cole, R., Eckenrode, J., Kitzman, H., Luckey, D., et al. (1998). Long-term effects of nurse home visitation on children's criminal and antisocial behavior: 15-year follow-up of a randomized controlled trial. *Journal of the American Medical Association, 280*(14), 1238-1244.

Ooms, T. (1990). Families and government: Implementing a family perspective in public policy. *Social Thought, 16*(2), 61-78.

Ooms, T., & Preister, S. (1988). *A strategy for strengthening families: Using family criteria in policy making and program evaluation.* Washington, DC: Family Impact Seminar.

Rice, R. M. (1977). *American family policy: Content and context.* Milwaukee: Family Service America.

St. Pierre, R. G., Layzer, J. I., & Barnes, H. B. (1996). *Regenerating two-generation programs.* Cambridge, MA: Abt Associates.

State Legislative Leaders Foundation. (1995). *State legislative leaders: Keys to effective legislation for children and families.* Centerville, MA: Author.

Walsh, F. (1995). From family damage to family challenge. In R. H. Miskell, S. H. Lusterman & S. H. McDaniel (Eds.), *Integrating family therapy: Handbook of family psychology and system theory* (pp. 587-606). Washington, DC: American Psychological Association.

Weiss, Carol H. (1999). Research-Policy Linkages: How much influence does social science research have? *World Social Science Report.* Paris: UNESCO.

Key Resources

Anderson, E., Skinner, D. A., & Letiecq, B. L. (2004). *Teaching family policy: A handbook of course syllabi, teaching strategies and resources* (2nd ed.). Minneapolis, MN: National Council on Family Relations.

Bellah, R. N., Madsen, R., Sullivan, W. M., Swidler, A., & Tipton, S. M. (1996). *Habits of the heart: Individualism and commitment in American life.* Berkeley: University of California Press. (Original publication 1985).

Bogenschneider, K. (2006). *Family policy matters: How policymaking affects families and what professionals can do* (2nd ed.). Mahwah, NJ: Erlbaum.

Bogenschneider, K. (2000). Has family policy come of age? A decade review of the state of U.S. family policy in the 1990s. *Journal of Marriage and the Family, 62*(4), 1136-1159.

Bogenschneider, K., & Ittig, M. (2006). *Family policy matters: How policymaking affects families and what professionals can do* [Instructor's manual]. Mahwah, New Jersey: Erlbaum.

Bogenschneider, K., Olson, J. R., Mills, J., & Linney, K. D. (2006). How can we connect research with state policymaking? Lessons from the Wisconsin Family Impact Seminars. In K. Bogenschneider, *Family policy matters: How policymaking affects families and what professionals can do* (2nd ed.) (pp. 245-276). Mahwah, NJ. Erlbaum.

Doherty, W. J. (2000). Family science and family citizenship: Towards a model of community partnership with families. *Family Relations, 49*(3), 319-325.

National Council on Family Relations. (2000). *Public policy through a family lens: Sustaining families in the 21st century.* Minneapolis, MN: Author.

Gross, E., Bogenschneider, K., & Johnson, C. (2006). How to conduct a family impact analysis. In K. Bogenschneider, *Family policy matters: How policymaking affects families and what professionals can do* (2nd ed.) (pp. 305-311). Mahwah, NJ: Erlbaum.

Smith, J. A. (1991). *The idea brokers: Think tanks and the rise of the new policy elite.* New York: Free Press.

Skinner, D. (n.d.). *Teaching family policy*. Retrieved February 24, 2008, from http://www.familyimpactseminars.org/index.asp?p=2&page=teachingfamilypolicy

Zimmerman, S. L. (1988). *Understanding family policy: Theoretical approaches*. Newbury Park, CA: Sage Publication.

Related Websites

The Policy Institute for Family Impact Seminars: www.familyimpactseminars.org

Putting Family First: www.familylife1st.org

WELPAN: www.irp.wisc.edu/initiatives/outreach/welpan.htm

About the Author

Karen Bogenschneider, Ph.D., is Rothermel Bascom Professor of Human Ecology at the University of Wisconsin-Madison, Family Policy Specialist in University of Wisconsin Extension, and Executive Director of the Policy Institute for Family Impact Seminars. E-mail: kpbogens@wisc.edu; Web: www.familyimpactseminars.org.

Portions of this article appeared in *Family Policy Matters. How Policymaking Affects Families and What Professionals Can Do* (2006) by Karen Bogenschneider. Reproduced by permission of Taylor and Francis Group, LLC, a division of Informa plc.

Professional Ethics and Practice

Glen Palm

A middle school teacher teaching a family life class concluded a presentation of different family structures that introduced single parent families, blended families, and gay and lesbian families. A student asks the teacher what she thinks about gay and lesbian families. The teacher holds strong religious beliefs about the immorality of gay and lesbian lifestyles. She has been trying to teach acceptance of family diversity in the class, but her personal belief system is in conflict with this value. How should she answer the student?

A young woman is applying for a job in a social service agency to work with families who are in a battered women's shelter. She has just completed her B.S. degree in family studies and has applied for the provisional CFLE certification. She has done some practice teaching with a parent support group for parents of toddlers but has limited experience working with families. None of the other staff has any experience doing parent education and she would be in charge of creating a parent education program for the women and their children. She really needs a job and this sounds like an exciting opportunity, but she is not sure if she has the skills and experience to work with this particular group of parents and children. What should she do?

A mother of a three-year-old in your parent education group tells the group about a new strategy that she uses to keep control over their child while her husband is away on business trips. She has purchased a wooden paddle at her husband's request and tells the child that daddy will paddle him when he gets home if he doesn't behave. She feels this new technique has been very effective. How do you respond as a parent educator?

The family life educator is likely to encounter difficult ethical situations like those described above on a regular basis. The field of family life education has struggled to establish ethical guidelines to guide practitioners facing situations like those described above (Powell & Cassidy, 2006; Brock, 1993; Leigh, Loewey & Lester, 1986; and Kerchoff, 1964). Professionals who practice family life education may receive information on ethics from different professional groups such as family studies researchers, early childhood education, or counseling. The fields of counseling and family therapy have developed codes of ethics through different professional organizations (American Counseling Association, 2005; American Association for Marriage and Family Therapy, 2001) and early childhood educators have also defined ethical standards (National Association for the Education of Young Children, 2005). Family life educators through the Certified Family Life Educator (CFLE) program of National Council on Family Relations (NCFR) are expected to develop the critical skills for ethical thinking and practice. This group has adopted the Minnesota Council on Family Relations (MCFR) *Guidelines for Ethical Thinking and Practice* (MCFR, 2009). These guidelines and the ethical decision-making process will be the basis for exploring important

CURRICULUM GUIDELINES: PROFESSIONAL ETHICS & PRACTICE

An understanding of the character and quality of human social conduct, and the ability to critically examine ethical questions and issues as they relate to professional practice. Based on knowledge of:

1. understanding the formation of social attitudes and values;
2. recognizing and respecting the diversity of values and the complexity of value choice in a pluralistic society;
3. examining value systems and ideologies systematically and objectively;
4. understanding the social consequences of value choices; and
5. recognizing the ethical implications of social and technological changes.

questions around ethical thinking and practice for contemporary family life educators (see Related Websites). The issues to be examined include: Why is ethics important for Family Life Educators (FLE); Theories that inform family life education guidelines for ethical decision-making; Ethical decision-making as a process; Tips for new family life education practitioners; and Future issues and challenges around integrating ethics into family life education practice.

Importance of Ethical Thinking and Practice in Family Life Education

As we enter the 21st Century, ethical thinking and practice is particularly relevant to the evolving field of family life education for a number of important reasons.

The *growth and maturity of the field* means that the age of innocence is past and family life practitioners have to acknowledge that they can do harm. Doherty (1995) in his conceptual framework about involvement with families describes the different levels of involvement that family life educators may encounter in working with families. As educators move from the second level of giving information to level three of addressing emotional family issues in a more direct manner, or level four of brief family system interventions, the possibility of doing harm to family members also increases (for further discussion see pp. 233-239).

As family life educators *work with more diverse families* and complex family systems they will encounter diverse family values and parenting practices that are more likely to conflict with the current understanding of effective and non-abusive parenting practices. Increased diversity of beliefs and practices will lead to ethical dilemmas where conflicts between principles will challenge practitioners (Palm, 1994).

Society will hold family life educators *more accountable as professionals* as we move towards greater involvement with families. More intense scrutiny about the effectiveness of FLE practice as well as the moral character of practitioners will follow from emerging professionalism and the trend of greater accountability for educational programs.

The *increase in the number of programs* (Carter, 1996) along with the intensity and complexity of family life education demands clearer standards for our moral behavior as well as a public and professional dialogue about ethical thinking and practice within the field

Ethical Theories and Family Life Education

Ethics is a complex branch of philosophy that has produced many different theories about how to define moral thinking and behavior (Freeman, 2000). The current set of ethical guidelines developed by MCFR (2009) represents a unique integration of different ethical theories. The MCFR document on Ethical Thinking and Practice combines concepts from three different theoretical traditions. These include a principles approach, relational ethics, and virtue ethics (Freeman, 2000). The different approaches are integrated into a model of creative tension that balances absolutist and relativist tendencies. This integration is incorporated into the decision-making process for discussion of ethical dilemmas (MCFR, 2009).

The code of ethics approach has been the most prevalent way for professional groups to articulate and monitor ethical behavior (e.g., Minnesota Board of Teaching, 1997); American Association of Marriage and Family Therapy Code of Ethics, (2001). Codes of ethics carefully define professional conduct through the delineation of broad principles. Codes do not always offer clear directions in the face of ethical dilemmas where two principles in the code come into conflict with each other or when codes tend to reflect past problems in a profession (Corey, Corey, & Callanan, 1988). The strength of a code of ethics is that it carefully describes expectations for professional behavior and reflects important professional values. The downside

Ethical Decision-Making Process (MCFR, 2009)

Step 1. Identification of Relationships

Step 2. Application of Principles

Step 3. Identification of Contradictions/Tensions

Step 4. Identification of Possible Solutions

Step 5. Selection of Action(s)

Note: for more detail regarding this process see Ethical Thinking and Practice for Family and Parent Educators on pp. 233-239.

is that most codes are not grounded in theories and that professionals often are not familiar with the code because it may not be used on a regular basis.

There are two different approaches to ethics; the first is mandatory ethics, which includes compliance with the law and a specific code of moral conduct for a profession. The second approach is aspiration ethics, which is more than compliance with the law and a code of ethics. The aspiration ethics approach encourages individuals to be sensitive to the effects of their intervention on the welfare of others. They strive to follow a set of ideal standards in their practice. The MCFR (2009) guidelines were designed in the spirit of aspiration ethics versus mandatory ethics.

One of the three theoretical frameworks to ethics that the MCFR guidelines employ is a principles approach to ethics. The specific principles were derived through several workshops with family life education practitioners who identified in an inductive manner general principles they would use in addressing specific ethical dilemmas. The guidelines describe an ideal level of practice that is defined through a set of specific principles that reflect important professional values. This provides the advantage of a code of ethics through a clear description of expectations and aspirations for professional conduct. The major limitation to this principles approach is the lack of enforcement by a professional body.

A second theoretical framework to ethics is relational ethics, which forms the basis for organizing ethical principles in the MCFR (2009) approach. "The use of relational ethics is critical to working with individuals and families. The principles of relational ethics form a basis for understanding the specific ethical dilemmas and guide practice first and foremost towards the development of caring and respectful relationships with all family members" (MCFR, 2009, p. 4).

This focus on relationships is very similar to Feminist Ethics (Freeman, 2000), which focuses on moral judgments from the female orientation of care versus a male orientation, which stresses justice. Relationships are also at the heart of feminist ethical thinking (Gilligan, 1982; Noddings, 1984). The MCFR guidelines for developing caring and respectful relationships are outlined as a developmental process. The relational approach defines a relational context for understanding how to apply and interpret ethical principles. The combination of these two disparate approaches to ethics provides a creative tension between the more absolutist tendency of the principles approach and the relativist tendency of the relational approach.

The third theory that is incorporated into the MCFR's version of ethical thinking and practice is virtues ethics. Virtue ethics is focused on the person of the family life educator and their moral competence (Doherty, 1991). Professional behavior has most often focused on tech-

CHILDHOOD — *Within the context of the family system*

Professional Ethics and Practice

- Taking responsibility for actions
- Consequences of actions for self and others
- Discovering spirituality
- Respect for all persons
- Gaining new rights and responsibilities with age
- Rights of all persons

Multicultural • Gender Fair • Special Needs Aware

Reciprocal interactions between family and ecosystem

ADOLESCENCE — *Within the context of the family system*

Professional Ethics and Practice

- Developing a personal ethical code
- Exploring personal spirituality
- Personal autonomy and social responsibility
- Interrelationship of rights and responsibilities
- Ethical principles as one kind of value
- Ethical values as guide to human social conduct
- Complexity and difficulty of ethical choices and decisions
- Ethical implications of social and technological change

Multicultural • Gender Fair • Special Needs Aware

Reciprocal interactions between family and ecosystem

ADULTHOOD — *Within the context of the family system*

Professional Ethics and Practice

- Establishing an ethical philosophy of life
- Acting in accordance with personal beliefs with consideration for others
- Continued growth in personal spirituality
- Personal autonomy and social responsibility
- Interrelationship of rights and responsibilities
- Ethical principles as one kind of value
- Ethical values as guide to human social conduct
- Complexity and difficulty of ethical choices and decisions
- Assisting in the formation of ethical concepts and behavior in others
- Ethical implications of social and technological change

Multicultural • Gender Fair • Special Needs Aware

Reciprocal interactions between family and ecosystem

LATER ADULTHOOD — *Within the context of the family system*

Professional Ethics and Practice

- Personal autonomy and social responsibility
- Continued growth in personal spirituality
- Acting in accordance with personal beliefs with consideration for others
- Interrelationship of rights and responsibilities
- Ethical principles as one kind of value
- Ethical values as a guide to human social conduct
- Assisting in the formation of ethical concepts and behavior in others
- Complexity and difficulty of ethical choices and decisions - quality of life issues, end of life issues
- Protection from exploitation
- Ethical implications of social and technological change

Multicultural • Gender Fair • Special Needs Aware

Reciprocal interactions between family and ecosystem

nical competence. Moral competence or virtues which are defined as "dispositions to do the right thing for the right reasons" are much more difficult to assess or measure. The virtues that were identified through numerous workshops with family life practitioners in the original work of the MCFR Ethics Committee turned into a long laundry list of virtues. The group decided to focus on three specific virtues that would be most relevant to family life education practice in the current social context. These were:

- **Caring** - the disposition to support the well being of family members as decision-makers in their own lives.
- **Prudence or Practical Wisdom** - the ability to understand competing needs in complex situations and make decisions based on reflection and consultation with peers.
- **Hope/Optimism** - the disposition to focus on the strengths and positive potential of family members and other individuals and to maintain a positive attitude in the face of adversity.

The integration of virtues ethics is complementary to relational ethics and identifies important internal moral characteristics that are relevant for family life educators. The three different ethical theories are combined in a creative manner that helps to balance the general tendencies towards absolutism and relativism.

Ethical Decision-Making

One of the greatest challenges for professional ethics is to create a practical and relevant approach to decision-making. Individuals in a field can use the ethical principles that have been defined as a guide for moral practice. However, the principles by themselves do not resolve ethical dilemmas. The ethical dilemma is a difficult situation where at least two competing principles appear to be in direct conflict. This is when ethical decision-making becomes most important and relevant. Ethical principles could be seen as hierarchically ordered where conflict is resolved by the order or priority of the principle when there is a conflict. For example, doing harm to children would be seen as more important than protecting parent rights to their own style of discipline. The MCFR (2009) approach to ethical decision-making involves a process that includes consideration of relationships, virtues, and principles to create solutions that are thoughtful and sensitive to a variety of factors (See the sidebar description of the case study process). This process has been designed to support individual practitioners in making thoughtful decisions about how to address ethical dilemmas. This process brings the wisdom of the profession in the identified principles along with the support and clear thinking of peers to problem-solve difficult situations.

Tips for New Professionals

The introduction of ethics is often done through a course on ethics in professions like counseling. Some practice with case studies helps to develop skills for new professionals. The following tips are presented to highlight common issues that new professionals in family life education may encounter in applying ethics to practice.

A difficult distinction to make when examining ethical issues is whether the situation is a true ethical dilemma or is an issue that could be resolved with good technical skills. This is especially difficult for new professionals as they begin to refine the technical skills of teaching and group facilitation skills. A true dilemma cannot be resolved with only good technical skills. Moral competence in understanding of ethical dilemmas in combination with good technical skills is the best way to approach difficult situations. For example, helping an immigrant family understand the problems with corporal punishment of children that has traditionally been used in their culture as an effective means of discipline is not acceptable in American society. The dilemma here is the conflict between respecting parents' values and choices, based on cultural differences and protecting children from harm. Without understanding the ethical dimensions of this situation the actions of a practitioner with excellent technical skills are diminished.

The relationship of law to ethics can also be a problem in addressing difficult ethical situations. Family life educators are likely to see legal obligations as the ultimate determination of good actions. Ethical principles and legal mandates can come into conflict and this conflict needs to be carefully examined. For example, Family Life Educators are mandated reporters of child abuse and neglect. The principle to follow legal mandates may come into conflict with a principle about respecting family cultural values and different ideas about monitoring children's behavior. Typically, obeying laws will lead to the right action, but the other principles in conflict with the law should not be automatically discounted or dismissed. In the process of honoring law, one must still look for ways to express understanding and respect for other principles.

Difficult ethical situations take time to process and problem-solve. In processing ethical dilemmas educators must consider the implications of different actions and different relational contexts. Most practitioners have the tendency to move directly into the problem-solving mode. The decision-making process described in the MCFR (2009) document provides the benefit of thoughtful reflection of both principles and relationships in a peer group setting. If you don't understand the original conflicts in principles and don't consider all of the relationships involved in addressing the problem, quick solutions can create unintended new problems.

Future Challenges and Next Steps for Family Life Educators

The practice of family life education by diverse groups such as psychologists, social workers, family therapists, and human service paraprofessionals creates confusion around ethical practice. It has been difficult to establish clear boundaries of practice and ethical responsibility in this context. As the field becomes more defined through specific standards for family and parent education, it will be easier to describe clear boundaries of practice and professional ethical guidelines. A better understanding of the collaborative interface with other professions will also support ethical thinking and practice in family life education.

The changing models of services such as family literacy programs (St. Pierre, Layzar, & Barnes, 1995) and fatherhood programs influence the intensity of services and the levels of involvement (Doherty, 1995) that practitioners encounter. Parent and family education in a family literacy program is a prime example of program changes. The populations served by a family literacy program may include new immigrant families with limited education and English, or American families with multiple needs trying to break out of generational cycles of poverty and illiteracy. The family life educator will encounter diverse values and family structures that create ethical challenges as well as the need for new knowledge and technical skills. The intensity of services in family literacy programs also puts parent and family educators in contact with families for several hours a month, including center-based services and home visits. This intensity of service translates to higher levels of involvement (Doherty, 1995) and the need to work in collaboration with other professionals including family therapists, adult educators, and early childhood educators. This level of involvement, intensity, and complexity creates more opportunities for ethical issues and potential dilemmas.

A third challenge for family life educators will be getting administrators to provide time, resources, and leadership in promoting ethical thinking and practice as an expected part of a program. Keeping ethical awareness alive after a set of guidelines has been defined is an ongoing challenge. The National Association for the Education of Young Children (NAEYC) has been an excellent model for keeping ethics alive through the publication of regular articles that feature difficult ethical situations and different responses to these situations by early educators (Feeney & Freeman, 1999; NAEYC Ethics Panel, 1998; Feeney, Freeman, & Morevick, 2000). The MCFR Ethics committee has also used case studies published in Views (Palm, 1999) to report on the application of the decision-making process to specific ethical dilemmas.

The final issue for family life education is enforcement. Should the current approach to ethics evolve into a code of ethics that is enforced by an official group of NCFR? What are the advantages of having a formal system of enforcement versus self-monitoring of ethical conduct? Is the decision-making process adequate or the best way for the profession to handle difficult ethical situations?

In summary:

- *Ethics is a habit, a deeply ingrained way of thinking that permeates our interaction with family members and other professionals.* It becomes part of our moral character. It helps us to be both moral and effective professionals.
- *Ethics is an alive and evolving process.* It is not a code of behavior that is carved in stone or only identifies obvious immoral practices to avoid. It must change with evolving family needs, changing boundaries of practice, and expanding research on families and effective family life education practice.
- *Ethics provide support for being moral family life educators through the consensus of professional thinking about important values and principles.* Individual moral responsibility can be supported by the wisdom and authority that comes through a set of professional ethical guidelines.
- *Ethics is a group of professionals processing difficult situations to generate insights and moral strategies.* This approach brings professional synergy and creativity to ethical decision-making in addition to individual moral responsibility.

References

American Association for Marriage and Family Therapy. (2001). *AAMFT code of ethics.* Washington, DC: Author.

American Counseling Association. (2005). *ACA code of ethics: 2005.* Washington, DC: Author.

Brock, G. (1993). Ethical guidelines for the practice of family life education. *Family Relations, 42*(2), 124-127.

Carter, N. (1996). *See how we grow: A report on the status of parenting education in the U.S.* Philadelphia, PA: The Pew Charitable Trusts.

Corey, G., Corey, M. S., & Callanan, P. (1988). *Issues and ethics in the helping professions* (3rd ed.). Pacific Grove, CA: Brooks/Cole Publishing Co.

Doherty, W. J. (1991, Winter). Virtue ethics: The person of the therapist. *AFTA Newsletter*, 19-21.

Doherty, W. J. (1995). Boundaries between parent and family educator and family therapy: The levels of family involvement model. *Family Relations*, *44*(4), 353-358.

Feeney, S., & Freeman, N. (1999). *Ethics and the early childhood educator: Using the NAEYC code*. Washington, DC: National Association for the Education of Young Children.

Feeney, S., Freeman, N., & Morevick, E. (2000). *Teaching the NAEYC code of ethical conduct*. Washington, DC: National Association for the Education of Young Children.

Freeman, S. J. (2000). *Ethics: An introduction to philosophy and practice*. Belmont, CA: Wadsworth.

Gilligan, C. (1982). *In a different voice*. Cambridge, MA: Harvard University Press.

Kerckhoff, R. K. (1964). Family life education in America. In H. T. Christiansen (Ed.), *Handbook of marriage and family* (pp. 881-911). Chicago: Rand McNally.

Kipnis, K. (1987). How to discuss professional ethics. *Young Children*, *42*(4), 26-30.

Leigh, G., Loewey, I., & Lester, M. (1986). Caveat emptor: Values and ethics in family life education and enrichment. *Family Relations*, *35*, 573-580.

Minnesota Board of Teaching. (1997). *Code of ethics*. St. Paul, MN: Minnesota Department of Education.

Minnesota Council on Family Relations. (2009). *Ethical thinking and practice for parent and family educators*. Minneapolis, MN: Ethics Committee, Parent and Family Education section.

National Association for the Education of Young Children Ethics Panel. (1998). What would you do? Real-life ethical problems early childhood professionals face: How do you know if you should suspect child abuse? *Young Children*, *53*(4), 52-54.

National Association for the Education of Young Children. (2005). *Code of ethical conduct and statement of commitment*. Washington, DC: Author.

Noddings, N. (1984). *Caring: A feminine approach to ethics and moral education*. Berkeley, CA: University of California Press.

Palm, G. (1994, Winter). Developing ethical guidelines for family educators. *Views*, 12-13.

Palm, G. (1999, Spring). Ethical dilemma: Culture and gender issues in the early childhood classroom, *Views*, 18-21.

Powell, L. H., & Cassidy, D. (2007). *Family life education: An introduction* (2nd ed.). Long Grove, IL: Waveland Press.

St. Pierre, R., Layzer, J., & Barnes, H. (1995). Two generation programs: Design, cost, and short-term effectiveness. *The future of children: Long term outcomes of early childhood programs*, *5*(3), 76-93.

Key Resources

Doherty, W. J. (1996). *Soul searching: Why psychotherapy must promote moral responsibility*. New York: Basic Books.

Feeney, S., & Freeman, N. (1999). *Ethics and the early childhood educator: Using the NAEYC code*. Washington, DC: National Association for the Education of Young Children.

Feeney, S., & Kipnis, K. (1998). *Code of ethical conduct and statement of commitment.* Washington, DC: National Association for the Education of Young Children.

Feeney, S., Freeman, N., & Morevick, E. (2000). *Teaching the NAEYC code of ethical conduct.* Washington, DC: National Association for the Education of Young Children.

Freeman, S. J. (2000). *Ethics: An introduction to philosophy and practice*. Belmont, CA: Wadsworth.

Minnesota Council on Family Relations. (2009). *Ethical thinking and practice for parent and family educators*. Minneapolis, MN: Ethics Committee, Parent and Family Education section.

Noddings, N. (1984). *Caring: A feminine approach to ethics and moral education*. Berkeley, CA: University of California Press.

Powell, L. H., & Cassidy, D. (2007). *Family life education: An introduction* (2nd ed.). Long Grove, IL: Waveland Press.

Related Websites

American Association for Marriage and Family Therapy: ww.aamft.org/resources/LRM_Plan/Ethics/index_nm.asp

American Counseling Association: www.counseling.org/Resources/CodeOfEthics/TP/Home/CT2.aspx

American Psychological Association: www.apa.org/ethics

Code of Ethics for Minnesota Teachers: www.revisor.leg.state.mn.us/rules/?agency=188

National Association for the Education of Young Children: www.naeyc.org/about/positions/PSETH05.asp

National Education Association: www.nea.org/code.html

About the Author

Glen F. Palm, Ph.D., CFLE is professor and chair of the Child and Family Studies at St. Cloud State University and a licensed parent educator in Minnesota. E-mail: gfpalm@stcloudstate.edu.

Family Life Education Methodology

JEAN ILLSLEY CLARKE AND
DAVID J. BREDEHOFT

Dear Jean and David,

You probably do not remember me, but I was a student in a parenting class you co-led five years ago. At the time, I was trying to figure out how to parent two young children, but as an added bonus, you inspired me to go back to college, get a degree, and become a family life educator.

Soon I will be responsible for leading my own family life education groups. I know I had good preparation, but I am apprehensive that I won't know what to do! Are there some things the two of you could suggest that might help?

Sincerely,

Stumped in Springfield

Dear Stumped,

We are thrilled you are becoming a family life educator and know that you have many gifts to share with learners across the entire life span! Yes, we have some concrete ideas to help you begin and some things you should remember as you become a seasoned professional in the field. As you read please consider which of these ideas will support you right now and which you will utilize as you become more experienced in your career.

Sincerely,

Jean Illsley Clarke, CFLE and David J. Bredehoft, CFLE

Planning and Implementing Family Life Education Programs

Keep in mind that families are systems (Burr, Day & Bahr, 1993; Day, Gilbert, Settles & Burr, 1995; Satir, 1988), and that effective family life educators always visualize families as systems moving across the life span with changing needs depending on the age and stage of a family. The *Framework for Family Life Education* (Bredehoft, 1997, 2001) presents the family lifecycle along with needs, stressors, and demands for each family age and stage. This model will be helpful in laying the groundwork for planning and evaluating your family life education (FLE) programs. Remember, planning and design of quality FLE programs is the equivalent of building a sturdy foundation in the construction of a building. Everything that follows depends on it. There is no substitute for good planning!

The Planning Wheel

The planning approach we suggest you use is *The Planning Wheel* (Clarke, 1998). You will find this six-step method of planning, leading and evaluating a learning experience very helpful because the planning wheel takes into account evaluation and underlying values at the same time the plan is developed. This is a circular model; evaluation is built in, not added on (see The Planning Wheel Model in Figure 1 and application in Figure 2).

Program Effectiveness and Evaluating Family Life Education Materials

In conjunction with the planning wheel you may want to use additional FLE program evaluation techniques (Weiss & Jacobs, 1988; Cooke, 1991; Powell & Cassidy, 2007; Treichel, 2009). For example, Weiss and Jacobs' (1988) Five-Tiered Approach to Program Evaluation may be incorporated to add greater evaluation specificity (for further discussion of this model see Treichel, (2009). Asking specific evaluation questions described by Patton (1987) is also helpful: (1) "Who is the audience for the evaluation?" "Who are the stakeholders?" (2) "What do we need to know about the program?" (3) "How will we do the evaluation?" (4) "How will we determine what the information gathered means?" (5) "How will we use the evaluation results?"

Figure 1. The Planning Wheel Model

Step 1 **I BELIEVE THAT:** Think through your and your agency's basic values.

Step 2 **WHAT I WANT:** Identify, in a general way what you hope to accomplish, and what the results of a needs assessment indicate.

Step 3 **END PRODUCT:** Identify the specific behavioral outcomes you will plan for. Differentiate between means goals and ends goals.

Step 4 **HOW TO DO IT:** Decide what learning experiences to offer.

Step 5 **CARRY OUT THE PLAN:** Do it – lead the workshop, teach the class, run the project.

Step 6 **EVALUATE:** Evaluate the outcome.

Continue the process by returning to step 1. Be aware that you made value judgments each time you moved from one step to the next. Follow through each of the five steps.

Slick does not equal substantive

Evaluation and selection of FLE materials and resources is often challenging for beginning professionals. One thing we have learned is that "slick does not equal substantive." The value of the program is in the content and the process, not in the packaging. Use the planning wheel (Figure 1) to assist you in deciding whether or not to use a curriculum resource by asking the following questions:

Step 1: What are the underlying values/theories supporting this curriculum? Do you understand its philosophical foundations (Morgaine, 1992; Heath, 2000)?

Step 2: What are the explicit and implicit goals of this curriculum?

Step 3: Does the specific material presented meet the needs of your population (diversity?)? Does the process fit the level of involvement (Doherty, 1995) you deem appropriate? Does it have empirical support?

Step 4: Are the processes consistent with the goals?

Step 5: Are the directions clear and specific enough for you to present this curriculum?

Step 6: Does this curriculum adequately meet your needs?

CURRICULUM GUIDELINES:
FAMILY LIFE EDUCATION METHODOLOGY

An understanding of the general philosophy and broad principles of family life education in conjunction with the ability to plan, implement, and evaluate such educational programs. Based on knowledge of:

1. planning and implementing family life education programs;
2. evaluating family life education materials, student progress, and program effectiveness;
3. using a variety of educational techniques in the presentation of a family life education program;
4. sensitivity to others to enhance educational effectiveness;
5. sensitivity to community concerns and values and an understanding of the public relations process; and
6. understanding the relationship between one's personal values/beliefs and family life education areas.

Sensitivity – An Essential Ingredient for Success

Sensitivity to community concerns and values

Sometimes community concerns are specific and highly visible. The recent devastating storm or the closing of a business that left many people unemployed can impact not only the economy but also the emotional climate of a whole community. The racially motivated attack raises not only emotional issues but also challenges people to think about community values.

Figure 2. Planning Wheel Application

Will You Do a Six-hour Workshop for Foster Parents?

1. I BELIEVE THAT

a. Foster parents and foster children are important.
b. The job of foster parents is to provide an environment in which the child can thrive.
c. Some of the information I have would be helpful to foster parents in supporting a child's social and emotional development: i.e., the emotional aspects of developmental stages, ways to build self-esteem, optional ways of handling discipline, anger and sexuality.
d. Foster parents know what they need better than I know what they need.
e. Foster parents can learn lots from each other.

The **best** way to set goals for this workshop is to ask the hiring agency and the foster parents which of my offerings they want. (They selected developmental stages and handling anger.)

2. WHAT I WANT

I want each foster parent attending:

a. to hear a review of emotional needs and appropriate expression of anger for each developmental stage.
b. to have the opportunity to focus on optional ways of handling anger in each developmental stage and to share their experiences.
c. to choose if they want to make behavior changes that they think will help their foster children.

A **good** way to achieve my general goal is to present one activity for each developmental stage and to invite people to participate in as many as they like.

3. END PRODUCT

WHAT: Information about the six developmental stages, affirmations for each, and appropriate and inappropriate expressions of anger in each.
HOW MUCH: Information for each of six stages.
BY WHEN: By close of 6-hour workshop.
BY WHOM: By each foster parent who chooses to participate

Since some people learn **best** by listening, some by doing, and some by seeing, it is **important** to offer all three opportunities.

4. HOW TO DO IT

I. ***Introduction and individual goal setting.***
II. ***For each of the six developmental stages:***
a. lecture and hand out information on emotional development, responsibilities, anger and affirmations.
b. role play optional ways of dealing with anger for each stage.
c. small group discussion of learnings, awarenesses, plans for new behaviors toward specific foster children.
III. ***Closing and evaluation.***

Each person has **the right** to experience the developmental stage he/she **needs** to focus on. Plan tasks carefully and distribute time evenly.

5. CARRY OUT THE PLAN

If a workshop is **worth** doing it is **worth** evaluating for immediate and for longer lasting results.

6. EVALUATE

a. Ask each participant to fill out evaluations based on (3).
b. After three months, ask agency workers to interview foster parents and foster children about parental behavior changes that the parent and child identified as helpful to the child's social and emotional development.

What did I learn from (6) to help me plan my next workshop?

Other community concerns are less obvious. Teen binging on alcohol may not make newspaper headlines but may be causing an undercurrent of concern in parts or all of a community.

The wise teacher is aware of these concerns and will decide how to address them. A validating acknowledgement that a concern exists? Part of a meeting offering some helpful strategy for consideration? A single meeting or a series of meetings to address the problem directly? A series of media messages? Website offerings?

Sensitivity to Others to Enhance Educational Effectiveness
Sensitivity to the people within the learning setting also involves being aware of both the visible and the invisible situations.

The visible ones are easy. Your careful adherence and repeated reference to the ground rules (Clarke, 1998) allows you to safely ask the bubbly person if she wants to share a celebration (Clarke, 1997). You keep an eye on the stressed looking fellow who came late and find a time to ask quietly if he is okay. Because you have shown a warm acceptance of differences and a consistent respect for individual needs, people can feel free to say "yes" or "no" to your invitations.

Some aspects of cultural and individual diversity (see Allen & Blaisure, (2009) are not obvious. It is these less visible factors that challenge us to be constantly aware of our own prejudices and presumptions. Consider who would be in your class if it were a reflection of the whole population. In a group of ten you could expect approximately:

- **3** who have a direct connection with alcoholism
- **2** who have adopted, have been adopted, or have relinquished a child
- **2** who have been sexually abused
- **4** who have experienced physical or psychological abuse
- **3** who have dyslexia
- **4** who are directly affected by divorce
- **1** who holds far left or far right political or religious views
- **1** who is foreign born
- **1** who is gay or lesbian
- **2** who have moved recently

This list adds to more than ten but one person can fit in more than one category. These figures were synthesized from a variety of sources. In addition, you may have someone who just lost or just got a new job or someone who is immersed in plans for a family celebration. You could have one to three people of mixed race, a war veteran, someone who is depressed or mentally ill, is grieving, or is in deep shame. Skin color will not tell you who has been detained in a camp or tortured.

It is your job to be so respectful of each individual that people will be comfortable enough with you to be willing to hear challenging content. It is not your job to "make people comfortable" by refraining from offering material because it might offend someone.

A small amount of personal revelation can put a group at ease and model techniques of being sensitive to others. For example, you might say that since your co-leader is worried about a sick relative you will be doing more of the leading than usual, or that, since you have just received some special recognition, you invite the group to celebrate briefly with you. This also models that sharing celebrations and concerns can usually be done respectfully in a short period of time.

One of the most exciting aspects of becoming a family life educator (and we are all becoming no matter how long we have been doing it) is the challenge to continually increase our ability to appeal to a wide diversity of learning styles.

Looking in Your Toolbox

Honoring Learning Style Preferences
List the theories and techniques you know and identify the ones you already use. We expect you are familiar with the theory of Andragogy (Knowles, Holton & Swanson, 2005) and the Experiential Learning Cycle (Kolb, 1983). You know the importance of *room arrangement* (Hall, 1990). Posting ground rules and goals at every meeting models for parents the importance of posting rules in the home, and it honors the *visual* learners. Your clear language supports the *auditory* learners and an activity that involves movement helps those with a *kinesthetic* preference get the learning into their bodies. You also make clear whether you are using *means goals* or *ends goals* and whether activities are to be done by *clock time* or *task time* (Clarke, 1998).

Your list will probably include *inductive* and *deductive* learning preferences, *introverted* and *extroverted* styles (Barron-Tieger, Tieger & Ellowich, 1997), and the *abstract*, *concrete*, *sequential*, *random* preferences of the Gregoric model (Tobias,

1994). You may recognize your strengths in the 5 Ps of highly effective educators, *Protection, Permission, Potency, Practice* and *Perception* (Clarke, 2000a, 2000b, 2001a, 2001b, 2001c, 2001d).

You may already be proficient at *bridging* people from the outside world into the learning setting and from one piece of content to another. From your own learning experiences you may be acutely aware of the need to create *indirect learning* experiences (Clarke, 2000c) and to use *technology* in a way that supports a specific learning objective. Technology is simply the means to an end; it is not an end in itself. A PowerPoint presentation that compares statistics can be very helpful, but nothing replaces singing as a way of learning a song. Films can present challenging material, but only individual *introspection* or safe *sharing* makes space for the individual to connect the concepts with real life experiences. The more you attend to those basic principles of group dynamics, the more learning flourishes.

Adding to Your Toolbox

Incorporating new research about group dynamics is a challenge many experienced family educators welcome and test, for example, the research about group sizes (Dunbar, 1996; Clarke, 2002b). In *Grooming, Gossip and the Evolution of Language,* Dunbar sites many studies that suggest that each group size has special functions. This information can help the group leader plan effective learning experiences, and can also help participants build or enhance their support systems.

Two for pair bonding

Two – the pair bond number is important, whether in establishing and maintaining a working relationship, a friendship, or a loving commitment. Many people do not feel connected to a larger group until they have established at least one satisfactory dyad relationship within it.

Three or four for conversation or discussion

Four is identified as the most functional number for a conversation. In Dunbar's view, conversation is vitally important for the establishment of friendships, allies, and support people. It is the primary way people stroke each other and judge trustworthiness. Three is okay for a conversation, but Dunbar notes that, when a fifth person is added, one person often becomes marginalized, or two people start a separate conversation. Notice how often four people dominate a discussion in a larger group.

Six to get the job done

Six is the ideal number for a working group. Six people can easily divide tasks. If there are more than six it often takes much longer to agree on a course of action.

Ten or more to brainstorm

Six provides enough variety for task accomplishment, but ten or more provide sufficient divergent thinking for a productive brainstorm session.

Twelve for teamwork or empathy

Twelve (or 10 to 15) seems to be the ideal number of people to build a strong team connection in order to reach a common goal. Sports teams and juries are examples. Also, 12 (or 10 to 15) is the number Dunbar identifies as the usual number of people each individual holds in his or her personal "empathy group." This is the person's close inner circle, the people most counted upon for support, loyalty, and intimacy. These are friends with whom one feels a strong connection.

When we limit the length of our lectures, and create many ways for people to interact in groups of two, three, four, six, and twelve, we provide opportunities for people to find friends for the personal "empathy" groups and to add people to their larger group (perhaps 150) called "community" or their "extended group" of 1,500 to 2,000.

Since we no longer live in simple tribal communities that have natural connections with each other, each of us has to form our empathy group and our community group as best we can. Family life educators can remember not only to let people talk directly with each other, but also to be sure they wear nametags. This helps people, especially those whose learning style preference is visual, to fix names with faces. For people who have moved recently or whose movements have been restricted, these opportunities to connect with others are an especially important way to help build support systems.

New Knowledge

While you are learning new techniques, you also are adding new areas of content. For example, learning about the exploding knowledge of how the brain works. As your knowledge becomes broader and deeper, resist the temptation to teach everything you know. Remember that if you present five items at once, the learners will be connecting all five (or feeling overwhelmed) because nine vectors are in play (Clarke, 2002a). A vector is "energy" the learner directs to each fact or related idea. Better to mention the five, ask people to put three aside while you connect two (one vector), then add the third (three vectors), then the fourth (six vectors), then the fifth (nine vectors).

We recommend that you explore one or two techniques at a time. As those become automatic, add one or two more. Nothing replaces sound planning beforehand and nothing adds to your flexibility in the learning situation like a well-stocked toolbox of techniques. However, no matter how many excellent techniques you use, the greatest gift you bring to learners is yourself, so remember to take excellent care of yourself.

The Relationship between One's Personal Values/Beliefs and Family Life Education

As Powell and Cassidy (2007) point out, "In order to be effective educators, they [family life educators] must have thoroughly considered where their beliefs lie" (p. 41), as well as "be in touch with their own feelings or biases or both" (p.39). To help you more fully understand the relationship between your values and beliefs and family life education, consider the following:

- What are your values, beliefs, and philosophy of FLE (Cherington, 2000)? Each participant will have different values and beliefs because they have had a unique life journey.
- Know yourself. What are your learning style preferences and do you balance them with others when you teach?
- Professional boundaries. How much self-disclosure is effective and appropriate (Doherty, 1995)?
- Personal values determine your process, underlying theories, and choice of content (Heath, 2000).
- Self care. Are you, as the teacher, taking care of yourself both in the large sense and before each learning event?
- How do you respond to values and beliefs that differ from yours? Always be respectful of differing values and beliefs (Duncan & Goddard, 2005). Be clear about the difference between a law that everyone must follow and a value. Help people to recognize informal norms that govern behavior (Payne, 1998).
- What are your ethical guidelines as a family life educator (Palm, 2009; Adams, Dollahite, Gilbert and Keim, 2001)?

In Closing

Dear Stumped in Springfield,

We are confident that you will use our suggestions in a way that will work for you. Keep learning and growing and stay in touch regarding your teaching successes!

Best wishes,

Jean Illsley Clarke, CFLE and David J. Bredehoft, CFLE

References

Adams, R. A., Dollahite, D. C., Gilbert, K. R., & Keim, R. E. (2001). The development and teaching of the ethical principles and guidelines for family scientists. *Family Relations, 50*, 41-48.

Barron-Tieger, B., Tieger, P. T., & Ellowich, M. E. (1997). *Nurture by nature: Understanding your child's personality type – and become a better parent*. New York: Little Brown & Co.

Allen, W., & Blaisure, K. R. (2009). Family life educators and the development of cultural competency. In D. J. Bredehoft & M. J. Walcheski (Eds.), *Family life education: Integrating theory and practice*(2nd ed.) (pp. 209-219). Minneapolis, MN: National Council on Family Relations.

Bredehoft, D. J. (Ed.). (1997). *The framework for life span family life education* (2nd ed.) [Poster]. Minneapolis, MN: National Council on Family Relations.

Bredehoft, D. J. (2001). The framework for life span family life education revised and revisited. *The Family Journal, 9*(2), 134-139.

Burr, W. R., Day, R. D., & Bahr, K. S. (1993). *Family science*. Pacific Grove, CA: Brooks/Cole.

Cherington, M. (2000, November). The subtleties of inclusion in parent education. In *Family information services professional resource materials* (p. 57). Minneapolis, MN: Family Information Services.

Clarke, J. I. (1997). *Growing up again: Leader's guide*. Seattle, WA: Parenting Press, Inc.

Clarke, J. I. (1998). *Who, me lead a group*? Seattle, WA: Parenting Press, Inc.

Clarke, J. I. (2000a, November). The importance of being positive – the five p's. In *Family information services professional resource materials* (pp. 54-56). Minneapolis, MN: Family Information Services.

Clarke, J. I. (2000b, September). Facilitation skills that build self-esteem: Offering protection. In *Family information services professional resource materials* (pp. 42-43). Minneapolis, MN: Family Information Services.

Clarke, J. I. (2000c, May). Facilitation skills that build self-esteem: Indirect learning. In *Family information services professional resource materials* (pp. 42-43). Minneapolis, MN: Family Information Services.

Clarke, J. I. (2001a, January). How you know what you know. In *Family information services professional resource materials* (pp. 1-3). Minneapolis, MN: Family Information Services.

Clarke, J. I. (2001b, March). Permission to think. In *Family information services professional resource materials* (pp. 13-15). Minneapolis, MN: Family Information Services.

Clarke, J. I. (2001c, May). The perfect way to learn: Practice. In *Family information services professional resource materials* (pp. 27-28). Minneapolis, MN: Family Information Services.

Clarke, J. I. (2001d, September). Perception – what is really going on here? In *Family information services professional resource materials* (pp. 39-40). Minneapolis, MN: Family Information Services.

Clarke, J. I. (2002a, March). Vectors: How many ideas at once? In *Family information services professional resource materials* (pp. 1-3). Minneapolis, MN: Family Information Services.

Clarke, J. I. (2002b, Winter). What size group do you belong to? In *CFLE Network: 14*(1), 4, 10. Minneapolis, MN: National Council on Family Relations.

Cooke, B. (1991, March). Family program evaluation basics. In *Family information services professional resource materials* (pp. 10-14). Minneapolis, MN: Family Information Services.

Day, R. D., Gilbert, K. R., Settles, B. H., & Burr, W. R. (1995). *Research and theory in family science.* Pacific Grove, CA: Brooks/Cole.

Doherty, W. J. (1995). Boundaries between parent and family education and family therapy. *Family Relations, 44*, 353-358.

Dunbar, R. (1996). *Grooming, gossip and the evolution of language*. Boston, MA: Faber and Faber Publishing.

Duncan, S. F., & Goddard, H. W. (2005). *Family life education: Principles and practices for effective outreach.* Thousand Oaks, CA: Sage.

Hall, E. T. (1990). The hidden dimension. New York: Anchor.

Heath, H. (2000). *Using your values to raise your child to be an adult you admire*. Seattle, WA: Parenting Press, Inc.

Knowles, M. S., Holton, E. F., & Swanson, R. A. (2005). *The adult learner: The definitive classic in adult education and human resource development* (6th ed.). New York: Butterworth-Heinemann.

Kolb, D. (1983). *Experiential learning: Experience as the source of learning and development*. Upper Saddle River, NJ: Prentice Hall.

Morgaine, C. A. (1992). Alternative paradigms for helping families change themselves. *Family Relations, 41,* 12-17.

Palm, G. (2009). Family life educators and the development of cultural competency. In D. J. Bredehoft & M. J. Walcheski (Eds.), *Family life education: Integrating theory and practice* (2nd ed.) (pp. 191-197). Minneapolis, MN: National Council on Family Relations.

Patton, M. Q. (1987). *How to use qualitative methods in evaluation*. Thousand Oaks, CA: Sage Publications.

Payne, P. K. (1998). *A framework for understanding poverty* (rev. ed.). Highlands, TX: RFT Publishing.

Powell, L. H., & Cassidy, D. (2007). *Family life education: Working with families across the life span* (2nd ed.). Long Grove: IL: Waveland Press, Inc.

Satir, V. (1988). *The new peoplemaking*. Palo Alto, CA: Science and Behavior Books.

Tobias, C. (1994). *The way they learn*. Colorado Springs, CO: Focus on the Family Publishers.

Treichel, C. (2009). In the best interests of children and their families: Merging program development and program evaluation. In D. J. Bredehoft & M. J. Walcheski (Eds.), *Family life education: Integrating theory and practice* (2nd ed.) (pp. 221-231). Minneapolis, MN: National Council on Family Relations.

Weiss, H. B., & Jacobs, F. H. (1988). *Evaluating family programs*. New York: Aldine de Gruyter.

Key Resources

Bredehoft, D. J. (Ed.). (1997). *The framework for life span family life education* (2nd ed.) [Poster]. Minneapolis, MN: National Council on Family Relations.

Clarke, J. I. (1998). *Who, me lead a group*? Seattle, WA: Parenting Press, Inc.

Clarke, J. I. (1998). *Growing up again: Leader's guide*. Seattle, WA: Parenting Press, Inc.

Family Information Services. 12565 Jefferson St, NE, Suite 102, Minneapolis, MN, 55434; 800-852-8112 (in U.S.), 763-755-6233 or Fax: 763-755-7355, e-mail: staff@familyinfoserv.com, website: www.familyinfoserv.com/

Heath, H. (2000). *Using your values to raise your child to be an adult you admire*. Seattle, WA: Parenting Press, Inc.

Knowles, M. S., Holton, E. F., & Swanson, R. A. (2005). *The adult learner: The definitive classic in adult education and human resource development* (6th ed.). New York: Butterworth-Heinemann.

Parenting Press Inc. *Parent Educator Resource Shelf.* P.O. Box 75267, Seattle, WA 98125, 800-992-6657, FAX: 206-364-0702, website: www.parentingpress.com

Related Websites

CFLE Certification: www.ncfr.com/cert/index.asp

Children, Youth and Family Consortium: www.cyfc.umn.edu/

Family Information Services: www.familyinfoserv.com/

The Gottman Institute: www.gottman.com/

Life Innovations, Inc: www.lifeinnovations.com

National Parent Information Network (NPIN): www.fcps.net/fcs/?prcItem=160

How Much is Enough? Homepage: www.overindulgence.info

Zero to Three: www.zerotothree.org

About the Authors

Jean Illsley Clarke, Ph.D., CFLE is a parent educator, teacher trainer, the author of *Self-Esteem: A Family Affair*, and co-author of *Growing Up Again: Parenting Ourselves, Parenting Our Children, How Much is Enough? Everything You Need to Know to Steer Clear of Overindulgence and Raise Likeable, Responsible, and Respectful Children* and the *How Much is Enough? Leader Guide*. E-mail: Jiconsults@aol.com.

David J. Bredehoft, Ph.D., CFLE is Professor of Psychology and Family Studies and Chair, Department of Social and Behavioral Sciences at Concordia University, St. Paul, MN. He is the editor of *The Framework for Life Span Family Life Education (2nd ed.)*, coeditor of *Family Life Education: Integrating Theory and Practice*, and coauthor of *How much is enough? Everything you need to know to steer clear of overindulgence and raise likeable, responsible, and respectful children.* E-mail: bredehoft@csp.edu.

Family Life Education Teaching and Practice Resources

Section III

Family Life Educators and the Development of Cultural Competency

William D. Allen and
Karen R. Blaisure

This article explores how cultural diversity must increasingly become a critical component of family life education (FLE) curricula and programming. In doing so, the authors first identify three important assumptions concerning cultural competency and family life educators (FLEs). Second, important key terms are defined for the reader. Third, the authors demonstrate how to apply a diversity lens to family life education. The article concludes with suggestions for continuing the journey towards cultural competence in the field of family life education.

Responding to Diversity

In response to the growing ethnic, socio-economic, and structural diversity in the population of the United States, FLEs, researchers and practitioners are rejecting monolithic or universal conceptions of family life and are pursuing contextual understandings of families and collaborative practices with families (Demo, Allen, & Fine, 2000; Dilworth-Anderson, Burton, & Turner, 1993; Dilworth-Anderson & McAdoo, 1988; Myers-Walls, 2000; Thompson, 1995). For example, the importance of ethnicity in understanding families has been highlighted in publications such as *Family Ethnicity: Strength in Diversity* (McAdoo, 1999), *Black Families* (McAdoo, 2007), and *Ethnicity and Family Therapy* (McGoldrick, Giordano, & Garcio-Preto, 2005).

FLEs are focusing an ever-increasing amount of attention on ethnicity, gender, and sexual orientation in educational practices (Allen, 1995; Berke & Wisensale, 2005; Lewis, 1995; S. Marks, 1995; Thompson, 1995) and clinical practice (Bean, Crane, Russell, & Lewis, 2002; McGoldrick, 1998). Educational practices draw attention to familial experiences that are shaped by family structure, process, gender, race, ethnicity, culture, and social class, and by combinations of these factors. Personal experiences of FLEs, in turn, influence research, theory construction, and practice (Demo, Allen, & Fine, 2000). A number of resources are now available to educators and family life practitioners seeking to incorporate aspects of family diversity into their work. (For example, a collection of course syllabi on family diversity are available from the Ethnic Minority Section of the National Council on Family Relations; contact NCFR at www.ncfr.org).

Assumptions Regarding Cultural Competence and Family Life Educators

This article is based on several important assumptions about cultural competency and family life educators:

1) *Given the increasing complexity of family life, FLEs have a critical role to play in promoting family well being in the 21st Century.*

2) *As society's families become increasingly more diverse, FLEs must acquire skills and knowledge that allow them to work effectively and ethically.*

3) *Cultural competence is an essential component of professional FLE competence. FLEs must be able to function effectively and ethically in increasingly diverse settings.*

There are a number of ways to operationalize these assumptions. One such approach is to incorporate the "diversity lens" discussed in the second edition of the *Framework for Life Span Family Life Education* (Bredehoft, 1997, 2001). This Framework directs family life educators to be multicultural, gender fair, and aware of special needs. In this model, the "diversity lens" becomes the "mortar between the bricks of life's stages." It is a necessary and vital part of all family life education. FLEs incorporate family characteristics (e.g., life stage, composition, and cultural contexts) into their understanding of whom they are serving while also guarding against over-simplification. This approach demands careful consideration of "what is to be taught, to whom [it] will be taught, as well as how to teach [it]" (Myers-Walls, 2000; Myers-Walls, Dunn, & Myers-Bowman, 2003).

Feminist family theory can also be an organizing principle that guides the exploration of families and the diversity of familial experiences. FLEs working from a feminist perspective ascribe to values of equality and respect for all families, social justice and action, self-determination, and responsibility for one's beliefs and the implications of those beliefs (Bubolz & McKenry, 1993). Walker, Martin, and Thompson (1988) identified six indicators of a feminist approach to family life education: "recognition of the cultural context, responsiveness to the vulnerable, participation and equality, celebration of diversity, clients' perspectives of problems and solutions prevail, and empowerment of clients" (p. 18). Feminist pedagogical practices of promoting dialogue, using personal experiences, offering choices, and engaging in personally relevant activities and assignments encourage those involved to recognize culturally-bounded assumptions and biases, plurality of family life, and personal responsibility (Blaisure & Koivenun, 2003). Several writers have described how to apply feminist approaches and values to educational settings (e.g., Allen & Baber, 1992; Baber & Murray, 2001; MacDermid, Jurich, Myers-Walls & Pelo, 1992; Walker, 1996).

Effective family life education must be undertaken by culturally competent, reflexive practitioners who think contextually and from a global perspective. Such an expectation sets a personal and professional agenda while acknowledging that its pursuit is life-long (Talbot, 1996). The exploration of diversity and culture as it shapes family life is also a dynamic process. Effective FLEs constantly acknowledge the diversity in families' lives (their own and those of others). They do this while avoiding reliance on static lists of group characteristics that are, at best, incomplete, and at worst, risk stereotyping families' experiences. Thus, to be effective FLEs, we must continually *practice* cultural competence. The next section begins by defining the terms that we will use to explore cultural competence in the context of family life education.

Definitions

The lack of consistency in language about diversity has often hampered understanding and development of effective programming and interventions. Terms such as race, culture and ethnicity are often used interchangeably making understanding and working with diversity unnecessarily confusing. Therefore, to have a meaningful discussion of the benefits of weaving diversity into the fabric of family life education, several key terms must be defined (ethnicity, culture, family, and cultural competence).

Ethnicity

For the purposes of this article, a distinction will be drawn between ethnicity and culture. *Ethnicity* is defined as the inner sense of identity or connection with others we perceive to be similar to us. Ethnicity can be a "common ancestral origin" or be based on one or more national or cultural characteristics (Sue et al., 1998, p. 10). For example, many people of African descent in the United States think of themselves as *African American* or *Black*, while many Native American Indians identify themselves collectively as *Indian*. Ethnicity can also arise from the shared sense of identity that comes from a common belief system. Followers of Jesus Christ typically call themselves *Christians*, while those who follow the Islamic faith may call themselves *Muslims*. As in the case of historical heritage or country of origin, what binds these groups together is their sense of shared history or common destiny.

Thus, ethnicity can be thought of as the perceived commonality within a particular group that shapes their perception of the world and their interactions in it. This commonality may also arise from physical characteristics, such as skin color, or from other shared attributes that individually or collectively produce a shared identity. Although some refer to this *social* construct as "race," many scholars have suggested avoiding this term because it suggests *genetic* differences in human beings that do not exist (for a discussion of inherent problems in using the term "race" see Marger, 1997; Banton & Harwood, 1975; J. Marks, 1995; Montagu, 1974).

The perception of shared identity or commonality among ethnic group members may also shape the perceptions and even behaviors of those outside of group. Often, the differences in groups' perceptions of themselves versus those around them account for differences in the way groups treat each other (as in the case of institutional racism). A final but important note about ethnicity is that there is typically as much diversity *within* as *between* ethnic groups. Therefore ethnic groups should never be seen as monolithic or completely homogeneous.

Culture

In this article, *culture* is differentiated from ethnicity. Culture is defined as "an integrated pattern of human behavior that includes thoughts, communications, actions, customs, beliefs, values, and institutions of a racial, ethnic, religious, or social groups" (Cross, Bazron, Dennis, & Isaacs, 1989, p. iv). If ethnicity is the *inner* sense of shared identity, culture is the *outward* reflection of an individual's or a group's identity. Culture may also be a reflection of other demographic attributes such as socioeconomic status, geography, gender, or generation (e.g., adolescence).

As an example, food or music may be expressions of the inward identification many individuals feel with similar others. Therefore, reggae and salsa music could be cultural reflections of West Indian American immigrants or Puerto Rican Americans, respectively. These groups are clearly not the only ones who appreciate these particular genres. Indeed, members of these groups might not like the genres at all, providing an example of intra-group diversity. However, reggae and salsa could typically be seen as outward expressions of each group's sense of shared identity.

As in the example of music presented above, food, dress and even speech patterns can also be cultural expressions of deeper individual or group identifications. Like music, these expressions are not determined solely by ethnicity. An important distinction here is that unlike ethnicity, which tends to be relatively static (one's place of origin probably will not change), culture is more dynamic and typically subject to evolving over time. Thus as individuals age they tend to move through various cultural stages: the cultures of childhood, adolescence, young adulthood, middle age, and later adulthood. Choices of dress, food, and preferences in art and expression often change as they progress through these stages. Gender, marital status, and socio-economics also shape the cultural contexts in which people live. Moreover, while most individuals develop a unified sense of who they are (e.g., ethnic identity), they typically operate simultaneously in a variety of cultural contexts. Thus, persons who identify themselves as an Asian Americans may simultaneously profess a love of pizza, the play "Fiddler on the Roof," and rap music.

Individual and family diversity are experienced in an almost endless array of intersecting social categories. Predicting how these demographic attributes may shape a particular individual's overall identity, self-perceptions, and behaviors is difficult, if not impossible. This difficulty is not only due to the sheer number of possible contributing factors, but to possible interactions between biological predispositions and psychosocial factors. The family science field is moving beyond the simplistic notion that membership in any specific ethnic-cultural group or other demographic category (e.g., gender) is powerful enough to exclusively bind family members either to each other, or to the ethnic group. Indeed, social and cultural influences outside a family may undermine (or alternatively reinforce) ethnic and cultural connections within a family. For example, Marks and Leslie (2000) suggest "racial identities and alliances may be overshadowed by gender or social-class differences… [and] competing identities…may easily overshadow the sense of a common identity as women" (p. 407).

Family

An obvious and central topic to consider from a diversity lens is the definition of *family*. Definitions of family vary and their implications affect the daily lives of people. Currently, the definition of what constitutes a family can determine who can or cannot marry, how families can form, who can inherit wealth, or who can have a say in the medical treatment of a loved one. Myers-Walls (2000) identifies a danger associated with a "vague definition" of families, primarily that FLEs risk relying on a "default norm" for family that excludes all those who do not fall within an unconscious personal definition. Marks and Leslie (2000) warn, "disciplines that deal with 'families' must have an inclusive reach and remain ever alert to the question of who gets left out by how we see and define social reality" (p. 403). They raise a question that all FLEs address, at least implicitly: What is the "nonreducible aspect of family—one essential element that, if absent, would signal for each of us a nonfamily status?" While this essential element may vary from FLE to FLE, the need to "remain ever alert to the question of who gets left out by how we see and define social reality" remains (p. 403). For example, an FLE's definition of family might affect the degree to which cohabiting heterosexual or gay parents are welcomed to a parenting class, or whether couple education programs are open to cohabiting couples or those in other, non-traditional relationships.

Cultural Competence

Finally, the term cultural competence describes practices that reflect an understanding and appreciation of diverse ethnocultural contexts, and the value such diversity brings to our lives and work. In their discussion of the role of leadership in promoting equity, Benjamin and Benjamin (personal communication, April 4, 2002) trace the concept to the work of the Cultural Competence Resource Committee at Georgetown University in the 1980's (see also Cross, Bazron, Dennis & Issacs, 1989). Benjamin and Benjamin define cultural competence as "a set of congruent behaviors, attitudes, and policies that come together in a system, agency, or amongst professionals… [that enable them] to work effectively in cross-cultural situations." They elaborate that the term competence "…implies having the capacity to function effectively".

Culturally competent organizations become consistent in the development and implementation of services designed to meet culturally specific (as well as generally beneficial) needs. Cross et al. (1989) further suggest that culturally competent systems of care effectively:

1) incorporate the importance of culture,
2) assess cross-cultural relations,
3) recognize the dynamics that result from cultural differences.

The term cultural competence is sometimes misused in a way that implies that these practices can be perfected. This is problematic because the increasing diversity in society makes such "perfection" highly unlikely. For the same reason, it is unlikely that practitioners can "achieve" cultural competence as the result of attending a single course or workshop. The authors of this article suggest that cultural competence is more accurately conceived as a process that motivates practitioners and organizations to remain proactive in their efforts to be effective with and inclusive of the widest spectrum of families.

Applying a Diversity Lens

What does it mean to assume a diversity lens when doing family life education? How does one practice family life education in a manner sensitive to and respectful of the myriad of ways individuals and families can differ from one another?

Several theorists have explored pathways to greater cultural competence in research (Dilworth-Anderson, Burton, & Turner, 1993), education (Myers-Walls, 2000), and practice (McGoldrick, 1998). Wiley and Ebata (2004) offer many practical ideas for incorporating cultural competency into the work of FLEs, including raising consciousness, curriculum development, program delivery, and engagement and dissemination strategies. This section focuses on applying the diversity lens to family life education across a variety of settings.

Sue, Arredondo and McDavis (1992) elaborated a systematic approach for moving practitioners toward higher levels of cultural competence. It involved establishing multicultural counseling "competencies and standards" that included dimensions of awareness, understanding and skills to function within and adapt to diverse cultures. Key components included the pursuit of self-awareness of one's own ethnic and cultural context(s), gaining an understanding of the contexts of others, and acquisition of appropriate, relevant intervention strategies. These authors also theorized three dimensions in which the practice of multicultural competence should occur: 1) beliefs and attitudes, 2) knowledge, and 3) skills (see Table 1).

Table 1. Conceptual Framework of Cross-Cultural Counseling Competencies*

Counselor's awareness of own assumptions and values
- Beliefs
- Knowledge
- Skills

Understanding the worldview of culturally different clients
- Beliefs
- Knowledge
- Skills

Developing appropriate intervention strategies and techniques
- Beliefs
- Knowledge
- Skills

*Adapted from Sue, Arrendando and McDavis, 1992.

As suggested earlier in this article, given the increasing diversity in American society, it is doubtful that any single practitioner could become expert at working in all-possible cultural contexts. We believe a more pragmatic approach is for FLEs to develop cultural competence by gaining the understanding and skills in the three contexts elaborated by Sue et al. (1992). This process requires a mindful, conscientious dedication to the ethical importance of the individual practitioner's personal and professional development. It also demands an understanding of and respect for the worldviews, values, and aspirations of the range of families FLEs meet in their settings.

Practicing Reflexivity

A first step on the road to cultural competence is to become aware of how the personal assumptions, biases, values, learned prejudices and fears about difference affect a professional's practice (Sue et al., 1998). *Reflexivity* is a means by which FLEs can explore the connection between themselves and their work, so that their work becomes more effective. Reflexivity is a process of becoming aware of oneself and one's own cultural experience. It includes one's own thinking and feelings related to individual and family diversity. Reflexivity also promotes an understanding of how these psychological and emotional processes have developed and a willingness to take responsibility for the implications resulting beliefs, feelings, and behaviors have on others (Allen & Farnsworth, 1993). Personal experiences are honored without generalizing them to others; the experiences of others are honored without denying our own. The goal is to know ourselves and how we have come to occupy our unique set of ethnocultural contexts.

Bennett's (1993) "Model of Cultural Competency" encourages the practice of reflexivity in developing intercultural sensitivity by "[p]erceiving behavior, values, and identity itself as a process of constructing reality [and] by reducing reification and the assumptions of absoluteness, centrality, and universalism that usually accompany reification" (p. 66). Bennett's six stages move from ethnocentrism (i.e., denial, defense, minimization) to ethnorelativism (i.e., acceptance, adaptation, integration). Strategies to promote reflexivity and movement along these stages can be incorporated into FLE practice.

For example, exposing oneself to culturally diverse events and trainings can encourage movement from denial (i.e., not perceiving differences, benign stereotyping, intentional distancing from others) to defense (i.e., when differences are experienced as threatening). Building cultural self-esteem, allowing for a balanced cultural pride, emphasizing the good in cultures, and using group activities can assist movement from defensiveness to the next stage, minimization (i.e., when similarities are valued more than differences, leading to trivialization of differences and implicit assumptions that all should be—or are—like the dominant group). Awareness of cultural factors that influence behavior and the possible dissonance between one's own cultural base(s) and those of others, facilitates movement toward the first stage in ethnorelativism, acceptance.

Practicing acceptance through participating in ongoing groups with diverse members encourages growth toward adaptation. At the following stage, adaptation is demonstrated through empathy and pluralism (i.e., a commitment to understanding others within contexts and operate successfully in other culture) and is fostered through living in another culture for a substantial time. However, sensitivity to one culture may not translate to another, so providing opportunities for personal growth in empathy and transferring adaptation to other cultures maybe useful. Those in the integration stage challenge themselves with more intensive experiences with other cultures and may commit to internationalism or multiculturalism. The integration stage is a launching point for possibilities that we have yet to envision.

Those who have experienced oppression and those from dominant groups may navigate the stages differently. For example, those who have experienced oppression are not typically in denial that they have been oppressed. However, for this group, the experience of oppression may generalize into a rigid expectation of vulnerability and, at worst, futility (Pinderhughes, 1989). FLEs must take the possibility of all of these having effects on their activities when working cross-culturally.

This model is based on the following assumptions: cultural understanding occurs through contact, a culture can only be understood through examining other cultures, and "cultural difference is neither good not bad, it is just different, although some cultural behaviors may be more adaptive than others to particular environmental conditions" (p. 46). Difference is not perceived as threatening but often is experienced as enjoyable and is sought after, eliciting a reflexive stance of "curiosity rather than animosity" (p. 48).

All of the above applies collectively to organizations, such as agencies and educational institutions, as well as to individuals. Organizations must also be reflexive about their history and current operations. The factors that shape organizational development also influence design, implementation, and evaluation of family life education. As in the case of individuals, organizations can only understand the increasing diversity in clientele by first recognizing the social and cultural contexts in which they exist.

Acquiring the Understanding and Skills to Function within and Adapt to Diverse Cultures

The second step in Sue et al.'s (1998) process is for FLEs to begin to learn the cultural contexts of others. This process includes developing knowledge and understanding of others' worldviews, cultural practices, values, history and context (Dilworth-Anderson, Burton, & Turner, 1993; McAdoo, 1999). Developing understanding and appreciation of other ethnic and cultural groups increases empathy for others, while simultaneously challenging insularity and ethnocentrism. The process of exploring diversity is a balance between generalizing the attributes learned about a given group with the realization that within-group differences exist. It is helpful to remember that there is often as much diversity within groups as between them.

This understanding is translated into *skills* to interact in respectful and useful ways and to build and implement appropriate Family Life Education programs that employ culturally appropriate techniques and strategies. Interpersonal skills must convey respect and knowledge of a culture. For example, addressing family members in the proper order, use (or avoidance) of eye contact, and the appropriate time allotted for building rapport through general conversation, all may vary from depending on the ethnic or cultural background. Understanding the preferred interactional patterns of the particular group with whom one is working is vital to success. A cultural guide may be imperative for effective work, including establishing trust and credibility (e.g., refuge and immigrant families, families who practice a religion unfamiliar to the FLE). In some cases, only an FLE who is a member of the group may be accepted. However, most diverse groups have demonstrated a high degree of tolerance for working with and receiving services from members of other ethnic or cultural groups.

Conceptual skills orient FLEs to meta-issues, such as learning styles, educator roles, and paradigms. Using information on learning styles as described by McCarthy (1996), Myers-Walls (2000) suggested that FLEs identify their own preferred learning style, then practice and become comfortable with the other styles, and then integrate all of them into a given situation. In terms of the role of an educator, FLEs can also assume the role of an "expert," a "collaborator," or a "facilitator" when working. These roles parallel the different paradigms that are present in family life education: instrumental/technical, interpretive, and emancipatory (Morgaine, 1992). An *expert* has information and skills for participants to learn that are intended to improve the quality of life. An FLE as a *collaborator* shares responsibility for the programming with participants. An interpretive paradigm guides FLEs to explore personal, family, and cultural meanings of family experiences. As a *facilitator*, an FLE functions as a resource for participants and helps with group process while assuming the goal is to assist participants in using their own knowledge to change external conditions. Comfort with these paradigms and educator roles can allow FLEs to use them flexibly, as audiences and situations demand.

Thinking Contextually and Globally

Daily work reflects the self-awareness gained, the understanding of other cultural contexts, and the acquired interpersonal and conceptual skills. The phrase, "Think globally, act locally" can be applied to family life education. All programs and practice are local, in that they must be nested in or developed within the local context to be responsive to population needs. To act locally, FLEs must understand and be conversant in the local cultures. This capability may require research or FLEs' deliberate efforts at experiencing different ethnic and cultural experiences and traditions (Sue et al., 1998).

Global awareness is critically important for cultural competency. Knowledge of the historical forces that have shaped the United States (U.S) and international processes such as immigration patterns are also key attributes. Without these, uninformed practitioners are a little like toddlers attempting to do pole-vaulting before they have learned to walk. FLEs typically work with refugees, migrant workers, families extended across nations, immigrants, and families with unemployed members. If FLEs fail to broaden their thinking to a global level, they may miss the contexts in which local families live. Given the greater mobility of families, those contexts of meaning are increasingly global and have sociopolitical dimensions.

For example, after the terrorist attacks in the United States of September 2001, many Arab American families in the U.S. feared to venture out in public, wary of possible reprisals from overzealous individuals or groups. Their fears were justified given the national levels of grief and xenophobia. This dilemma also indirectly affected Muslim families from other parts of the world, and non-Muslims whose customs may have been perceived as "Arab" or "Muslim." In many cases, the tragic events and tensions affecting families throughout the United States created unique, additional stresses for these families and for other groups of families as well, such as those with members in the military. Yet is it also important to note that there were reports by Arab Americans receiving messages of support and concern from neighbors, co-workers, and employers (Beitin & Allen, 2005).

Just knowing about the terrorist attacks would not be enough to help such families regain their equilibrium and sense of agency in troubled times. Depending on their socioeconomic and ethno-cultural location, practitioners may alternatively need to use innovative approaches or to engage non-traditional allies. Understanding the religious and ethnic influences that led to the events and the range of worldviews that families throughout the nation hold could facilitate family life educators' efforts to help specific families.

In discussing Sue et al.'s (1992) third step, it is useful to consider attributes of our national character that might help or hinder the process of developing culturally appropriate intervention strategies. Among the positive attributes are the spirit of creativity and innovation that have fostered achievements in both the sciences (e.g., space exploration, medicine) and the arts (e.g., rock, jazz music). All of these can help reduce the fear of the "unknown" that prevents many practitioners from courageously embracing the diversity around them.

Turning to potentially negative attributes, those of the U.S. majority culture are not always the most patient of people. The desire for quick, simple answers to complex questions often results in the development of deeper, more protracted problems. Related to these faults is the tendency for dichotomous thinking that often impedes the identification of alternatives. This tendency is a prime culprit in the inability to identify common ground between groups, or to understand the diversity within diverse groups. For some members of privileged groups (e.g., whites, heterosexuals, or the affluent), feelings of guilt, anger, or helplessness may inhibit growth (Helms, 1992). Recognizing such feelings as normative and refusing to succumb to the paralysis of self-recrimination can help provide the motivation for resuming one's development. Practitioners who overcome these problems can develop the competencies to serve the families in their settings.

Continuing the Journey

What is next for the field of family life education along this journey of cultural competence? The field would benefit from continued development of cultural competencies in four areas: empirical accounts and reports, applications, organizational development, and professional expectations.

Increasing Cultural Competency

First, the field benefits from continued focus on how FLEs are successfully increasing their cultural competencies. Empirical accounts and reports from the field provide insight into how FLEs are incorporating a diversity lens in their work, and how they are personally growing in multicultural awareness, understanding, and skills. What are the lessons being learned from those practicing in the field?

Movement in this direction is occurring, for example, within the United States Department of Agriculture Cooperative State Research, Education and Extension Service. Over the course of two years, Cooperative Extension in Pennsylvania published a quarterly newsletter, *Diverse Issues*, for Extension professionals. This newsletter included five regular features:

- diversity in people (e.g., the Amish, rural/urban/suburban communities, gay and lesbian families, how child-rearing practices vary across populations);
- diversity in the workplace (addressed working with diverse others);
- diversity activities (to be used with youth or adult groups to encourage awareness of diversity);
- diversity resources (reviews of educational materials, clip art, and websites prepared for diverse groups); and
- diversity around the state (highlights of efforts of Extension professionals' diversity activities).

A third of the newsletter recipients reported using it for their own development; while another third included the content in county newsletters, media, and Extension meetings (Ingram & Radhakrishna, 2002). FLEs could benefit from further research on the day-to-day diversity practices of FLE professionals. Using ethnographic and in-depth interviewing methods, researchers could document effective practices of Extension professionals as they work with the populations in their counties.

The work of Bean, Perry, and Bedell (2002) provides an example of lessons learned in therapeutic settings. They document how combining a literature review with personal development help non-African American therapists work effectively with African American clientele. This approach illustrates the value of using insights gained through the first two steps of Sue et. al.'s (1998) process to shape culturally appropriate interventions. Several of Bean, Perry, and Bedell's (2002) 15 guidelines assume that practitioners will have successfully reflected on their own ethnocultural contexts. This reflexivity allows practitioners to avoid defensiveness and to overcome their fear of joining with clients in what may well be new ways for both clients and practitioners.

This article echoes points raised throughout the elaboration of Bean, Perry, and Bedell's (2002) guidelines (e.g., such as "maintaining a broad definition of family" and including family structure and roles). Another example would be these authors' suggestion that clinicians specifically address issues of "racism and its effects" on the lives of the families they work with. This approach, along with de-emphasizing artificial power dynamics (i.e., clinician over client) and the willingness to meet families in their own environments when possible, enhance the credibility of practitioners seeking to cross cultural boundaries.

Applications

A growing number of materials for families and FLEs are available, including on-line resources in English, Spanish, and other languages (e.g., www.cyfernet.org; www.clas.uiuc.edu; http://osu.orst.edu/dept/ehe/; http://extension.missouri.edu/parentlink/index.htm; www.extension.umn.edu/topics.html?topic=3). Examples of diversity as a topic include *Families of All Kinds: A Guide for Parents* (Olsen, 1994) and *A Guide for Leaders* (Olsen, 1995). More documentation is necessary of the efforts underway to provide families with resources and programs on increasing cultural competency and the effectiveness of these efforts.

Several FLEs have developed programs materials tailored to specific ethnic and cultural communities. For example, Blackman (2002) has developed The African American Marriage Enrichment Program, one of two empirically-based practice models that make up the African American Family Life Education Program [c]. The marriage enrichment program uses a culturally competent approach to helping couples develop skills for a healthy relationship. It has been widely presented at national forums such as the Smart Marriages Conference (Blackman, 2007). The second model focuses on parenting education. The African American Family Life Education Program © represents a good illustration of collaboration between a Certified Family Fife Educator and several community stakeholders, in this case the Indiana University School of Social Work, two local agencies (the Wishard Health Services and the M.L. King Center) and a local faith community (Robinson Community AME Church). (See also AAFLE program description at www.aafle.org).

Faculty and staff affiliated with the Center for Family Research at the University of Georgia have been studying the contextual factors that promote health and positive development in families within rural African American communities. Their research has resulted in the development of prevention programs responsive to family and community strengths, including Strong African American Families and the Program for Strong African American Marriage (www.cfr.uga.edu; Brody et al., 2004; Hurt et al., 2007).

Grandparent Resource Site Initiative is a collaboration among FLEs, local agencies serving families providings kinship care, and the Kellogg Foundation. Ten Grandparent Resource Centers have been established nationwide in which staff and advisory groups collaborate in offering culturally sensitive services to grandparents and the grandchildren they are raising (Dannison & Smith, 2003; www.wmich.edu/grs).

For FLEs in higher education, recent faculty accounts from the field of family science (e.g., see works noted earlier) and related fields, such as higher education (see www.diversityweb.org) offer practical strategies and models for diversifying curricula. The Carnegie Foundation for the Advancement of Teaching (see www.carnegiefoundation.org) provides direction and resources for K-12 schools and institutions of higher education that commit to fostering the scholarship of teaching and learning.

Cultural Competency in Organizations

Third, FLEs can promote organizational cultural competency where they work and volunteer. As suggested earlier, FLEs seeking to help organizations increase their cultural competency should find Sue et al.'s (1998) work helpful. Integrating a variety of sources, Sue et al. (1998) offers six characteristics of multicultural competent organizations.

1) The organization values the diversity of personnel and clients, and consequently, recognizes that values, behaviors, communication styles, attitudes will differ. Differences within and between groups are acknowledged. While European American group characteristics are respected as one of many possible identities, they are not used as the standard against which others are judged.

2) The organization is able to engage in self-assessment or cultural auditing. Those within the organization recognize the importance of better understanding how the system has been influenced by cultural factors and how unexamined biases, assumptions, and values require exploration. Assessment may include the organization's services, products, processes and context.

3) The organization has a clear vision. Personnel know and share a common vision of what it means to be cultural competent.

4) The organization understands the dynamics that may occur when moving toward cultural competency. For example, conflict may arise when two or more groups attempt to better understand each other and work toward eliminating racism, sexism, heterosexism and other forms of oppression. Leaders need to respond creatively, flexibly, and allow for mistakes, as personnel become "pioneers" in change.

5) Organizations allow cultural knowledge to permeate all sections and duties of the workplace. Everyone has access to and makes use of cultural knowledge in their work.

6) Organizations continually adapt to diversity. As clients change, the organization responds by developing and implementing additional culturally appropriate services.

Beyond these steps may be a necessary shifting an agency's "operating assumptions" so that culturally-specific services and programs emerge from the worldview of the local community (Uttal, 2006). To be culturally-specific, an organization may be called on to shift its orientation from client-centered to community-based, particularly when the local community does not differentiate among community development, social support, and individual development. Uttal suggests such a shift entails a number of practices.

1. Personnel need the autonomy and support to acknowledge cultural and material circumstances of audience when designing programs.
2. Redesign program materials to fit the knowledge of the audience.
3. Add topics of interest to the curriculum (e.g., a group with a large group of immigrant families may need immigration information included in even though the topic does not appear connected to the program).
4. Rely on dialogical rather than didactic interactions to better understand the worldview of the participants and thus make necessary changes to a program.
5. Encourage all staff at all levels of an organization to examine how programmatic changes can actually help to meet broader goals of an organization.

Professional Expectations

Finally, cultural competency should continue to be incorporated as a formal part of the certified family life education program. (see www.ncfr.org for more information on becoming a Certified Family Life Educator). Training for cultural competency should include all aspects of research, training and practice in order to encourage reflexive practitioners who continually work on increasing their cultural competency. As academic programs educate students in the ten family life education content areas for the certification of family life educators (NCFR, 1984), conscious integration of diversity and cultural competency is necessary.

For example, in lessons on ethics for professional practice (one of the ten content areas; NCFR, 1984), instructors can explore the importance of personal reflexivity, understanding, and skills to the development of cultural competency. Instructors can incorporate models of ethnic, gender, and sexual identity development and cultural competency development into human growth and development, ethics, or family life education methodology courses. As part of the FLE certification process, applicants could demonstrate work undertaken to become more culturally competent.

Progress was made in this area with the inclusion of "multicultural—gender fair—special-needs aware" within the *Framework for Life Span Family Life Education* (Bredehoft, 1997, 2001). FLEs involved in future revisions of the framework may wish to consider replacing "special needs" with "particular needs" or another term to better represent that all families have needs rather than creating a dichotomy between needs and special ones. For example, historically families in privileged positions were considered the model or default family against which others were judged and studied. However, in a vivid account, Marks (2000) "problematizes" family privilege and entitlement and argues for their inclusion in research agendas. Privilege and entitlement neither demand awareness of or attention to diversity, nor responsibility for changing oppressive conditions. Families can perpetuate prejudice and insularity, not only to the detriment of "others" but also to the detriment of their members. Not only can family privilege and entitlement become topics of study, they can also become topics of concern for family life educators. It is important to note that no individual or family fits solely into one category or another (i.e., totally privileged or totally disadvantaged), but experiences a unique intersection of benefits and harms (Marks & Leslie, 2000; see also Collins, 1990; hooks, 1996; Lorde, 1984).

Summary

Cultural competency is central to the work of family life education. As the population of the United States continues to diversify, practitioners must effectively cross-cultural boundaries to be effective. Thus, rather than being rare or occasional occurrences, these types of crossings will increasingly define which individuals and organizations have meaningful roles guiding and empowering families in the 21st Century.

Guidance in developing cultural competency is available both from within the family life education field, and from other disciplines. One approach is the use of a "diversity lens" to build cross-cultural understanding. Another approach begins with developing personal awareness and reflexivity. These combine with knowledge of others and their values, and the acquisition of cross-cultural skills that facilitate understanding. This synthesis of awareness, knowledge and skills is the essence of cultural competence.

The authors have attempted to demonstrate how family life educators and practitioners can enrich their work by embracing these principles. Through this process of deliberate attention to diversity in its many forms, FLEs can move towards higher levels of cultural competence and professional excellence. However, the benefits reach far beyond the improvement of our work. Ultimately, it is the families whose lives we touch who are empowered by this attention to diversity. If our work validates and honors them and their roots, together we can cultivate a spirit of hope that future generations will see their differences as a healthy resource for strengthening communities.

References

Allen, K. R. (1995). Opening the classroom closet: Sexual orientation and self-disclosure. *Family Relations, 44*, 136-141.

Allen, K. R., & Baber, K. M. (1992). Starting a revolution in family life education: A feminist vision. *Family Relations, 41*, 378-384.

Allen, K. R., & Farnsworth, E. B. (1993). Reflexivity in teaching about families. *Family Relations, 42*, 351-356.

Baber, K. M., & Murray, C. L. (2001). A postmodern feminist approach to teaching human sexuality. *Family Relations, 50*, 23-33.

Banton, M., & Harwood, J. (1975). *The race concept*. New York: Prager.

Bean, R. A., Crane, D., & Lewis, T. L. (2002). Basic research and implications for practice in family science: A content analysis and status report for U.S. ethnic groups. *Family Relations, 51,* 15-21.

Bean, R. A., Perry, B. J., & Bedell, T. M. (2002). Developing culturally competent marriage and family therapists. *Journal of Marital & Family Therapy, 28*, 153-164.

Bennett, M. J. (1993). Toward ethnorelativism: A developmental model of intercultural sensitivity. In R. M. Paige (Ed.) *Education for the intercultural experiences*, pp. 21-71. Yarmouth, ME: Intercultural Press.

Berke, D. L., & Wisensale, S. K. (Eds.). (2005). *The craft of teaching about families: Strategies and tools*. Binghamton, NY: Haworth Press.

Blackman, L. C. (2002). The African American Marriage Enrichment Program©: How to make your good thing better. *Social Work Today*, *2* (3), 14–18.

Blackman, L. C. (2007, June/July). *African American marriage enrichment.* Presented at the 2007 Smart Marriages Conference. Denver, CO.

Blaisure, K. R., & Koivenun, J. (2003). Family science faculty members' experiences with teaching from a feminist perspective. *Family Relations, 52*, 22-32.

Bredehoft, D. J. (Ed.). (1997). *The framework for life span family life education* (2nd ed.) [Poster]. Minneapolis: National Council on Family Relations.

Bredehoft, D. J. (2001). The framework for life span family life education revisited and revised. *The Family Journal: Counseling and Therapy for Couples and Families, 9*, 134-139.

Beitin, B. K., & Allen, K. R. (2005). Resilience in Arab American couples after September 11, 2001: A systems perspective. *Journal of Marital and Family Therapy, 31*, 251-268.

Brody, G. H., Murry, V. M., Gerrard, M., Gibbons, F. X., Molgaard, V., McNair, L., et al (2004). The strong African American families program: Translating research into prevention programming. *Child Development, 75*, 900-917.

Bubolz, M. M., & McKenry, P. C. (1993). Gender issues in family life education: A feminist perspective. In M. E. Arcus, J. D. Schvaneveldt & J. J. Moss (Eds.), *Handbook of family life education: Foundations of family life education Vol. 1.* (pp. 131-161). Newbury Park, CA: Sage.

Collins, P. H. (1990). *Black feminist thought: Knowledge, consciousness, and the politics of empowerment* (*Perspectives on Gender, Vol. 2*). Cambridge, MA: Unwin Hyman.

Cross, T., Bazron, B., Dennis, K. & Isaacs, M. R. (1989). *Towards a cultural competent system of care: A monograph on effective services for minority children who are severely emotionally disturbed, Volume I*. Washington, DC: CASSP Technical Assistance Center, Georgetown University Child Development Center.

Dannison, L., & Smith, A. (2003). Custodial grandparent community support program: Lessons learned. *Children and Schools, 25*(2), 87–95.

Demo, D., Allen, K. R., & Fine, M. A. (Eds.). (2000). *Handbook of family diversity*. New York: Oxford University Press.

Dilworth-Anderson, P., Burton, L. M., & Turner, W. L. (1993). The importance of values in the study of culturally diverse families. *Family Relations, 42*, 238-242.

Dilworth-Anderson, P., & McAdoo, H. P. (1988). The study of ethnic minority families: Implications for practitioners and policymakers. *Family Relations, 37*, 265-267.

Helms, J. (1992). *A race is a nice thing to have: A guide to being a white person or understanding the white persons in your life*. Topeka, KS: Content Communications.

Hurt, T.R., Beach, S. R. H., McNair, L. D., Fincham, F. D., & Murry, V. M. (2007, November). *Dissemination of couples' interventions: Experiences from ProSAAM*. Paper presented at the annual conference of the National Council on Family Relations, Pittsburgh, PA.

Ingram, P. D., & Radhakrishna, R. (2002). Evaluating a diversity educational resource in cooperative extension. *Journal of Extension, 40*(1). Retrieved May 5, 2002, from http://www.joe.org/joe/2002february/iw2.html

Lewis, E. A. (1995). Toward a tapestry of impassioned voices: Incorporating praxis into teaching about families. *Family Relations, 44*, 149-152.

Lorde, A. (1984). *Sister outsider*. Trumansberg, NY: The Crossing Press.

MacDermid, S. M., Jurich, J. A., Myers-Walls, J. A., & Pelo, A. (1992). Feminist teaching: Effective education. *Family Relations, 41,* 31-38.

Marger, M. (1997). *Race and ethnic relations: American and global perspectives* (4th ed.). Belmont, CA: Wadsworth.

Marks, J. (1995). *Human biodiversity: Genes, race, and history*. New York: Aldine de Gruyter.

Marks, S. (1995). The art of professing and holding back in a course on gender. *Family Relations, 44,* 142-148.

Marks, S. (2000). Teasing out the lessons of the 1960s: Family diversity and family privilege. *Journal of Marriage and the Family, 62*, 609-622.

Marks, S. R., & Leslie, L. A. (2000). Family diversity and intersecting categories: Toward a richer approach to multiple roles. In D. H. Demo, K. R. Allen & Mark A. Fine (Eds.), *Handbook of family diversity* (pp. 402-423). New York: Oxford University Press.

McAdoo, H. P. (1999). *Family ethnicity: Strength in diversity* (2nd ed.). Newbury Park, CA: Sage.

McAdoo, H. P. (2007). *Black families* (4th ed.). Thousand Oaks, CA: Sage.

McCarthy, B. (1996). *About learning*. Schaumburg, IL: Excel.

McGoldrick, M. (Ed.). (1998). *Re-visioning family therapy: Race, culture, and gender in clinical practice*. New York: Guilford Press.

McGoldrick, M., Giordano, J., & Garcio-Preto, N. (Eds.). (2005). *Ethnicity and family therapy* (3rd ed.). New York: Guilford.

Montagu, A. (1974). *Man's most dangerous myth: The fallacy of race* (5th ed.). New York: Oxford University Press.

Morgaine, C. A. (1992). Alternative paradigms for helping families change themselves. *Family Relations, 41*, 12-17.

Myers-Walls, J. A. (2000). Family diversity and family life education. In D. H. Demo, K. R. Allen & Mark A. Fine (Eds.), *Handbook of family diversity* (pp. 359-379). New York: Oxford University Press.

Myers-Walls, J. A., Dunn, J., & Myers-Bowman, K. S. (2003). *Cultural Characteristics Questionnaire: What does your target population look like?* In D. J. Bredehoft & M. J. Walcheski (Eds.), *Family life education: Integrating theory and practice* (pp. 186-188). Minneapolis, MN: National Council on Family Relations.

National Council on Family Relations. (1984). *Standards and criteria for the certification of family life educators, college/university curriculum guidelines, and content guidelines for family life education: A framework for planning programs over the life span.* Minneapolis: Author.

Olsen, C. S. (1994, December). *Families of all kinds: A guide for parents.* Manhattan, KS: Cooperative Extension Services, Kansas State University.

Olsen, C. S. (1995, April). *Families of all kinds: A guide for leaders.* Manhattan, KS: Cooperative Extension Services, Kansas State University.

Pinderhughes, R. (1989). *Understanding race, ethnicity, and power: The key to efficacy in clinical practice.* New York: Free Press.

Sue, D. W., Arredondo, P., & McDavis, R. J. (1992). Multicultural competencies/standards: A pressing need. *Journal of Counseling and Development, 70*, 477-486.

Sue, D. W., Carter, R. T., Casas, J. M., Fouad, N. A., Ivey, A. E., & Jensen, M. (1998). *Multicultural counseling competencies: Individual and organizational development.* Thousand Oaks, CA: Sage.

Talbot, D. M. (1996). Multiculturalism. In S. Komives & D. Woodard (Eds.) *Student services: A handbook for the profession* (3rd ed.). San Francisco, CA: Jossey-Bass.

Thomas, J. (1995). Toward inclusive curriculum: Identifying bias and exclusivity in family life education curriculum material. In D. J. Bredehoft (Ed.), *Family life education curriculum guidelines,* (2nd ed., p. 15). Minneapolis: National Council on Family Relations.

Thompson, L. (1995). Teaching about ethnic minority families using a pedagogy of care. *Family Relations, 44*, 129-135.

Uttal, L. (2006). Organizational cultural competency: Shifting programs for Latino immigrants from a client-centered to a community-based orientation. *American Journal of Community Psychology, 38*, 251-262.

Walker, A. (1996). Cooperative learning in the college classroom. *Family Relations, 45*, 327-335.

Walker, A. J., Martin, S. S. K., & Thompson, L. (1988). Feminist programs for families. *Family Relations, 37*, 17-22.

Wiley, A. R., & Ebata, A. (2004). Reaching American families: Making diversity real in family life education. *Family Relations, 53*, 273-281.

About the Authors

William D. Allen. Ph. D., L.M.F.T. is a licensed marriage and family therapist and proprietor of Healing Bonds, a private practice in Minneapolis, MN. In addition to his work with social service agencies and government, he conducts family research and is on the adjunct faculty of the Family Social Science Department of the University of Minnesota. E-mail: ballen@umn.edu.

Karen Blaisure, Ph. D., CFLE, L.M.F.T. is a professor in the Department of Family and Consumer Sciences, Western Michigan University. Her research areas include group and online education programs for separating parents. She also facilitates programs for couples and a weekend course on family life and the military. E-mail: karen.blaisure@wmich.edu.

In the Best Interests of Children and Their Families: Merging Program Development and Program Evaluation

Christa J. Treichel

"Do family life education programs make a difference?" With the appropriate design and data collection approaches, the program evaluation process provides evidence to answer this question; a question that is important to the general public, to funders, policymakers, and the academic and research communities—many stakeholders with different interpretations of what this question means. Evaluation is also for the practitioner who strives to offer valuable, effective services that meet the needs of families. This article will demonstrate how the evaluation process generates information that satisfies the needs of family life educators (FLEs) and other family life education professionals while enriching the lives of children and their families.

Evaluation as a Diverse and Expanding Field

Evaluation approaches have proliferated in the last few decades (Chelimsky & Shadish, 1997; Stufflebeam, 2001). One reason for the growth in evaluation techniques is their application in an ever-growing number of settings. Many of us are familiar with the use of program evaluation in the fields of social work, public health, education, youth development, or family life education. However, evaluation is now being applied in other less familiar settings. For example, businesses evaluate the value of employee assistance services (Maiden, 1988). Police officers use evaluation results to determine whether their community policing programs improved the public's perceptions of police officers (Sadd & Grinc, 1994). Environmental organizations study the effectiveness of a new project focusing on improving water quality. Contemporary art museums evaluate their efforts to attract different populations through various initiatives. Ecumenical religious groups examine the feasibility of an affordable housing project within a particular geographical area. It is not uncommon to attend the American Evaluation Association's annual conference and meet evaluators from the World Bank, the U.S. Department of Defense, the

U.S. General Accounting Office, the National Science Foundation, the United Nations, or the World Health Organization. While this disciplinary diversity has its advantages, it also poses challenges in that the breadth of approaches and terminology is overwhelming—or at least confusing—for a family life educator who finds out that program evaluation is now part of his or her program description.

This leads to the three purposes of this article. The first purpose is to help practitioners understand the differences and similarities between evaluation and research. The second purpose is to suggest that practitioners engage in the process of conducting an evaluability assessment early in the life of their family life education program. An evaluability assessment is a process whereby evaluators work with program staff to get them ready for program evaluation (Patton, 1997). It provides valuable information to practitioners thinking through the components of their program, how they function, and how the program enriches the lives of children and their families. The third purpose is to advocate the merging of evaluation processes with program development. Toward this end, Jacobs' Five-Tiered Approach to evaluation (1988) is presented as a tool practitioners can apply in their work with family life education programs. The Jacobs' model links the stages of program development with parallel evaluation tasks. These three purposes provide the family life educator with a broad picture of evaluation, its connection to planning and implementation processes, and its value in answering questions about the benefits of family life education.

Defining Evaluation and Distinguishing it from Research

What is evaluation? It depends whom you ask. The *Standards for Evaluations of Educational Programs, Projects, and Materials* (Joint Committee on Standards for Educational Evaluation, 1981, pp. 12-13) defines evaluation as the "…systematic investigation of the worth or merit of some object." The "object" is defined as a program, a project, or materials. Programs are defined as educational activities offered for an indefinite period of time (like a university's continuing education program) whereas a project consists of activities offered for a shorter period of time (a two-day workshop about a particular instructional strategy). Materials evaluation focuses on studying books, curricula, videos, workbooks, or study guides.

This definition of evaluation and the distinctions between programs, projects, and material is still useful today. Patton (1997) expanded on this seminal definition by focusing on how evaluation is used. Patton states "Program evaluation is the systematic collection of information about the activities, characteristics, and outcomes of programs to make judgments about the program, improve program effectiveness, and/or inform decisions about future programming" (1997, p. 23). Patton suggests that making a judgment may not be the end result or the only reason for conducting an evaluation. Furthermore, Patton challenges stakeholders to understand why something is being studied and what will be done with the judgments that are made. Focusing on the practical purpose of evaluation use raises the need for an important distinction between research and evaluation.

The terms research and evaluation are often used synonymously. While it may seem like an exercise in semantics to debate their differences, words do influence our actions. For example, some FLEs feel pressured by funders, by their supervisors, or by their colleagues to engage in research activities as compared to evaluation activities. Many are under the impression that it is their responsibility to carry out a study characterized by a longitudinal experimental design with sophisticated sampling approaches (e.g., they manage a home visiting program with a caseload of 22 mothers and their children). In addition, they feel obligated to carry out studies that generate conclusions, produce findings that are generalizable across families, and that result in causal statements like, "Our home visiting program caused decreased rates of child abuse and neglect." Family life educators who believe this is their responsibility usually feel panicked, overwhelmed, or frustrated. Their professional experience in this setting tells them that a scientific research study of their program is not feasible.

While we have many questions in the field of family life education that call for research studies, "pure research" is often beyond the resources and expertise of smaller, non-profit organizations (Pietrzak, Ramler, Renner, Ford, & Gilbert, 1990). Furthermore, the results of a research study do not help a practitioners to understand the degree to which their program is of benefit to families, to help improve the program, or make decisions about what should be done next month (Patton, 1997).

In my work with practitioners, it has been helpful to discuss the differences and similarities between evaluation and research. Contextually-bound, evaluation results are useful for the specific situation studied but it is usually not the purpose to generalize these results to a larger population. Program evaluation is intended to provide practitioners with the practical information needed to make program decisions and improvements—and usually with a fairly quick turnaround of the results. Practitioners need to answer questions like, "Would the parents prefer peers or professionals as group leaders?" or "What did parents learn from our discussion?" or "Are parents more comfortable meeting in their homes for public nurse health visits or would they prefer to come to the clinic?" To summarize, evaluation results are of great value to practitioners when real issues drive the questions and when the results are used to make decisions and improve programs.

Research on the other hand is an inquiry process directed toward a different end. The process of scientific research generates information that helps researchers test theories or laws, generates information to help them draw conclusions, and allows them to generalize their findings to other people or situations not directly studied (Worthen & Sanders, 1987). Patton (1997) summarizes the differences and similarities of research and evaluation by saying that research aims to produce knowledge and truth whereas evaluation provides information that supports action.

Research and evaluation do have some things in common. Both are disciplined forms of inquiry and both are systematic in terms of data collection and analysis approaches. Researchers and evaluators share similar methods—interviews, document review, surveys, or observations; methods that may be qualitative or quantitative in nature. In both inquiry processes, researchers and evaluators use information or data as the basis of their studies (Patton, 1997; Worthen & Sanders, 1987).

I believe all family life education programs should be evaluated. Families who join programs may enroll because they have a crisis or simply because they want to engage in activities they think will benefit their families. Whatever the reason, practitioners want to meet these needs and program evaluation offers a process to ensure that this occurs.

Getting Started: Evaluability Assessments

Developing a family life education program is a serious undertaking. Family life educators create programs motivated by a desire to create positive change in the life of a child, a teenager, a parent, or for the family. The goal may be to help families acquire new information, change their belief system, gain different skills, or improve their life circumstances.

There is a process in the field of evaluation called an "evaluability assessment" (Wholey, 1977). Regardless of the program's goal, an evaluability assessment helps FLEs strengthen the conceptual design of their program and increase the likelihood that families will benefit from its activities. It also can prevent a misguided use of resources preventing an organization from taking on an evaluation study prematurely.

When an organization conducts an evaluability assessment, they ask and answer several questions. What do we want to offer families (in terms of programming or services)? What do we expect families to gain from this experience? How will the program activities we offer lead to the outcomes we want for families? Are our ideas plausible? How will we provide evidence of our program's success? Are we well-positioned to take on an outcomes evaluation study? In order to answer these questions, the next section of this article breaks the evaluability assessment processes into four steps: 1) creating a program theory, 2) creating a logic model, 3) identifying outcomes and indicators, and 4) assessing the organization's readiness for summative evaluation activities.

Articulating a Theory of Change

To begin the process of an evaluability assessment, practitioners spend time developing a "theory of change" (sometimes referred to as a theory of action) (Jacobs, Kapuscik, Williams, & Kates, 2000). A theory of change explains how a program works to produce benefits for families (children, youth, or adults). It makes the change process transparent because it pushes practitioners to be clear about how change is expected to occur while participants are involved in the program's services or activities. When an evaluation is implemented to study program benefits but the theory of change is not developed, it results in a "black box" (Chen, 1990). A black box occurs when FLEs can identify the outcomes families experience by participating in the program, but do not understand why or how the results occurred. In addition, a black box approach does not help FLEs understand whether the program was implemented in the way it was originally designed. Furthermore, if the results of the program were positive, how can FLEs recreate this success when they are unsure about how the outcomes occurred in the first place?

In contrast to the black box, Killion (2002) explains that developing a theory of change creates a "glass box," or a clear description of the program. The glass box illuminates program operations and benefits while providing a reasonable, logical explanation of how outcomes are linked to these operations. When using Killion's "glass box" approach to program evaluation FLEs are more likely to:

1) produce useful insights for improving the program
2) clarify important program elements
3) understand the necessary conditions for success
4) understand program limitations
5) prevent program slippage, dilution, or deterioration
6) contribute to the field's knowledge of effective programming approaches
7) help colleagues with replication

In *New Approaches to Evaluating Community Initiatives*, Kagan (1989) summarizes the benefits of using a theory of change; benefits for practitioners and evaluators:

> First, the approach is aligned with family support [family life education] in that it captures the non-linearity and iterative nature of the programs. Rather than expecting defined and static interventions, the theory of change approach welcomes the diversity and changeable nature of interventions. It regards critical contextual factors not as theoretical nuisances, but as important variables to be understood and examined. In respecting the role of context, the approach appreciates, rather than tolerates, variation within and across sites—a critical element in

Figure 1. Sample Logic Model

Program Audience Group of people for whom the family support programming is designed for	**Long-Term Desired Outcome** Social or economic condition or status change	**Intermediate Outcomes** Practice changes or behavior adoption necessary to change conditions and achieve long-term outcomes	**Short-Term Outcomes** Participant engagement, and changes in knowledge, attitudes, skills, aspirations necessary for taking action and achieving intermediate outcomes	**Family Support Programming** Services, interventions or activities which are expected to bring about desired outcomes	**Resources Needed** Finances, people and materials which are needed to implement the planned program
Non-custodial fathers, ages 18-25 years	Dads will be involved parents and support their child's healthy growth and development. Dads will demonstrate basic parenting skills.	Dads will demonstrate effective communication and conflict resolution skills. Dads will value co-parenting. Dads and moms will agree to co-parent. Dads will establish legal fatherhood. Dads will develop custody/visitation agreements. Dads will spend time with their babies.	**Engagement Outcomes** Dads understand the importance of being involved in their baby's life. Dads will accept help. Dads will show up for program. Dads will agree to work with legal system to establish paternity. Dads will agree to mediation with their baby's mom to facilitate co-parenting. Dads will complete program. **Learning Outcomes** Dads will have knowledge of child development and appropriate discipline approaches. Dads will have knowledge of the process of establishing legal fatherhood. Dads will have knowledge of co-parenting. Dads will have knowledge of communication and conflict resolution processes and skills.	Legal Services Parent Education Mediation Services Transportation Food	Lawyers Parent Educators Mediators Parent Education Curriculum Meeting Space Office Space for Staff Food Transportation Baby Supplies Referral Network Financial Resources

Note: Format for this sample developed by the FRIENDS National Resource Center for Community Based Family Resource and Support Programs.

> family life education programs. The approach is responsive to interventions that are multi-, not uni-, dimensional—precisely the kinds of interventions that are found in most family support programs.
>
> But perhaps the most appealing aspect of the theory of change approach is that it is as helpful to program personnel as it is to evaluators. By demanding precise thinking about the purpose and outcomes of various activities, the process of building a theory of change forces program staff to examine their own assumptions and beliefs about what works, for whom, and under what conditions. With the evaluators and participants present, activities that are and are not likely to yield the desired outcomes can be identified and the program refined accordingly. In this respect, the process is valued by providers. (pp. 115-116)

Logic Models as Blueprints of Theories of Change

A theory of change is perhaps best represented in a visual manner via a logic model (see Logic Model Resources Appendix at the end of this chapter). A logic model is a mental map of the program. In developing a logic model, FLEs inventory the resources provided; identify the activities families engage in; and connect resources, program activities, and the range of outcomes they expect as a result of participating (ideally on one sheet of paper). Some FLEs are very enthusiastic about this idea and create elaborate maps that go beyond describing the program's basic components and outcomes by illustrating contextual elements affecting families. Others use a series of "if-then" statements to help readers of the logic model understand the relationships between certain activities and results while others try to represent the dynamic nature of their programs by creating maps that look like flow charts.

A logic model is an effective communication tool because it provides someone unfamiliar with the program (a funder, a board member, or a new staff person) an orientation to its essential components, how participants move through the program, and the results families are meant to experience. Logic models are also essential in organizing the evaluation process. It reminds family life educators and evaluators to pay attention to the program's process as much as the results. Data collected over time can inform the further development of the program's theory of change so it becomes a learning tool for FLEs. When used in this manner, the logic model can be useful to both internal and external audiences.

It is not the intention of this article to explain how to develop logic models, as there are many good resources available for practitioners (see Logic Model Resources Appendix). In addition, many evaluators offer this service as part of their consultation work. However, a logic model is given in Figure 1 to provide the reader with an understanding of what a basic logic model looks like.

Developing promotional outcomes and indicators in the logic model

Outcomes are an essential component of the theory of change and the corresponding logic model and yet, evaluators have not used this term consistently. Terms like results, performance measures, benefits, milestones, benchmarks, targets, goals, impacts, indicators, and objectives are all used interchangeably, which are different from outcomes: immediate, short-term, initial, intermediate, or long-term. The decision about which terms to use is less important than building a common understanding of these terms amongst the workgroup.

Family Support America (2005) defines an outcome as a desired condition of well-being for children, families, and communities. An outcome grows out of the question, "What do we want for children and families who participate in this program?" After the evaluability assessment phase has been completed and the evaluation design is being developed, evaluators and FLEs also create indicators. An indicator is a measure that helps to quantify the achievement of an outcome. Identifying an indicator grows out of the question, "How do we know if we are making progress on this outcome?" "What evidence do we have that leads us to believe we're moving in the right direction?

Developing outcomes and indicators that are promotional in nature is a relatively new trend in the field of family life education. This trend emerged from taking a strengths-based or empowerment approach to working with families (Dunst, Trivette, & Deal, 1988; Garbarino, 1982; Rappaport, 1981, 1987; Zigler & Berman, 1983). Instead of viewing families as problems in need of fixing, families are viewed as having strengths that they bring to the relationship formed between the family life educator and the family members. While family life educators' interactions with families may be changing, the outcomes used to describe the results we want to see for families and the data we collect to chart our progress (indicators) has been slow to follow.

With support from the Robert Wood Johnson Foundation, Family Support America (2005) worked with states involved in its *States Initiative Project* to advance using promotional outcomes and indicators at the federal, state, and local level. Examples of promotional outcomes and indicators contrasted with traditional outcomes and indicators are provided in Figure 2. It is

Figure 2. Contrasting Promotional and Traditional Outcomes and Indicators

Promotional Outcomes and Indicators	Traditional Outcomes and Indicators
Outcome: Children succeeding in school **Indicator:** Percent of parents actively engaged in their children's learning and education	**Outcome:** Children failing in school **Indicator:** Percent of children failing standardized tests, involved in federal programs (like Title I), or dropping out of school
Outcome: Youth development **Indicator:** Percent of youth whose families set clear expectations, rules, and consequences	**Outcome:** Problem youth **Indicator:** Percent of youth involved in the juvenile justice system, teen pregnancies, or rates of substance use
Outcome: Stable families **Indicator:** Percent of parents who have someone to rely on (a support network)	**Outcome:** Unstable families **Indicator:** Percent of parents experiencing depression or involved in the mental health system
Outcome: Supportive community **Indicator:** Percent of individuals volunteering in their community	**Outcome:** Unhealthy community **Indicator:** Crime rates, poverty rates, unemployment rates, housing vacancy rates

Note: Family Support America (2005). Evaluation and family support: Promotional outcomes and indicators. Chicago, IL: Family Support America.

interesting to note that extensive data collection systems have been created to measure how children, youth, parents, and communities are failing while little has been done to measure strengths that exist among these different populations.

While articulating a theory of change, creating a logic model, and developing promotional outcomes and indicators may seem like basic tasks most organizations would complete independently, evaluators often find themselves facilitating these processes in the early stages of an evaluation project.

During this process, it is not uncommon to discover that FLEs do not share the same beliefs about how their program works. Often FLEs have not had the chance to articulate their beliefs. Differing beliefs occurs for many reasons. Sometimes it results from staff working in the program for different lengths of time (they see the program operating differently because of their experiences). Sometimes divergent beliefs occur when staff is involved in providing direct services off-site and they do not have time to gather and develop a common understanding of how the program operates. Or from grant writers working on extremely tight deadlines frame the program and its outcomes without necessary staff input. It is important for FLEs to see the multiple benefits gained by spending time conducting an evaluability assessment.

After developing a theory of change, mapping out a logic model, and identifying promotional outcomes and indicators, family life educators have reached the final stages of an evaluability assessment. At this point, staff may want to determine whether a commitment exists to continue with programming and the corresponding evaluation tasks. If they choose to move forward Jacobs (1988) Five-Tiered Approach to evaluation provides a valuable framework to guide the next steps of the process.

The Five-Tiered Approach to Evaluation

The Five-Tiered Approach (FTA) was originally created with family life education programs in mind. Regardless of whether the program is small and relatively new, or large and well-established, FLEs will find this model a welcome approach to evaluation for several reasons. First, Jacobs (1988) approaches the concept of evaluation from a broad perspective. The FTA model includes needs assessment evaluation, formative evaluation, and summative evaluation. Second, the FTA presents evaluation activities in a developmental fashion that mirrors how programs evolve over time. Third, as a program matures, Jacobs advises FLEs to evaluate on a deeper level in order to provide evidence that supports increased investment in the program over time. The model assumes that as programs develop, organizations must build in a variety of resources (time, money, and skills) to address increasing evaluation tasks. Fourth, although progression through the tiers appears to be sequential, Jacobs acknowledges the need for flexibility in the real world where programming occurs. Jacobs suggests that practitioners using the FTA will likely combine evaluation activities from more than one tier, cycle back through tiers, or return to the first tier and reassess strengths and needs as the community changes over time. Fifth, Jacobs encourages practitioners to adopt the view that evaluation is a process, not an event. By linking evaluation tasks to each stage of program development, the FTA makes it clear that program development and evaluation are parallel paths that should be integrated.

Jacobs' Five-Tiered Approach includes: 1) Needs assessment, 2) Monitoring and accountability, 3) Quality review and program clarification, 4) Achieving outcomes, and 5) Establishing impact (see Figure 3). The following section describes each tier in detail.

Level One: Pre-implementation Tier

Before a program is implemented, a case needs to be made that the program is justified, feasible and appropriate for the intended audience. Assessments are usually conducted by organizations as a means of gathering evidence to make their case to funders or the community. In level one of the FTA, Jacobs outlines several types of assessments that FLEs may use: prospective assessments (implemented before a program is established or revised), retrospective assessments (conducted after the program has been implemented), and evaluability assessments (described earlier in this article).

Many scholars (Kretzmann & McKnight, 1993; Rossi & Freeman, 1993) distinguish between three types of prospective assessments that may be used during the programs' pre-implementation phase (needs assessment, demand assessment, or asset-based community development approach.

The type of assessment most practitioners are familiar with is referred to as a *needs assessment*. Rossi and Freeman define a needs assessment as a type of study where others (often family life educators) describe what they think somebody else needs (usually a group of people who are perceived to be "at-risk" of some problem). A second type of assessment is called a *demand assessment* (Rossi & Freeman, 1993). A demand assessment involves potential participants describing what they want or need and the types of supports they are most likely to use. Kretzman and McKnight (1993) postulate the third type of assessment which is critical of society's tendency to focus on people's needs, problems and deficiencies. Instead, Kretzman and McKnight propose an *asset-based community development approach* believing that strong communities are built through a process of mapping the assets, skills, and abilities of citizens and institutions at a local neighborhood level. These three types of prospective assessments do not need to be mutually exclusive. A pre-implementation study might blend the best aspects of all three types of assessments described here.

Thoroughly conducting a prospective assessment usually takes time—time that may not be available when funders or political leaders want to act quickly. This situation places FLEs in an difficult position—funding is available, political will is

Figure 3. The Five-Tiered Approach to Program Evaluation

Evaluation Level	Purpose of Evaluation	Audiences	Tasks	Types of Data to be Collected and Analyzed
Level 1 Implementation Tier	1. To document the need for a particular program within community 2. To demonstrate the fit between community needs and proposed program 3. To provide "data groundwork"	1. Potential funders 2. Community/citizen groups	1. Detail basic characteristics of proposed program 2. Conduct community needs assessment to support establishment of such program 3. Revise proposed program coordinated to assessed needs	1. Locally generated statistics that describe populations and needs for service (including public/personal costs of not providing the program) 2. Interviews with community leaders on seriousness of problem 3. Interviews or survey data from prospective participants
Level 2 Accountability Tier	1. To document program's a. utilization b. entrenchment c. penetration into target population 2. To justify current expenditures 3. To increase expenditures 4. To build a constituency	1. Funders, donors 2. Community leaders, media	1. Describe accurately program participants and services provided 2. Provide accurate cost information per unit of service	1. Client-specific monitoring data 2. Service-specific monitoring data a. Case material b. Data from interviews with clients indicating clients' needs and responses c. Community (nonuser) reactions to program
Level 3 Program ClarificationTier	1. To provide information to program staff to improve program	1. Program staff 2. Program participants	1. Question basic assumptions: what kinds of services for whom and by whom? 2. Clarify and restate program's mission, goals, objectives, and strategies	1. Content of staff meetings, supervision sessions, interviews with staff 2. Observation by staff of program activities and staff process 3. Previously collected staff and service data 4. Interview data from parents on desired benefits to program 5. Client satisfaction information
Level 4 Progress Toward Objectives Tier	1. To provide information to staff to improve program 2. To document program effectiveness	1. Staff members 2. Program participants 3. Funders 4. Other programs	1. Examine outcomes (short-term) objectives 2. Derive measurable indicators of success for a majority of the outcome objectives 3. Decide on data analysis procedures 4. Assess differential effectiveness among individual clients 5. Assess community awareness among individual clients	1. Interview material regarding individual client's progress toward objectives 2. Standardized test scores for clients, where applicable 3. Client-specific information from criterion-referenced instruments 4. Client satisfaction data 5. Evidence of support/resistance to program in community
Level 5 Program Impact Tier	1. To contribute to knowledge development in the substantive fields of child development, family process, organizational theory, and/or to the refinement of evaluation practices 2. To produce evidence of differential effectiveness among alternative program approaches 3. To suggest program models worthy of replication.	1. Academic and research communities 2. Policymakers at federal, state, and local levels 3. General public, through the media 4. Potential program directors and funders	1. Delineate specific impact objectives that are to be achieved, presumably through the accretion of short-term objectives' success 2. Identify measures(s) that can assess enduring and/or lifestyle changes among participants 3. Develop evaluation plan that reflects common understanding among evaluator(s), program personnel, contractor (if different from program)	1. Quantifiable client-specific data, including standardized test results collected over time (longitudinal client data) 2. Control group data or comparison group standards 3. Qualitative client data, including record reviews, client interviews, etc. 4. Cost-effectiveness information, necessary for planning program replication

on their side, but the information needed to plan a well-designed program is lacking. One option may be to move forward with programming and conduct a retrospective assessment (Jacobs, Kapuscik, Williams, & Kates, 2000). A retrospective assessment allows practitioners to go through a process (examining needs, demands, or assets) shortly after the program has been implemented. Information collected during a retrospective assessment allows FLEs to go through the planning phase again. It also allows them to gather needed data that can be used as a baseline for future evaluation efforts.

Level Two: Accountability Tier

At the second tier, programs are operating and evaluation provides information to family life educators for monitoring purposes. Family life educators working with programs at this stage should be able to provide a clear description of the participants, program activities and staffing, and costs for delivering these services.

In order to describe program participants, an array of family characteristics will need to be documented depending on the type of program, funding requests and what FLEs want and need to know. For example, in a program designed for babies and their mothers, it might be important to know how many mothers and babies are enrolled; their ages; and perhaps some information regarding the mothers' educational background, income, employment situation, or family status. In a program for parents who have a child with special needs, more information might be gathered about the child: the type of special need and supportive services the family is accessing to help care for their child. Family life educators working with immigrant or refugee families might be interested in other types of information. What is the family's country of origin? Did the family come directly from their country of origin to the United States or did they spend time in a refugee camp? How long has the family lived in their current location and in the United States? Which languages do families speak?

Collecting information to describe the program participants' demographics serves several purposes. First, it allows FLEs to determine whether they are reaching the audience of people they hoped would be involved in the program. Second, it demonstrates integrity on the part of the organization when staff respond quickly and accurately to inquiries about who is participating. Third, having a clear sense of who the intended audience is makes it easier to build a referral network with other practitioners.

In addition to describing the participants, it is valuable for family life educators to be able to specify programming activities and the staff involved in delivering these activities. Again, FLEs often develop a plan for who will be working in the program and what will be offered to families before the program is actually funded and implemented. The changes that occur in program activities and staffing patterns from the time the funding proposal is written to the time activities are delivered can be dramatic. Sometimes change is a result of staff turnover or because the original plans were too ambitious and need to be scaled down. Sometimes the full amount of money requested for programming was not awarded to the organization and programs are redesigned to accommodate available funds. Or, practitioners offering the same program in a different site may customize it to respond to be more responsive to family needs (i.e., single-parent families in Site A versus blended families in Site B). Regardless of the reasons for the change, being clear about the current program operations and staffing patterns allows FLEs to create the "glass box" Killion (2000) describes and explain how outcomes (data collected at Level Four) are or are not achieved.

Most family life educators know how much it costs to offer a program but some cannot speak to the costs on an individual or per family basis. As professionals, we have a reasonable sense of what it costs for some approaches to working with families but not for others. How much does it cost to send a public health nurse to visit every family in a rural county with a newborn? Using a sliding fee scale, how much should a two-parent family pay to take part in a parent education and support group for one year? Which is more cost-effective: a therapeutic preschool setting for a child with behavior problems or family therapy?

Why is it necessary to document the costs of providing programming? Usually, information about costs of programming or services is linked in some way to whether the cost is worth the benefit that was produced. Sorting out the issue of costs and benefits is part of understanding the bigger question of which programs are of greatest benefit to which families. Decision-makers want to know the answer to this question because it is an important issue related to program replication.

What costs information should family life education programs be tracking? At a minimum, organizations should strive to monitor the following four elements involved in determining costs:

1) The amount of fiscal support receiving for the program (grants, contracts, reimbursements);
2) The amount of money resulting from fundraising activities (capital campaigns, board fundraisers, publications sales);
3) Indirect or in-kind support (volunteer time or donated supplies); and
4) Program operating costs (personnel, overhead, operations, or supplies) (Jacobs et al., 2000).

Level Three: Program Clarification Tier

Evaluation data collected at level three provides FLEs with information to improve the program. Program staff operating in this tier will continue to focus on collecting formative data and revisiting some of the questions asked earlier in levels one and two. However, the questions need to go deeper at level three. Fortunately, practitioners at this tier usually have more experience and more data to work with because the program has been established for a longer period of time. For example, while one of the tasks in the second tier was to describe the demographics of the parents involved in the program, practitioners would be wise to start gathering more information about the parents' experiences. How are parents benefiting (or not) from being involved in the program? Do parents believe the program is worth their time? Are parents satisfied with the program?

Besides gathering information from parents, FLEs may observe the program as it operates, lead discussions about program operations during staff meetings, or review the results of monitoring data collected at levels two and three with staff and administrators. The purpose of asking deeper questions at tier three not only serves as ongoing program monitoring function, it allows staff to question some of their basic program assumptions (e.g., Is this the right package of services for these families?). Ideally, data collection at this tier provides family life educators with information that can improve the program.

Level Four: Progress Toward Objectives Tier

At level four, the program has been operating for an even longer period of time and FLEs will begin to shift the focus away from formative to summative evaluation tasks. While information is still needed for program improvement, FLEs should also be ready to take a look at the effectiveness of their program. Family life educators employed in programs at this level are often motivated to collect information about the success of their program that goes beyond their anecdotal stories. External audiences (funders, legislators, and FLEs in the field) usually expect that programs at this tier should be able to provide evidence of their accomplishments.

One of the ways to study program effectiveness involves collecting objective data about the changes participants experience while in the program or the progress they make toward goals (Jacobs, 1988). Collecting summative evaluation data allows FLEs to capitalize on all the evaluation work done in previous tiers. If an assessment was conducted prior to program implementation, baseline data now exists for comparison purposes at this level. Family life educators are able to accurately describe the demographic characteristics of families, the services offered to them, and provide accurate data about how much this service costs to offer the program to a family. Agency staff is familiar with this information, it is complemented by information collected from families about their perceived program benefits, and whether they are satisfied with the services. With this groundwork in place, it makes sense to study short-term outcomes of the program identified as part of the logic model. Studying these outcomes begins to answer the question, "Are we making a difference?"

For the first time, family life educators may look to an external evaluator to provide consultation around designing and conducting an evaluation project. An evaluation consultant can help family life educators design a study that is appropriate for the program and their participants. A consultant can help identify the indicators that will provide evidence about whether participants are achieving the desired outcomes. Agency staff might ask the consultant to help with the design of methods and procedures to collect data (if existing tools are not available or appropriate), with the analysis of the data, and reporting and dissemination tasks. A skilled evaluator working with an engaged and enthusiastic group of family life educators can respond to level four type questions from external audiences. "Why do some families achieve the outcomes while others do not?" "Why do parents on one side of the county get involved at a much higher rate compared to other neighborhoods?" "Why are some parents less satisfied with the program?"

Level Five: Program Impact Tier

The evaluation tasks associated with level five are sophisticated, complex, and may last several years. All previous evaluation efforts bear fruit at this tier. According to Jacobs (1988), few smaller-scale organizations reach this tier of evaluation because of program demands. At this level it is more common to see nationally replicated programs teaming with university faculty or larger research firms to carry out program impact studies. Studies of programs like the Perry Preschool Project (Berrueta-Clement, Schweinhart, Barnett, Epstein, & Weikart, 1984), Parents as Teachers (Owen & Mulvihill, 1994), the Comprehensive Child Development Program (St. Pierre, Layzer, Goodson, & Bernstein, 1999), or the Nurse Home Visitation Program (Olds, Henderson, Kitzman, Eckenrode, Cole, & Tatelbaum, 1999) are examples of level five evaluation projects.

The purpose of level five evaluation differs from the others. In a sense, the lines between evaluation and research begin to blur at this tier. While evaluation information gathered at other levels is useful to the organization and its family life educators, the results of evaluation at this tier are much more directed toward external audiences. For example, federal or state level decision-makers may use information gathered at this tier to determine which types of programs are most worthwhile to fund (e.g., targeted versus universal home visiting programs or placement versus reunification services for children in the maltreatment system). Non-profit administrators might use the results to help them select a program to implement in the future. Academic faculty or researchers collect and use program impact data in order to answer the question, "Is this local program ready for replication on a broader level?" Funders use the results of these studies to select effective programs that meet their "research-based" criterion. And finally, the family support field relies on these studies to advance the work of all family life educators.

Concluding Thoughts about the Evaluation Process

Many family life educators value Patton's practical focus on the utilization of evaluation results. "[Evaluation is]...the systematic collection of information about the activities, characteristics, and outcomes of programs to make judgments about the program, improve program effectiveness, and/or inform decisions about future programming" (1997, p. 23). However,

Preskill and Torres (1999) take Patton's philosophy to the next level and write that the goal of evaluation should also involve "...developing a community of practitioners who inquire daily about their progress and use their learning to improve themselves and the organization" (p. xix).

This philosophy supports the pragmatic use of evaluation results, but assumes that the discussion should not stop at this point. Preskill and Torres believe that the evaluative inquiry process should focus on questioning and debating the value of what is done in organizations. Integrating programming and evaluation, using evaluation results for program improvement, and employing the evaluative inquiry process as a means for personal and organizational learning are lofty goals. Yet, when family life educators merge program development and program evaluation they are doing because it is in the best interests of children and their families.

References

Berrueta-Clement, J. R., Schweinhart, L. J., Barnett, W. S., Epstein, A. S., & Weikart, D. P. (1984). *Changed lives: The effects of the Perry Preschool Program on youths through age 19.* Ypsilanti, MI: High/Scope Educational Research Foundation.

Chelimsky, E., & Shadish, R. (1997). *Evaluation for the 21st century: A handbook.* Thousand Oaks, CA: Sage.

Chen, H. (1990). *Theory-driven evaluations.* Newbury Park, CA: Sage.

Dunst, C., Trivette, C., & Deal, A. (1988). *Enabling and empowering families.* Cambridge, MA: Brookline Books.

Family Support America. (2005). *Evaluation and family support: Promotional outcomes and indicators.* Chicago, IL: Author.

Garbarino, J. (1982). *Children and families in the social environment.* New York: Aldine Publishing.

Jacobs, F. H. (1988). The five-tiered approach to evaluation: Context and implementation. In H. B. Weiss & F. H. Jacobs (Eds.), *Evaluating family programs* (pp. 37-68). Hawthorne, NY: Aldine de Gruyter.

Jacobs, F. H., Kapuscik, J. L., Williams, P., H., & Kates, E. (2000). *Making it count: Evaluating family preservation services.* Medford, MA: Tufts University.

Joint Committee on Standards for Educational Evaluation. (1981). *Standards for evaluations of educational programs, projects, and materials.* New York: McGraw Hill.

Kagan, S. L. (1989). Using a theory of change approach in a national evaluation of family life education programs. In. K. Fulbright-Anderson, A. C. Kubisch & J. P. Connell (Eds.), *New approaches to evaluating community initiatives: Vol. 2. Theory, measurement, and analysis* (pp. 113-122). Washington, DC: The Aspen Institute.

Killion, J. (2002). *Assessing impact: Evaluating staff development.* Oxford, OH: National Staff Development Council.

Kretzman, J. P., & McKnight, J. L. (1993). *Building communities from the inside out: A path toward finding and mobilizing a community's assets.* Evanston, IL: Center for Urban Affairs and Policy Research, Northwestern University.

Maiden, R. P. (1988). Employee assistance program evaluation in a federal government agency. *Employee Assistance Quarterly, 3*(3/4), 191-203.

Olds, D. L., Henderson, C. R. Kitzman, H. J., Eckenrode, J. J., Cole, R. E., & Tatelbaum, (1999). Prenatal and infancy home visitation by nurses: Recent findings. In R. E. Behrman (Ed.), The Future of Children, *Home visiting: Recent program evaluations* (pp. 44-65). Los Altos, CA: David and Lucile Packard Foundation.

Owen, M. T., & Mulvihill, B. A. (1994). Benefits of a parent education and support program in the first three years. *Family Relations, 43*, 206-212.

Patton, M. Q. (1997). *Utilization-focused evaluation: A new century text.* Thousand Oaks, CA: Sage.

Peisher, A., Sewell, M., & Kirk, R. (2001). *Outcome accountability for family life education programs* (Vol. 2) [Workbook and Instruments]. Chapel Hill, NC: FRIENDS National Resource Center for Community Based Family Resource and Support Programs.

Pietrzak, J., Ramler, M., Renner, T., Ford, L., & Gilbert, N. (1990). *Practical program evaluation: Examples from child abuse prevention.* Newbury Park, CA: Sage.

Preskill, H., & Torres, R. T. (1999). *Evaluative inquiry for learning in organizations.* Thousand Oaks, CA: Sage.

Rappaport, J. (1981). In praise of paradox: A social policy of empowerment over prevention. *American Journal of Community Psychology, 9*, 1-25.

Rappaport, J. (1987). Terms of empowerment/exemplars of prevention: Toward a theory for community psychology. *American Journal of Community Psychology, 15*(2), 121-128.

Rossi, P. H., & Freeman, H. E. (1993). *Program evaluation: A systematic approach.* Newbury Park, CA: Sage.

St. Pierre, R. G., & Layzer, J. I., Goodson, B. D., & Bernstein, L. S. (1999). The effectiveness of comprehensive case management interventions: Evidence from the national evaluation of the Comprehensive Child Development Program. *American Journal of Evaluation, 20(1),* 15-34.

Sadd, S., & Grinc, R. M. (1994). Innovative neighborhood-oriented policing: An evaluation of community policing programs in eight cities. In P. O. Rosenbaum (Ed.*), The challenge of community policing: Testing the promise* (pp. 27-52). Thousand Oaks, CA: Sage.

Stufflebeam, D. (2001). Evaluation models. *New directions for evaluation, 89 (Spring)*, 7-98.

Wholey, J. S. (1977). Evaluability assessment. In L. Rutman (Ed.), *Evaluation research methods: A basic guide* (pp. 41-56). Beverly Hills, CA: Sage.

Worthen, B. R., & Sanders, J. R. (1987). *Educational evaluation: Alternative approaches and practical guidelines.* White Plains, NY: Longman, Inc.

Zigler, E., & Berman. W. (1983). Discerning the future of early childhood intervention. *American Psychologist, 38*, 894-906.

Logic Model Resources Appendix

FRIENDS-National Resource Center for Community-Based Child Abuse Prevention. Evaluation Toolkit Resources. Retrieved January 14, 2008 from www.friendsnrc.org/resources/print.htm.

United Way of America. (1996). *Measuring program outcomes: A practical approach (*0989). Retrieved January 14, 2008 from www.unitedwaystore.com.

W. K. Kellogg Foundation. (1990). *W. K. Kellogg foundation logic model development guide.* Retrieved January 14, 2008 from www.wkkf.org/default.aspx?tabid=101&CID=281&CatID=281&ItemID=2813669&NID=20&LanguageID=0

About the Author

Christa J. Treichel, Ph.D., is the President of Cooperative Ventures, an evaluation consulting firm working in partnership with community non-profit organizations, schools, government, hospitals, and cultural organizations to improve programming for children, youth and families. Email: treic004@umn.edu.

Ethical Thinking and Practice for Parent and Family Life Educators

DEVELOPED BY THE ETHICS COMMITTEE, MINNESOTA COUNCIL ON FAMILY RELATIONS

REVISED BY ADA ALDEN, BETTY COOKE, AND GLEN PALM

Parent and family life educators face difficult ethical issues on a daily basis regarding parenting practices that may be harmful to children, responding to parent remarks about their partners, or sharing information about a family with a professional in another agency. Some of these situations may be resolved by reviewing general principles of good practice with a colleague, while others may reveal a true ethical dilemma.

Parent and family educators are working with complex family systems, diverse belief and value systems and a variety of social institutions and agencies. Many face these issues in relative isolation and with limited guidance from an emerging field. This document was developed to offer a thoughtful and balanced approach to understanding ethical principles and a concrete process for using them to address difficult ethical issues and dilemmas.

History

The information on ethics described here was developed by the Ethics Committee of the Minnesota Council on Family Relations. This group has studied ethical thinking and behavior for parent and family life educators since 1992. This journey has involved an initial needs assessment of Minnesota parent and family educators, several workshops to develop and field test an inductive process for identifying guidelines and virtues for parent and family educators and consultation with professionals from other fields. The process led to new understandings and the development of a multi-perspective approach to ethics. The blending of the traditional ethical principles approach with virtues ethics and relational ethics was an outcome of meetings with Dr. William Doherty, Professor in Family Social Science at the University of Minnesota, who has adapted virtues and relational ethics to the field of family therapy. These three different approaches provide different, but compatible, lenses for understanding ethical practice. Together they provide a unique approach to ethics for parent and family life education.

A second set of workshops was developed to test and refine the integration of the three approaches and "fine tune" a case study process for generating ethical thinking and solutions. The guidelines and case study process presented here are a result of several workshops during 1995-1997, where practitioners applied the guidelines to case studies. The Ethics Committee has used input from these workshops to edit and refine the principles. The ethics process has been shared with both state and national audiences from 1997-2002 through workshops at local and national conferences. NCFR has published this information as part of a resource booklet for family life educators.

In 2007 the CFLE program went through a transition with the initiation of an exam as a new criterion for certification. The question about adopting an official code of ethics for CFLE came up during this time and the revision of the original MCFR document as a working code of ethics was proposed as a way to meet this need for CFLEs. A code of ethics provides an additional indicator of professionalism as the CFLE program continues to evolve and gain recognition. This document should be seen as a foundation for the CFLE code of ethics that could be adopted and revised as needed.

Integration of Three Approaches to Ethics

The ***relational ethics approach*** provides a starting place for understanding relationships as the context for making ethical decisions. This perspective allows for a careful examination of the multiple relationships that parent and family life educators encounter as a step towards applying principles. Parent and family life education professionals also see it as a guide for action. Striving for caring relationships in all professional interactions is the goal of relational ethics. Relational ethics provides a clear understanding of the immediate state of a relationship as well as goals for establishing a caring relationship. It provides both process and content for ethical behavior. General principles for developing caring, respectful relationships with family members are outlined in the section on Relational Ethics.

The ***principles approach to ethics*** has been linked to the relational ethics approach by organizing principles around the concept of relationships. This allows parent and family life educators as a group to articulate important principles that can guide interactions with different populations. The principles are intended to guide parent and family educators in everyday decisions and actions.

The third approach to ethical thinking involves the more individual lens of ***virtues ethics***. It attempts to fill in a gap in our current way of defining professional behavior that tends to focus more on technical competence than on moral character. Good practice in family life education should be tied to internal standards of excellence as well as external behavior. Virtues are "dispositions to do the right thing for the right reason."

Virtues can be defined on two different levels. The first level identifies core virtues that are necessary for every profession. These include virtues such as justice, truthfulness and courage. Their implementation varies over time and in specific professions. The second level includes those virtues that are essential for ethical practice in the current social context for parent and family life education.

Three essential virtues have emerged from the discussions between Ethics Committee members and practitioners:

1. **Caring**: A disposition to enhance the welfare of family members as agents in their own lives.
2. **Prudence/Practical Wisdom**: The ability to understand competing needs and decisions based on reflection and consultation.
3. **Hope/Optimism**: A disposition to look at the strengths of family members and other individuals and to see positive potential in situations related to family life.

These dispositions provide family life educators with internal strengths to think and behave in an ethical manner.

The strengths of a multi-perspective approach depend not only upon the richness of having different perspectives but also the dynamic tensions that keep a balance between absolutism and relativism. The creative tensions in this approach include (1) a balance between the dynamic nature of relationships and the more static nature of principles, (2) a balance between the individual in the context of a relationship and the group in thoughtful reflection of important principles and (3) a balance between wisdom of the past, learnings of the present and striving to be good in the future. These tensions provide a dynamic balance to ethical thinking as it continues to evolve through reflection and refinement.

Relational Ethics: An Introduction

The use of relational ethics is critical to work with families. The principles of relational ethics form a basis for understanding specific ethical dilemmas and guide practice first and foremost towards the development of caring and respectful relationships with all family members. Some of the important principles that assist family life educators towards this end are:

1. The parent and family life educator's relationship with individual family members, peers and the community is both the context and the point of contact for our ethical thinking and actions. This means that parent and family life

educators will focus on relationships in understanding ethical issues and depend upon the development of caring relationships to guide movement towards ethical actions.

2. Parent and family life educators bear the primary responsibility to initiate a relationship built on trust, caring and understanding. All relationships are two-way interactions and parent and family life educators cannot assure that all their relationships will be positive. However, parent and family life educators will model acceptance, caring and understanding towards family members and peers while pursuing a mutually respectful and caring relationship.

3. All relationships have predictable stages of development. Parent and family life educators will adjust their practice to their understanding of the state and stage of a relationship.

4. Parent and family life educators will bring a knowledge base of general principles about children and youth, parenting, family and community systems to share with family members. Parent and family life educators will work in collaboration with parents to understand how these principles apply to individual family members and situations.

5. Parent and family life educators will set boundaries on their relationships with family members and be responsible for potential negative influences of care taking beyond these limits. The intensity of relationships will vary but the good family life educator will be vigilant of his/her responsibility to nurture interdependence between family members and other community systems.

In many ways the caring and respectful relationships that parent and family life educators build with family members are analogous to healthy parent-child relationships. Parent and family life educators need to take the major responsibility for initiating healthy relationships and must work to maintain these relationships. In many cases relationships with adults quickly assume a stance of mutual respect and understanding. In other cases there may be a number of barriers that make this relationship more difficult to build into an egalitarian and respectful relationship. Parent and family life educators must continue to develop an understanding of the relationship process and how to best facilitate healthy relationships among family members, colleagues and themselves.

Ethical Principles for Parent and Family Life Educators

I. Relationships with Parents and Families

1. We will be aware of the impact we have on parents and family relations.
2. We will strive to understand families as complex, interactive systems where parents have the primary responsibility as educators, nurturers and limit-setters for their children.
3. We will respect cultural beliefs, backgrounds and differences and engage in practice that is sensitive to the diversity of child-rearing values and goals.
4. We will help parents and other family members recognize their strengths and work with them to set goals for themselves, their children and others.
5. We will respect and accept parents and other family members for who they are, recognizing their developmental level and circumstances.
6. We will support and challenge parents to continue to grow and learn about parenting and their child's development.
7. We will communicate respectfully and clearly with all family members.
8. We will communicate openly and truthfully about the nature and extent of services provided.
9. We will support diverse family values by acknowledging and examining alternative parenting practices that support healthy family relationships.
10. We will include parents/other family members as partners in problem solving and decision-making related to program design and implementation.
11. We will be proactive in stating child guidance principles and discipline guidelines and encourage non-violent child rearing.
12. We will create data privacy and confidentiality guidelines respectful of family members and protective of their legal rights.
13. We will provide a program environment that is safe and nurturing to all family members.
14. We will ensure that all family members have access to and are encouraged to participate in family education.

15. We will support family members as they make decisions about the use of resources to best meet family needs.
16. We will support healthy interpersonal relationships among all family members.
17. We will encourage family members to explore their values and promote healthy sexuality in their family.

II. Relationships with Children and Youth

1. We will treat children and youth with respect and sensitivity to their needs and rights as developing persons.
2. We will strive to understand children and youth in the context of their families.
3. We will do no harm to children and youth and insist on the same from others.
4. We will advocate for children and youth and their best interests at the same time that we work with the parents and other family members.
5. We will provide environments that are respectful of children and youth and sensitive to their developmental and individual needs.
6. We will support the right of all children and youth to have access to quality education, health and community resources.

III. Relationships with Colleagues and the Profession

1. We will value and promote diversity in staff.
2. We will provide staff with policies and support systems for addressing difficult situations with family members, colleagues and others.
3. We will follow data privacy policies that meet legal standards and are based on respect for family members.
4. We will follow the mandatory reporting of abusive family behavior in a respectful and prudent manner.
5. We will define our role as parent and family life educators and practice within our level of competence.
6. We will recognize the difference between personal and professional values in our professional interactions.
7. We will support the ongoing development of a knowledge base that guides us towards ethical and effective practice.
8. We will be committed to ongoing professional development to enhance our knowledge and skills.

IV. Relationships with Community/Society

1. We will be knowledgeable about community resources and make and accept informed, appropriate referrals.
2. We will be aware of the boundaries of our practice and know when and how to use other community resources for the benefit of family members.
3. We will communicate clearly and cooperate with other programs/agencies in order to best meet family needs.
4. We will advocate for laws and policies that reflect our changing knowledge base and the best interests of parents, families and communities.
5. We will respect and uphold laws and regulations that pertain to our practice as parent and family life educators and offer expertise to legal authorities based on professional knowledge.

Introduction to Process:

This process is provided as one concrete way for small groups of parent and family life educators to carefully examine an ethical dilemma using the approaches described earlier. It is critical to practice ethical thinking in this concrete manner to become familiar with both the principles and the process. This process can be done in approximately one hour as a part of staff meetings.

Process Steps:
Steps 1 through 4 focus on ethical thinking. This is important; give it plenty of time. Practitioners tend to leap to brainstorming possible actions/solutions before thoroughly engaging in the process.

Step 1. Identification of Relationships: Identify important relationships in the situation using the educator role as the primary focal point.

a. What is the relational field – what are all potential relationships in the case?

b. What is the primary caring relationship the educator needs to address in this case? (Examples: educator to family member, educator to group, educator to another staff person)

c. What do we know about this relationship – quality, stage of development, etc.?

Step 2. Application of Principles: Look over the list of principles to identify those that apply to the important relationship(s) in this situation. Decide which principles may be relevant to guiding ethical behavior. Are there any additional principles that might apply? Which are the 3-4 most relevant principles? Why? (Spend some time alone to select principles before discussing in small group.)

Step 3. Identification of Contradictions/Tensions: What are some potential/ actual contradictions or tensions among or between relevant principles?

Step 4. Identification of Possible Solutions: Brainstorm possible actions by the parent and family life educator – keeping in mind the relationship(s), the relevant principles, and the virtues.

Step 5. Selection of Actions: Select one action or combination of actions to use that reflects adherence to the ethical principles. All of the principles are important and should be addressed in a thoughtful and respectful manner.

Application of the Process to Real Life Dilemmas/Case Studies

The following real life ethical dilemma was discussed by a group of parent and family life educators, early educators and administrators using the case study process. This scenario illustrates how the case study process can be applied to make thoughtful decisions about ethical challenges.

CASE STUDY EXAMPLE: Culture and Gender Issues in the Early Childhood Classroom

A mother and her son attend an Early Childhood Family Education (ECFE) class for four year olds. They are from Somalia. The mother has limited English but participates well in the parenting class by listening and talking at length when asked a question. She is quietly involved with her son during parent-child interaction time. Her son loves the children's room. He is eagerly involved in most areas of the room, with a clear preference and a strong interest in the housekeeping area. During parent-child time, mom steps back when her son enters the kitchen area.

At the home visit, the parent educator meets the father and siblings. It is clear that only the father is going to speak with the parent educator, with only a brief "hello" from the mother. The parent educator is treated respectfully and positively. The father says he is thankful that his son is in the class and he hopes he will continue to learn English, letters and numbers.

After a few weeks, the father sends a message indicating that his son is not to play in the kitchen area. Household work is not for boys and Somali males have nothing to do with such activities. There was no discussion of the housekeeping area at the home visit.

Staff Discussion

The group began the discussion by jumping immediately to suggesting strategies, but they were directed back to the process. It is common when staff members discuss an ethical dilemma that they want to solve the problem and look for an immediate solution or action. A true ethical dilemma does not have a quick and easy resolution because important ethical principles are in conflict or tension with each other.

Steps 1: Identify Important Relationships

The group identified that the important relationships were with the mother, father and the child. The relationships with the mother and child are more established through their regular attendance at the ECFE class. The relationship with the father has been positive but limited to one home visit. The father appears to be the decision-maker in the family and maintaining a positive relationship with him will be important.

Step 2: Identify Relevant Ethical Principles

The staff identified the relevant principles for this situation in Part I: Relationships with Parents and Families:

I.2. We will strive to understand families as complex, interactive systems where parents have the primary responsibility as educators, nurturers and limit-setters for their children.

I.3. We will respect cultural beliefs, backgrounds and differences and engage in practice that is sensitive to the diversity of child-rearing values and goals

I.10. We will include parents/other family members as partners in problem solving and decision-making related to program design and implementation.

I.13. We will provide a program environment that is safe and nurturing to all family members.

In Part II: Relationships with Children and Youth, three principles were identified.

II.4. We will advocate for children and youth and their best interests at the same time that we work with the parents and other family members.

II.5. We will provide environments that are respectful of children and youth and sensitive to their developmental and individual needs.

II.6. We will support the right of all children and youth to have access to quality education, health and community resources.

Step 3: Identify Contradictions/Tensions between Principles

The first proposal was that Principle I.3, respect for cultural beliefs, would be most important. Several people murmured agreement. It then became apparent that this principle was in conflict with Principle II. 5, providing environments sensitive to a child's/youth's developmental and individual needs. No one approved of removing the kitchen area from the environment or of restricting the child when others had free choice. Many important questions were raised during this discussion of principles.

- How Americanized does the family want to be?
- Are they here permanently or just for a year of two?
- Could we leave it to mother to restrict the child?
- Is the Housekeeping area important and a cultural value for other families?
- What other dramatic play areas could there be?

There was also discussion that males should be taught to cook and clean as a matter of self-sufficiency and gender equality. Children learn a great deal through the dramatic play in the housekeeping area. In this situation the staff could help the father to see the benefits of learning that the kitchen play area provided for his son.

The staff struggled with the concept and boundaries of cultural respect. Should families from other cultures adapt to American culture and respect the housekeeping area as an important part of the American preschool environment and curriculum? If American children were attending a Japanese school, would we expect them to remove their shoes out of respect for the culture? It was noted that at U.S. military child care centers, the sand table often contains tanks, planes and "army guys". This type of play is culturally relevant, yet when asked, most of the staff members involved in this discussion would not enroll their child in a program that had a "gun corner" or a learning center that included guns. Cultural values embedded in the environment and activities of a preschool became apparent in the discussion. It was clear that some values were important to the staff such as equality, respect for household tasks and respect for cultural differences and that they were in conflict or tension in this particular situation.

These questions helped the group see the potential contradictions and tensions between principles. Many staff members wanted to say that protecting culture was the most important principle. They were sensitive to the issue of people being asked to deny their culture. They valued diversity and respected families' differences. However, when they had to defend the strategies that using only Principle 1.3, respect for cultural diversity, would entail, they realized that their primary goal was to provide a diverse and responsive environment for children. This included allowing children free choice, responding to children's interests and teaching children about "real life." Understanding the tensions between these two principles set the stage for considering possible solutions.

Step 4: Identify Possible Solutions

As the staff discussed strategies and implications, the following question arose: If we are unable to assist the family in becoming comfortable with our curriculum, is taking the stance we have chosen worth the risk of losing the child from the program?

The following strategies were proposed:

- Discuss with the family about what children learn through the housekeeping area. Indicate that this is the area that consistently has the most social interaction. This may be particularly good for their son's develop of language.
- Make a strong statement that one of our goals is to be respectful of family culture. Let the family know that staff would never insist that the child play in that area.
- Ask the parents if they had ideas on how to resolve this situation.
- Inform the parents that their son would be observed to see what aspect of the housekeeping area he seemed to be most interested in and then try to offer different play settings that would address those interests.
- Inform the parents that the kitchen area would not always be part of the classroom. The staff said they could be comfortable with the kitchen area being absent 1/3 to 1/2 of the year.
- Thank the parents for bringing this dilemma to staff and giving them the opportunity to consider the issue. Explain that this was a learning experience for all the staff in understanding different cultural values.

Step 5: Select an Action(s)

This case led to selecting a number of the identified options to implement. The first was to talk to the parents about the issues and see if they had ideas for resolving the situation. The early childhood teachers would add new dramatic play props to transform the housekeeping area into a variety of different dramatic play opportunities for the children. Discussing with the parents about what children learn through the dramatic play and why the housekeeping area is part of the environment was the final action the staff would take.

PRACTICE CASE STUDIES

The following two case studies are presented as examples for practitioners to use to practice the process on their own.

Case Study 1: Mother, Daughter, Father Dilemma

In one mother-child pair in your class for toddlers and their parents, the toddler has several developmental delays and the mother has some, too. The mother alludes to the father being abusive. In talking with others who deal with the mom, you have been made aware of the dominance of the father and his family. How can you support the mom and daughter without causing upset in the family relationships? You have been told that the father will pull the family from any support if he feels threatened. What does the "good" family educator do?

Case Study 2: Twin Dilemma

As a parent educator for an Early Childhood Family Education class you meet with colleagues in early childhood special education who tell you about a family with twins. One of the twins is a child with typical developmental needs; the other is a child with Down syndrome. The early childhood special education staff feels that the child with Down syndrome would be best served at home with services provided by special education staff. The staff is focused on best practices for the child in need of their expertise, special education. The special education staff recommends the mother bring only the typically developing child to class.

You agree that the child with Down syndrome would be best served with in-home services. You also think the mother should be allowed to bring both children to the regular ECFE parenting class. The special education staff does not think that is necessary. However, you see that the family is a system and recognize that this is a mother of two children and a family of four to consider. What does the "good" family educator do?

References

Doherty, W. J. (1992). Virtues ethics: The person of the therapist. *AFTA Newsletter*, 19-21.

Feeney, S., & Kipnis, K. (1985). Public policy report: Professional ethics in early childhood education. *Young Children*, *40*(3), 54-58.

Kipnis, K. (1987). How to discuss professional ethics. *Young Children*, *42*(4), 26-30.

Radomski, M. A. (1986). Professionalization of early childhood education. *Young Children*, *41*(5), 20-23.

Palm, G. (1994, Winter). Developing ethical guidelines for family educators. *Views*, 12-13.

Palm, G. (2003). Ethics. In D. J. Bredehoft & M. J. Walcheski (Eds.), *Family Life education: Integrating theory and practice* (2nd ed.) (pp. 125-130). Minneapolis, MN.

Minnesota Council on Family Relations Ethics Committee Members

Ada Alden, Ed.D., CFLE, Dawn Cassidy, M.Ed., CFLE, Betty Cooke, Ph.D., CFLE, Marietta Rice, M.A., Glen Palm, Ph.D., CFLE, Joyce Schultenover, Kathy Zanner, M.S., LMFT, Anne Stokes, Ed.D., and **Sue Stoner, M.A.**

This document serves as the guidelines for ethical thinking and practice for the National Council on Family Relations (NCFR) Certified Family Life Educator (CFLE) program.

The Development and Teaching of the Ethical Principles and Guidelines for Family Scientists

Rebecca A. Adams, David C. Dollahite.
Kathleen R. Gilbert, and Robert E. Keim

Our society is more pluralistic, faster paced, and more mobile than in the past. Family roles and structures are evolving, and there is deep disagreement on family issues, values, and the definition of "family" itself. Because of the complex, sensitive, and personal nature of the family, family professionals have a distinct relationship with society. Unlike telephone solicitors or used-car salespersons whose motto may be "Let the buyer beware," family professionals are expected to be trustworthy, competent, and ethical (Arcus, 1999; Keith-Spiegel & Koocher, 1985; Leigh, Lowen, & Lester, 1986).

In the past, when family life was less complex, the sentiment among some family professionals seemed to be that no ethical code was needed. Family scholars, however, have shown that psychoeducational interventions used in family education and enrichments are increasingly popular, potent, and potentially harmful (Brock, 1993; Doherty, Lester, & Leigh, 1986). For example, educators who teach about families can lead students to explore their personal lives in ways that can lead to positive growth and development. At the same time, however, the interaction also can open emotional wounds that are still unhealed. Similarly, therapists who counsel individuals and families and researchers who gather data from individuals and families can have a powerful impact on the emotional welfare of their clients and research participants.

The literature also indicates that university professors who teach the value and emotion-laden content found in family courses have serious ethical obligations and often experience complex ethical dilemmas (Allen & Crosbie-Burnett, 1992; Knaub & Meredith, 1991; Quoss, 1993; Swartzlander, Pace & Stamler, 1993). For example, a significant unique ethical issue for teachers of family life courses in formal educational settings involves the potentially troubling combination of highly personal and value-laden information and evaluating the work of the student for a grade (Brock, 1993; Lee, Weber, & Knaub, 1994). Many family professionals indicate they find themselves unprepared to adequately respond to the ethical dimensions of the cultural and structural complexities of today's families (Knaub & Meredith; Quoss). Responding to the growing need for a code of ethics that would guide the professional conduct of its members, the Family Science Section of the National

Council on Family Relations (NCFR) undertook the task of developing a code. This article (a) describes the developmental process of the *Ethical Principles and Guidelines for Family Scientists* adopted by NCFR, unanimously approved at the April 1998 board meeting; (b) reviews the literature on ethics education and applies principles from other disciplines to the family science context; and (c) delineates the ethical principles and guidelines themselves (see Appendix A).

The Development of Ethical Principles and Guidelines

The NCFR was founded in 1938 as an informal organization "a welcomed relief from the big, disciplined, aloof organizations to which most of us belong" (Walters & Jewson, 1988, p.iii). Membership was interdisciplinary and included participants in such areas as law, sociology, religion, home economics, marriage counseling, psychology, medicine, and education.

A constitution was developed, but a code of ethics was not. In retrospect, such a code may not have been needed because the purpose of the organization as defined by the constitution was "to advance the cultural values that are now principally secured through family relations for the advantage of the individual and strength of the nation" (Walters & Jewson, p.1). The time was not ripe to ask the questions: Which cultural values? What family structure?

The NCFR was not alone in lacking a code of ethics at that time. The American Psychological Association (APA) established an ethics committee in 1938, but an official code was not adopted until 1953 (Keith-Spiegel & Koocher, 1985).

The perception of the NCFR as an informal organization continued into the 1960s, when Jessie Bernard wrote, "[NCFR] is an association of professionals but not a professional association of professionals... Its members come together to think about problems, to teach one another, to learn from one another" (Bernard, 1964, p.29). Many NCFR members belonged to other professional organizations, such as the APA, the American Sociological Association, and the American Association for Marriage and Family Therapy. Each had its own codes of ethics and served as the primary professional organization for its members.

At the same time Bernard argued that NCFR was not a professional organization, interest in professionalizing it appeared to grow. For example, concern for professional competency regarding teaching about families lead to the establishment in 1964 of a committee on Standards and Certification for Family Life Educators. Even though a chapter in the *Handbook of Marriage and the Family* (Kerckhoff, 1964) urged the field of family life education to develop a code of ethics, interest focused on other issues of professionalization, and no membership code of ethics was addressed (Walters & Jewson, 1988).

In his presidential address at the 1982 NCFR annual meeting, Wesley Burr "struck terror in the hearts of traditionalists in the family field" (Walters & Jewson, 1988, p. 115) by suggesting that the study of family be recognized as a separate discipline, albeit a young discipline. He also suggested that it met five of the seven criteria needed to be considered a unique discipline and should be considered a newly emerging one (Burr & Leigh, 1983). Although response to Burr's proposal was mixed, many family scholars and practitioners began thinking of themselves as part of an emerging discipline and profession, and the Family Discipline Section (now called the Family Science Section) was formed within NCFR.

At the 1992 NCFR annual meeting, Family Science Section members voted and approved, as a top priority, the development and adaptation of a code of ethics for its membership. Section Chairperson, Kathleen R. Gilbert, appointed Rebecca A. Adams to chair the newly established Ethical Code Committee with David C. Dollahite and Robert E. Keim as committee members.

Through the ensuing year, the committee studied codes of ethics from other professional disciplines and associations discussed the professional arenas in which Family Science Section members operated, studied the value of a professional code of ethics, and began formulating possible ethical statements for family scientists. As the committee members discussed the developing document, they came to think of it as a "living document" that would be flexible enough to respond to emerging ethical concerns. It also was decided that the document should be considered a set of "ethical principles and guidelines" rather than a "code of ethics" because of the diverse professional activities represented by family scientists and because the document was meant to be educational and sensitizing rather than a legalistic code with enforcement potential.

The initial draft, along with the "living document" concept, met with favorable responses when presented at the section business meeting the following year. To provide for maximum input from all section members, the draft was published in the December 1995 issue of the *NCFR Report* (Adams, Keim, & Dollahite, 1995), and mailed to all section members for feedback. The document was then modified and presented at the 1996 section meeting. Section members were given an additional year for input. The final draft, along with related changes in section bylaws, was then approved as the Family Science Section Ethical Principles and Guidelines by a mail-in vote of the section membership.

While the document was in the review process, committee members and the section chairperson received numerous inquiries about the possibility of NCFR, as a whole, adopting the guidelines. Principal among those was NCFR Executive Director, Mary Jo Czaplewski, who had provided extensive feedback throughout the developmental process. Section members were receptive to the broader application of the guidelines but were concerned about relinquishing control because of concerns about lack of an interested body to periodically revise the document. Therefore, they approved that the section chairperson at the time, Rebecca A. Adams, propose the guidelines to the Board, with the section maintaining some continued responsibility for their ongoing development.

This was done at the April 1997 meeting of the NCFR Board of Directors, and the overall interest of the Board was positive. The guidelines were printed again in the *NCFR Report* (Adams, Keim, & Dollahite, 1997), and input by the entire NCFR membership was invited. In addition, NCFR Section Chairs were asked to include discussion of the Ethical Principles and Guidelines at their section business meetings at the November 1997 Annual Conference, and the NCFR attorney was asked to review them regarding liability issues. Surprisingly, there were few minor revisions recommended from the general membership, section chairs, and attorney. This suggests the principles and guidelines adequately addressed the kinds of concerns most members felt were important. Following these efforts, including making the minor revisions suggested, the *Ethical Principles and Guidelines for Family Scientists* were unanimously approved at the April 1998 meeting of the NCFR Board of Directors.

The eight ethical principles and 51 specific ethical guidelines are intended to apply to *all* members of NCFR in the roles as family life educators, therapists, researchers, professors, employees of agencies, and citizens of their communities. Of course, NCFR members and students who also are members of other professional associations are bound by the ethical codes of those bodies. For example, parent and family educators who obtain the Certified Family Life Educator (CFLE) designation from NCFR are expected to abide by 33 Ethical Guidelines for Parent and Family Educators. Less than 20% of the nearly 3,800 members of NCFR are CFLEs, however (personal communication, Dawn Cassidy, CFLE Program Director, May 2000). We encourage the many NCFR members who practice some type of family life education, but who are not CFLEs, to obtain the document titled *Tools for Ethical Thinking and Practice in Family Life Education* from the NCFR office and incorporate those ethical guidelines into their work. (In addition to the Ethical Guidelines for Parent and Family Educators, this booklet contains an excellent discussion on relational ethics, an article on the levels of involvement by William Doherty, a "Case Study Process" that can help educators teach ethics, and a set of Competencies for Family Life Educators created by Weber State University that has ethical implications.)

Implications for Ethics Education

Postmodernism has brought much-needed attention to the importance of recognizing and appreciating variation in family life. An unintended negative consequence of postmodernism is the tendency for some students to wonder whether there are *any* legitimate standards of moral, responsible, or ethical professional behavior – other than to be tolerant of all people's choices and conditions. Teaching ethical principles and guidelines that ground students in a way of thinking and acting as ethical family professionals can help diminish this unintended consequence.

Garner and Smith (1991) argued that "all who teach are involved in ethics education either by design or by default. Our implicit ethical perspective is shown in countless everyday behaviors and decisions" (p.11). It appears that the only question is how consciously and effectively we will teach ethics to our students. An important study (Knaub & Meredith, 1991) of ethical issues among 357 family scientists selected from the Family Science, Family Therapy, and Education and Enrichment sections of NCFR provides empirical evidence for the need for both ethical guidelines and for explicit education in ethical behavior. The authors reported that:

1. Seventy-six percent of respondents stated that they had experienced a serious ethical dilemma in their work.
2. Of those in the entire sample who said they had faced a serious ethical dilemma, only 47% said that their educational preparation had helped them resolve it.
3. Of the family therapists in the sample (who are required to have course work in ethics), 71% said their ethics education helped them resolve the dilemma.
4. Professors and graduate students in nonclinical family programs indicated that they felt poorly prepared to deal with ethical questions.
5. When asked if they believed that family life educators should have a code of ethics, 96% answered yes.
6. Family professionals who had not studied ethics believed that course work in this area would have been helpful.

These data suggest both a fundamental need for better education on ethical principles and guidelines and a strong desire on the part of family life professionals for ethical guidance. Now that a set of ethical principles and guidelines has been adopted by NCFR, it is the responsibility of family professionals who belong to that association to educate and encourage one another, as well as future family scientists, in ethical reasoning and action. This is no small challenge, as Knaub and Meredith (1991) stated:

> The need for competent instruction may cause the profession difficulty. As revealed in the study, professors feel ill-prepared to deal with ethical dilemmas; yet, it is professors who must design and teach practical ethics to upcoming family scientists. How will this lack (or perceived lack) of education be corrected? (p. 19)

We present below suggestions on ethics education based on a review of relevant literature. Given the diversity of programs and contexts in which ethics education occurs, the emphasis will be on concepts and principles rather than on specific pedagogical strategies.

Ethics Education: Goals and Principles

The literature on ethics education includes philosophy, theory, and application to various domains (i.e., counseling, education, research). Professional ethics are both highly dependent on the specific professional context in which the work is done, and they are extremely complex and value laden (Craig, 1991; Kitchener, 1986; Knaub & Meredith, 1991; Leigh et al., 1986). Thus it is not sufficient to ask students to read an article or book about ethics in general or about another professional context, for example, and expect them to be well educated on the ethical principles they should know and the dilemmas that they may face as family professionals. Broad, superficial, or out-of context discussions of ethics will not adequately prepare students for the complex, value-laden, diverse, and changing professional arenas in which they will work (Craig; Knaub & Meredith). In addition, general discussions are less likely to elicit strong commitments to ethical behavior (Arcus, 1980).

Garner and Smith (1991) stated that "Ethics education has a transdisciplinary quality that makes it everyone's concern and no one's exclusive domain" (p. 10). The good news is that the surge of interest in professional ethics in the 1970s and 1980s produced numerous ethical codes and institutionalized ethics curricula in graduate clinical programs. This means that graduate programs in family therapy likely are comparable to the strong ethics education curricula in law, medicine, business, and nursing. The bad news is that all of this has not yet resulted in a comprehensive and coherent body of scholarship that can clearly guide the teaching of professional ethics in the family field to non-clinical family science students.

Thus, despite repeated calls in the last 3 decades of the 20th century for greater attention to ethics among various leaders in the family field, particularly among family life educators (e.g., Brock, 1993; Czaplewski & Jorgensen, 1993; Leigh et al., 1986), and despite the fact that ethics is 1 of 10 "subject areas" of which knowledge is required to become a CFLE, a well-developed literature on ethics education specifically for family professionals is not available. In fact, Margaret Arcus appears to be the only family scholar to have provided a sustained discussion of ethics education relating to family issues (Arcus, 1980, 1984, 1999; Arcus & Daniels, 1993). In her most recent article, Arcus (1999) argued that:

> This relative lack of attention to ethics education in the family science literature is an important omission because many who are responsible for this curricular development and implementation in family science programs may have little or no preparation in ethics and ethics education. (p. 50)

The lack of a more vibrant literature on ethics education in family science suggests that family science scholars and educators may not believe that ethics are as important to the preparation of family professionals as is topical content, scholarly methods, and pedagogical methodology. This assumption, if true, has troubling implications for the integrity of the family field and for the way current and future professionals feel about their responsibilities. It implies that those who train others to work with families do not believe strongly in the importance of a coherent, thorough, well-researched, and philosophically defensible approach to teaching ethics. Thus, we believe that the development of a scholarship on ethics education in family science is crucial for the well-being of the field, our students, and those we serve as family professionals.

Next, we draw from this literature as well as from scholarship on ethics education in other helping professions to briefly discuss some of the most useful ideas from this literature with implications for ethics education for family professionals. Those who teach in this area are encouraged to consult these and other sources of ethical guidance.

For a principles-based educational approach. Krager (1985) suggested five principles relating to the development of ethical behavior:

1. *Respect autonomy* by helping others make their own choices.
2. *Do no harm* by avoiding actions that hurt others or place them at risk.
3. *Benefit others* by acting in ways that contribute to the welfare and growth of other individuals and society.
4. *Support fairness and justice* by serving all persons fairly and equally and by disregarding irrelevant factors when treating others.
5. *Maintain fidelity* by keeping promises, being honest, and maintaining commitments.

Brock (1993) summarized the ethical principles typically found in the helping professions as including: (a) practice with competence, (b) do not exploit, (c) treat people with respect, (d) protect confidentiality, and (e) do not harm (p. 126). Arcus (1999) encapsulated the ethical concepts in the *Life Span Framework For Family Life Education* (NCFR, 1997), which include:

> respect for persons, the interrelationship of rights and responsibilities, taking responsibility for actions, ethical values as one kind of values and as guides to human social conduct, personal autonomy and social responsibility, the complexity and difficulty of ethical choices, the ethical implications of social and technological change, and developing a personal code. (p. 53)

Although there are additional principles that can and have been articulated, a curriculum that considers a set of ethical principles such as these will certainly be more effective than one without such a framework. The *Ethical Principles and*

Guidelines for Family Scientists adopted by NCFR incorporate a principles-based philosophy where underlying ethical principles such as those above are adapted to the specific contexts in which family professionals work.

Acting ethically does not simply involve learning a set of rules. Instead, it entails embracing a way of thinking and acting that is based in principle, while also being sensitive to context and oriented toward personal well-being and growth. One pedagogical strategy that may be helpful is for students to formulate underlying personal ethical principles that they can use to help them make reasoned and moral ethical choices in their future professional responsibilities.

Kitchener (1986) outlined four goals for ethical education that have important implications for educating family professionals. These include:

1. Stimulating ethical sensitivity: This involves helping students increase their awareness of the complex and various ethical issues that may confront them as professionals. Kitchener suggested, "This task cannot be relegated to a single class. Rather, it requires the commitment of an entire faculty to identify and raise moral issues as they appear in their classes and in practice" (p. 308). This argues strongly for an integrated approach to ethical education for family science students in which the faculty coordinate their efforts, and each has a stake in the teaching process. Whereas many programs that teach ethics have an excellent course in this area, they also should teach professional ethics "across the curriculum," if they want to seriously impact their students in this important area (Craig, 1991).
2. Improving ethical reasoning: According to Kitchener, improving students' ethical reasoning involves strengthening their ability to move beyond a sense of "moral intuition" and helping them acquire the critical thinking tools to be able to competently analyze and judge ethical problems. This presumes an understanding of the theories of applied ethicists on issues such as ethical justification in the helping professions (Drane, 1982) and of ethical decision making (Kitchener, 1984, 1985, 1986).
3. Developing moral responsibility: Kitchener stated that developing students' moral responsibility involves helping students make and justify ethical decisions about specific cases called ethical dilemmas. It also involves helping students better understand "the responsibilities of professionals involved in making ethical decisions" (p. 309).
4. Coping with ethical ambiguity: Developing students' attitudes and skills for coping with ethical ambiguity involves "introducing students to the true ambiguity that often surrounds ethical choices" (p. 309), including the fact that acting ethically can be painful, difficult, and frustrating.

Table 1. Degree of Ethics Education in Undergraduate Family Programs

0	No discussion of ethics in any context
1	Random discussion of ethics in one or more courses
2	Superficial but regular treatment of ethics in one or more non-required courses
3	Thorough treatment of ethics in a unit of one non-required course
4	Thorough treatment of ethics in units of more than one non-required course
5	Entire course on ethics as a non-required class
6	Nonacademic ethics seminar or lecture series required for all students
7	Thorough, consistent treatment of ethics in unit of one required course
8	Required, academic, full-credit course on ethics
9	Integration of ethics across required curriculum without one thorough course
10	Integration of ethics across curriculum including one required, thorough course

Other Pedagogical Issues

Degrees of ethics coverage in curriculum. Table 1 presents a model of the degrees of professional ethics education that can exist in undergraduate family programs. Given the number of complex legal, moral, and ethical issues facing professionals in the family field, an ideal approach to ethics education may be the combination of systematic coverage of ethics across the curriculum that includes a required course with thorough, systematic coverage of ethics (number 10 in Table 1). Programs differ in mission and resources, however, so although it is possible to suggest the foregoing as an ideal, the reality is that most programs likely will not find that approach feasible. Given the constraints under which most family studies faculty operate, as well as the ever-expanding knowledge base, ethics education usually is taught as a unit of a broader course (often a capstone, professionally oriented teaching-methods course), rather than as an entire class devoted to ethics (Haemmerlie & Matthews, 1988; Quoss, 1993). Regardless of their situation, faculties could use the framework in Table 1 to assess the degree of their current ethics coverage, to consider what other options exist, and to consider the best way to increase the quality of their ethics education. The fact that coverage of ethics often is limited to a couple of weeks in the context of another class suggests the need for creative pedagogy that goes beyond the superficial treatment of a crucial set of issues.

Thinking critically with and about an ethical code.

Craig (1991) warned that "the greatest possible danger may come from an unquestioning acceptance of any code, standard, or set of practices" (p. 6). Thus, while acquainting our students with the *Ethical Principles and Guidelines for Family Scientists,* we also must teach them how to reason ethically with and think critically about that set of principles and guidelines. This is no easy task because "integration of personal and approved standards of behavior within the society and profession requires significant reflection and self-examination" (Craig, p. 3).

The pedagogical power of the ethical dilemma case study approach

Most ethics educators agree that the most effective, efficient, and enjoyable general approach is to use well-chosen ethical dilemmas (case studies) that allow dynamic discussion of ethical principles and guidelines. One benefit of the case study approach is its ability to engage affective as well as cognitive dimensions (Arcus, 1999). Lee et al. (1994) also made a compelling case for this pedagogy:

> Case studies developed around ethical issues such as these provide students with opportunities to discuss alternative actions they might take, predict likely consequences, evaluate potential outcomes, and establish general ethical principles to apply in other situations. By analyzing such issues as undergraduates, students should be better equipped to make more ethical decisions as professionals. (p. 29)

Important readings

For those who have not taught a course or a unit on ethics for family professionals, the reference list of this article is a good place to start for helpful information about ethics education. The single most important article is by Arcus (1999). It provides an excellent application of the ethics education work of scholars such as Callahan (1980), Nash (1996), and Thiroux (1986) to family science curricula. Another excellent article is by Quoss (1993). These two articles are important reading for all who wish to effectively teach ethics to undergraduate family science students. We also strongly recommend others (i.e., Brock, 1993; Doherty, 1995; Doherty et al., 1986; Knaub & Meredith, 1991; Leigh et al., 1986). For example, Doherty's framework distinguishes levels of involvement for parent and family educators in relation to marriage and family therapy. This important contribution should be in the syllabus of any course or unit on ethics for family professionals because it clearly articulates the need to work within one's professional training and competence. In addition, it provides helpful and concrete examples.

Summary and Conclusions

For the majority of its existence, NCFR has been without a formal code of ethics. This was remedied in 1998, when the Board of Directors approved the *Ethical Principles and Guidelines for Family Scientists*, which had been earlier developed by the Family Science Section of NCFR. Although not legalistic, these guidelines are intended to be sensitizing and educational and can be used by all members of the organization in their own practice and in training their students for future work with families and their members.

Ethics education serves to prepare future professionals to relate ethically with their students or clients, as well as with persons within the profession itself. Thus, in addition to any emphasis on relevant vocational issues, including legal obligations, students need to learn "the moral principles that comprise a professional code of ethics" (Haemmerlie & Matthews, 1988). In other words, ethics education should not only provide our students with better vocational training, but it also should help them feel a part of an emerging profession dedicated to strengthening families.

Using the NCFR principles and guidelines, the Family Science Section is undertaking the next step of creating a bank of ethical dilemmas and case studies that can be utilized in ethics education. Lee et al. (1994) recommended that professional associations survey practicing professionals in their membership for information on the types of ethical dilemmas they experience. To begin the process, NCFR members or other professionals are invited to participate in this endeavor by contacting the first author.

References

Adams, R. A., Keim, R., & Dollahite, D. (1995). Ethical principles and guidelines for family scientists. *NCFR Report, 40*(4), 18-19.

Adams, R. A., Keim, R., & Dollahite, D. (1997). Ethical principles and guidelines for family scientists. *NCFR Report, 42*(3), insert, 1-4.

Allen, K. R., & Crosbie-Burnett, M. (1992). Innovative ways and controversial issues in teaching about families: A special collection on family pedagogy. *Family Relations, 41,* 9-11.

Arcus, M. E. (1980). Home economics and ethics. *Canadian Home Economics Journal, 30,* 178-182.

Arcus, M. E. (1984). Ethical inquiry and home economics education. In P. J. Thompson (Ed.), *Home economics teacher education: Knowledge, technology, and family change* (pp. 237-264). Bloomington, IL: Bennett and McKnight.

Arcus, M. E. (1999). Ethics education in family science: Strengthening programs in higher education. *Family Science Review, 12,* 49-64.

Arcus, M. E., & Daniels, L. B. (1993). Values and family life education. In M. E. Arcus, J. D. Schvaneveldt & J. J. Moss (Eds.), *Handbook of family life education: Vol. 1. Foundations of family life education* (pp. 76-105). Newbury Park, CA: Sage.

Bernard, J. (1964). Developmental tasks of the NCFR 1963-1988. *Journal of Marriage and the Family, 26,* 29-38.

Brock, G. W. (1993). Ethical guidelines for the practice of family life education. *Family Relations, 42,* 124-127.

Burr, W. R., & Leigh, G. K. (1983). Famology: A new discipline. *Journal of Marriage and the Family, 45,* 467-480.

Callahan, D., (1980). Goals in the teaching of ethics. In D. Callahan & S. Bok (Eds.), *Ethics teaching in higher education* (pp. 61-74). New York: Plenum Press.

Craig, K. E. (1991). Ethics: The heart of home economics. *Home Economics FORUM, 6,* 3-6.

Czaplewski, M. J., & Jorgensen, S. R. (1993). The professionalization of family life education. In M. E. Arcus, J. D. Schvaneveldt & J. J. Most (Eds.), *Handbook of family life education: Vol. 1. Foundations of family life education* (pp. 51-75). Newbury Park, CA: Sage.

Doherty, W. J. (1995). Boundaries between parent and family education and family therapy: The levels of family involvement model. *Family Relations, 44,* 353-358.

Doherty, W. J., Lester, M. E., & Leigh, G. K. (1986). Marriage encounter weekends: Couples who win and couples who lose. *Journal of Marital and Family Therapy, 12,* 49-61.

Dane, J. F. (1982). Ethics and psychotherapy. A philosophical perspective. In M. Rosenbaum (Ed.), *Ethics and values in psychotherapy* (pp. 15-50). New York: Free Press.

Garner, S. G., & Smith, D. J. (1991). Ethics: Clarity for home economics professionals. *Home Economics FORUM, 6,* 10-13.

Haemmerlie, F. M., & Matthews, J. R. (1988). Preparing undergraduates for paraprofessional positions: What, where, when, and how are ethical issues taught? *Teaching of Psychology, 15,* 192-194.

Keith-Spiegel, P., & Koocher, G. P. (1985). *Ethics in psychology: Professional standards and cases.* New York: Random House.

Kerckhoff, R. K. (1964). Family life education in America. In H. T. Christensen (Ed.), *Handbook of marriage and the family* (pp. 881-911). Chicago: Rand McNally.

Kitchener, K. S. (1984). Intuition, critical evaluation and ethical principles: The foundation for ethical decisions in counseling psychology. *Counseling Psychologist, 12*(3), 43-55.

Kitchener, K. S. (1985). Ethical principles and ethical decisions in student affairs. In H. J. Canon & R. D. Brown (Eds.), *Applied ethics: Tools for practitioners* (pp. 17-29). San Francisco: Jossey-Bass.

Kitchener, K. S. (1986). Teaching applied ethics in counselor education: An integration of psychological process and philosophical analyses. *Journal of Counseling and Development, 64,* 306-310.

Knaub, P. K., & Meredith, W. (1991). Ethical dilemmas experienced by family scientists: Implications for ethics education. *Home Economics FORUM, 6,* 14-19.

Krager, L. (1985). A new model for defining ethical behavior. In H. J. Canon & R. D. Brown (Eds.), *Applied ethics in student services: New directions for student services, No. 30* (pp. 32-34). San Francisco: Jossey-Bass.

Lee, C. L., Weber, M. J., & Knaub, P. K. (1994). Ethical dilemmas of human science professionals: Developing case studies for ethics education. *Journal of Family and Consumer Sciences, 86*(4), 23-29.

Leigh, G. K., Lowen, I. R., & Lester, M. E. (1986). Caveat emptor: Values and ethics in family life education and enrichment. *Family Relations, 35,* 573-580.

Nash, R. J. (1996). *"Real-world" ethics: Frameworks for educators and human service professionals.* New York: Teachers College Press.

National Council on Family Relations. (1997). *Family life education life span framework teaching resources.* Minneapolis, MN: Author.

Quoss, B. (1993). Ethical training in undergraduate family science programs. *Family Science Review, 6,* 105-113.

Swartzlander, S., Pace, D., & Stamler, V. L. (1993, February 17). The ethics of requiring students to write about their personal lives. *The Chronicle of Higher Education,* p. B1-B2.

Thiroux, J. P. (1986). *Ethics: Theory and practice* (3rd ed.). New York: Macmillan.

Walters, J., & Jewson, R. (1988). *The National Council on Family Relations: A fifty-year history, 1938-1987.* St. Paul, MN: National Council on Family Relations.

Appendix

National Council on Family Relations Ethical Principles and Guidelines for Family Scientists

These "Ethical Principles and Guidelines for Family Scientists" were drafted by the Family Science Section of National Council on Family Relations (NCFR) and adopted by the NCFR Board of Directors at its 1998 spring board meeting. The approach of providing general principles with illustrative guidelines was implemented because the guidelines are meant to be educational and sensitizing rather than a legalistic code with enforcement potential.

It is natural for guidelines to evolve as new issues and circumstances arise. Examples are offered because different concerns arise at various historical times. Thus, the examples help to identify specific issues so family scientists can become sensitive to them. When modifications or additions to the principles and guidelines seem appropriate, family scientists should make known their concerns or ideas to officers of the Family Science Section of NCFR. Although the Family Science Section is the professional association vehicle that helps to clarify and publicize ethical principles and guidelines, this document is intended for all individuals who consider themselves family scientists. This may include university students, social service professionals, educators, therapists, and administrators.

Purpose: These ethical principles and guidelines were developed to

- *inspire and encourage family scientists to act ethically,*
- *provide guidance in dealing with often-complex ethical issues,*
- *provide ethical guidance in areas that family scientists may overlook, and*
- *enhance the professional image and status of family scientists by increasing the level of professional consciousness.*

The principles that apply to family scientists in all their professional situations are included in the first section. The remaining sections relate to family scientists in specific professional arenas.

I. General Principles for Family Scientists

This section identifies general ethical principles that are relevant to family scientists in all professional settings.

Family scientists are respectful of all individuals, do not unethically discriminate, do not develop inappropriate intimate personal relationships in their role as family scientists, are sensitive to the complications of multiple role relationships, protect the confidentiality of their students or clients, and do not engage in sexual harassment.

Guidelines

1.01 Family scientists are respectful of others, show sensitivity to the dignity of all humans, and avoid all forms of exploitation.

1.02 Family scientists are not unethically discriminatory on the basis of gender, sexual orientation, age, marital status, race, religion, national origin, ethnicity, disability or socioeconomic status. We recognize that discrimination occurs in our society, and when done wisely for positive purposes it may be appropriate. For example, we may allow a student with a vision impairment to sit in the front row of the classroom.

1.03 When attempting to influence the behavior or attitudes of students or clients, family scientists should not use methods that involve undue influence, such as coercion or manipulation.

1.04 Family scientists segregate intimate personal relationships from their role as family scientists. Therefore, they do not develop inappropriate personal relationships with students, clients, or research subjects.

1.05 Family scientists are sensitive to the complications in dual and multiple role situations and are ethical in those roles. For example, family scientists may teach classes in which a son or daughter is enrolled. Others may have professional colleagues in a workshop where some form of personal evaluation is an expected outcome.

1.06 Family scientists protect confidentiality in their professional role as family scientists, whether it be in teaching, service, public speaking, writing, or consulting activities. For example, if family scientists share information with students about others, the confidentiality of those involved should be protected. This can be done by changing identifying information, creating composite cases, or summarizing information.

1.07 If information is shared with a family scientist that mandates reporting (such as child abuse or the possibility of extreme harm), such information is to be reported to the appropriate authorities. Whenever possible, individuals should be informed in advance of the family scientist's need to report.

1.08 Family scientists avoid sexually harassing all persons with whom they come in contact in a professional or personal setting. Sexual harassment involves unwelcome intimate and sexual advances, requests, or other conduct of a sexual nature that is used as grounds for providing benefits or services for terms of or conditions of employment, or for the purpose or effect of unreasonably interfering with an individual's learning or work performance or creating an intimidating, hostile, or offensive learning or working environment. Such things as inappropriate hugging, touching, or language are considered harassment.

1.09 Family scientists who belong to other professional organizations with more elaborate or role-specialized guidelines should abide by them. For example, professional family therapists should use the ethical guidelines of the American Association for Marriage and Family Therapy and medical doctors should utilize the ethical guidelines of the American Medical Association.

Principle II: Family Scientists Are Respectful of Students and Clients

Family scientists are respectful of diverse family forms. They are respectful of students' sensitivity when discussing personal family issues. Family scientists do not exploit the hierarchical relationship with persons they serve and are respectful of privacy issues.

Guidelines

2.01 When family scientists teach marital and family courses, they inform students that sometimes students in classes of this nature have painful memories of personal or family experiences. They should inform students of appropriate counseling resources available to them.

2.02 Family scientists recognize the strengths and weaknesses of various family forms and do not operate from a deficit perspective in discussing various family forms.

2.03 When giving examples, family scientists utilize examples with families from diverse cultures and forms.

2.04 When subjects are discussed in a course or class, including controversial issues, family scientists encourage an open, respectful, and thoughtful atmosphere that acknowledges and respects diversity of values, beliefs, and attitudes.

2.05 Family scientists do not insist that students agree with or adopt a particular perspective. In fairness to students, teachers should, where appropriate, divulge personal values and biases and label them as such.

2.06 When teaching, family scientists differentiate between knowledge and insight gained from clinical or personal experience and knowledge obtained from published theory or research.

2.07 Family scientists who are also clinicians do not pursue or allow clinical relationships to develop with students during the course of instruction. If students request clinical services, they should be directed to an appropriate provider of the clinical service.

2.08 Family scientists who are not clinicians do not cross into a therapeutic role while interacting with students. Family scientists make referrals for clinical services when appropriate.

2.09 Family scientists avoid any situation or the perception of any situation in which grades may be exchanged for favors of any kind.

2.10 Family scientists who ask (or allow) students in courses or classes to share personal and family experiences in class regularly remind students to treat any information received as confidential information not to be shared or discussed with anyone outside the classroom. The fact that confidentiality cannot be assured should be stated, however.

2.11 While teaching a for-credit course, family scientists do not make assignments that require students to divulge potentially painful personal or family experiences or information without providing an alternative assignment for those who do not wish to participate. An exception exists if the class is part of a professional training program that requires such educational activities.

2.12 When family scientists request (or require) students to obtain potentially sensitive and painful information from family members (e.g., in a genogram assignment) or others, students are carefully instructed and cautioned about potential harm and allowed to use their own discretion about which information to seek.

2.13 Family scientists do not coerce their students to participate as subjects in research. If students enrolled in courses do not wish to participate in or assist with research projects, they should be offered alternative assignments of equal value and be assured that their decision not to participate will in no way affect their grade.

2.14 In giving assignments in which students are required to discuss their values, family scientists develop grading criteria that do not include evaluation of the students' values.

2.15 When family scientists return papers or post scores, confidentiality of the students' grades are maintained. For example, scores should neither be posted nor papers returned in any hierarchical order of points earned.

2.16 Family scientists base material taught on what is appropriate for students, rather than solely on the instructor's personal or professional needs or interests, such as a research agenda.

Principle III: Family Scientists Abide by High Professional Standards

Family scientists are responsible for upholding high professional standards. They are encouraged to be cooperative with other family scientists in gathering and sharing of scientific information. They strive to keep current with material in their domain. They are ethical in representing their profession at their place of employment, as well as other settings.

Guidelines

3.01 Family scientists are supportive of and cooperative with other family scientists and the profession at large regarding the timely sharing of new ideas, theories, research findings, and innovative program developments.

3.02 Wherever possible, family scientists promote the profession in such a way that members can make contributions to society for the enhancement of families and the growth and development of individuals in various family settings.

3.03 Family scientists give proper credit or acknowledgement to the works of others when formally sharing that information.

3.04 Personal information gained from or known about a colleague is treated with discretion. Sharing the information with others should be done only for the welfare of the colleague, except where appropriate disciplinary action may be involved. When questionable professional or personal conduct may have a bearing on professional activities that concern initially should be discussed with the involved colleague(s) when feasible. If, in the judgment of the family scientist, that is not practical or resolution of the matter is not apparent, such behavior should be reported appropriately.

3.05 Family scientists are adequately prepared for their professional responsibilities. If there are professionally recognized standards of certification or licensing requiring experience, supervision, or additional education, family scientists seek such credentials.

3.06 Family scientists use the times under which they are under obligation to an employer for professional purposes.

Principle IV: Family Scientists Conduct Research Ethically

Family scientists contribute to society and to the profession through research and evaluation activities. When conducting research or evaluation, family scientists recognize that their ultimate responsibility is to the participants. Family scientists honestly report the findings of their study.

Guidelines

4.01 Family scientists conduct all aspects of the research process with respect for the dignity of those who participate in the research, and they ensure that those who assist in the research process do likewise.

4.02 Family scientists inform research participants of the purpose of their research, any potential risk of involvement, how confidentiality will be protected, the right to withdraw from the study at any time, the way the data will be used, and available referral resources if risks are involved.

4.03 Family scientists avoid "doing therapy" with research participants (unless therapy is a part of the research design). Researchers should provide a referral to an appropriate resource for those who request it.

4.04 Family scientists give credit to others for contribution to scholarship in proportion to the contributions made.

4.05 Family scientists do not manipulate research data for the purposes of supporting their views.

4.06 Family scientists use research money for the stated purpose described in the research proposal.

Principle V: Family Scientists Are Ethical in Their Interactions With Employing Organizations or Agencies

Family scientists are respectful of the internal policies and procedures of current and past employers. Family scientists seek to promote the highest standards of policies and practice by their employers.

Guidelines

5.01 When family scientists and those in training have information pertaining to an organization's internal activities or planning and the knowledge may hinder or harm the organization if known by outsiders, the information is treated as confidential unless these activities are unethical or harmful to others.

5.02 Family scientists abide by the policies and procedures of their respective employing organizations. Where such policies and procedures are believed to violate professional standards or cause unprofessional conduct by employees, attempts are made to rectify the situation. If such attempts are unsuccessful, concerns for the pertinent policies or procedures are reported to an appropriate governing or investigative body.

5.03 Family scientists cooperate with other community organizations that provide services to mutual clients. Family scientists do not share client information with other agencies, however, unless the client has given written permission or it is mandated by policy or law.

5.04 Family scientists are aware of other resources that may benefit their students or clients and make appropriate referrals.

Principle VI: Family Scientists Are Involved in Improving Society

Family scientists are advocates for individuals and families and participate in developing policies and laws that are respectful and empowering to them.

Guidelines

6.01 Family scientists are concerned for the general welfare of all individuals and families in society. Whether as professionals or private citizens, they engage in family advocacy at the local, state, and national levels.

6.02 Family scientists are encouraged to participate in developing laws and policies that are respectful of and empowering to all individuals and families and in modifying such policies and laws that are not.

Principle VII: Family Scientists Are Ethical When Reviewing Professional Writing

When a reviewer for a professional work, family scientists avoid conflicts of interest, read materials carefully and in their entirety, and evaluate them fairly.

Guidelines

7.01 Family scientists do not review articles where there is conflict of interest, such as when the work is that of a friend or in other instances in which they may feel a sense of obligation to the author.

7.02 Family scientists carefully read in their entirely materials that are accepted for review and provide explicit reasons for their evaluations.

Principle VIII: Family Scientists Understand and Abide by Ethical Principles and Assist Others in Doing So

Family scientists understand and abide by ethical principles, encourage and assist other family scientists to know and apply them, and teach ethical principles to students of family science.

Guidelines

8.01 Family scientists understand and abide by ethical principles.

8.02 Family scientists assist other family scientists to know and apply ethical principles by encouraging understanding and adherence to them and by their willingness to discuss the principles.

8.03 Family scientists teach students of family science to understand and abide by ethical principles in their professional roles.

8.04 Family scientists who are involved in an ethical dilemma consult with other family scientists about the situation. A written record of the problem, the resolution, and the justification for the resolution is given to another family scientists so that if one is accused of unethical conduct, the record can be used to demonstrate that the family scientist was aware of the ethical concern and dealt with it conscientiously.

8.05 Family scientists assist the profession to further identify and articulate ethical issues. Additional ethical principles and guidelines (beyond those included herein) are to be communicated to the chair of the Family Science Section of the National Council on Family Relations.

About the Authors

Rebecca A. Adams, Ph.D., CFLE is an Associate Professor in the Department of Family and Consumer Sciences, Ball State University, Muncie, IN. E-mail: badams@bsu.edu.

David C. Dollahite, Ph.D., CFLE is a Professor at the School of Family Life, Brigham Young University, Provo, UT. E-mail: Dave_dollahite@byu.edu.

Kathleen R. Gilbert, Ph.D., CFLE is an Associate Professor in the Department of Applied Health Science, Indiana University, Bloomington, IN. E-mail: gilbertk@indiana.edu.

Robert E. Keim, Ph.D., CFLE is Professor Emeritus in the School of Family, Consumer, & Nutrition Sciences, Northern Illinois University, Dekalb, IL. E-mail: KeimBob@aol.com.

This article was originally published in *Family Relations*, 2001, *50*, 41-48, and is reprinted with permission.

Boundaries Between Parent and Family Education and Family Therapy

The Levels of Family Involvement Model

William J. Doherty

Perhaps no issue has plagued the profession of parent and family education more than how to distinguish education from therapy. In order to define a unique terrain for parent and family education, theorists have struggled, without success, to stake out its conceptual differences from therapy. Practitioners, for their part, have continually wrestled with the question of how deeply to go into the feelings and experiences of individuals who are participating in parent and family education activities, without crossing the boundary into family therapy.

Progress on this issue has been scanty for nearly a century. Following a decade that witnessed the consolidation of parent education in the United States, Lindeman and Thurston (1935, as cited in Brim, 1965) wrote that "parent educators are now searching for that new line of demarcation which reveals where education leaves off and psychotherapy begins" (p. 13). Brim (1965) saw little progress three decades later. His own distinction between education and therapy specified that education focuses on conscious (and near-conscious) aspects of the personality of the learner, whereas therapy focuses on the unconscious aspects of personality. Although this distinction may have made sense when Brim was writing the first edition of his book in the mid-1950s, an era when psychoanalytic therapy dominated therapy practice and family therapy was not yet visible, it cannot be sustained in an era when many models of psychotherapy deliberately avoid dealing with unconscious processes.

The last three decades have not yielded any better resolution of the problem. In their authoritative *Handbook of Family Life Education,* Arcus, Schvaneveldt, and Moss (1993) articulated, but did not try to resolve, the ongoing tension between "educational approaches and therapeutic ones" (p. 22). However, the authors raised two important questions that the present article seeks to answer: "Is there a legitimate *conceptual* distinction between these two approaches, or do they simply reflect different points along some continuum? How would clarification of this issue influence the nature of family life education?" (p. 23). The present article argues for a continuum approach to working with families, rather than a dichotomous approach, and suggests that this clarification has important implications for parent and family education.

If education for family life were viewed as a regular academic subject such as geography or mathematics, the distinction between education and therapy would be easy: the former deals with cognitive knowledge only, whereas the latter deals with personal and experiential issues. The problem is that contemporary definitions of parent and family education universally involve a personal and experiential component: the feelings, motives, attitudes, and values of the learners are central foci in the process (Arcus et al., 1993; Darling, 1987). This personal element distinguishes a parent education group from, say, a standard college course in child development.

Here, then, is the conundrum: In order to accomplish its purpose, parent and family education must have more personal depth than other forms of education, but too much depth or intensity risks harming participants, or at least scaring them away. Participants must be able to tell their stories, express their feelings and values, and be encouraged to try out new behaviors. However, if they recount in detail their most traumatic memories, ventilate their most painful and unresolved feelings, or take major behavioral risks, the experience can be damaging.

Why damaging? First, if the context of the program is defined as educational, not clinical, the participant does not enroll expecting highly intense interactions and searing personal disclosures. If such experiences occur, the participant might be overwhelmed emotionally and feel unsafe, even if the disclosures are completely voluntary. Second, if the educator has received the standard training in parent and family education, he or she is not equipped to deal with such intense personal issues, and is likely to feel anxious, incompetent, or legally liable if the interaction gets out of hand. Third, if the interaction occurs in a group setting, the experience is likely to disturb other participants and drive them away from the group.

Every experienced parent educator, for example, has faced the situation where a mother in a parent education group suddenly reveals her own childhood abuse memories and becomes very emotional. The parent educator knows that the boundaries of parent education are being stretched at such moments. The most obvious way to avoid such incidents-to stay at a cognitive level and not encourage expressions of feelings and personal stories among participants-does not seem an adequate solution.

The challenge is to have both depth and limits in parent and family education. A dichotomous distinction between education and therapy is not especially helpful in meeting this challenge, because such a sharp distinction implies a cognition-emotion split, as if education deals only with the cognitions and therapy only with the emotions-neither of which is true, because cognitions and emotions are thoroughly intertwined in both endeavors. This dichotomy leaves out the middle ground between giving information and working intensively with the most serious family problems. This article argues that only a continuum approach to the distinction between education and therapy holds the possibility of capturing the required nuances. Such an approach shows how therapy and parent and family education occupy different levels of intensity in work with families. It also allows us to conceptualize differences of levels within parent and family education itself.

The Levels of Family Involvement (LFI) model, as adapted for parent and family educators, applies primarily to direct work with parents and other family members who are dealing with children. The term *parent and family education* refers to activities, whether one-to-one or in groups, designed to enhance the competence of parents, couples, or other family members in their parenting or co-parenting roles. These activities include didactic programs, parent support and educational groups, more intensive groups for teen parents and other high-risk parents, and home visitation programs for families who are hard to reach through centers. Although the model can be adapted to classroom settings for children, adolescents, and college students, and to couple and marriage enrichment activities, these contexts are outside of the scope of present discussion.

Background of the Levels of Family Involvement Model

The model was originally developed for training family physicians who work with families experiencing illness and disability (Doherty & Baird, 1986, 1987). These professionals face a similar dilemma to that of parent and family educators: They inevitably work with family members in emotional distress but are not equipped by mission, training, and scheduling logistics to engage in intensive family therapy. The LFI Model has provided a way to conceptualize a moderate degree of depth or intensity in physicians' work with families, that is, not merely informational but not as intensive as therapy. The model has been adopted widely in family medicine training and has been operationalized in a series of research studies assessing the degree of family-centered skill in academic family physicians and family practice residents (Marvel, 1993; Marvel & Morphew, 1993; Marvel, Schilling, Doherty, & Baird, 1994). The model has also been applied to the work of school psychologists (Doherty & Peskay, 1992).

In 1993, the LFI Model for physicians was adapted to parent and family education and refined in a focus group and a series of workshops with parent and family educators in Minnesota. Model programs are being developed, and training videotapes have been produced. This article provides the first written description of the LFI Model for parent and family educators. (Training tapes on the LFI Model are available for purchase at a modest cost from the Cavanaugh Early Childhood Family Education Center, 5400 Corvallis Ave. N., Crystal, MN 55429).

Levels of Family Involvement for Parent and Family Educators

The five levels of the LFI Model are arranged hierarchically from minimal involvement with families to family therapy, with the higher levels subsuming and going beyond the lower ones (see Appendix). The first and fifth levels are outside the mission of parent and family education; they are included to show what is on the other side of the boundaries of the field. The model refers to both group work with parents and one-to-one work.

Level One: Minimal Emphasis on Family

Level One describes programs or activities in which parents and other family members are included only for practical or legal reasons. At Level One, the educator does not see working with families as a professional skill to be developed. Educational and programmatic policies are created by professionals with little explicit attention to the needs of parents and family members, who are expected to support and cooperate with the professionals. Family conferences for children with difficulties are conducted in a school-focused manner instead of a partnership manner, with parents having relatively little input. Fortunately, Level One programs are increasingly being seen as inadequate ways to work with families and are even contrary to federal law in the case of children with special educational needs (Christenson & Conley, 1992).

Level Two: Information and Advice

Level Two involves collaborative educational activities with family members around the content knowledge of child development, parenting, and family life. At Level Two, the parent and family educator has good skills in communicating information clearly, eliciting questions, engaging a group in the learning process, and making pertinent and practical recommendations. Examples of appropriate Level Two activities in parent and family education include speakers' programs and one-time didactic workshops that engage family members in an informative and collaborative way. The principal strength of Level Two is that the parent and family educator can reach a large number of families with important information in a low-risk environment. The principal limitation of Level Two is that, because it avoids the affective and experiential domains and does not involve parents in personal discussion, it lacks sufficient depth to stimulate meaningful change in most cases.

Level Three: Feelings and Support

Level Three embraces the activities, knowledge, and skills of Level Two and adds to them the eliciting of the feelings and experiences of the parents and family members and the use of these personal disclosures as part of the educational process. Parent and family educators involved at Level Three are able to listen empathically, probe gently for feelings and personal stories, create an open and supportive group climate, engage in collaborative problem solving, and tailor recommendations to the specific situation of the parent or family member. Combining as it does the cognitive and affective domains in a nonintrusive manner, Level Three is the optimal level of intensity for most ongoing parent and family education activities.

Level Three interactions in parent and family education generally deal with the normative stresses of family life, rather than traumatic personal memories and experiences. Describing one's feelings about being spanked occasionally as a child is an example of the former; recounting one's sexual abuse history is an example of the latter. Thus, one Level Three skill is the ability to protect a parent or family member from too much self-disclosure, especially in a group setting. At Level Three, the parent and family educator must have a good awareness of, and comfort with, his or her own emotional responses, in order to be able to stay connected with parents without trying to rescue them or flee from them when they express painful feelings. The most common mistakes at Level Three are (a) moving too quickly back to the cognitive level because of personal discomfort; (b) cutting off a parent by turning the issue back to the group too quickly; (c) giving premature advice before the parent has had the chance to tell the story and express feelings; and (d) probing too deeply into the sources of the parent's distress, thereby becoming too intrusive in an effort to help. When done well, however, the Level Three balancing of depth and limits is the hallmark of parent and family education.

The principal limitation of Level Three is that some parents' needs and problems are too intense to be worked with constructively in an educational/supportive approach. In a group setting, these parents may overwhelm other parents with a need for air time, or their problems may go far beyond parenting issues. In these situations, the parent and family educator might meet with the parent alone to discuss a referral to a therapist or might refer the parent to a more intensive Level Four parent education program.

Level Four: Brief Focused Intervention

Level Four subsumes Levels Two and Three and goes beyond by including an assessment and a planned effort to help the parent change a troublesome parenting problem, a broader family interaction pattern, or larger systems problem. Level Four is primarily suited for work with families with special ends, that is, populations of families who are in high-risk situations. These might include teen parents with family and peer problems, families involved in the mental health or child protective services systems, and parents facing the stress of a chronically ill or disabled child. Problems suitable for Level Four interventions generally go beyond one-to-one parent child issues to involve the parent's interactions with a co-parent, other family members, or professionals who are dealing with the child. Examples might include conflictual co-parenting with a divorced spouse, an interfering grandparent who is allied with one's spouse, or struggles with a child protective services caseworker.

At Level Four, parent and family educators have learned the skills of assessing family problems in their wider context and of developing basic interventions to ameliorate them. They have also done personal work to examine their feelings and relationships with their own family system and community systems, in order to avoid becoming triangulated with the parent against these people or groups in the parent's life.

In the LFI Model, Level Four is considered an elective competency level for parent and family educators, one that requires training beyond that normally provided in nontherapy graduate programs and other training settings. It represents the upper boundary of parent and family education practiced by a minority of professionals who choose to work with special populations of parents and seek special training in family assessment and basic family interventions. Furthermore, Level Four requires a clear contract with the parent or group of parents to engage in more intensive work than in standard Level Three information and support activities.

Experience suggests that the most common mistakes at Level Four are: (a) moving into this depth without realizing it and then getting stuck or overwhelmed, (b) not having an agreement with the parents to engage in this kind of problem solving discussion, (c) not spending sufficient time at Level Three before moving into assessment and intervention, and (d) staying at Level Four when it is not helping. On the last point, at Level Four intervention for a troublesome family interaction should be attempted only for a limited time, say, one discussion and a follow up. If this degree of intervention is not being helpful, and if the problem is serious enough, the educator should refer the family for therapy and return to Level Three involvement. If the family does not accept a therapy referral, the parent and family educator should remain at Level Three so as not to offer problem-solving help that cannot be useful.

Because Level Four is a more intensive involvement than what generally occurs in parent and family education, it is important to specify its limits as well. Level Four deals only with issues of parenting, not marital functioning, psychological disorders, or personality problems of adults. Thus, co-parenting issues are appropriate to address but marital issues are not. Anger management with children is appropriate, but anger management with one's mother-in-law or boss is not. Self-defeating thoughts about oneself as a parent or co-parent are grist for Level Four work, but self-defeating thoughts about one's body image are not. Level Four remains focused on the goals of the parent and family education program.

Given that the LFI Model suggests that Level Three should be the typical level of involvement for parent and family educators, it is reasonable to ask why Level Four is appropriate at all. Is it too intensive for parent and family education? This article argues that, as parent and family educators increasingly are asked to work with families with special needs and multiple stressors, the boundaries of the field are already being extended beyond informational and supportive services. Teen mothers, for example, may not be helped sufficiently with a strictly Level Three group because the members need a more active problem-solving approach to the complex relationships they are dealing with as teens, co-parents, students, and often as welfare recipients. Another example is a group program for incarcerated fathers, whose needs require a more in-depth involvement by the parent educator than a standard Level Three group. In any case, the parent and family educator working at Level Four is likely to be involved in collaborative professional relationships with family therapists and other professionals, who are usually working with the same families. Level Four is inherently collaborative, both with families and with other professionals.

In a group setting, Level Four differs from Level Three in the amount of time allocated to individual parents each session. For example, in a 90-minute group meeting, the parent educator and the group might work with a particular parent for 20-30 minutes to help this parent understand a problem and explore steps to address it. Such intensive focus on an individual parent is not generally part of Level Three groups, and indeed might be inconsistent with the norms for sharing air time in many parent education groups. However, this intensive focus on particular parents is essential for Level Four groups. Experience has indicated no difficulty with group process as long as all the parents have agreed to be in a problem-solving group where they will share time over the course of the group's ongoing meetings. Alternatively, a primarily Level Three group might be able to handle an occasional Level Four discussion with a parent who is facing an acute parenting problem; in that case, the parent educator should obtain the parent's and the group's permission to focus a segment of the group's time on that parent's situation.

The most common misapprehension about Level Four is that, because it is the most intensive level of parent and family education, it must be the preferred level of involvement. This notion is no more true than the assumption that surgery is generally preferable to less invasive treatment. Experience with the LFI Model in Minnesota suggests that Level Four is the exception rather than the rule in parent and family education. It is an approach that requires careful programmatic decision making, staff preparation, acceptance by the parents and family members who participate, and close working relationships with therapists and other professionals in the community. Just like all the other levels, Level Four interventions can be done in groups or in one-to-one interactions. The chief dangers of Level Four occur when the educator is drawn unaware and unprepared into family interventions by dint of the family's serious problems and by a frustration over the limits of informational and supportive efforts to help the family.

Level Five: Family Therapy

Level Five is outside the boundaries of parent and family education. Family therapy generally involves an extended series of family sessions aimed at treating serious psychological and family problems by stimulating significant change in family interaction patterns. Whereas Level Four is confined to parenting related issues, Level Five may move beyond parenting into couple relationship issues, family of origin problems, and mental disorders in individual family members. The skills specific to Level Five are those dealing with the management of intense personal distress or interpersonal conflict and ambivalence or resistance to change among family members. When family members see a therapist, they know they are in mental health treatment and not in an educational program, although education is also likely to occur.

Each of the levels beyond Level One also has a set of skills used in relating to outside services and service providers. At Level Two the parent and family educator is knowledgeable about community resources such as therapy services and makes information about them available in written form to participants. At Level Three, the parent and family educator adds the ability to detect when a family might require a referral and the ability to tailor the referral to the unique situation of the parent and family. At Level Four, the parent and family educator knows family therapists and other family professionals and services, and is able to orchestrate a referral by educating both the family and the professionals about what to expect from each other.

Use of the LFI Model in Parent and Family Education

The LFI Model can be used in several ways. First, it can be used descriptively to characterize the depth or intensity of a particular group or one-to-one interaction with a parent or other family member. Was the group primarily at Level Two or Level Three? Did the educator move into Level Four for several minutes? Did the actual level fit the parent and family educator's goal for the parent education activity or did the actual interaction undershoot or overshoot the desired level?

Second, the LFI Model can be used to establish goals for the kinds and range of family services offered by a parent and family education program. One program might define its offerings as primarily Level Three parent groups, with an occasional Level Two public lecture. Another program might decide also to offer special Level Four services in addition to its standard Level Three activities; Level Four parent groups, for example, could be created and clearly defined as problem-solving groups for parents whose needs are not being met in Level Three groups.

Third, the model can be used to describe the competency of a parent and family educator in different kinds of work with families. To what extent does this individual possess the knowledge, personal development, and skills required for each level? Some parent and family educators with traditional education backgrounds, for example, might be much more comfortable at Level Two than at Level Three, whereas those with prior counseling training might already have many Level Four skills.

Fourth, the model can be used to define training and professional development goals for programs and for individual parent and family educators. For example, a program staff might want to bolster every educator's Level Three skills, while offering Level Four training to one or two individuals if they are interested in working with high-risk families. One assumption of the model is that each level past Level One involves skills that can be developed and honed over a professional lifetime. It seems particularly important to assist parent and family educators in becoming increasingly more skilled at Level Three work with families, because this work is the heart of parent and family education. The next section deals with the process and content of training.

Implications for Training

Most training programs in human development and family relations, family life education, and child development appear to provide good grounding in Level Two knowledge, personal development, and skills. However, it appears that most of these training programs do not give sufficient attention to the knowledge, personal development, affective skills, and group process skills required for Level Three. Many students finish with perhaps one course in group process and little in the way of supervised experience in communicating with parents and other family members about emotionally-charged issues. The result is that most parent and family educators enter their first position prepared well at Level Two and not well at Level Three.

How can parent and family educators be trained at Level Three? Level Three knowledge is best developed and maintained through courses on family systems, family stress, and group process. Level Three personal development is best developed and maintained – either in graduate programs or in-service training programs – through support groups and mutual feedback sessions in which parent and family education students and practitioners can process their own emotional reactions to parents, other family members, and groups. Level Three skills require systematic practice and supervision, including techniques such as role playing, co-facilitation of groups, peer observation, teacher observation, and video observation of one's own work. There is no substitute for careful observation, coaching, and feedback on performance if one is to develop good Level Three skills, and no substitute for a trusting support group if one is to process the personal feelings that Level three work inevitably generates in educators. A strictly content-oriented training program cannot adequately prepare professionals for affective work with families.

Level Four competency requires advanced course work on family systems and basic course work on family assessment and family interventions. The personal development aspect involves sorting out one's own family issues and one's relationships with other professionals and community systems. Level Four personal development and skills can best be learned through an apprenticeship with a Level Four parent and family educator, with consultation from a Level Five family therapist. When there are no Level Four parent and family educators in a program, then a family therapist should do the initial apprenticeship training. The involvement of a family therapist in training and ongoing consultation is essential for the safety and security of Level Four work and for backup for the parent and family educators. It is crucial, moreover, that the family therapist be thoroughly familiar with the mission and scope of parent and family education and be willing to learn from the parent and family educators about the needs of parents in their setting.

Implications for Research and Evaluation

The LFI Model, which has been operationalized in research on physicians, can potentially be used for research on parent and family education. Marvel et al. (1994) refined a coding system for assessing the level of involvement of family physicians' interactions with patients and families in family practice office settings. Working from videotapes, two coders achieved 73% agreement on the highest level of involvement found in the session. This coding system, which can also be used with audiotapes and possibly with live observation, could be adapted fairly readily to parent and family education to assess such issues as (a) the fit between programmatic goals for parent groups versus the actual level achieved, (b) the effectiveness of a staff training program, (c) the evaluation of student competency, and (d) the relationship between level of involvement and outcomes and satisfaction of participants.

A specific research idea for parent and family education would address the question of the appropriate balance of informational and affective exchanges in Level Three work. At this time, it is not clear whether an optimal Level Three parent group would have, for example, a 50-50 split between informational and affective exchanges, or an 80 informational and 20 affective split, or vice-versa. Perhaps the optimal balance would vary considerably from group to group. The LFI Model could be used to study the work of a number of parent and family educator *exemplars* – individuals widely respected for their skill – to determine the balance they use in their work with groups and individuals. This kind of research, although not prescriptive for every parent and family educator or for every context, could nonetheless provide some bench marks about what the best parent and family education looks like at Level Three in different settings and with diverse groups of parents.

A self-report assessment of competency in the levels is not likely to be valid. Research and experience with the LFI Model among different professional groups have indicated that many professionals believe they are practicing at higher levels than they appear to be when actually observed. Self-assessment, however, can be useful in establishing a partnership in training goals when participants are asked which content areas they would like to learn more about and which skills they would like to enhance.

Conclusion

This article has proposed a way to address a nagging concern in the field of parent and family education: the distinction between education and therapy. The proposed way out of the century-long impasse is to delineate levels of intensity within parent and family education, and then to distinguish the most intense level of education from therapy. Inevitably, there is some overlap between Level Four Brief Focused Intervention and Level Five Family Therapy, particularly in an era when therapy is becoming briefer and more problem-focused and parent and family education is becoming more expansive in its scope. The way to avoid professional turf struggles at the interface is to make sure that Level Four parent and family educators are well-trained and to establish collaborative links between parent and family educators and family therapists. Family physicians and obstetricians have had these linkages for decades; family physicians manage normal pregnancies and deliveries, consult with obstetricians on borderline cases, and refer high risk cases to obstetricians.

The effort to distinguish parent and family education from therapy requires that distinctions be made among kinds of parent and family education. Indeed, the failure to distinguish different kinds of intensity in parent and family education may have inhibited the development of a clear distinction from therapy. This article has made a case for Level Three as the ideal degree of intensity for ongoing parent and family education activities, because it combines information and affect; Level Two is appropriate primarily for one-time informational presentations, and Level Four is a specialized kind of work for a subset of families with special needs. There is much more to be done to bring all parent and family educators up to speed in knowledge, personal development, and skills required to practice at Level Three.

The LFI Model awaits further application to the classroom teaching of parent and family education. It would appear that Level Four would be too intensive for these settings but at Level Three would be highly appropriate, given the scope of recommended content for parent and family education for children and adolescents (Arcus, 1987). The model also needs study of its applicability to diverse populations of families, some of whom may prefer programs at different levels of intensity.

The most controversial aspect of the model is its inclusion of Level Four within the scope of parent and family education. However, the case can be made that if the field is to adapt to the growing needs of families, then it will have to face the challenge of preparing some of its practitioners for more in-depth work with families who can benefit from the unique blend of information, support, and nonintrusive problem solving that Level Four can offer. This development in the field will inevitably involve parent and family educators more closely in collaborative relationships with other professionals serving families in the community, thereby increasing the visibility of parent and family education as a valuable service to a broad range of families and a valuable resource for family therapists and other family service professionals. Whatever the eventual consensus about the place of Level Four, however, a clearer definition of the scope of practice for parent and family education is a development long awaited and much needed.

References

Arcus, M. (1987). A framework for life span family life education. *Family Relations, 36,* 5-10.

Arcus, M. E., Schvaneveldt, J. D., & Moss, J. J. (1993). The nature of family life education. In M. E. Arcus, J. D. Schvaneveldt & J. J. Moss (Eds.), *Handbook of family life education: Foundations of family life education, Vol. I* (pp. 1-25). Newbury Park, CA: Sage.

Brim, O. G. (1965). *Education for child rearing.* New York: Free Press.

Christenson, S. L., & Conoley, J. C. (Eds.). (1992). *Home-school collaboration.* Silver Spring, MD: The National Association of School Psychologists.

Darling, C. A. (1987). Family life education. In M. A. Sussman & S. K. Steinmetz (Eds.), *Handbook of marriage and the family* (pp. 815-833). New York: Plenum.

Doherty, W. J., & Baird, M. A. (1986). Developmental levels of family-centered medical care. *Family Medicine, 18,* 153-156.

Doherty, W. J., & Baird, M. A. (Eds.). (1987). *Family-centered medical care: A clinical casebook.* New York: Guilford.

Doherty, W. J., & Peskay, V. E. (1992). Family systems and the school. In S. L. Christenson & J. C. Conoley (Eds.), *Home-school collaboration* (pp. 1-18). Silver Spring, MD: The National Association of School Psychologists.

Marvel, M. K. (1993). Involvement with psychosocial concerns of patients: Observations of practicing family physicians on a university faculty. *Archives of Family Medicine, 2,* 629-633.

Marvel, M. K., & Morphew, P. K. (1993). Levels of family involvement by resident and attending physicians. *Family Medicine, 25,* 26-30.

Marvel, M. K., Schilling, R., Doherty, W. J., & Baird, M. A. (1994). Levels of physician involvement with patients and their families: A model for teaching and research. *The Journal of Family Practice, 39,* 535-544.

Appendix

Levels of Family Involvement for Parent and Family Educators

Level 1: Minimal Emphasis on Family
Interactions with parents are institution centered, not family centered. Families are not regarded as an important area of focus, but parents are dealt with for practical or legal reason.

Level 2: Information and Advice
Knowledge Base: Content information about families, parenting, and child development.

Personal Development: Openness to engage parents in collaborative ways.

Skills:

1. Communicating information clearly and interestingly.
2. Eliciting questions.
3. Engaging a group of parents in the learning process.
4. Making pertinent and practical recommendations.
5. Providing information on community resources.

Level 3: Feelings and Support
Knowledge Base: Individual and family reactions to stress, and the emotional aspects of group process.

Personal Development: Awareness of one's own feelings in relation to parents and group process.

Skills:

1. Eliciting expressions of feelings and concerns.
2. Empathetic listening.
3. Normalizing feelings and reactions.
4. Creating an open and supportive climate.
5. Protecting a parent from too much self-disclosure in a group.
6. Engaging parents in collaborative problem-solving discussion.
7. Tailoring recommendations to the unique needs, concerns, and feelings of the parent and family.
8. Identifying individual and family dysfunction.
9. Tailoring a referral to the unique situation of the parent and family.

Level 4: Brief Focused Intervention
Knowledge Base: Family systems theory.

Personal Development: Awareness of one's own participation in systems, including one's own family, the

Skills:

1. Asking a series of questions to elicit a detailed picture of the family dynamics of a parent's problem.
2. Developing a hypothesis about eh family systems dynamics involved in the problem.
3. Working with the parent for a short period of time to change a family interaction pattern beyond the one-to-one parent/child relationship.
4. Knowing when to end the intervention effort and either refer the parent or return to level three support.
5. Orchestrating a referral by educating the family and the therapist about what to expect from each other.
6. Working with therapists and community systems to help the parent and family.

Level 5: Family Therapy
This level is outside the scope and mission of parent and family education. The following description is offered to show the boundary between Level 4 parent and family education and Level 5 family therapy.

Knowledge Base: Family systems and patterns whereby distressed families interact with professionals and other community systems.

Personal Development: Ability to handle intense emotions in families and self and to maintain one's balance in the face of strong pressure from family members or other professionals.

Example Skills:

1. Interviewing families or family members who are quite difficult to engage.
2. Efficiently generating and testing hypotheses about the family's difficulties and interaction patterns.
3. Escalating conflict in the family in order to break a family impasse.
4. Working intensively with families during crises.
5. Constructively dealing with a family's strong resistance to change.
6. Negotiating collaborative relationships with other professionals and other systems who are working with the family, even when these groups are at odds with one another.

About the Author

William J. Doherty, Ph. D., CFLE, is Professor in the Department of Family Social Science and Director of the Citizen Professional Center at the University of Minnesota. E-Mail: bdoherty@umn.edu.

This article was originally published in *Family Relations*, 1995, *44*, 353-358, and is reprinted with permission.

Certified Family Life Educator Exam Content Outline

This outline represents the content included within the Certified Family Life Educator (CFLE) Exam. The National Council on Family Relations' *University and College Curriculum Guidelines* and *Competencies for Family Life Educators,* developed by faculty at Weber State University, provided the foundation of the document. Schroeder Measurement Technologies and the NCFR Subject Matter Experts Committee incorporated these concepts into a survey which was distributed to current Certified Family Life Educators who were asked to rate the importance of each knowledge, skill or ability to competent practice. The results of the survey, which was completed by 47% of all active Certified Family Life Educators, were used to establish the content outline that became the foundation of the CFLE Exam

I. Families & Individuals in Societal Contexts

a Identify the characteristics, diversity, & impact of local, national, & global social systems

b Identify factors (e.g., media, marketing, technology, economics, social movements, natural disasters, war) influencing individuals & families from both contemporary & historical perspectives.

c Identify factors that influence the relationship between work & family life

d Identify social & cultural influences affecting dating, courtship, partner/marital choice & relationships, family composition, & family life

e Recognize the reciprocal interaction between individuals, families, & various social systems (e.g., health, legal, educational, religious/spiritual)

f Assess the impact of demographics (e.g., class, race, ethnicity, generation, gender) on contemporary families

II. Internal Dynamics of Families

a Recognize & define healthy & unhealthy characteristics pertaining to:

1 Family relationships

2 Family development

b Analyze family functioning using various theoretical perspectives

c Assess family dynamics from a systems perspective

d Evaluate family dynamics in response to normative & non-normative stressors

- e Evaluate family dynamics in response to crises
- f Facilitate & strengthen communication processes, conflict-management, & problem-solving skills
- g Develop, recognize, & reinforce strategies that help families function effectively

III. Human Growth & Development Across the Life Span

- a Identify developmental stages, transitions, tasks, & challenges throughout the life span
- b Recognize reciprocal influences
  - 1 Individual development on families
  - 2 Family development on individuals
- c Recognize the impact of individual health & wellness on families
- d Assist individuals & families in effective developmental transitionse Apply appropriate practices based on theories of human growth & development to individuals & families

IV. Human Sexuality

- a Recognize the biological aspects of human sexuality
  - 1 sexual functioning
  - 2 reproductive health
  - 3 family planning
  - 4 sexually transmitted infections (STIs)
- b Recognize the psycho-social aspects of human sexuality
  - 1 characteristics of healthy & ethical sexual relationships
  - 2 nterpersonal dynamics of sexual intimacy
  - 3 risk factors (e.g., substance abuse, social pressures, media)
- c Address human sexuality from a value-respectful position

V. Interpersonal Relationships

- a Recognize the impact of personality & communication styles
- b Recognize the developmental stages of relationships
- c Analyze interpersonal relationships using various theoretical perspectives
- d Develop & implement relationship enhancement & enrichment strategies
- e Develop & implement effective communication, problem solving, & conflict management strategies
- f Communicate aspects of relationships within the context of their developmental stages

VI. Family Resource Management

- a Identify personal, familial, professional, & community resources available to families
- b Recognize the reciprocal relationship between individual/family/community choices & resources
- c Apply value-clarification strategies to decision-making
- d Apply goal-setting strategies & evaluate their outcomes
- e Apply decision-making strategies
- f Apply organizational & time management strategies
- g Apply basic financial management tools & principles
- h Inform individuals & families of consumer rights, responsibilities, & choices of action/ advocacy
- i Apply stress management strategies

VII. Parenting Education & Guidance

- a Promote healthy parenting from a systems perspective
- b Promote healthy parenting from a child's & parent's developmental perspective
- c Apply strategies based on the child's age/stage of development to promote effective developmental outcomes

- d Identify different parenting styles & their associated psychological, social, & behavioral outcomes
- e Promote various parenting models, principles, & strategies
- f Evaluate the effectiveness & appropriateness of various parenting strategies
- g Recognize various parenting roles (e.g., father/mother, grandparents, other caregivers) & their impact on & contribution to individuals & families
- h Recognize parenting issues within various family structures (e.g. single, blended, same-sex)
- i Recognize the impact of societal trends on parenting (e.g., technology, substance abuse, media)
- j Recognize the influence of cultural differences & diversity
- k Identify strategies to advocate for children in various settings (e.g. schools, legal system, healthcare)
- l Recognize the various pathways to parenting & their associated issues & challenges, (e.g. assisted reproduction, adoption, childbirth, blending)

VIII. Family Law & Public Policy

- a Identify current law, public policy, & initiatives that regulate & influence professional conduct & services
- b Identify current laws, public policies, & initiatives that affect families
- c Inform families, communities, & policy makers about public policies, initiatives, & legislation that affect families at local, state, & national levels

IX. Professional Ethics & Practice ROFESSIONAL ETHICS & PRACTICE

- a Demonstrate professional attitudes, values, behaviors, & responsibilities to clients, colleagues, & the broader community, that are reflective of ethical standards & practice
- b Evaluate, differentiate, & apply diverse approaches to ethical issues & dilemmas
- c Identify & apply appropriate strategies to deal with conflicting values
- d Demonstrate respect for diverse cultural values & ethical standards

X. Family Life Education Methodology

- a Employ a variety of current educational strategies
- b Employ techniques to promote application of information in the learner's environment
- c Create learning environments that are respectful of individual vulnerabilities, needs, & learning styles
- d Demonstrate sensitivity to diversity & community needs, concerns, & interests
- e Develop culturally-competent educational materials & learning experiences
- f Identify appropriate sources for evidence-based information
- g Develop educational experiences
  - 1 needs assessment
  - 2 goals & objectives
  - 3 content development
  - 4 implementation
  - 5 evaluation/outcome measures
- h Promote & market educational programs
- i Implement adult education principles into work with families & parents
- j Establish & maintain appropriate personal & professional boundaries

About the Authors

National Council on Family Relations: Family Life Education Subject Matter Expert Committee -

Ada Alden, Ed.D., CFLE, Deborah Cashen, CFLE, Jean Illsley Clarke, M.A., CFLE, Carol Darling, Ph.D., CFLE, Bryce Dickey, M.S., CFLE, Michael Fleming, Ph.D., CFLE, Benita Jasper, M.A., CFLE, Kristy Jones, M.S., CFLE, Richard Glotzer, Ph.D., CFLE, Mary Kay Stranik, M.S., Kathleen Tesi, M.S., CFLE and **Dawn Cassidy, M.Ed., CFLE.**

Index

D

E

F

M

N

O

P